AP* WORLD HISTORY
ALL ACCESS®

Genevieve Brand, M.A.

Research & Education Association
Visit our website: www.rea.com

Planet Friendly Publishing
✔ Made in the United States
✔ Printed on Recycled Paper
Text: 30%   Cover: 10%
Learn more: www.greenedition.org

GREEN EDITION ®

At REA we're committed to producing books in an Earth-friendly manner and to helping our customers make greener choices.

Manufacturing books in the United States ensures compliance with strict environmental laws and eliminates the need for international freight shipping, a major contributor to global air pollution.

And printing on recycled paper helps minimize our consumption of trees, water and fossil fuels. This book was printed on paper made with **30% post-consumer waste**, and the cover was printed on paper made with **10% post-consumer waste**. According to the Environmental Paper Network's Paper Calculator, by using these innovative papers instead of conventional papers, we achieved the following environmental benefits:

Trees Saved: 35 • Air Emissions Eliminated: 8,772 pounds
Water Saved: 7,083 gallons • Solid Waste Eliminated: 2,657 pounds

Courier Corporation, the manufacturer of this book, owns the Green Edition Trademark.
For more information on our environmental practices, please visit us online at **www.rea.com/green**

Research & Education Association

61 Ethel Road West
Piscataway, New Jersey 08854
E-mail: info@rea.com

AP WORLD HISTORY ALL ACCESS®

Published 2014

Printed in the United States of America

Library of Congress Control Number 2011943702

ISBN-13: 978-0-7386-1025-2
ISBN-10: 0-7386-1025-9

Contents

Chapter 1: Welcome to REA's All Access for AP World History   1

Chapter 2: Strategies for the Exam   7

Unit I: Technological and Environmental Transformations, to c. 600 BCE

Chapter 3: Big Geography and the Peopling of the Earth   35

Chapter 4: The Neolithic Revolution and Early Agricultural Societies   43

Chapter 5: The Development and Interactions of Early Agricultural, Pastoral, and Urban Societies 53

Unit II: Organization and Reorganization of Human Societies, c. 600 BCE to c. 600 CE

Chapter 6: The Development and Codification of Religious and Cultural Traditions 83

Chapter 7: The Development of States and Empires   97

Chapter 8: Emergence of Transregional Networks of Communication and Exchange   119

Unit III: Regional and Transregional Interactions, c. 600 CE to c. 1450

Chapter 9: Expansion and Intensification of Communication and Exchange Networks   133

Chapter 10: Continuity and Innovation of State Forms and Their Interactions 145

Chapter 11: Increased Economic Productive Capacity and Its Consequences 159

Unit V: Industrialization and Global Integration, c. 1750 to c. 1900

Unit VI: Accelerating Global Change and Realignments, c. 1900 to the Present

About Our Author

Genevieve Brand has been a full-time professional writer and editor in the field of education for more than 20 years. She earned her B.A. in English and political science, with distinction in English and with honors in the liberal arts, then went on to earn her M.A. in English while also teaching creative and expository writing at the Ohio State University.

Since then, Ms. Brand has had a long and distinguished career as a developer and writer of educational materials for leading publishers worldwide.

About Research & Education Association

Founded in 1959, Research & Education Association (REA) is dedicated to publishing the finest and most effective educational materials—including study guides and test preps—for students in middle school, high school, college, graduate school, and beyond.

Today, REA's wide-ranging catalog is a leading resource for teachers, students, and professionals. Visit *www.rea.com* to see a complete listing of all our titles.

Acknowledgments

REA would like to thank Larry B. Kling, Vice President, Editorial, for supervising development; Pam Weston, Publisher, for setting the quality standards for production integrity and managing the publication to completion; John Paul Cording, Vice President, Technology, for coordinating the design, development, and testing of the REA Study Center; Diane Goldschmidt and Michael Reynolds, Managing Editors, for coordinating development of this edition; S4Carlisle Publishing Services for typesetting; and Weymouth Design and Christine Saul for cover design.

We would also like to thank Jay P. Harmon, AP World History teacher at The Woodlands Christian Academy, The Woodlands, Texas, for his technical review of the book.

Welcome to REA's All Access for AP World History

A new, more effective way to prepare for your AP exam.

There are many different ways to prepare for an AP exam. What's best for you depends on how much time you have to study and how comfortable you are with the subject matter. To score your highest, you need a system that can be customized to fit you: your schedule, your learning style, and your current level of knowledge.

This book, and the free online tools that come with it, will help you personalize your AP prep by testing your understanding, pinpointing your weaknesses, and delivering flashcard study materials unique to you.

Let's get started and see how this system works.

How to Use REA's AP All Access

The REA AP All Access system allows you to create a personalized study plan through three simple steps: targeted review of exam content, assessment of your knowledge, and focused study in the topics where you need the most help.

Here's how it works:

Review the Book	Study the topics tested on the AP exam and learn proven strategies that will help you tackle any question you may see on test day.
Test Yourself & Get Feedback	As you review the book, test yourself. Score reports from your free online tests and quizzes give you a fast way to pinpoint what you really know and what you should spend more time studying.
Improve Your Score	Armed with your score reports, you can personalize your study plan. Review the parts of the book where you are weakest, and use the REA Study Center to create your own unique e-flashcards, adding to the 100 free cards included with this book.

Finding Your Weaknesses: The REA Study Center

The best way to personalize your study plan and truly focus on your weaknesses is to get frequent feedback on what you know and what you don't. At the online REA Study Center, you can access three types of assessment: topic-level quizzes, mini-tests, and a full-length practice test. Each of these tools provides true-to-format questions and delivers a detailed score report that follows the topics set by the College Board.

Topic-Level Quizzes

Short online quizzes are available throughout the review and are designed to test your immediate grasp of the topics just covered.

Mini-Tests

Two online mini-tests cover what you've studied in each half of the book. These tests are like the actual AP exam, only shorter, and will help you evaluate your overall understanding of the subject.

Full-Length Practice Test

After you've finished reviewing the book, take our full-length exam to practice under test-day conditions. Available both in this book and online, this practice test gives you the most complete picture of your strengths and weaknesses. We strongly recommend that you take the online version of the exam for the added benefits of timed testing, automatic scoring, and a detailed score report.

Improving Your Score: e-Flashcards

With your score reports from our online quizzes and practice test, you'll be able to see exactly which topics you need to review. Use this information to create your own flashcards for the areas where you are weak. And, because you will create these flashcards through the REA Study Center, you'll be able to access them from any computer or smartphone.

Not quite sure what to put on your flashcards? Start with the 100 free cards included when you buy this book.

After the Full-Length Practice Test: Crash Course

After finishing this book and taking our full-length practice exam, pick up REA's *Crash Course for AP World History*. Use your most recent score reports to identify any areas where you are still weak, and turn to the *Crash Course* for a rapid review presented in a concise outline style.

REA's Suggested 8-Week AP Study Plan

Depending on how much time you have until test day, you can expand or condense our eight-week study plan as you see fit.

To score your highest, use our suggested study plan and customize it to fit your schedule, targeting the areas where you need the most review.

	Review 1-2 hours	Quiz 15 minutes	e-Flashcards Anytime, anywhere	Mini-Test 30 minutes	Full-Length Practice Test 3 hours, 5 minutes
Week 1	Chapters 1-5	Quiz 1	Access your e-flashcards from your computer or smartphone whenever you have a few extra minutes to study. Start with the 100 free cards included when you buy this book. Personalize your prep by creating your own cards for topics where you need extra study.		
Week 2	Chapters 6-8	Quiz 2			
Week 3	Chapters 9-11	Quiz 3		Mini-Test 1 (The Mid-Term)	
Week 4	Chapters 12-14	Quiz 4			
Week 5	Chapters 15-18	Quiz 5			
Week 6	Chapters 19-21	Quiz 6			
Week 7				Mini-Test 2 (The Final)	
Week 8	Review Chapter 2 Strategies				Full-Length Practice Exam (Just like test day)

Need even more review? Pick up a copy of REA's *Crash Course for AP World History*, a rapid review presented in a concise outline style. Get more information about the *Crash Course* series by visiting *www.rea.com*.

Test-Day Checklist

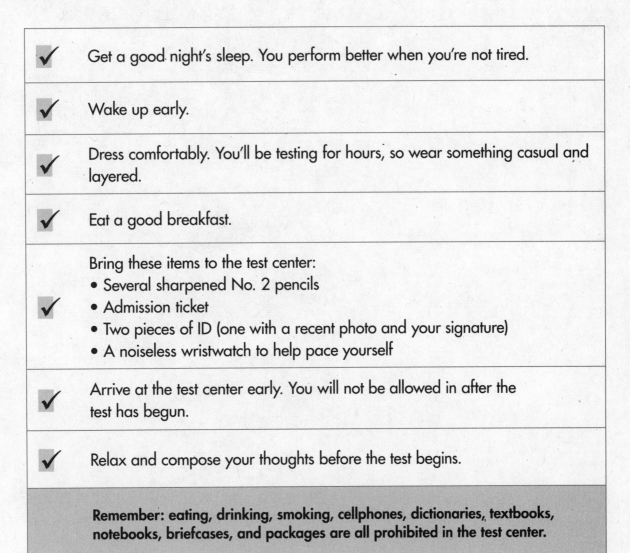

✓	Get a good night's sleep. You perform better when you're not tired.
✓	Wake up early.
✓	Dress comfortably. You'll be testing for hours, so wear something casual and layered.
✓	Eat a good breakfast.
✓	Bring these items to the test center: • Several sharpened No. 2 pencils • Admission ticket • Two pieces of ID (one with a recent photo and your signature) • A noiseless wristwatch to help pace yourself
✓	Arrive at the test center early. You will not be allowed in after the test has begun.
✓	Relax and compose your thoughts before the test begins.

Remember: eating, drinking, smoking, cellphones, dictionaries, textbooks, notebooks, briefcases, and packages are all prohibited in the test center.

Strategies for the Exam

What Will I See on the AP World History Exam?

One May morning, you stroll confidently into the school library where you're scheduled to take the AP World History exam. You know your stuff: you paid attention in class, followed your textbook, took plenty of notes, and reviewed your coursework by reading a special test prep guide. You can identify major technological advances, explain the characteristics of different civilizations around the globe, and describe the similarities and differences among various instances of political, economic, and social change. So how will you show your knowledge on the test?

The Multiple-Choice Section

First off, you'll complete a lengthy multiple-choice section that tests your ability to not just remember facts about the various eras of world history, but also to apply that knowledge to interpret and analyze historical information. This section will require you to answer 70 multiple-choice questions in just 55 minutes. Here are the major time periods with accompanying major themes found on the AP World History exam:

- Period 1: Technological and environmental transformations (to about 600 BCE)

- Period 2: Organization and reorganization of human societies (from about 600 BCE to about 600 CE)

- Period 3: Regional and transregional interactions (from about 600 CE to about 1450 CE)

- Period 4: Global interactions (from about 1450 CE to about 1750 CE)

- Period 5: Industrialization and global integration (from about 1750 CE to about 1900 CE)

- Period 6: Accelerating global change and realignments (from about 1900 CE to the present)

So being able to name which dynasty led China in building much of the Great Wall (the Ming Dynasty, but you know that, right?) will not do you much good unless you can also explain how the Great Wall both reflected and influenced the development of the Chinese civilization as a whole. It sounds like a lot, but by *working quickly and methodically* you'll have plenty of time to address this section effectively. We'll look at this in greater depth later in this chapter.

The Free-Response Section

After time is called on the multiple-choice section, you'll get a short break before diving into the free-response, or essay, section. This section requires you to produce three written responses in 130 minutes. Like the multiple-choice section, the free-response portion of the exam expects you be able to *apply your own knowledge to analyze historical information,* in addition to being able to provide essential facts and definitions. One of these free responses will require you to interpret several primary source documents to create a historical argument. This is known as the document-based question, or DBQ. The next free-response item will ask you to use your historical knowledge to explore how a broad issue, such as technology or population movement, has shaped the world over time. This is known as the continuity and change-over-time essay. The final free-response question will require you to compare how two or more civilizations have dealt with one another or with a major historical issue. This question is called the comparative essay.

What's the Score?

Although the scoring process for the AP exam may seem quite complex, it boils down to two simple components: your multiple-choice score plus your free-response score, which account for your performance on the change-over-time and comparative essays and the DBQ. The multiple-choice section accounts for one-half of your overall score, and is generated by awarding one point toward your "raw score" for each question you answer correctly. The free-response section also accounts for one-half of your total score. Within the free-response section, each essay question counts equally toward your overall score for the section. Trained graders read students' written responses and assign points according to grading rubrics. The number of points you accrue out of the total possible will form your score on the free-response section. For the AP World History exam, these rubrics direct graders both to score your ability to provide an adequate response and to provide one that goes above-and-beyond. In order to receive consideration on these extra measures of excellence, however, you must first write an essay that meets the basic level of competence.

The College Board reports AP scores on a scale of 1 to 5. Although individual colleges and universities determine what credit or advanced placement, if any, is awarded to students at each score level, these are the assessments typically associated with each numeric score:

5   Extremely well qualified

4   Well qualified

3   Qualified

2   Possibly qualified

1   No recommendation

Section I: Strategies for the Multiple-Choice Section of the Exam

Because the AP exam is a standardized test, each version of the test from year to year must share many similarities in order to be fair. That means that you can always expect certain things to be true about your AP World History exam.

Which of the following phrases accurately describes a multiple-choice question on the AP World History exam?

(A)   always has four answer choices

(B)   may rely on a map, photo, or other visual stimulus

(C)   more likely to test interpretation and application content than names and dates

(D)   all of the above*

> Did you pick "all of the above?" Good job!

What does this mean for your study plan? You should focus more on the application and interpretation of various historical events and periods than on nuts and bolts such as names and dates, because the exam will not directly test your ability to memorize these types of details. Note that the AP World History exam presents you with four

---

*Of course, on the actual AP World History exam, you won't see any choices featuring "all of the above" or "none of the above." Do, however, watch for "except" questions. We'll cover this kind of item a bit later in this section.

answer choices for each multiple-choice item. This gives you slightly more time to answer each multiple-choice question than you may be accustomed to, but also reflects the exam's high level of required reading and interpretation.

The historical thinking skills tested on the AP World History exam require you to evaluate, compare, and describe historical developments in chronological and geographical contexts within one society and/or between or across multiple societies.

This means you should pay particular attention to political, social, and economic connections between and among societies over time. Below is a sample multiple-choice question that requires you to make these connections.

Sample Question:

Which of the following statements best describes Asia's relations with Europe from 1500–1850 C.E.?

(A)   European powers colonized all of Asia, including Japan, during this period.

(B)   European powers colonized all of Southeast Asia, but not South and East Asia during this period.

(C)   European powers defeated China in the Opium Wars, colonized India and large parts of Southeast Asia but for Thailand, and Japan pursued a policy of isolationism during this period.

(D)   European powers colonized India and traded with Japan, but failed to develop colonies in Southeast Asia.

The correct answer is (C). After the British defeat of China in the Opium Wars, Britain dominated trade in China. Britain colonized India, while France colonized Indonesia. Thailand remained free of European domination, and the Tokugawa expelled foreigners and pursued a policy of isolationism.

Types of Questions

You've already seen a list of the general content areas that you'll encounter on the AP World History exam. But how do those different areas translate into questions?

Question Type	Sample Question Stems
Cause and Effect	*Which of the following best describes the impact on slavery of the development of colonies in the New World?*
Change and Continuity	*Which statement does NOT describe changes in Latin America since World War II?*
Charts, Graphs, and Tables	*Based on the information in the graph, which statement best analyzes migration trends in Asia during the mid-nineteenth century?*
Compare and Contrast	*Which of the following statements best describes India during the reign of Akbar as compared to China during the late Ming dynasty?*
Definition/Identification	*Which of the following statements best describes Homo sapiens neanderthalensis?*
Fact	*Which of the following countries was the last to abolish slavery?*
Photograph	*The photograph above of a modern-day Buddhist temple in Thailand best displays what historical process?*
Political Cartoon	*Which of the following statements best describes the viewpoint of the creator of this political cartoon?*
Primary Source	*"If the spring of popular government in time of peace is virtue, the springs of popular government in revolution are at once virtue and terror... Subdue by terror the enemies of liberty, and you will be right, as founders of the Republic. The government of the revolution is liberty's despotism against tyranny."* *In what period of the European history does this quotation originate?*

Throughout this book, you will find tips on the features and strategies you can use to answer different types of questions.

Achieving Multiple-Choice Success

It's true that you don't have a lot of time to finish this section of the AP exam. But it's also true that you don't need to get every question right to get a great score. Answering just two-thirds of the questions correctly—along with a good showing on the free-response section—can earn you a score of a 4 or 5. That means that not only do you not have to answer every question right, you don't even need to answer every question at all. By *working quickly and methodically,* however, you'll have all the time you'll need.

Plan to spend just over 45 seconds on each multiple-choice question. You may find it helpful to use a timer or stopwatch as you answer one question a few times to help you get a handle on how long 45 seconds feels in a testing situation. If timing is hard for you, set a timer for ten minutes each time you take one of the 15-question online quizzes that accompany this book to help you practice working at speed. Let's look at some other strategies for answering multiple-choice items.

Process of Elimination

You've probably used the process-of-elimination strategy, intentionally or unintentionally, throughout your entire test-taking career. The process of elimination requires you to read each answer choice and consider whether it is the best response to the question given. Because the AP exam typically asks you to find the *best* answer rather than the *only* answer, it's almost always advantageous to read each answer choice. More than one choice may have some grain of truth to it, but only one—the right answer—will be the most correct. Let's examine a multiple-choice question and use the process of elimination approach:

Before jumping into a question based on a photograph or drawing, take a moment to study the image. Determine some basic facts about what you see, such as in which region of the world the item or place shown originated and which period of time it most likely reflects. This frame of reference will help you further analyze the image to answer the question.

The image above shows a tablet written in

(A) ~~Arabic~~

(B) Cuneiform

(C) ~~Hebrew~~

(D) ~~Sanskrit~~

> You should have noticed that this tablet seems to be quite ancient, so it probably shows a very early form of writing. Arabic is a relatively modern language, so you can eliminate that option. The writing shown uses a pictographic system. Hebrew uses an alphabetic system, and Sanskrit has used a variety of alphabetic and syllabic systems. Thus, neither of these choices can be correct, leaving only (B) as a possibility.

Students often find the most difficult question types on the AP exam to be those that ask you to find a statement that is *not* true or to identify an *exception* to a general rule. To answer these questions correctly, you must be sure to carefully read and consider each answer choice, keeping in mind that three of them will be correct and just one wrong. Sometimes you can find the right answer by picking the one that just does not fit with the other choices. If three answer choices relate to civilizations that flourished during the Classical period, for example, the correct answer choice may well be the one that relates to a civilization that became powerful during the early Medieval period. Let's take a look at a multiple-choice question of this type.

Which of the following statements is NOT a correct description of medieval monasticism?

(A) The Benedictine philosophy of *ora et labora* inspired the copying and preservation of ancient manuscripts.

(B) Nuns were not instrumental in the spread of Christianity.

(C) Anglo-Saxon abbesses were very powerful.

(D) European monks and nuns often lived according to mixed rules prior to the reforms of Benedict of Aniane.

> To answer a NOT or EXCEPT question correctly, test each option by asking yourself: *Is this choice true? Does this correctly state a fact about medieval monastic life and its influence?* You may wish to physically cross off answer choices as you eliminate them. Notice that only choice (B) states something in a negative way. This should tip you off to consider this option carefully. You might remember that at least one nun took part in a Christian mission. Thus, this statement is *not* true.

Predicting

Although using the process of elimination certainly helps you consider each answer choice thoroughly, testing each and every answer can be a slow process. To help answer the most questions in the limited time given AP test takers, you may find it helpful to instead try predicting the right answer *before* you read the answer choices. For example, you know that the answer to the math problem two-plus-two will always be four. If you saw this multiple-choice item on a math test, you wouldn't need to systematically test each response, but could go straight to the right answer. You can apply a similar technique to even complex items on the AP exam. Brainstorm your own answer to the question before reading the answer choices. Then, pick the answer choice closest to the one you brainstormed. Let's look at how this technique could work on a common type of question on the AP World History exam—one with a visual stimulus.

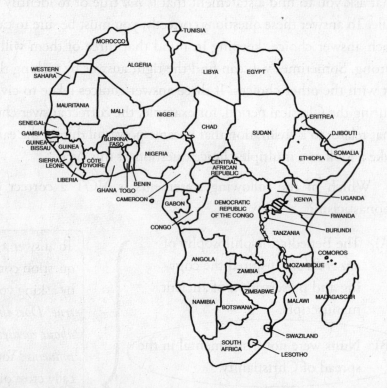

Read the question and look at the map. Take note of which countries are represented on the map. Pay close attention to the locations of borders and the names of different nations. Ask yourself, *When did Africa take on this form? Is this a modern map, or does it reflect a specific historical period?* You may wish to look closely for specific places that you know fell under colonial rule, for example. Are these places shown in their colonial state, an earlier one, or a later one?

Look carefully at the map on the previous page. This map represents Africa

(A) before 1880.

(B) in 1900.

(C) 1915-1949.

(D) post-1950.

> Make a prediction about which time period this map represents. Then look for your prediction among the answer choices.

What should you do if you don't see your prediction among the answer choices? Your prediction should have helped you narrow down the choices. You may wish to apply the process of elimination to the remaining options to further home in on the right answer. Then, you can use your historical knowledge to make a good guess.

Learning to predict takes some practice. You're probably used to immediately reading all of the answer choices for a question, but in order to predict well, you usually need to avoid doing this. Remember, the test maker doesn't want to make the right answers too obvious, so the wrong answers are intended to sound like appealing choices. You may find it helpful to physically cover up the answer choices to a question as you practice predicting. This will ensure that you don't sneak a peek at the choices too soon.

Sometimes, though, you might need to have a rough idea of the answer choices in order to make a solid prediction or be prepared to refine your prediction, especially when there are a lot of possible ways to interpret a question. Let's examine another question with a visual stimulus to practice predicting in this way.

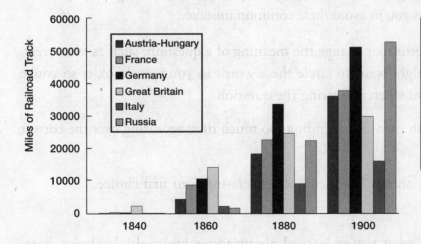

> This chart could support any number of conclusions. Take a moment to make some broad generalizations about its content, such as, *countries experienced uneven levels of growth* or *Italy had the least development overall.*

Read the question and look at the chart. Quickly skim the answer choices to see if they give you any guidance. Notice that all of the answer choices deal with Germany, Great Britain, and Russia. You can see that you should focus your predictions on trends relating to these three countries. Ask yourself, *How did each country's railroad tracks grow over time? Which country or countries had the most track overall early in the Industrial Era? Which country or countries had the most track overall late in the Industrial Era?* Then make a prediction about the chart.

What does the chart on the previous page illustrate?

(A) Germany had the greatest number of railroads prior to 1860.

(B) Great Britain clearly held the lead in industrialization after 1860.

(C) Russia lagged behind Great Britain in industrialization, when measured by railroad tracks, after 1880.

(D) Russia and Germany eclipsed Great Britain in miles of railroad created after 1880.

Consider each of the possible answer choices. Ask yourself, *Does this choice match with the prediction I made about what this map shows?* Then select the answer choice that most closely matches your prediction.

Avoiding Common Errors

Remember, answering questions correctly is as important as answering every question. Work at a pace that allows you to avoid these common mistakes:

- Missing key words that change the meaning of a question, such as *not, except,* or *least.* You might want to circle these words in your test booklet so you're tuned into them when answering the question.

- Overthinking an item and spending too much time agonizing over the correct response.

- Changing your answer but incompletely erasing your first choice.

Some More Advice

Let's quickly review what you've learned about answering multiple-choice questions effectively on the AP exam. Using these techniques on practice tests will help you become comfortable with them before diving into the real exam, so be sure to apply these ideas as you work through this book.

- Big ideas are more important than minutiae. Focus on learning important historical concepts, causation, and connections instead of memorizing names and dates.

- You only have about 45 seconds to complete each multiple-choice question. Pacing yourself during practice tests and exercises can help you get used to these time constraints.

- Because there is no guessing penalty, remember that making an educated guess is to your benefit. Remember to use the process of elimination to narrow your choices. You might just guess the correct answer and get another point!

- Instead of spending valuable time pondering narrow distinctions or questioning your first answer, trust yourself to make good guesses most of the time.

- Read the question and think of what your answer would be before reading the answer choices.

- Expect the unexpected. You will see questions that ask you to apply information in various ways, such as picking the wrong idea or interpreting a map, chart, or even a photograph.

Section II: Strategies for the Free-Response Section of the Exam

The AP World History exam always contains three free-response questions in its second section. This section allows you 130 minutes to respond to all three of these questions. The first question will always require you to interpret a series of primary source documents to make a historical argument. The second question will ask you to examine how broad historical topics have experienced change and continuity over time in one or more civilizations. Finally, the third question will require you to discuss similarities and differences among civilizations and their histories. Let's examine these three forms of free-response questions in turn.

Taking on the Document-Based Question

The document-based question, also known as the DBQ, will present you with an essay prompt along with several written or visual primary source documents. Before you can begin writing, you must spend 10 minutes reviewing the documents. You may take notes on the documents in your DBQ booklet. DBQs rarely present you with documents with which you are already familiar, so don't worry if you have no prior knowledge of the subject matter. Using historical skills, like grouping and finding the author's point of view, is what will matter most. Let's take a look at a typical DBQ.

DIRECTIONS: The following question is based on accompanying Documents 1–4. Read the documents and write an essay that:

- Has a relevant thesis and supports that thesis with evidence from the documents.

- Uses all of the documents.

- Analyzes the documents by grouping them in as many appropriate ways as possible. Do not simply summarize the documents individually.

- Takes into account the sources of the documents and analyzes the authors' points of view.

- Identifies and explains the need for at least one additional type of document.

You may refer to relevant historical information not mentioned in the documents.

All DBQs will start with a series of directions similar to these. Be sure to address each of the bulleted points on this list. Although some points, such as including a thesis and using all of the documents, may seem obvious, you're probably less accustomed to suggesting additional sources of information that would clarify historical ideas or present alternate viewpoints in your writing.

Using documents 1–4, analyze the effects of the Mongol occupation of Russia from the 13th through the 15th century.

- *Primary source from French ambassador William of Rubruck describing the Mongols in Russia, ca. 1255*

- *Excerpt from "Mongol Charter of Immunity Granted to the Church" (1267)*

- *Excerpt from* Tver Chronicle, *1237*

- *Excerpt from the* Chronicle of Novgorod *describing a Mongol invasion*

> This list tells you the typical types of documents that you might see on a document-based question. An actual item would provide text passages or images on which you could base your analysis. Remember, you will have a 10-minute reading period at the beginning of the time allotted for the document-based question during which you are required to read and consider the documents. Use this time wisely by thoroughly examining the documents and taking good notes in your test booklet.

Remember, you do not need to have a great deal of knowledge outside what is presented in the documents to perform well on this type of question. Graders will primarily look for your ability to construct a solid thesis-based discussion based on the information given in the documents. A good essay will include an analysis of the points of view of at least two or three creators and combine information from the documents in various ways to draw conclusions and support arguments. You may draw on your historical knowledge to expand your interpretation, but you can receive a solid score without including a great deal of extra information.

Step One: Evaluating Primary Source Documents

Although each document-based question is different, you can follow the same steps in order to answer all of them effectively. Because this particular type of question requires you to draw on the documents provided, you should first evaluate your sources in the context of the essay question given on the exam; the mandatory 10-minute reading period on the exam ensures that you have the chance to do just that. Remember, when interpreting primary sources, you should think about the author or creator of the work. Ask yourself, *What was the author's intention? What biases did the author have? Is the author reliable? What was the historical context in which this document was produced?* Keep in mind that even seemingly bland documents such as law decrees are products of their time and place. Religious declarations, for example, exist strongly in their historical context and should be considered just as critically as a diary entry.

Take notes and mark up the documents as you consider them. Circle key ideas or points that you may wish to include in your argument, and jot down ideas and historical connections in the margins of your booklet. This is a good time to brainstorm, but try to stay focused on the question presented in the essay prompt.

Step Two: Developing an Outline

The test maker gives students 40 minutes on top of the reading period to plan and write the DBQ essay. Even though time is relatively short, you should dedicate five minutes to developing a simple outline to guide your writing. Creating a simple outline will allow you to organize your thoughts, brainstorm good examples, and reject ideas that don't really work once you think about them. Your outline should include a thesis statement and the main points you wish to include in your essay. To help organize your essay, you may wish to divide your ideas paragraph by paragraph, or list them in the order in which you plan to discuss them. In your outline, add references to the specific documents you wish to include in your argument to help you remember what you've read. You will need to cite these documents by name or author as you write, so including this information here will ease the writing process. Make your outline short, to the point, and complete, and by following it, your response will naturally have the same qualities.

Perhaps the most important part of your outline is your thesis statement. Your thesis statement should be a clear, direct response to the question posed in the essay prompt. Including a relevant and well-supported thesis is the single most important step you can take to achieving a good score in this section. You'll lose one point on your essay if you do not state your thesis. To help you generate a suitable thesis, restate the question with your answer in a complete sentence. For this particular DBQ, you should consider how the Mongol occupation of Russia influenced those two civilizations. For example, you might say, *The Mongol Empire used its unique military prowess to occupy and reshape life in Russia during its long occupation of that nation.*

Step Three: Writing a Response

Once you've written a good outline, stick to it! As you write your response, you'll find that most of the hard work is already done, and you can focus on *expressing your ideas clearly, concisely, and completely.* Remember, too, that the essay scorers know what information has been provided in the documents. Don't waste time and effort quoting the contents of the documents unless you are adding your own interpretation; if you do so, however, be sure to clearly cite each source. Also be sure to include all of the major ideas from your outline and to stick to the topic. You'll have plenty of time to complete your essay if you don't get distracted and follow your plan.

As you're writing your responses, keep in mind what the AP Readers will see when they sit down to consider your answers weeks from now. Expressing your ideas clearly and succinctly will help them best understand your point and ensure that you get the best possible score. Using your clearest handwriting will also do wonders for your overall score; free-response graders are used to reading poor handwriting, but that doesn't mean they can decipher every scribble you might make.

Be sure to state your thesis clearly and succinctly in the opening paragraph of your essay. This will highlight your main argument from the start and let scorers know what they're looking for throughout the rest of the essay. Restating your thesis and main points at the conclusion of the essay is another good practice.

Step Four: Revising Your Response

Even the best writers make mistakes, especially when writing quickly: skipping or repeating words, misspelling names of people or places, and neglecting to include an important point from an outline are all common errors when you're rushed. Reserving a few minutes at the end of your writing period will allow you to quickly review your responses and make necessary corrections. Adding skipped words or including forgotten information are the two most important edits you can make to your writing, because these will clarify your ideas and help your score.

A Sample DBQ Response

After you've read, considered, outlined, planned, wrote, and revised, what do you have? A thoughtful written answer likely to earn you a good score, that's what. Review the sample response given below to help you understand what a well-planned, thoughtful DBQ essay should contain.

The Mongol Empire used its unique military prowess to occupy and reshape life in Russia during its long occupation of that nation. The documents provided reveal many things about the Mongols and their occupation of Russia. For one thing, document

#1 points to the order and discipline among the Mongol forces that account for their conquests. Chingiz Khan (also known as Genghis Khan), the greatest Mongol leader, established a clear chain of command among his forces and instilled within them a sense of unity and discipline. He did this partly by promising loot to his conquering troops and, as we see in this document, partly by the threat of death for shirkers.

Mongol soldiers were not paid; they relied on loot to make a living. That is one thing that attracted them to war. Fear of deadly punishment kept them fighting once the battle began. Because the Mongols were a nomadic people, Mongol fighters did not have the burden of being away from "home," a trial soldiers in their empires before and after the Mongols did have to deal with.

In addition to being fierce and disciplined fighters, the Mongols employed weaponry and tactics that gave them advantages over their foes. As we see in document #2, Mongol men made bows and arrows and tended to horses. This reminds us that Mongols fought with powerful bows and arrows, and they fought mainly on horseback. Infantry were no match for them. Document #2 also suggests that Mongol women accompanied men during their campaigns, and Mongol men and women divided some tasks and shared others. As in the majority of the world's societies until modern times, Mongol men dominated in the public sphere, and women cared primarily for homes and children.

In the western part of their empire, the Mongols remained in Russia the longest. Document #3 reveals how ruthless the Mongols could be and how little they cared about sacred places when in battle. Document #3 also shows that, as was common before the modern period, the Russians interpreted the Mongols' ruthlessness as God's punishment for sin.

Following conquests, the Mongols usually allowed locals to run their own affairs, so long as they paid tribute and homage to the khan—the Mongol who ruled a region of the vast empire. Mongols would sometimes adopt the dominant religions of the regions they conquered. In China, many became Buddhist; further west, many became Muslim. In Russia, churches were exempt from paying taxes. This tolerance for local institutions is expressed in document #4, where we read that Russian church property "should be neither occupied, expropriated, alienated or destroyed [by Mongols]."

Of course, praying for and adhering to the rules of the Mongols required Russians to, at least, appear to have changed their opinions of the Golden Horde, as the Mongol occupiers were called. At first, the Mongols were seen by the Russians as pagan, lawless, and godless scourges used by God to punish the people. Now Mongols had to be tolerated and prayed for. Sometimes, during the occupation, Russians would rise up against the Mongols, as we see in document #5. When this happened, Mongol ruthlessness returned: Russians were slaughtered and towns were burned.

The Mongol empire lasted into the sixteenth century, when it disintegrated as all empires eventually do. But the empire had very important long-term consequences. One major consequence is that this empire, which spread from East Asia into Eastern Europe, made it easier for goods, missionaries, merchants (such as Marco Polo), and adventures to travel the Silk Highway. This led to increased interest in Asia among Europeans and to a rising level of commercial exchange between Asia and Europe. This set the stage for the Age of Discovery, which would lead to the global empires of the French, Dutch, Portuguese, Spanish and British. In a sense, the Mongol empire begat several empires whose actions would, in turn, create many modern nations.

Taking on the Continuity and Change-Over-Time Essay

You've conquered the DBQ, and now you're ready for the next stage of the free-response section: the continuity and change-over-time essay. Like the DBQ, your success on this essay will hinge on your ability to make and support a thesis-based historical argument. Unlike the DBQ, however, you'll draw exclusively on your own historical knowledge to explore big-picture themes, such as technology, population movements, trade, cultural shifts, environmental changes, and so on. Often, the continuity and change-over-time essay will allow you to select from among several options to discuss in your essay. This allows you to play to your strengths by picking the group you feel the most confident writing about.

As the name suggests, this essay asks you to develop an argument on how one or more civilizations underwent broad change over a stated period of time as it relates to a given theme. To do this, you need to compare and contrast information across time to find similarities and differences from one period to the next. Then you'll need to thoughtfully analyze the causes and consequences of this continuity and change. Let's look at a typical continuity and change-over-time essay.

Cultural mixing and cultural clashes are among the most common themes in human history. Focusing on the period 1300 to 1600, discuss the cultural mixing and cultural clashes involving one of the groupings below.

- *Protestants, Catholics, and Jews in Western Europe*

- *Muslims and Hindus in India*

- *Spaniards, Africans, and Aztecs in Mexico*

Because the most important thing that you must do to score well on these essays is to respond fully to the essay prompt, you should begin by asking yourself what, exactly, the essay wishes you to do. You may choose to rephrase the prompt in your own words. For example, this essay prompt could be rephrased as: *How did cultural interaction among people in one of the given groups shape history between 1300 and 1600?*

Step One: Developing an Outline

With no primary sources to evaluate, you can skip straight to prewriting on the continuity and change-over-time essay. The test maker allows you 40 minutes to address this essay and suggests you spend five minutes on outlining and planning, but no reading period is mandated.

The continuity and change-over-time essay does not require the same level of analysis as the DBQ, but does draw on a greater level of your own historical knowledge. You may choose to organize your outline by paragraph or by main idea to help you brainstorm major details and ideas to include for each required section. Be sure to include a thesis statement in your first paragraph to make sure the AP Reader understands your argument right off the bat. Then include one or two major ideas or details in each of your supporting paragraphs. Use as many paragraphs as you need to discuss fully the information you wish to present. Write these main points in your outline so you don't forget them when it comes time to write. Your final paragraph should contain a conclusion that wraps up your ideas and restates your thesis.

Step Two: Writing a Response

All the same rules apply when writing answers to the continuity and change-over-time essay as did on the DBQ, although you don't need to worry about citing your sources or suggesting additional resources. Stick to your outline, stick to the point, and stick to the topic to produce the best and most concise response possible. The AP exam isn't a term paper, so you're not being scored on spelling and grammar. However, don't forget to include transition words to help guide the AP Reader through your argument and to follow the ideas you brainstormed in your outline.

Step Three: Revising Your Response

Remember that essay graders are not mind readers, so they will only grade what's on the page, not what you thought you were writing. At the same time, remember, too, that essay graders do not deduct points for wrong information, so you don't need to spend time erasing errors. Just write a sentence at the end of your essay or, if you've skipped lines, on the line below that corrects your mistake.

A Sample Response

How would you have answered the essay question given earlier in the chapter? Review this sample response to see what one good response looks like. Remember, there's no one right answer to a given essay question, although high-scoring responses will always be based on accurate historical facts. You may choose to interpret those facts in a way that's out of the ordinary as long as you adequately support the ideas in your thesis.

When Spaniards met Africans and purchased them as slaves from other Africans, and when the Spaniards and their slaves met Aztecs in present-day Mexico, violence and conquest were inevitable. But that conquest would lead to a new culture in the New World.

By 1500, Muslims who had occupied Iberia (Portugal and Spain) for centuries were pushed out. At this same time, Jews were being expelled from Spain, partly as a result of the Spanish Inquisition. These experiences of conflict provide some context for the conquest of what would come to be called New Spain. At the same time, Europeans from France, Portugal, and the Netherlands, as well as from Spain, were pursuing Asian wealth in the form of spices and silk, for example. They also sought gold and glory for their monarchs as well as souls to convert to Christianity. It was en route to Asia that the Portuguese and Spaniards came upon the New World—the West Indies, the Caribbean, and North, Central and South America.

West Africans (from present-day Senegal to Nigeria) had enslaved one another for a long time before Europeans capitalized on the slave trade. European traders provided commodities to tribal leaders in exchange for slaves. The Spaniards brought Africans to the New World with one generation of Columbus's landfall in 1492.

Unlike some indigenous peoples in the New World, the Aztecs were a sedentary people—that is, they established settlements and remained in them for long periods of time. The Aztecs employed sophisticated irrigation systems and used fertilizer to grow crops. They had highly organized political and religious structures. Yet given the limits on their knowledge, they were capable astronomers; the Pyramid of the Sun was the largest pyramid in the world. The Aztec capital, Tenochtitlan, was larger than the Spanish capital of Madrid.

Like the Spaniards and slave-selling African tribes, the Aztecs were conquerors. Just as the Spaniards had conquered Muslims and put great pressure on Jews, so had the Aztecs conquered and put great pressure on other Native groups. When the Spaniards and Aztecs met, conflict was inevitable.

The striking thing is that the Aztec empire, which had many thousands of fighters at its disposal, was toppled in a few years by a few hundred Spaniards. How was this possible? The most important weapon the Spaniards had was European disease, especially smallpox, which killed many more Aztecs than Spanish weapons did. The West Africans, who had contact with Europeans long before 1519 (the year the conquistador Hernán Cortés arrived in Mexico), were more able to survive European diseases. This is a major reason that Spaniards (and other Europeans) turned to African slave labor—the Aztecs and other Natives died quickly from disease.

Another thing the Spaniards had in their favor was advanced technology in the form of guns, cannons, and swords. They also had ferocious dogs and horses, the latter of which the Aztecs had never seen before. These weapons contributed to an Aztec belief that the Spaniards had extraordinary spiritual power. A third thing the Spaniards had on their side was the hatred Native groups had for the Aztecs. Like the Spaniards and Africans, the Aztecs enslaved conquered peoples, and some conquered people were used as human sacrifices in Aztec religious rituals. The Spaniards made use of the idea that "the enemy of my enemy is my friend" and convinced Native groups to help defeat the Aztecs. Of course, many of these Natives would soon die of disease.

After the conquest of the Aztec empire, a new culture began to emerge in present-day Mexico. Very few Spanish women accompanied the mostly young men who went to conquer and settle New Spain. This led to widespread intermarriage between Spanish men and indigenous women and to the creation of people who would be called mestizos, *people of mixed ethnicity. Hundreds of Spanish words were absorbed by Nahuatl, the language spoken by the Aztecs, but the indigenous language did not die out; officials in New Spain often kept records in Nahuatl. The Spaniards' Catholicism became the religion of New Spain. This was made easier to accept by the Spaniards' practice of building churches on sites where Aztec gods had been honored before.*

Since 1600, the descendents of the Spaniards, Africans, Aztecs (and other indigenous peoples) have forged unique Latin American cultures. Catholicism in Mexico today looks and feels different from Catholicism in the United States. This is largely because of indigenous influence.

Taking on the Comparative Essay

Part C of the free-response section presents you with your final challenge—the comparative essay. This essay shares several similarities with the continuity and change-over-time essay. Like its predecessor, the comparative essay focuses on broad historical themes and asks you to consider similarities and differences. However, instead of discussing those similarities and differences across time periods, you'll investigate them in the context of one or more historical civilizations. Another handy similarity to the continuity and change-over-time essay is the test maker's frequent inclusion of choice. Again, you may be able to pick from a series of options which specific example you'll discuss, allowing you to present the one about which you know the most.

Writing and supporting a clear thesis is again a key to your success in the comparative essay. You must also include relevant, direct comparisons between the groups identified and offer logical analyses for the reasons behind these similarities and differences. To further bolster your argument, be sure to include substantive historical evidence. Consider, too, whether you can place your comparisons within a broader global context. Doing this may help you garner additional points toward your free-response score. Let's look at a typical comparative essay.

Analyze similarities and differences in the basic features of the religions given in one of the following groupings:

- *Hinduism and Judaism*

- *Confucianism and Christianity*

- *Islam and Buddhism*

Again, try restating the question in your own words to help you get started. Then ask a series of questions to drill down further. For example, you may ask, *What characteristics do the two religions in any pair have in common? What basic points do they agree on? What differences do they have? What basic points do they disagree on? How do the historical and geographical situations of these religions match up? How do they draw apart?*

Step One: Developing an Outline

Like the continuity and change-over-time essay, the test maker allows you 40 minutes to address this essay prompt. Again, you should plan to spend five minutes on outlining and planning. Your first decision, if needed, should be which grouping you wish to discuss. Remember that picking a group about which you have adequate knowledge of all the members will help you more than picking one that contains one member about which you know a lot and another about which you know very little.

You may find it easier to consider specific similarities and differences first, and then use those notes to develop a thesis. To do this, set up a simple T-chart listing each group separately. Identify direct comparisons or contrasts between the two groups in a row within the chart. Study the details you have brainstormed. Then make a generalization about what you have written. This generalization may serve as the basis for your thesis statement.

Step Two: Writing a Response

By this time, you may be getting tired. Don't let an achy hand or a dragging brain keep you from writing clearly, concisely, and neatly. Be sure to follow your outline. If you've done your prewriting well, executing your essay should be simple: just present the ideas and evidence you've noted in a logical way. Remember, showing and analyzing direct comparisons and contrasts is a big part of your score for this essay. Include words and phrases to show these relations, such as *like, similarly, in the same way, however,* and *on the other hand.* Key words like these help AP graders understand your argument and help emphasize how well you have organized your ideas.

Step Three: Revising Your Response

If you're feeling pressed for time at the end of the writing period, focus on completing only the most important revisions. Make sure that your thesis is stated clearly early in your essay. Add missing words that are needed to make your writing comprehensible. Be sure that transition words that show the comparisons and contrasts in your argument are sprinkled liberally throughout your paragraphs. All of these steps will be more beneficial to your overall score than making sure you've used the spelling *Koran* or *Qur'an* consistently throughout your essay.

A Sample Response

Based on the samples that you've seen thus far in this chapter, you are probably starting to get a good idea of what a solid, well-written response looks like. How might you answer the comparative essay prompt presented earlier? Read through the following sample response. Pay attention to how the writer quickly states her thesis and provides direct comparisons and contrasts between the religions discussed. Take note, too, of how the writer provides additional information to place the discussion in a global context.

Buddhism and Islam are quite complicated and, although, they are very different, they have some commonalties. Buddhism and Islam both provide their adherents with comprehensive outlooks on life, they both address the big questions of human existence—such as "How can I live a good life?"—and they both place at their centers individuals who acquired the truth and preached it to others. These individuals— Buddha Gotama and Mohammed—are essential to Buddhism and Islam, but they, themselves, are not worshipped. This is one key difference these religions have from Christianity, whose central figure is Jesus Christ, whom Christians believe is God.

The Buddha Gotama (also called Siddhattha or Sidhartha) lived in India in the sixth century BCE. (According to tradition, twenty-five Buddhas preceded him.) After standing up to significant temptation and after lengthy meditation, Buddha Gotama entered a transcendental realm. He could have stayed in that realm but decided instead to preach the Dhamma—the truth about the world. Part of the Buddhist truth is that suffering is an illusion that is brought on by impermanent human desires.

Compared to Buddhism, Islam is a new religion. According to Muslim tradition, in the late sixth century CE, near Mecca, Mohammed meditated through the night. He was disturbed by the polytheistic religious practice he saw in Arabia. At one point an angel told him to write down what the angel said. These writings became the Koran, which Muslims around the world are still encouraged to read in Arabic. According to Islam, Mohammad was the last and greatest of God's prophets on earth. He had been preceded by other important prophets such as Abraham, Moses, and Jesus, but none of these were as great as Mohammed. This is one important differ- ence between Islam and Judaism, which does not recognize Mohammad as a great prophet. Also, Muslims are strictly monotheistic, and to them, the Christian idea of the Trinity equals polytheism.

Islam spread quickly through Arabia, the rest of the Middle East, and North Africa, and it remains the dominant religion in those regions. Muslims occupied Spain beginning in the eight century, and they remained there for centuries. By the eleventh century, Muslims were moving into Afghanistan and India.

Islam spread primarily as a result of conquest, but also as a result of proselytism and of the conversion of local leaders. Buddhism, on the other hand, began in India, but it never was the dominant religion there. (Hinduism and Islam gained more adherents.) Buddhism became more dominant in other parts of Asia, such as Vietnam, Thailand, and Cambodia.

Traditional Buddhists do not believe that individuals possess souls. Indeed, they believe that the idea of the "self" is an illusion. For Buddhists, their primary goal is to achieve "awakening"— freedom from the cares and concerns of this impermanent life. If a Buddhist achieves a desire-free life, then he or she has achieved nirvana, an eternal realm of selfless perfection. Traditional Muslims, on the other hand, believe in human souls, and they believe that people who do not submit to the will of Allah (i.e., God) will suffer in hell, about which the Koran (the Muslims' most important book) has a lot to say. People who do submit to the will of Allah will go to a paradise after this life. The word Islam means "submission." The western concept of "free will" is not important to traditional Muslims.

Muslims are required to adhere to the Five Pillars of Islam. The first pillar is the Muslim's confession of faith—that there is only one God and that Mohammed is his prophet. The second pillar involves prayer five times a day, facing Mecca. The third pillar calls for alms to be given to assist the poor. The fourth pillar requires fasting from dawn to dusk during the month of Ramadan. The fifth pillar calls on all Muslims to make at least one pilgrimage to Mecca in their lifetimes, if they are able to do so.

Buddhists believe in the "middle way"—not going to extremes. This means, for example, that people should avoid both gluttony and extreme fasting. Buddhists call for meditation under the direction of an experienced practitioner, which leads to ethical behavior and the elimination of earthly desire. Buddhists discourage clouding the mind with drugs and alcohol, sexual immorality, and harming living things.

While Buddhism and Islam have some features in common, they have very different approaches to life.

Some More Advice

What have you learned about the free-response section? Keep these ideas in mind as you prepare for the AP World History exam. Becoming comfortable with these techniques will make you feel confident and prepared when you sit down to take the exam in May.

- Remember that the DBQ, the continuity and change-over-time essay, and the comparative essay questions require different approaches. You should be mentally prepared to address all of these essay types.

- Be sure to read thoroughly and evaluate all of the sources given with the DBQ. Make notes in your test booklet, and think of additional information to further contextualize the provided sources.

- Make a clear and concise outline before you begin writing. This will help you organize your thoughts and speed up the actual writing process.

- Stay on topic and answer the question! Addressing the question fully is the single most important way to earn points on this section.

- Handwriting is important and must be legible! If the AP Reader can't read your writing, you'll get no points, even if your response is correct.

- Leave a few minutes to quickly review and revise your answers. You don't need to check the spelling of every single word, but you do need to make sure that all of your ideas made it onto the page. Skipping lines while you write will leave room for you to add important words and ideas, and make it easier for the scorer to read your handwriting.

Two Final Words: Don't Panic!

The free-response questions can and probably will ask you about specific historical concepts and examples you haven't thought about in much detail before: The relationship between the Reformation and later political revolutions in Europe and the Americas, perhaps? The connections between democratic movements of Eastern Europe and Southeast Asia in the late twentieth century? The possibilities are practically endless. Remember that all free-response questions seek to test your knowledge of big-picture historical themes and concepts and not your ability to write a list of battles or recite the names of Egyptian pharaohs from the Old Kingdom until the Ptolemaic era. Applying what you know about broad historical causation to these specific scenarios will help you get a great score, even if you're never thought much about the particular event presented in the question.

Unit I: Technological and Environmental Transformations, to c. 600 BCE

Big Geography and the Peopling of the Earth

Prehistory refers to the vast period of time before approximately 3000 BCE, when written records first appeared in Mesopotamia. **History**, essentially, is the time during which there are written records of human activities. The historic era represents a small fraction of the human past, from 3000 BCE to the present time. The terms *prehistoric* and *historic* do not so much describe the sorts of cultures that existed as they describe the ways that modern historians study them. The historical method emphasizes the use of written primary sources or firsthand accounts of the past. Traditionally, the written record has been considered the most important kind of primary source, whereas in the prehistoric periods, scholars must rely on fossil evidence and **artifacts**, or objects actually made by human hands.

Key Terms

artifacts	Paleolithic era
cave of Lascaux	polydaemonism
history	polytheism
hominid	prehistory
Homo sapiens	savanna
hunter-gatherers	Venus figures

The Paleolithic Era

Human cultures first appeared in the latter part of the **Paleolithic era**, which means "Old Stone Age." This name is derived from abundant evidence that stone was the primary medium out of which early hominids (human-like creatures) and, later, *Homo sapiens,* made tools. Although the Paleolithic era lasted much longer than all historical periods combined, historians know the least about this time period and its early humans. The main reasons for our limited knowledge about them is that, because they lived so long ago, many of their artifacts and traces of their lives have been eradicated by time and the natural processes of Earth and weather. There's also the stark fact that they did not have organized systems of writing.

By the end of the Paleolithic era, in about 10,000 BCE, humans' general physical appearance and mental capacity had evolved to nearly the same degree that they are at present. For approximately 30,000 years, *Homo sapiens* (the modern human species) had successfully competed with other hominids for meat and desirable places to take shelter. *Homo sapiens'* enlarged brain, their erect posture, which allowed them the free use of their hands, and their opposable thumbs enabled them to make and use tools and weapons with increasing sophistication. With implements, humans were no longer at a disadvantage to rival predators with greater strength and speed and lethal teeth and claws, such as wildcats and wolves. In addition, their development of language helped humans to develop small communities characterized by cooperation and a form of social organization. The advantages that humans had developed made them superior to other animals and paved the way for them to become the masters of their environments.

The first humans likely originated in the **savannas,** or grassy plains, of East Africa, where the climate was pleasant, food was plentiful, and animals that could be domesticated were abundant. These early humans were hunters and gatherers. The hunters were very skillful at capturing and killing wild animals, while gatherers learned which wild fruits, berries, and nuts were edible, nonpoisonous, and nutritious. The development of tools and other innovations greatly helped humans in both hunting and gathering. Humans first used stones and later, metals, to make tools and weapons, and they gradually learned, through experience, new techniques to gather and store food more efficiently.

TEST TIP

Do not try to cram for the AP World History exam. Study for the exam throughout the school year and begin to study comprehensively for the test at least six weeks before the scheduled exam day—or even earlier if you are involved in many other activities.

Migration and Adaptation

Migration, a major theme of world history, began in prehistory. During the Paleolithic period, humans gradually migrated from Africa to parts of the Middle East, Europe, Asia, and Australia, and from Asia to North and South America. Small bands of humans migrated from Africa to the Middle East about 100,000 years ago, to Australia by about 40,000 years ago, and to the east by about 25,000 years ago. Other groups migrated about 15,000 years ago to North America across the Bering Strait using a strip of land that once connected Siberia with the Americas. By 10,000 BCE, humans had reached South America. These migrations probably resulted from the necessity of following animal herds for sustenance and of finding other new sources of food.

Humans were highly creative in adapting to and surviving in a variety of climates and terrains as they moved from their origins in the grassy plains of Africa to vastly different geographical settings and climates, ranging from deserts to dense forests to the frigid northern tundra. In these new environments humans encountered many new species of animals and plants, as well as new weather patterns and terrain. They successfully met the challenges they faced by refining and adapting their simple, all-purpose tools and weapons into a variety of specialized implements, with each being suited to a particular environment and specific purpose, from hunting, disassembling animal carcasses, fishing, and harvesting wild plants to building makeshift tents and other forms of shelter.

Humans in different areas of the world progressed, independently of one another, beyond the all-purpose stone-and-wooden hand axes and flint tools of earlier times and began making extensive use of animal bones, antlers, and ivory to craft much more specialized tools. These tools included harpoons for fishing; large leaf-shaped and grooved spears with shafts for hunting large game; javelin tips; scrapers for scraping fur from animal hides, meat from animal bones, and bark from trees; and various types of reworked blades with handles. Humans also made bone needles to sew animal hides into clothing and tents, wove bags for carrying items from plant fibers and animal hair, and fashioned leather straps for various purposes. They made boats of various constructions, each adapted to the body of water it was meant to traverse and the natural materials that were available to make it.

Adaptation to New Environments

Groups of **hunter-gatherers** who migrated to the tropical and subtropical coastlands of Europe and Asia probably adapted most easily to their new environments because they did not face the challenges of significantly new and different environmental conditions. These areas had comfortable climates that did not present extremely difficult challenges related to shelter, as well as plentiful plants, fish, and wild game.

In contrast, humans who migrated to northeastern Europe and even farther north to the tundra needed much more creativity to develop specialized innovations to adapt to these harsh environments. Some constructed pit houses, dwellings dug into the ground with roofs made of animal hides or logs filled in with tightly packed soil, and they learned to sew animal hides and fur into warm clothing and tents using needles made of animal bones. They were forced to become even more efficient hunters, as plants were scare and many of the wild animals they encountered, such as mammoths, were very large.

Migrations to Australia and overseas to Asia provide clear evidence of the abilities of early humans not only to adapt to new environments, but also to plan and execute the necessary preparations to do so. They would have had to design and build boats suitable for the journey through eastern seas and have sophisticated knowledge of how to navigate. They also would have needed knowledge of what supplies they needed to take with them to survive a journey whose destination they could not have known. Burial sites, tools, and other artifacts found in southern Australia and dating back to around 30,000 BCE indicate that the human population grew rapidly once humans had settled there. This could only have happened because the humans who originally landed there adapted extremely rapidly to the geographic features, climate, animals, and plants there, which were vastly different from those of Eastern Africa.

DIDYOUKNOW?

Scientists have discovered that Ötzi, the 5,000-year-old iceman whose mummified remains were found in the Alps of Northern Italy in 1991, enjoyed a meal of ibex (wild goat) less than two hours before his death. In addition to the red meat, scientists also found wheat grain, animal hair, and fly parts in Ötzi's stomach contents as well as ash particles, which may indicate that the red meat was cooked over a fire.

Fire

By this time, humans had learned to control fire, which they used in many ways to adapt to new environments. Without fire it would have been impossible for humans to remain warm in the northern areas to which they wandered. Because of its light and warmth, fire was the center of small campsites in every geographical setting. Humans used fire as a natural protective deterrent for predatory animals, and as means to defend themselves against these animals and to chase them away.

Humans also made use of fire to prepare food, especially animal flesh, their only source of protein. Cooked meat was easier to digest than raw meat, and it was also easier to preserve, which was a great help in warding off the constant threat of hunger. Fire was also used to defrost frozen meat in cold climates. Another early use of fire was to burn mature vegetation and thereby encourage the growth of more delicate and desirable young plants, which attracted the plant-eating animals that humans wanted to capture and eat. Humans used fire to treat animal hides to make clothing and various types of shelters, as well as to harden the wooden tools and weapons that they made. For all of these reasons, fire reduced mortality rates among humans.

Social Structure

In the late Paleolithic era, humans in widely varied environments had similar social structures. Their lives centered on survival; they spent most of their time capturing, collecting, and preparing food, and making implements to assist them in these activities and to build and maintain their shelters. They traveled in small hunter-forager groups with authority based on family relationships. Although these groups were led by men, they generally were characterized by gender equality, as women played an equally important role in the survival of the groups. Men were valued as hunters and women were valued as equally skillful gatherers. There were no real distinctions in social status, because there was no opportunity for these people to accumulate wealth. The few possessions that they owned were necessary for survival and had to be carried everywhere they went. The groups, however, were generally well organized and purposeful; many of them developed specialized practices, as well as tools and weapons, that focused exclusively on hunting single species of animals and harvesting specific plants.

Most of these groups remained mobile, traveling as the seasons changed and the animal herds moved on to new pastures. They tended to set up camps for only a few weeks before again moving on. Occasionally, different groups would meet during their travels and exchange ideas and experiences.

Beliefs and Art

The Paleolithic era was characterized by a blossoming of creative activities that were highly symbolic. Humans created a variety of artwork, including paintings, carved figures, jewelry, decorative headgear, and masks. Through artistic expression, humans represented the natural world around them symbolically. Archaeological interpretations of much of their artwork indicate that the people of the late Paleolithic era believed in spirits, sacred places, and an afterlife. Cave paintings and artifacts indicate that they practiced a form of religion called **polydaemonism**, the belief in many spirits, as opposed to the practice of **polytheism**, the belief in many gods.

Much of the art of this period also reflects the emphasis on the hunt. One of the most famous examples is the **cave of Lascaux** in France, with remarkably realistic and colorful paintings of mainly large animals, such as reindeer and bison. Early humans derived their daily sustenance from the hunt, and there are many aspects of the

DIDYOU**KNOW?**

The paintings in the cave of Lascaux were created between 15,000 and 17,000 years ago, near Montignac, France. However, they were not discovered until 1940, when four teenagers followed their dog through the narrow passage of the cave.

cave art that suggest it had a magical, ritualistic function. The location of the art, for example, is puzzling. The cave of Lascaux is very long, deep, and narrow, and much of the art is painted in very hard-to-reach places. There are often several layers of paintings, one on top of another. This suggests that the actual location of the cave was sacred, as artists tended to return there repeatedly. There are also nick marks on the walls, suggesting that early humans reenacted the hunt there. There are very few images of humans in these caves, and those that exist seem to have animal characteristics as well. These images indicate the close relationship between early humans and the natural world upon which they depended for their daily survival.

These cave images also appear to represent a world full of spirits that inhabit rocks, trees, water, and animals, which seemed to be able to communicate with humans. As part of their polydaemonism, humans of this era likely thought of themselves simply as other parts of the natural world. A sense of separateness of humans from nature that characterizes later religions did not seem to be part of their belief system.

Other objects commonly found in Paleolithic caves across Eurasia are carved **Venus figures,** such as the Laussel Venus and the Venus of Willendorf. These figurines are clearly feminine and have exaggerated female body parts associated with fertility. There are no identifiable features on their faces, making them appear to be generalized symbols of fertility rather than images of individual women.

Much of the artwork of the late Paleolithic people is difficult to interpret with any kind of certainty, partly because they left no written records. Still, their artwork, especially the cave paintings, indicate that these humans clearly had developed sophisticated thought processes and had a desire to express themselves artistically. They must have intended to leave behind lasting images about their lives, activities, and the world around them, and also to go back themselves periodically to look at and ponder the images that they had created.

In contrast, there is no evidence to suggest that any of the humans of the late Paleozoic developed a system of writing. They did, however, make certain markings on various surfaces, such as dots and different types of lines. These might represent some form of systematic record-keeping or observations of events, or information about the natural world. Perhaps they were primitive calendars or counting systems. Although early humans certainly communicated with language, very little is known about how it developed or spread from one community to another.

By 8000 BCE, humans inhabited parts of all the large landmasses on Earth. They had traveled to and settled in these various locations independently of one another and at different times. Some groups of humans spent increasingly longer periods of time in particular areas and became more settled, especially in coastal areas, where the climates were pleasant and food was abundant. Consistent with their continued and progressive adaptation to new challenges and higher levels of thought processes, humans in these areas developed ways to increase and maintain their food supplies even further. Some built cages made of sticks and set them in shallow waters to trap and contain live fish. Others took care of plant species that were the most desirable food sources by clearing weeds from around them and scaring away birds and other animals to prevent them from eating them. Such practices were likely the earliest beginnings of farming.

As the areas that humans occupied expanded, their populations also increased. However, individual hunter-gatherer communities remained small, while the number of communities and the areas of settlement throughout the world increased.

TEST TIP

During the exam, make sure to read all of the possible answer choices for the multiple-choice questions. Just because you think that you know the correct response, do not automatically assume that it is the best answer. By reading each answer choice, you will be sure that you are not making a mistake by jumping to a conclusion.

The Neolithic Revolution and Early Agricultural Societies

The **Neolithic era**, whose name means the "New Stone Age," began somewhere around 10,000 BCE and continued until about 3500 BCE. During this era, new and more complex economic and social systems emerged independently and gradually in different parts of the world, leading to drastic changes in human societies. Humans continued to create more refined and sophisticated tools and techniques for the activities of their daily lives, but more importantly, they developed the beginnings of agriculture and established permanent agricultural villages. Humans were able to permanently settle because they were successful in cultivating crops and domesticating animals.

The emergence of agricultural societies probably resulted, at least in part, from the climatic changes of the last Ice Age, about 14,000 years ago, when glaciers shrank and receded northwards. Sea levels and temperatures throughout the world rose significantly, and the Northern Hemisphere experienced increases in rainfall. These conditions were ideal for the rapid growth of meadows and forests across much of the Northern

Key Terms

basin irrigation	pastoralism
Fertile Crescent	patriarchal social systems
maize	river valleys
Mesoamerica	sedentary
Mesopotamia	slash-and-burn agriculture
metallurgy	terracing
Neolithic era	

Hemisphere. In turn, populations of various animal species in these areas thrived. Many species of large game animals probably migrated to the new pastures in the north; the distribution of wild rice and other grains on which these humans depended shifted to the north as well, both of which depleted the food supply of hunter-gathers in some parts of the Middle East and Africa.

TEST TIP

Work out a study routine and stick to it. Be consistent and use your time wisely.

The Beginnings of Agriculture

In some areas in the Northern Hemisphere, there was such an abundance of desirable plant and animal species that bands of hunter-gatherers who had followed animal herds there decided to settle, as there was no necessity to continue to move throughout the year from place to place. The settlements became villages, and for the first time in prehistory, humans in different parts of the world and at different times independently adopted a **sedentary** lifestyle based on agriculture. The domestication of animals was crucial to the success of agriculture. A variety of animals, such as dogs and herding animals, were tamed in different ways for different purposes.

The major areas where agriculture began to emerge were the **river valleys** of Mesopotamia, Egypt, South Central Asia, and northern China, as well as in Papua New Guinea, Mesoamerica, and the Andes of Peru, which did not have major river valleys but, instead, had smaller rivers and streams located near oceans. Between about 7000 BCE and 2500 BCE, agricultural villages were thriving in all of these places.

Mesopotamia

Mesopotamia was located in Southwest Asia between the Tigris and the Euphrates Rivers; in fact, the word *Mesopotamia* means "the land between two rivers." The rivers provided an abundant source of water and very fertile silt for the nearby plains, which were ideal conditions for agriculture, except for the damage caused by unpredictable floods. The first settlements in Mesopotamia, known as the **Fertile Crescent**, date back to about 5000 BCE. Small groups of people who had previously gathered wild grains and other edible plants began to work cooperatively to care for the plants by weeding the areas in which they grew, scaring away birds and other wild animals, and irrigating these areas, which were the beginnings of domesticated fields. These early farmers later worked together to clear nearby northern plains to prepare them for the distribution of plant seeds to increase crop yields. They then selected and planted the seeds of the most desirable plant species, and cultivated, harvested, and stored them. They learned how to grow crops, mainly barley and wheat, that produced larger and more nutritious grains than those that grew wild. At the same time, the people in the settlements of the Fertile Crescent domesticated and bred sheep, goats, pigs, and cows, controlling and managing these animals in a manner similar to the ways in which they changed the environment for agricultural purposes.

As these settlements grew in northern Mesopotamia, farmers looked to the south for additional fields. The environment there was significantly different; it was hotter, drier, and did not receive sufficient rainfall to support the growth of crops. Farmers worked in organized groups to first clear the land and then to irrigate the new fields by diverting the slow-moving water from the Euphrates River through streams to the new fields.

TEST TIP

Beginning in May 2011, the AP exam stopped penalizing test takers for incorrect responses to multiple-choice questions. Entering a response for every question—even a wild guess—may help improve your score.

Nile River Valley

Similar agricultural communities became established in various other river valleys throughout the world. By 3000 BCE in Egypt, which the ancient Greek historian Herodotus called the "gift of the Nile," people had developed agricultural communities based on a very small but fertile strip of land only ten to twenty miles wide. During the summer months, heavy rains in the Ethiopian Highlands produced flooding along the Nile River, which caused an annual period of flooding of the Nile as it passed through Egypt. Unlike the erratic flooding that occurred in Mesopotamia, the flooding of the Nile was regular and predictable, and the floodwaters deposited very fertile soil, enabling agriculture to flourish. In addition to grains, the Egyptians grew a variety of fruits and vegetables. They used much more sophisticated irrigation techniques than the Mesopotamians did. **Basin irrigation**, the Egyptians' basic system, involved a series of dikes that held back the floodwaters during periods of adequate rainfall and canals that allowed the water to flow to fields beyond the fertile strips of land along the river during periods of insufficient rainfall. Two main advantages of basin irrigation were that no further irrigation was needed for winter grain crops and the nutrient-rich silt made fertilization unnecessary. Egyptian farmers of this era domesticated goats, sheep, pigs, cattle, and geese.

Indus River Valley

By about 2500 BCE, the people of the Indus River Valley, in what is now northern India, were cultivating wheat, rice, yams, beans, peas, and bananas, as well making use of domesticated sheep, goats, pigs, oxen, and chickens. The floods of the Indus River deposited nearly twice as much silt along its riverbanks as did the Nile, creating an extremely fertile environment for farming. However, the floods were unpredictable, so farmers built earthen walls and canals to try to prevent floodwaters from washing away their crops in the fields. In the dry plains north of the valley, people depended on the domestication of cattle and water buffalo rather than crops.

Yellow River Valley

By about 4000 BCE, agricultural villages based on the cultivation of millet (small grain crops), rice, onions, and fruit, and on the domestication of pigs, appeared in the Yellow (Huang He) River Valley in northeastern China. Although the Chinese historically referred to the Yellow River as "China's Sorrow" because of the widespread destruction and loss of life caused by its unpredictable floods, the floods did deposit rich silt along the riverbanks, which was a great advantage for the growth of agriculture in this area. To try to prevent large-scale damage to their crops from flooding, farmers collectively built levees to hold back some of the floodwaters.

Papua New Guinea

Perhaps even earlier than 5000 BCE, the people of Papua New Guinea, located along smaller rivers that drained into the Pacific Ocean in northeastern Australia, were cultivating bananas, yams, taro (a root and leafy green vegetable), and other plants. These people constructed small basins for the cultivation of water-tolerant plants and island beds for plants that required drier conditions. They drained their swamp gardens by digging ditches that drained into large channels.

Mesoamerica

The first agricultural settlement in **Mesoamerica** (which includes most of present-day Mexico, Guatemala, Nicaragua, Honduras, Costa Rica, and Honduras), evolved in the central highlands of Mexico. This settlement was not in a river valley, but rather in a large plateau region that received adequate rainfall for the cultivation of maize (corn). By about 7000 BCE, the Tehuacán people had learned how to domesticate the most desirable species of maize (corn), which they planted in addition to squash, beans, and peppers. Once it was planted, maize did not require much care until harvesting. Tehuacán farmers did not have domesticated animals, as did early agricultural communities in other parts of the world.

The cultivation of maize spread to surrounding areas in Mesoamerica. The climate in the area to the northwest of the Tehuacán settlement was dry and received insufficient rainfall to sustain their crops of maize, so the people there built irrigation channels leading from streams to the fields.

The Andean People of Peru

The Andes people of South America, in what is now Peru, settled in the arid coastal valleys along the Pacific Ocean and in the highlands of the Andes Mountains. In the highlands the land was fairly level and there was sufficient water for cultivating crops. Farmers there grew maize, and they were the first people to cultivate potatoes. The highlands also contained large grazing areas for the llamas and alpacas that the Andean farmers domesticated. The coastal areas did not receive adequate rainfall for the successful cultivation of crops, so the farmers of the highlands made use of extensive irrigation and **terracing** to increase the food supply to those coastal areas.

DIDYOUKNOW?

All Mesoamerican cultures played a ritualistic ball-court game around 1000 BCE. There were different versions, but the game was usually played using a hard rubber ball on an I-shaped field with side walls. Players kept the ball in play, not by striking the ball with their hands or feet but with their knees, elbows, and hips. The game was ominously sacrificial: The captain of the losing team was beheaded.

Social Structure

All of the early permanent agricultural settlements that emerged during the Neolithic Revolution required communities to work together in more complicated ways and on much greater scales than did their predecessors, the hunter-gatherers. Organized groups cleared large areas of forests, plains, and rocky ground to make way for fields in which to grow crops, and they constructed irrigation and drainage systems to sustain the crops. There may have been some specialization of labor, depending on strength, intelligence, or other abilities. However, it is likely that these communities' social structures were egalitarian, similar to those of the hunter-gatherers.

Slash-and-Burn Agriculture

Not all agricultural societies were sedentary. In the rain forests and jungles of Central and South America, western Africa, and different areas of southern Asia, some people used a form of farming called **slash-and-burn agriculture.** Farmers would arrive at a piece of land, cut down all the vegetation, and, once it dried up, they would burn it to clear a field for the cultivation of food plants. The soil in a burned piece of land was very fertile at first, as the ashes added nutrients to the soil, but the nutrients were soon depleted as a result of overfarming. When the yield from the land began to diminish, the farmers moved on to another piece of land, which was subjected to the same slash-and-burn method.

Slash-and-burn agriculture, as well as the resulting overhunting of wild animals within the same geographical areas, had significant negative effects on the new environments in which early humans temporarily settled. The destruction of these environments was perpetuated by the continuous and frequent movements of the migratory farmers.

Pastoralism

During the Neolithic era, a new type of society and economy called **pastoralism** developed in Afro-Eurasia in parts of what is known as the Great Arid Zone. This swath of dry and semi-arid land extended from the beginning of the Sahara Desert in western Africa to Manchuria in northern China.

Pastoralists did not settle into villages, but were organized into communities that followed animal herds, just as early hunter-gatherers did. However, pastoral nomads domesticated the herds of goats, sheep, cattle, camels, horses, and reindeer that they followed. Pastoral nomads journeyed along the extensive migratory routes of animal herds from pasture to pasture as the seasons changed. They had few possessions, carrying with them only implements, clothing, and makeshift shelters that they needed for survival. They subsisted mainly on the products of their livestock: meat and dairy products. Some pastoral nomads planted crops with rapid growth cycles to supplement their diets, while others did not.

Generally, pastoralism had less of a negative impact on the environment than permanent agricultural villages did. However, some pastoralist communities with large herds of animals damaged fragile grasslands in Africa and Eurasia by staying in the same place too long and allowing their animals to overgraze. This resulted in the erosion of the top layers of soil and the exposure of underlying soil with insufficient nutrients to sustain new plant growth. These areas often took years to recover.

The Transformation of Human Societies

Once humans mastered various environments throughout the world by domesticating plants and animals, they not only had reliable and abundant food supplies, but also surpluses in many cases. The people of agricultural and pastoralist communities began to have longer life spans and higher rates of reproductivity, and thus the populations of these communities grew rapidly. Whereas the world population in 8000 BCE was probably about 5 million, by 600 BCE it had risen to at least 120 million, with some historians placing this number even higher.

By about 2500 BCE, the people of the large river valley societies and other agricultural societies were living and working together in large, dense communities. There were more than enough people to tend to crops and animals, and as a result, other, specialized occupations developed, including merchants, artisans, builders, priests, and soldiers, or warriors. A hierarchy of social classes emerged in both agricultural and pastoral communities, including an elite class that had greater wealth, power, and privileges than other classes. In addition, gender differences became more pronounced, with men becoming more and more dominant. Men took over the responsibilities for most of the activities related to agricultural production and the care of animals, while women raised the children, cooked, and performed domestic tasks. **Patriarchal social systems** developed: men were the leaders and had the power within families, economies, and societies.

Although pastoralists did not have permanent settlements, some did acquire wealth and status by trading animal hides, dairy products, wool, and even their services as soldiers and bodyguards for farm products or manufactured goods from people in agricultural communities. However, there was a growing distinction between agriculturalists, who had permanent settlements and the nomadic pastoralists, who did not own land or houses. This would lead to a recurring pattern throughout history in which peaceful trading was accompanied by violent encounters between agriculturalists and pastoralists.

TEST TIP

Don't forget to break up your essay into several paragraphs so you can make your argument clearer and easier to understand. Introduce just one main idea at the beginning of each paragraph, and use the remainder of that paragraph to support your main idea with relevant historical evidence.

Technological Innovations

People continued to make innovations in toolmaking, building, and techniques for accomplishing a variety of tasks, leading to further specialization of labor, which, in turn, led to further sophistication and efficiency in agriculture, trade, and transportation. Specialization of labor had developed by about 4000 BCE in the following five major areas:

Pottery

Once agriculture had taken hold, a need developed for containers in which to store and cook food. Thus, pottery making was likely the first specialized craft to develop. The concept of the wheel was probably first introduced in the making of pottery in the form of a potter's wheel. This implement was perfected gradually, perhaps first from some type of moving platform on which a potter would turn a pot before going on to shape another side of it and thereby avoid having to get up and walk around it. Eventually, potters developed simple revolving wheels as part of their craft.

Plows

The plough was probably the first tool that humans used to perform work that was not solely a result of their own muscles. Plows enabled humans to efficiently cultivate much greater areas of land and greatly increase agricultural productivity.

Woven Textiles

Early textile makers developed spindles to twist plant fibers and animal hairs together and to spin these fibers and hairs into thread. They then arranged the threads in rectangular, crisscross patterns to weave pieces of flat cloth. Eventually, the loom was invented and improvements were made to increase efficiency and precision. Depending on the types of fibers available in different environments, textile makers used flax, wool, and silk to produce clothing, rugs, and tents.

Metallurgy

Copper was the first metal to be mined and hammered into shapes to make knives, axes, hoes, other tools, weapons and, later, jewelry. People who worked with copper eventually found that heating the copper made it more malleable and allowed them to work more precisely with it and therefore to make products of much higher quality. The discovery of bronze as an alloy of copper and tin led to even greater improvements in the production of tools and other implements, as bronze was harder than copper and could be shaped into sharper cutting edges.

Wheels

The wheel is often said to be the most important invention of early technology. Wheels were likely first used in pottery making, and then later for vehicles and plowing. The first wheels used for transportation were made from wood in Mesopotamia. Although wheels were used on chariots drawn by pack animals in some communities at this time, transportation by water was still much more efficient than transportation by land.

These technological innovations paved the way for further new developments in agricultural societies. Originally, the people of each household made only the tools, weapons, pots, containers, and clothing that they needed for themselves. However, individuals or families who became especially skillful in certain crafts began to make implements and goods beyond their own needs and to trade them for other goods.

The Development and Interactions of Early Agricultural, Pastoral, and Urban Societies

Civilization

The development of organized agriculture, along with the domestication of animals, led to the development of urban centers; as some historians have remarked, "Without agriculture there is no culture." The establishment of agricultural communities created a stable supply of food and therefore more leisure time for people to continue to make innovations in producing implements, as well as to produce art and pursue other interests.

Key Terms

Amun-Re	myth of Osiris
Chavin	Olmecs
civilization	Rig Veda
Code of Hammurabi	Royal Road
cuneiform	Sanskrit
Epic of Gilgamesh	satrapy
foundational civilizations	Shang dynasty
Great Pyramid at Giza	Sumerian
Harappan	The Book of the Dead
hieroglyphs	Torah
Hittites	ziggurat
Hyksos	Zoroastrianism

The abundant food supply also created a need for new containers and techniques with which to cook, preserve, and transport food. Agriculture enabled humans to stay in one place, giving rise to civilization. The word civilization is derived from the Latin word civilis, meaning "political or civic." A **civilization** is the term generally used by historians to refer to a large society that has major cities and is a powerful state.

Foundational Civilizations

Foundational civilizations were much bigger and denser than the early farming communities of the Neolithic period; therefore, significant changes emerged and evolved in the ways in which people lived and worked. The exchange of ideas and information within these newly emerging civilizations led each one to develop a unique cultural style. However, all of these foundational civilizations were alike in significant ways:

- Their societies were centered around cities. By 2250 BCE, eight cities in the world had populations of at least 30,000 people, and by 1200 BCE, there were about sixteen.

- They all had agricultural surpluses that allowed for the specialization of labor. Rather than spending their time in agricultural activities, some people were able to take up full-time specialized occupations and professions, such as artisans, architects, merchants, soldiers, and priests.

- They all developed complex institutions, including centralized governments, laws, armies, and religious hierarchies.

- They all were characterized by some form of social hierarchy. Social stratification enabled the emergence of elite classes. In addition, gender differences widened, with men assuming power over women politically and socially.

- They all developed forms of written records and more sophisticated forms of art, architecture, and engineering; monumental buildings were constructed, including temples, palaces, city walls, and tombs of rulers.

- They all had sophisticated economic organizations that grew out of the increasing need to conduct trade, and long-distance trading relationships developed alongside the intensification of trade within and between civilizations, as well as with pastoralists.

Foundational civilizations developed in various locations throughout the world where agricultural villages flourished. These villages' populations swelled, and they grew to be large, urban centers that dominated the areas around them. Some of these early cities developed into the first states, which grew and eventually had to compete with other states for additional land and natural resources. Those states that were located in the most desirable geographic locations produced great amounts of surplus food, as well as other goods, which led to flourishing trade networks and eventually a desire to expand their territories by conquering nearby states. Such expansions were the beginnings of empire building.

While great empires are usually most remembered for the brilliance of their development and the accomplishments during their days of glory, it is important to keep in mind that no empire has ever lasted; a great truth of history is that all empires have declined and eventually come to an end. A common thread in both the rise and fall of all empires is the interactions with other cultures. In the case of the early river valley civilizations, these interactions began in a positive way: increased trade led to greater wealth and therefore greater power, as well as the sharing and diversification of cultures. However, the desire for and preoccupation with ever-greater wealth, power, and conquests led to both internal and external conflicts. In addition, interactions with negative consequences resulted from another recurring historical theme: often-unwanted migrations of nomadic peoples who seized control of the areas in which they settled. Even as the foundational civilizations thrived, they were vulnerable to large migrations into their territories between about 2500 and 1000 BCE that would play a major role in weakening these civilizations.

Mesopotamia, in the Tigris and Euphrates River Valley

Mesopotamia is known as "the cradle of world civilization." It is the earliest known civilization, and Mesopotamians produced the earliest written records, including the first unified code of law. Mesopotamians also invented the wheel, the calendar, and the clock. Mesopotamian writing is called **cuneiform,** a word that means "wedge shaped" writing. Cuneiform was written on clay tablets with wedge-shaped instruments called styluses. Throughout its history, several different peoples conquered Mesopotamia and established empires there.

The first settlements in Mesopotamia date back to 4000 BCE. Geography played an important role in the creation of the Mesopotamian worldview. The flooding of the Tigris and Euphrates Rivers was unpredictable and disastrous; flooding often destroyed city-states in an instant. Many creation stories from the region, such as the *Epic of Gilgamesh*, describe a disastrous flood that wiped out Earth; these stories were likely based on actual events. The constant and unpredictable flooding partially accounts for the very grim view of life that is evident in the *Epic of Gilgamesh*, in which the first immortal man, Utnapishtim, tells the hero Gilgamesh that the god Enlil sent the flood because humans were too noisy and irritated the gods. When Utnapishtim survives, Enlil is enraged and rewards him with immortality, a gift Utnapishtim assures Gilgamesh is no favor. Every day, he says, is like every other day, the days continuing on in dreary bleakness without end.

Another contributing factor to the overall pessimism of Mesopotamian culture was the competition for land and water resources. Because of the need for large amounts of land, there were fairly wide separations among settlements. Several independent city-states arose in southern Mesopotamia, such as Uruk, where the Sumerian king recorded the beginning of the reign of Gilgamesh in 2700 BCE and Ur, the original home of Abraham, the patriarch of the Hebrews.

Southern Mesopotamia was known as Sumer. Each of its city-states had its own government, customs, and deities. Their common customs and culture are referred to as **Sumerian.** Empires did not arise in Mesopotamia until Sargon the Great unified the region in 2340 BCE. The competition for land and water rights led to almost continuous conflict between city-states. In fact, the earliest recorded treaty in world history resolved a conflict over irrigation rights between the Sumerian city-state of Lagash and its neighbors.

The geographical features of Mesopotamia contributed to the lack of stability, as there were no natural barriers to protect the city-states from outside invaders.

Throughout Mesopotamian history, there was a constant stream of conquering peoples, such as the Hittites and Assyrians. Combined with the continuous conflict between city-states, Mesopotamians never developed a continuous and long-lived empire. Rather, Mesopotamian history is one of constant invasion and conquest and is the story of successive cultures that borrowed from each other.

The importance of the rivers as well as the ideology of warfare is reflected in Mesopotamian mythology. According to the creation myth of the Mesopotamians, in the beginning, Ocean and Chaos began to merge, but Chaos tried to make herself supreme. Marduk, the creator god, killed Chaos by splitting her in half, from which came the heavens and the Earth. The tears that flowed down her face from the pain became the Tigris and the Euphrates Rivers. Marduk then kneaded the wet earth and created humans. As we have seen, according to the *Epic of Gilgamesh*, eventually the gods grew weary of the noise made by the troublesome humans and sent a flood to destroy them. The gods sent a heavenly bull to inflict revenge on Gilgamesh for his refusal to marry the goddess Ishtar, but instead it kills his friend Enkidu. On his death-bed, Enkidu had a vision of the underworld, and he told Gilgamesh that there the kings were servants of the gods, and all one can find there is dust and darkness. Enkidu tells Gilgamesh that the gods play with humans like puppets on strings, having a contest to see what misery they can inflict. From the creation myths to the collapse of the Assyrian empire in 612 BCE, the devastating flooding of the rivers and the bleak nature of brutal warfare colored Mesopotamian culture. Mesopotamians were not sure they could even turn to the gods for compassion; they were simply at the mercy of a brutal environment whose purpose and plan they did not know.

Although the Mesopotamians were pessimistic about the benevolence of the gods, they continued to worship them devoutly and perform sacrifices to them. In the *Epic of Gilgamesh*, the goddess Siduri tells Gilgamesh to "live for the moment," and to learn to enjoy every minute of life. The Mesopotamians were never sure of what the future held, but they tried to find happiness in the moment and protection by offering whatever sacrifices they could to the gods.

Every city-state had at its center and its highest point a stepped, pyramid-like temple called a **ziggurat.** Religious ceremonies were performed there, but scribes also learned to read and write there in the eddubas or "tablet houses," so called because Sumerians wrote on clay tablets. At the foot of each ziggurat there was a marketplace. The king, who was also the chief priest, controlled this important religious and social center. Mesopotamian society was a theocracy, a system of government in which religion and politics were not separate. In Mesopotamia, the chief priest-king was considered to be semidivine. The fact that the ziggurat was the center of education, religion, government, and trade illustrates that the Sumerians, like many other peoples of the ancient world, did not distinguish among history, mythology, religion, or other areas as separate endeavors or areas of knowledge. The following time line summarizes the main empires of ancient Mesopotamia.

Chronology of Empires in Mesopotamia	
2340 BCE	Sargon the Great establishes the Akkadian Empire.
1800 BCE	The Amorites conquer Mesopotamia and establish their capital at Babylon. During this period, Hammurabi compiles the first unified code of law, the Code of Hammurabi.
1500 BCE	The Hittites conquer the Babylonian Empire.
1000 BCE	The Assyrians conquer Babylon and establish their capital at Nineveh, where the tablets recording the *Epic of Gilgamesh* are later found.
612 BCE	The Chaldeans conquer the Assyrian capitol of Nineveh and establish the Neo-Babylonian empire. Its most famous ruler is Nebuchadnezzar.
539 BCE	The Persians under Cyrus the Great conquer the Chaldeans or Neo-Babylonians. The Persians would rule until the expansion of Islam engulfed the region in the seventh century CE.

The Akkadians

Sargon I (the Great) created the first true empire in Mesopotamia with his capital at Akkad. His empire is known as the Akkadian Empire. Sargon lived sometime around 2340 BCE. As a young man, he displayed prodigious abilities and became the cupbearer to Enmebaragesi, the king of Kish. The cupbearer was the king's most trusted servant; he tasted his food and drink to make sure it was not poisoned before the king ate it. Sargon, however, overthrew the king. He then proceeded to conquer important Sumerian city-states such as Uruk, Ur, Lagash, and also the Elamites.

Before and during Sargon's reign, Mesopotamian city-states engaged in trade with each other and with other civilizations, such as the Harappan people of the Indus Valley. Mesopotamians traded grain, wool, and textiles for gold, stone for building, spices, and wood. Early Mesopotamian trade probably influenced the gradual shift from a barter economy to commodities trading using silver or grain as payments. Although Sargon created an empire that lasted for two hundred years, it finally collapsed in 2100 BCE.

The Babylonians or Amorites

Around 1800 BCE, the Amorites, led by King Hammurabi, conquered much of Mesopotamia and destroyed whatever of Sargon's empire remained. At that time, the extent of Mesopotamian power increased from an area less than fifty miles in radius to one that extended from the Persian Gulf to beyond Turkey. The Amorite capital was Babylon, and the Amorites themselves are better known as Babylonians. Under the reign of King Hammurabi, Babylon was an economic and cultural crossroads of the ancient world.

King Hammurabi was most remarkable as being the earliest-known ruler who publically proclaimed an entire body of written law, addressing a variety of topics in civil, criminal, and commercial law, so that all of his people could read the laws and understand what was required of them. Consisting of 282 laws carved in forty-nine columns on a basalt stele, the **Code of Hammurabi** is extremely important in legal history. King Hammurabi did not try to address all possible legal situations, but rather to establish "laws of Justice" that clarified the rights of any "oppressed man."

The Babylonians were also notable for creating one of the Seven Wonders of the Ancient World: the beautiful, blue-tiled Gate of Ishtar that guarded the entrance to the city. They were pioneers in mathematics and created a base-60 number system, which still influences the world today, from the division of the hour into minutes and the minute into seconds, to the 360-degree circle. The Babylonians created a uniform standard of weights and measurements, which helped in the development of increasingly sophisticated and extensive trading systems. The Babylonians were also pioneers in astronomy, and they observed and recorded eclipses. They charted the movements of the planets, discovered satellites around Saturn, distinguished stars from planets, and knew that the true length of the solar year was 365 and 1/4 days. Their interest in astronomy was a result of their belief that planets had souls and were animate, and that their movements represented the will of the gods and foreshadowed events on Earth.

The Babylonians built incredible architectural works, such as the famous ziggurat dedicated to the god Marduk. The ziggurat in Babylon was built in seven layers representing the planets, all colored differently. The ziggurat served as an observatory as well as a religious temple. The height of the great ziggurat of Babylon may have been the basis for the biblical story of the tower of Babel.

The Hittites

The **Hittites** were one of the most important empires of antiquity to rule Mesopotamia. They were pastoral Indo-Europeans who invaded and conquered the Old Babylonian Empire in Mesopotamia in the sixteenth century BCE. The homeland of the Hittites was known as Hatti, in Central Anatolia. Archaeologists discovered a huge cache of 10,000 Hittite tablets in 1906 in the Hittite capital of Hattusas, located near the modern Turkish town of Boghazkoy, east of Ankara. The Hittites adopted many Mesopotamian customs while developing their own unique and sophisticated culture, which they also spread in the near East.

The Hittite Empire flourished from about 1600 to 1200 BCE. One of the most distinctive features of Hittite culture was their sense of loyalty to a state governed by laws that were much more advanced and humane than those of most other ancient cultures. Whereas the Code of Hammurabi and later Assyrian codes mandated an "eye for an eye" policy and often the death penalty, Hittite laws were far more merciful. The Hittites placed a high value on human life and the rights of individuals; they did not inflict humiliating punishments on members of their own society, nor did they torture or commit other atrocities against their enemies. Although kings ruled by right of heredity, the Hittites did not believe in the divine right of kings. The Hittite kings' duties included attending to the welfare of his people, waging war as commander-in-chief, and conducting religious ceremonies as the high priest.

The Hittites created monumental sculptures and buildings, including the best military architecture of the Near East. Their system of offensive-defense works was a unique type of fortification. The walls at Hattusa and Alaca display a very high level of craftsmanship and strategic contouring, despite being constructed in difficult terrain. The major characteristic of Hittite architecture was its perfectly asymmetrical ground plans. The Hittites used square piers as supports and did not use columns. They constructed large windows with low parapets set into the outer walls of buildings but not into the walls of courtyards. The five huge temples in Hattusa were among the finest monuments of their time. The largest was devoted to the weather god, Hatti, and the sun goddess, Arinna. The temple was a rectangular building with an inner court. An additional wing contains nine rooms, which were the places of worship.

The Hittites were the first people to work with iron and had access to large natural deposits of iron ore. They developed a smelting process, and the iron weapons that they made enabled them to become serious threats on the battlefield. They engaged in numerous wars with Egypt from 1300 to 1200 BCE. After the inconclusive battle of

Kadesh in 1275 BCE, the Hittites and Egyptians entered into a treaty, and the daughter of Hittite king Hattusilis III married Egyptian pharaoh Ramses II.

Like many other cultures, the Hittites were victims of famines and other natural disasters that occurred around 1200 BCE, and their empire fell into decline. It was finally destroyed by the invasion of the People of the Sea from the northeast.

TEST TIP

Choose the times and places for studying that work best for you. You might set aside a specific period of time after a certain activity or at night before going to sleep.

The Assyrians

Babylon fell to the Assyrians around 1000 BCE. The Assyrians created one of the first truly organized and well-trained armies; they were the first truly militaristic society in world history. Their most important god was Ashur, the god of war. Another reason for the Assyrians' success was the iron weapons they used, having adopted the Hittites' iron-making techniques. Soldiers were rewarded for every severed head they brought back from battle. They were ordered to take no hostages, and they often cut off the extremities of nobles and those in power, roasted people over slow fires, and deported entire populations. The Assyrians used cruel and repressive tactics even at home; they fueled their military machine by encouraging a high birth rate and made abortion punishable by death. Ashurbanipal was the most famous and brutal of Assyrian kings (d. 626 BCE). He was also noteworthy for his devotion to learning and created a library of 30,000 volumes.

The capital of the Assyrian Empire was Nineveh, and several tablets with portions of the *Epic of Gilgamesh* were found there dating to the ninth century BCE. The *Epic of Gilgamesh*, like almost every ancient text, was told orally for hundreds of years before it was written down by the Babylonians; the tablets found in Nineveh contain several versions of some of the tales in the epic and it is unclear how they all fit together.

As Assyrian cities such as Nineveh grew, the empire could no longer sustain urban populations through agriculture, which necessitated both trade for grain and other foods and the conquests of neighboring areas. The peoples of these areas were required to give the Assyrians tributes of food. The Assyrians' trading relationships with Egypt and Syria thrived, as did a wide-ranging system of trade with subjugated peoples. The Assyrians also developed an early silk industry.

In the eighth century BCE, the Assyrians destroyed Israel, the northern kingdom of the Hebrews. The Assyrian Empire collapsed in 612 BCE when the Chaldeans, Cimmerians, Scythians, and Medes united to capture their capital city of Nineveh. The Cimmerian and Scythian warrior horse nomads had originated in the steppes north of the Black Sea. The Scythians were predominantly horse archers who developed saddles, other equipment for their horses, and various weapons, including their uniquely short Scythian bows, which were ideal for battle on horseback. The Scythians dominated a vast area in Eurasia and the Middle East. They raided extensively in the Near East and eventually allied with the Medes of western Iran to destroy the Assyrian kingdom.

The Chaldeans or Neo-Babylonians

The Chaldeans restored much of the grandeur of the Babylonian empire and, for that reason, the Chaldean Empire is also known as the Neo-Babylonian Empire. Its most significant ruler was Nebuchadnezzar II, an absolute monarch who pursued a policy of relentless expansionism. He was a brilliant military tactician and was also prominent in international diplomacy, sometimes sending ambassadors to mediate conflicts. Nebuchadnezzar built up his enormous empire by ruthlessly subjugating neighboring peoples, including the Hebrews of Judea, the Syrians, and the people of Palestine. When threatened by rebellion, he committed atrocious acts. However, Nebuchadnezzar's court was magnificent and enormously wealthy, attended by astronomers and governmental officials who were all very well educated. Nebuchadnezzar ruled until his death in 562 BCE, at the age of about 80.

Nebuchadnezzar also restored the city of Babylon. He extended its fortifications, constructed a huge moat and an outer defensive wall, paved the ceremonial Processional Way with limestone, and built canals. The Hanging Gardens of Babylon, built on top of his palace, were known as one of the Seven Wonders of the Ancient World. Nebuchadnezzar reportedly had the gardens built for his wife, who was a Mede (the predecessors of the Persians); her homeland was a very lush and beautiful region with abundant vegetation. Nebuchadnezzar intended to replicate her homeland, and his engineers concealed hydraulic pumps in the columns of the palace to carry water to the trees on the top.

The Persians

The Persians were Indo-Europeans who established a vast, tolerant, and ecumenical empire in the sixth century BCE. Persia was known as Elam during Sumerian and Babylonian times; today it is known as Iran. Ancient Persia was bounded by the Indus Valley, the Tigris and Euphrates Rivers, and the Caucasus Mountains. The empire had a high plateau in its center; in the center of the plateau there were two large deserts. The Medes, who united earlier than the Persians, originally ruled Persia. In 550 BCE, Cyrus, chief of the Persian tribes, defeated the Medes. He then went on to conquer Anatolia on the coast of Asia Minor. Anatolia gave the Persians access to seaports and therefore to trade. Eventually, access to the sea would bring the Persians into conflict with the Greek colonies and the Greeks on the mainland. This series of conflicts is known as the Persian wars. The Persians then turned to Babylon and captured it in 539 BCE.

The Organization of the Persian Empire

The Persian Empire was organized into provinces, or satrapies. The land of the Medes was the first province, and at the height of Persian power, there were some twenty such satrapies, each ruled by a provincial governor. Governors could not become too powerful, as in each province there also was a military official. The Persian Empire was the first to govern many different cultural groups based on the principle of equality of rights and responsibilities for all. As long as the Persian subjects paid their taxes and kept the peace, the king did not interfere with local religions, customs, or trade relationships.

The king received tribute from the satraps, as well as recruits for the army. The Persian army was well trained and at its heart was an elite core of 10,000 soldiers known as the Immortals, so called because no matter how many died on the battlefield, the next day there were still 10,000 Immortals. The Immortals figured prominently in the Persian wars with the Greeks. Persian kings ruled by "election of the gods" and were just and tolerant of all religions. As the Persians were a very eclectic, tolerant, and prosperous culture, and they traded with most of western Asia along the Royal Road. The Royal Road was a 1,600-mile-long stretch of road, and it connected the capital of Susa to Sardis, a Greek port. In antiquity, the **Royal Road** took an ordinary person three months to traverse; however, there were 111 stations along the way, and royal couriers using fresh horses at each of these stations could travel the length of the road in a week. The Royal Road helped fuse the kingdom together, as did the imposition of an official language, Aramaic. There were two capitals of the Persian Empire, Susa and Persepolis.

Zoroastrianism

The Persians also contributed a religion known as **Zoroastrianism.** The prophet Zarathustra (628–551 BCE), referred to more commonly by the English name Zoroaster, founded Zoroastrianism. The main known text for this tradition dates from the third century BCE, and is known as the *Zend Avesta.* According to this much later text, in his youth, Zoroaster had visions and conversations with divine beings. He became a wandering preacher who urged the Persians to abandon sacrifice to all minor deities, and to be more humane toward animals in sacrifice. He taught a dualist religion, in which good battled evil. Good was symbolized by light, while evil was symbolized by darkness. Fire was thought of as divine, since it was a form of light. The god of good was Ahura Mazda, and immortal holy ones or forces of good, such as obedience, truth, law, and immortality, assisted him. His twin, Ahriman, was banished from heaven to hell, where he reigned as the principle of evil. Zoroaster urged the Persians to "turn from the lie to the Truth."

Zoroaster taught that people are creations of the good god and have the free will to turn toward either good or evil. In the end, humans will be judged according to the *Book of Life,* in which all deeds are recorded. Zoroastrian had a priesthood known as the Magi, who absolved sins and meted out atonement and repentance. Some historians argue that the Zoroastrian concept of good versus evil influenced Christianity, as did its concept of life after death, the importance of good works, and its cult of the Magi, who are mentioned in the Christian gospels as among the first visitors to the infant Jesus. Zoroastrianism became the state religion of the Persian Empire following the conversion of the Persian kings.

DIDYOUKNOW?

Despite being "protected" religious minorities, Zoroastrians, Christians, and Jews in Iran have suffered—and continue to suffer—government imprisonment, harassment, intimidation, and discrimination based on their religious beliefs. Such is the case of Youcef Nadarkhani, a 32-year-old Iranian who converted from Islam to Christianity and thus, subsequently, was sentenced to death in 2011 for refusing to renounce his Christian beliefs.

Egypt, in the Nile River Valley

The geography of the Nile River Valley created a stable and isolated region in which Egyptian culture could flourish uninterrupted by outside invaders. Consequently, the Egyptians developed a very positive view of life and the afterlife.

The Nile River is the longest river in the world. Three rivers meet to create the Nile as it flows through Egypt: The White Nile, originating in modern Uganda; the Blue Nile, originating in the highlands of modern Ethiopia; and the Atbara River. To the west of the Nile was the world's largest desert, the Sahara, which takes its name from the Arabic word for "tan," the color of the sand. North Africa was not very populous in antiquity and presented no threat of invasion. High cliffs protect the eastern side of the Nile. These natural barriers kept invaders out of the Nile River Valley before the arrival of the Hyksos in the Second Intermediate Period. These features of the Nile allowed the native culture to flourish without interference. During the Old Kingdom, bureaucracy remained unchanged for centuries and so did the basic way of life. Although the Egyptians had a more positive view of life and the afterlife than did the Mesopotamians, they also had a much more rigid social structure in which there was little mobility.

Historians have more information about ancient Egypt than they do about ancient Mesopotamia. Egypt's hot, dry climate contributed to the preservation of documents written on papyrus, whereas the clay tablets of Mesopotamia dissolved in floods. Archaeological evidence indicates that Egyptian **hieroglyphs** are the oldest form of writing, which was first developed around 3300 BCE and used by the Egyptians for the next 3,500 years. However, only a small segment of the Egyptian population—members of royalty, priests, and civil officials—used hieroglyphs, as the system was difficult to learn and time-consuming to write. The hieroglyphic system had between 700 and 800 basic symbols, called glyphs, which included one group that represented sounds and another group that represented objects or ideas. The number of glyphs continued to grow, especially in the latter part of the ancient Egyptian Empire as a result of the increase in the writing of religious texts. Hieroglyphs were written in long lines from right to left and from top to bottom.

Modern historians divide Egyptian history into three main periods based on the stability of the government, with two additional periods before and after. The three main periods of Egyptian history are the Old Kingdom, the Middle Kingdom, and the New Kingdom. The period before the Old Kingdom is the Archaic or Protodynastic era, and the period after the New Kingdom is the Late Period.

The Archaic/Protodynastic Era

The Archaic era began in 3100 and lasted until 2700 BCE. Herodotus, a Greek historian, and Manetho, an Egyptian priest, claimed that Menes founded the first dynasty in 3000 BCE and first united Upper and Lower Egypt. However, the Narmer palette, a decorated stone palette designed to hold cosmetics and discovered in the nineteenth century, credits Narmer with these deeds. Upper Egypt was the southernmost area along the Nile Valley, while Lower Egypt was the region nearest the Nile River Valley Delta. The Nile flows from south to north, which accounts for Lower Egypt being to the north of Upper Egypt. Egypt was the most stable when Upper and Lower Egypt were unified, and unification of these two regions helps to determine the dividing points between the various eras of Egyptian history.

The Old Kingdom

The Old Kingdom lasted from 2700 to 2200 BCE. During this period, Egyptian culture was unthreatened by outside invaders, although Egypt did develop trade relationships with numerous neighboring societies and continued to do so throughout its long history. In the Old Kingdom, goods from the Near East were brought to Egypt, as were foreign workers and artisans. Over time, Egypt began to trade with the Minoans, the Trojans, the early Greeks, the Arabs, the Nubians, and the Canaanites. Despite its thriving trading systems, Egypt was influenced very little by other cultures. This likely was a result of the Egyptians' general sense of cultural superiority over others with whom they came in contact.

During the Old Kingdom, Egyptians developed the cult of the pharaoh (a word that means "great house" and technically was not in use before the New Kingdom), established a sophisticated political bureaucracy, and built monumental constructions such as the pyramids. Egyptians considered their pharaoh to be fully divine and thought of him as a living god. The **myth of Osiris** created the cult of the pharaoh. Historians do not know whether Osiris was an actual historic figure, but the ancient Egyptians believed that he was. According to legend, Osiris was a ruler who was very much loved by his people. His brother Seth was jealous of him, and designed a special coffin for guests at a banquet to compete to see whom the coffin would fit, and it fit Osiris. Once he had climbed in, however, Seth sealed the coffin with molten lead and threw it in the Nile. It landed in a cedar tree in Byblos, where Seth then dismembered the body of his brother. Isis, the wife of Osiris, found him and created the first mummy from him. She regenerated him enough to conceive their son Horus, the falcon god. Horus then fought with Seth, making Horus the ruler of the living and Osiris the ruler of the underworld. Egyptians believed that when Horus would finally vanquish Seth, the personification of evil, Osiris would rule again forever. Just as Osiris was revived, so every pharaoh was revered as the lord of the underworld and as the living Horus while on Earth. Egyptians believed that when they passed into the underworld, Osiris himself would judge their deeds. They revered Isis as the goddess of fertility.

As a tribute to the immense power of pharaoh, the Egyptians built enormous pyramids to ensure the safe passage of the pharaoh's *ka* (which can be likened to modern ideas of the soul) and *ba* (a mirror image of the person's body and identity) in the afterlife and his unification with the sun god Re.

Around 2600 BCE, the pharoah Djoser and his architect Imhotep first constructed a stone pyramid at Saqqarah. Imhotep designed an innovative new type of pyramid with numerous stone mastabas, or tombs, stacked on top of one another in a staggered design, thereby creating the step pyramid. This was the largest building in the world when it was first constructed, and Imhotep was revered in Egypt and along the coast of Africa and Saudi Arabia as a god in his own right for this fabulous achievement.

Pharaoh Sneferu continued to experiment with pyramid building. At least two of his pyramids failed, such as the collapsed pyramid at Medun and the Bent Pyramid at Dashur, but he nonetheless perfected the techniques to eventually create a perfect, though smaller pyramid, the Red Pyramid. His children and grandchildren Khufu (called by the Greeks "Cheops"), Khefre (called by the Greeks "Chefren"), and Menkaure (called by the Greeks "Mycerinus") learned from his experiences and constructed the three Pyramids of Giza. The **Great Pyramid at Giza** is one of the Seven Wonders of the Ancient World and was the tallest building in the world until the Eiffel Tower was built. The Great Pyramid has several internal passageways that appear to be aligned with constellations and important stars, leading some to suggest that Egyptians constructed the pyramids to facilitate the union of the pharaoh as Osiris with the sun god Re.

The Egyptians had a positive view of afterlife, as reflected by the collection of poems known as ***The Book of the Dead***. According to one of the texts from this collection, known as "The Negative Confession," the Egyptians valued many of the same virtues as do many modern societies. The Egyptians considered beating one's family or slaves, stealing, and damming up the Nile so as to withhold life-giving water to be evil. The text also makes clear that one should not trespass on one's boundaries with the gods. The Egyptians believed that Osiris would reward good deeds with an afterlife that in many ways would be like life itself. The form of "The Negative Confessions," each of which begins with "I have not" and continues with the specific deed to be denied, was perhaps influenced the Hebrews' Ten Commandments, seven of which are in negative form.

By about 2100 BCE, the priests had become extremely powerful. The last pharaoh of the Old Kingdom, Pepi II, ruled for approximately ninety years. To balance the rising power of the priesthood with his own power, he gave away pharaonic power and decentralized the government. Although Pepi reigned for almost a century in this precarious state, his successors were unable to maintain power. The decline in the pharaoh's power can be seen in the title Pepi took as "Son of Re."

The First Intermediate Period

The First Intermediate Period lasted from 2200 to 2050 BCE. During this period, there was political chaos as four dynasties competed for power. There were two dynasties at Memphis and two more at Herakleopolis. Another dynasty developed in Thebes, which gradually managed to take control from the other centers of power in the First Intermediate Period. The main god of Thebes was Amun, and during this period the Thebans fused their mythology of Amun with that of the earlier god, Re. Amun-Re would be one of the most important deities worshipped throughout the remainder of Egyptian history.

The Middle Kingdom

The Middle Kingdom lasted from 2050 to 1652 BCE and represents the restoration of unity and stability after the collapse of the Old Kingdom. Mentuhotep II reunited Upper and Lower Egypt. Mentuhotep governed from Thebes, and favored the god Montu, a god of war.

The Second Intermediate Period

The Second Intermediate period lasted from 1567 to 1085 BCE. It was characterized by a series of ineffective rulers. For most of this period, Upper and Lower Egypt were not united and there was widespread civil warfare. The **Hyksos,** a pastoralist group of people who came from Palestine and perhaps from even farther to the east, established a rival dynasty during this period. The Hyksos, or "rulers of foreign lands," were also known as the "shepherd kings" and had actually had a presence in Egypt at Avaris for quite some time. Their settlements acquired a progressive adaptation of Egyptian culture. Although this was the first time that foreigners had controlled Egypt, the presence of the Hyksos often proved to be beneficial. Under the Hyksos, Egypt imported oils, furniture, and weapons from the Nubians, who lived in what is present-day southern

Egypt and the Sudan. Egypt also imported incense from Canaan as well as opium from Cyprus. Other trade commodities included figs, grapes, wine, and beer.

Later pharaohs would borrow the Hyskos' technique of fighting in chariots. Egyptians also benefited from the Hyksos' skill in bronze casting. In addition, the Hyksos preserved a number of papyri from ancient Egypt, including many famous medical texts. Several less-powerful Egyptian dynasties continued to rule during the Hyksos period.

The New Kingdom

The New Kingdom prospered from 1567 BCE until 1085 BCE. It began when Ahmose I defeated the foreign Hyksos and reunited Upper and Lower Egypt. Thebes was once again the capital of Egypt. The New Kingdom was a prosperous period marked by a new kind of pharaoh who excelled on the battlefield. Trade increased during the New Kingdom, particularly after Egypt and the Hittite Empire concluded one of several peace agreements. Trade and other interactions between the Egyptians and the peoples of the Middle East and the eastern Mediterranean, including the island of Crete, continued to thrive and expand. These contacts spread Egyptian influences, such as monumental architecture, art, and other cultural aspects, to these areas.

Thutmose I expanded Egypt to the south and to Palestine and Syria in the east. His daughter, Hatshepsut, became the most important of six women in Egyptian history to wield power as regent or, as in her case, as pharaoh. Hatshepsut ruled as regent for her stepson Thutmose III, and then declared herself pharaoh shortly after she took power. While other New Kingdom pharaohs concentrated on conquest, Hatshepsut sent an expedition to Africa and engaged in trade. The tutor of one of her daughters, Senenmut, also constructed for her a magnificent mortuary temple near that of Mentuhotep II of the Middle Kingdom in the Valley of the Kings. In the temple is a mural depicting her divine birth from the god Amun. Hatshepsut depicted herself as pharaoh not only in this story of her divine birth, but also in numerous statues, in which she appears as a sphinx, and also wearing the ceremonial regalia of the pharaoh.

Thutmose III defaced Hatshepsut's monuments several years after he took power and went on to become one of the greatest warrior-rulers of the New Kingdom. He led seventeen successful campaigns that greatly expanded the Egyptian Empire, invading Syria, Nubia, Sudan, Palestine, and Phoenicia. Although Thutmose III allowed the rulers of his conquests to remain in power, he ordered their sons to be taken to Egypt, where they were raised and immersed in the Egyptian culture. Once grown, they were sent home to their native homes and eventually ruled as Egypt's loyal vassals. Egypt enjoyed 100 years of prosperity and glory beginning with Thutmose III's reign.

The Egyptian Empire was at its peak under Amenhotep III, who ruled from about 1390 to 1350 BCE. The people of conquered lands sent him lavish tributes, and the Hittite and Babylonian kings sent gifts in return for gold. With its temples built for the sun-god Amon, Thebes was the most magnificent city in the world. During Amenhotep III's reign, Egypt was peaceful; he had little interest in conquests or other military activities. Instead, Amenhotep III was interested in the arts and in monument building, which he supported with the wealth gained from Egypt's flourishing foreign trade and extensive gold mining in Nubia.

During the reign of the next pharaoh, Amenhotep IV, the Egyptian Empire sharply declined as the result of his internal struggle with the powerful priests of the sun-god Amon. Amenhotep IV transformed the religion of Egypt by proclaiming the worship of the sun's disk, Aton, instead of Amon and all the other gods. He changed his name to Akhenaton, which means "devoted to Aton"; he left Thebes, the city of Amon, and established the new capital of Akhetaton; and he focused his attention on religious reform rather than on the protection of Egypt's frontiers. Amenhotep IV ignored the appeals of Egypt's vassal princes for protection against attacks, and they defected from the empire as a result. At the same time, the Amon priests encouraged dissension within Egypt. After Akhenaton's death, his nine-year-old brother, Tutankhamen, returned to Thebes and worshipped Amon, whose powerful priests essentially controlled him until he died at the age of 19.

Ramses II was the last ruler of the great Egyptian Empire. He ended the hundred years of conflicts between Egypt and the Hittites at the famous battle of Kadesh. Although Egyptian records paint this victory as a huge success, Egyptian accounts do not provide a completely accurate view of the battle itself. Ramses failed to conquer the Hittites or to drive them out of Syria, although he did regain Palestine for the Egyptian Empire. Nevertheless, he managed to negotiate an important treaty with them and sealed the alliance by his marriage to the Hittite king's daughter. The terms of the treaty are quite modern in terms of its provisions for a relationship of nonaggression, mutual aid against enemy attackers, and the extradition of fugitives. After Ramses II, the authority of the pharaohs gradually declined as the priests of Amon became more and more powerful.

The Hebrews

Also during the reign of Ramses II, the Hebrew Exodus from Egypt led by Moses also occurred. The Hebrews had originated in about 1850 BCE with Abraham, the founder of Judaism, in the Mesopotamian city of Ur. As a result of a famine, Abraham and his pastoralist people moved to the eastern Mediterranean region and established the land of Canaan, which is present-day Israel and Lebanon. During a severe drought there, the Hebrew people again migrated, this time to Egypt, where they were enslaved. After several generations, Moses led the Hebrew people from Egypt back to Canaan, which became the kingdom of Israel. Unlike other peoples of the time, the Hebrews were monotheistic: they believed in only one god. Judaism greatly influenced other cultures, although the Hebrews did not try to convert others to their religion, as they believed that they were the chosen people of their god. The customs of Judaism, such as an emphasis on moral behavior and prayer, eventually gave rise to two of the world's other major religions.

In 1200 BCE, another group of people, known as the People of the Sea, began to enter Egypt. Some People of the Sea had fought in the armies of Egypt, such as under Ramses II at the battle of Kadesh. Their arrival began the decline of Egypt's traditional power structure, which led to the Late Period.

The Late Period

Egypt entered a long period of decline in which it would become part of several other empires. In the seventh century BCE, the Assyrians conquered Egypt. In 525 BCE, the Persians conquered Egypt; and in the fourth century BCE, Alexander the Great would proclaim himself the "son of Re" and bring Egypt into the Hellenistic world.

TEST TIP

Before you read the answer choices for a multiple-choice question, try to answer the question mentally. Then read the answers choices and select the one that is closest (in meaning but not necessarily wording) to your answer.

The Indus River Valley

Mohenjo-Daro and Harappa

The Indus River is located in the northernmost reaches of the Indian subcontinent. Two important centers of civilization existed there: the twin capitals of Harappa and Mohenjo-Daro, nearly identical cities located 400 miles apart. The culture of this civilization is commonly called the **Harappan** culture, as most of the important discoveries came from the city of Harappa.

Historians still have not learned to decipher the language of the Harappa; their language was not related to Sumerian cuneiform, and many believe it was from the Dravidian family of languages. The Harappans recorded texts on tiny clay seals with images of animals. Artifacts from Harappa date back to 2500 BCE, and many aspects of Harappan culture resemble practices of modern Hinduism. Both Harappa and Mohenjo-Daro were well-planned cities, laid out on a grid with streets intersecting each other at right angles. City blocks and buildings were uniform in structure between Harappa and Mohenjo-Daro, suggesting a centralized government. Such organized building on such a massive scale would have needed an autocratic government with the ability to plan and supervise large numbers of laborers. The similarity of the structures within each city and between the cities also resembles the modern Hindu belief in the unity of all life. The homes of the upper classes, however, are clearly distinguishable from those of the workers. The cities were also noteworthy for their system of running water and sewers.

Both Mohenjo-Daro and Harappa had a heavily fortified citadel surrounded by a wall, which must have been constructed to protect the cities from attacks from outsiders who posed a threat. The citadels were built with a large-scale community effort. Later, Mohenjo-Daro and Harappa likely needed protection from nearby militant commercial competitor cities. However, despite their preparedness for attacks and possible invasion, the Indus civilization seems to have experienced long periods of peace and successful trading.

The Harappan emphasis on cleanliness, evident in their focus on a supply of running water, was unique in the ancient world. Only the Hebrews and Romans could equal it, and these were both later cultures. Their emphasis on cleanliness is also reminiscent of the modern Hindu water rituals of purification, such as bathing in the Ganges.

Life in the cities of the Indus civilization seems to have been mostly peaceful and well-ordered, exhibiting signs of a disciplined and well-ordered society with little violence. In Harappa, very few weapons have been found, but quite a number of toys have been discovered, suggesting that the culture had plenty of leisure time and therefore few enemies to worry about. These aspects of the Indus civilization also resemble many modern Hindu practices and beliefs, as modern Hindus have reverence for all life forms and they practice nonviolence. The earliest Hindu texts date from the later Aryan period, but given the similarity of Harappan practices to those of later Hinduism, historians speculate about whether the culture that wrote the Hindu texts, the Aryans, borrowed many beliefs and practices from the Indus River Valley culture.

The Decline of the Harappan Civilization

The Harappan civilization began to decline around 1900 BCE, when its ports were suddenly abandoned for reasons that are unknown. Simultaneously, the construction of their homes and buildings was less proficient, and the pottery declined in quality. Archaeological evidence indicates that parts of the city of Mohenjo-Daro had to be rebuilt several times after floods destroyed them. Large buildings in Mohenjo-Daro were subdivided and altered to accommodate small workshops and to provide shelter for a great many more people. Apparently, many more people had crowded into the city, possibly during a siege imposed by attackers, because of unrest in the surrounding countryside, or during major periods of flooding.

There is evidence of a later violent invasion in Mohenjo-Daro, including a cache of unburied skeletons with severe injuries, including dismemberment. In addition, the skeletons of people were found lying unburied in the streets where they had died. The city was never rebuilt or inhabited again. In Harappa, a much more gradual abandonment of the city took place.

There is evidence that excessive irrigation of the land in the Indus River Valley led to the buildup of salts and alkalines, which could have led to a drastic decline in the supply of food and other natural resources. Destructive floods probably also contributed to the decline of the Harappans. By 1800 BCE, a large group of Indo-European people, the Aryans, had migrated from Asia to India. They spread throughout the area and eventually gained control of northern India. A decline in the availability of food and other resources, severe flooding, and the presence of the Aryans all likely played a part in the demise of the Harappan culture.

The Vedic Period

The period from 1700 to 500 BCE is known as the Vedic period. The Aryans were part of an extremely widespread and important series of migrations. These Indo-European peoples spread throughout many parts of the world, including Greece, Iran, Italy, and numerous other locations. The Aryans who settled in the Indus River Valley were pastoralists who mainly relied on their large herds of cattle for subsistence. They introduced horses into the Indus Valley, which, surprisingly, the Harappans had not domesticated. At first, the Aryans had no interest in restoring the great Harappan cities or using the sophisticated irrigation systems and advanced agricultural technology of the Indus people. They did, however, adopt some Harappan beliefs and customs. Over time, the Aryans eventually came to depend on agriculture to support their communities.

In the Indus River Valley and other parts of India, the Aryans developed the set of traditions known as Hinduism. The word *Veda* means "knowledge." The Aryans wrote the Vedas in **Sanskrit,** and the earliest of the Vedic texts, the ***Rig Veda*** (a collection of 1,028 hymns), reveals much about their culture. Early Hinduism was extremely polytheistic in nature. In fact, it has been said that there are 330 million gods in Hinduism, although such a large number must be meant to convey the fact that Hinduism has a very large pantheon of deities that cannot in the end be counted. Hindu temples were elaborate structures containing thousands of carvings of gods and goddesses. Among the deities worshipped in the Vedic period were Shiva the destroyer god, Ganesha the elephant god, Krishna, and many others. The *Rig Veda* also records the formation of the castes from the self-sacrifice of the deity Purusha. The caste system did not exist in India before the arrival of the Aryans, who were in the minority of the population. The caste system evolved so as to subjugate the native population of India. The highest caste was the brahmin, or priests; then the kshatriya, or warrior, caste; then the vaisya, or the herders, farmers, traders, and merchants; and then sudra, or the slave and servant class. The class even below the sudra was the pariahs, or untouchables—those considered to be outside Indian society.

DID YOU KNOW?

In 700 BCE, the first university in the world was established in Takshashila, in the Indian kingdom of Gandhar. More than ten thousand students from Babylon, Greece, Syria, China, and other places studied approximately 68 subjects, including the Vedas, languages, philosophy, mathematical calculations, medicine, surgery, politics, warfare, astronomy, accounting, economics, music, and dance.

The Late Vedic or Brahamanic Age

The period from 1000 to 500 BCE is called the late Vedic or Brahamanic Age. As Hinduism evolved, many texts reflected a growing awareness of the unity of all reality. According to the Hindu concept of reincarnation, the atman lives eternally in innumerable bodies or life forms, and life is essentially about the growth of self-knowledge. The more one truly understands reality, the more one knows the true self, the atman, and the more one knows that the atman and the Brahman are one. Once one attains such knowledge, there is no longer a self at all, because the self becomes one with all reality.

Hinduism had no founder and no body of canonical texts that every Hindu had to practice. The concept of Brahman as the totality of reality allowed Hindus to accept any tradition as a path to enlightenment. Hindus believed that all people were Hindus, that all were on separate paths that would eventually meet in the same place, that reality in which all are one, Brahman. Three Hindu deities emerged as the most predominant: Brahma, the creator god; Vishnu, the preserver; and Shiva, the destroyer. These three deities represent the cyclic nature of all reality. From creation comes preservation, yet ultimately created things are destroyed. From the remnants of destruction, new life often comes, as when the charred remains of a forest fertilizes the ground for new growth.

By 600 BCE, the emergence of priestly and warrior elites marked the beginning of a new pattern of civilization in the Indus region. There was a renewal of trade, sophisticated urban lifestyles, and interest in artistic and architectural endeavors.

The Shang, in the Yellow River or Huang He Valley

The Yellow River is a very turbulent river, which the ancient Chinese people crossed by inflating goat skins and creating rafts from them. Chinese culture arose on the small plots in valleys around the Yellow River. The family unit cultivated these plots. The influence of early Chinese agriculture around the Yellow River is still felt in the importance of the family unit in Chinese society. The oldest male was the head of the Chinese family; next in order of importance were the sons, from oldest to youngest; last in importance were the women of the family, from the oldest, the mother, to the youngest daughter.

The chief crop cultivated in ancient and modern China was rice and millet. Rice is a very efficient source of nutrition, but it must be cultivated primarily by hand. Rice sprouts are allowed to grow into shoots and then transplanted by hand into flooded paddies, where they are later harvested by hand. Throughout Chinese history, the special care needed to cultivate rice has meant that the vast majority of Chinese lived in the countryside and worked at manual labor. Women played an important role in the fields, and were for centuries the most significant group of laborers in China. Just as historical records of the lives of women are scant, so too are records of the lives of the majority of the world's population, the peasants and laborers.

The Xia (Hsia) Dynasty

For many years, historians thought the Xia (Hsia) dynasty (before 2000 BCE to 1570 BCE) was a mythological dynasty. Its founder was a heavenly emperor, Yu, who taught the Chinese how to manage the flooding of the Yellow River. Yu left behind his family and walked through China for ten years in order to help his people. At the end of the ten years, he returned a cripple. The emperor Yu illustrates the Confucian notion of the self-sacrificing and virtuous emperor who rules for the good of society. Archaeolgists have recently unearthed artifacts that suggest that the Xia dynasty was actually a historic dynasty.

The Shang

The first solidly authenticated dynasty in Chinese history is the **Shang dynasty** (1570–1045 BCE), which was centered in the Yellow River Valley. The Shang used tortoise shells for divination and in their cult of ancestor worship. The chief priest was the oldest male in each family, and he would burn the shells and interpret the answers to the questions written on them depending on where the shell cracked. The use of tortoise shells in ancestor worship made literacy a necessity, and the Chinese were the most literate culture in the world for centuries.

The Shang were a warrior people who moved their capital several times. The walls of the city of Ao, their sixth capital, aptly show their warrior culture, as these walls were 30 feet thick in places. The Shang buried their warriors with jade, as they believed it had magical properties. Jade is not indigenous to the area dominated by the Shang, which means that they clearly had established trading networks outside their dominions. The Shang also placed ritual vessels in the tombs, and the Chinese skill in bronze casting was unequalled for centuries. The Shang also buried their warriors with live servants, in much the same way as the inhabitants of ancient Ur in Mesopotamia buried their royalty. A slave revolt in the eleventh century BCE overthrew the dynasty.

The Olmecs, in Mesoamerica

The **Olmecs** originated around 1500 BCE at San Lorenzo, south of present-day Veracruz, Mexico. Although they were originally an egalitarian society, by 1500 BCE, a small class of hereditary noble rulers had evolved. The Olmecs had a small class of craftsmen, but most were farmers who cultivated maize, squash, and beans, and also hunted wild game. The Olmecs were literate and had sophisticated knowledge of astronomy, which they used to predict agricultural cycles; their symbolic system influenced the Mayas. There were several Olmec centers scattered over a very large region, including coastal areas, mountains, and jungles, but, unlike most ancient civilizations, the Olmecs were not a politically unified people.

The Olmecs carved enormous stone faces and managed to move them into place, even though they did not have the use of wheels. They also constructed square buildings without using any type of mortar, as well as irrigation and drainage canals for their crop fields. The stone heads, as well as the stone statues of jaguar-like men that the Olmecs created, might have had some religious significance. The Olmecs were polytheistic, practicing religious rituals, including human sacrifices, and honoring shamans as healers. They also engaged in ritualistic ball games held in large, open courts, a feature shared by the Mayas, who were the heirs of Olmec culture. The Olmecs were very successful traders, ferrying their goods to central and western Mexico and to the Pacific Coast. They imported obsidian, from which they made weapons, iron ore, shells, and perishable goods. They exported pottery, rubber, cacao, and jaguar pelts.

San Lorenzo fell in 900 BCE, and La Venta then arose as a prominent Olmec center. La Venta is known for its 110-foot-high Great Pyramid. The Olmec culture was the foundation of the other later cultures in the classical period of 300 to 900 CE in Mesoamerica.

The Chavín, in Andean South America

By about 900 BCE, the **Chavín** people had developed a sophisticated culture based on agriculture in the highlands of the Andes, in what is now Peru. They had a centralized authority in the Mosna River Valley and spread their culture to other peoples along the Pacific Coast.

The Chavín constructed elaborate ceremonial centers with large stone buildings in the highlands and along the coast. The most significant of these was Chavín de Huántar, the Chavíns' religious and political center, constructed about 10,000 feet above sea level. Its architecture is characterized by massive raised platforms built of huge blocks of stone, beginning what was to become a long Peruvian building tradition. To protect the Chavín de Huántar from the flooding of the Mosna and Supe Rivers, the Chavín people built a series of drainage canals underneath it.

The Chavín had skilled craftsmen who worked with gold, silver, copper, and some alloys. Others made pottery, stone sculpture, and textiles with a variety of elaborate and distinctive designs. Their artwork is considered by many to be among the finest of any Andean cultures. Much of it is characterized by motifs that appear to represent a system of religious beliefs, including a worship of jaguars, as well as snakes and birds of prey. By 300 BCE, the Chavín culture was in decline, and its unifying influence in the Andean area was gone. However, the Chavín had a significant influence on the development of later Peruvian civilizations, including the Paracas and Nazca, and later, the Huari, Tiahuanaco, and Inca.

Growth, Change, and Interactions in the Earliest Civilizations

The expansion of cities into states and the empire-building that occurred in all of these early civilizations resulted from continuous and complex societal changes, as cultural values were intricately related to the natural environment, economic life, and politics, which also were continuing to evolve. All of these civilizations—with the exception of the Shang in China—became less and less culturally isolated and self-sufficient; they learned, changed, and became more diverse partly because of interactions with other societies, especially interactions involving trade and war. The mobility of pastoralists and their vital role in trade helped to link different agricultural and urban societies—both directly and indirectly—with one another and to expand networks of commercial and cultural exchanges.

However, the very interactions involving trade, including weapons—particularly among the empires of Mesopotamia, Egypt, and the Indus Valley and pastoralists—that led to their prosperity also made them more vulnerable and weakened them. Although the decline of the Harappan Empire in the Indus Valley probably was partly a result of destructive flooding and environmental damage caused by excessive irrigation, the invasion of the Indo-European Aryans and their conquest of the area around 1800 BCE almost certainly contributed to the disappearance of the Harappas. The empires of Mesopotamia and Egypt were still thriving at that time; however, beginning around 1500 BCE and continuing for another 1,000 years, both empires were invaded and threatened by Indo-European pastoralists from regions north of Mesopotamia. The changes that occurred during that period reflect a pattern that recurs again and again in history: interactions between and among different societies can be both beneficial and destructive.

The following table compares and contrasts some changing aspects of the Mesopotamian and Egyptian empires between about 1500 and 500 BCE.

Changes in the Empires of Mesopotamia and Egypt: 1567–600 BCE	
MESOPOTAMIA	**EGYPT**
Political Systems	• Outside invaders conquered the city-states, resulting in two separate political zones: in 1500 BCE, pastoral Hittites in the south (Babylon) and in 1000 BCE, Assyrians in the north. • Hittites interacted with other larger states and spread their culture; they were expansionist at first; later, King Muwatallish (began his reign in 1308 BCE) was concerned only with protecting the empire; well-organized militarily, but not brutal to those they conquered; had merciful laws. • Hittites had many wars against the Egyptians. • The Hittite empire collapsed around 1200 BCE after attacks from the People of the Sea. • The Assyrians conquered Babylon in 1000 BCE; they were one of the first military societies in the world; harsh laws within their own society; expansionist goals. • The Assyrian empire fell in 612 BCE to the united Chaldeans, Cimmerians, Scythians, and Medes.	• Outside invaders—the Hyksos—had taken over; political fragmentation challenged the power of the pharaohs; reunification into the New Kingdom in 1567 CE after the foreign Hyksos were defeated; unlike the Old Kingdom in being aggressively expansionist with warrior pharoahs—especially Rameses II, who reigned for 66 years, beginning in 1271 BCE. • Egyptians had many wars against the Hittites but Ramses II failed to conquer them; instead he negotiated a treaty with them and ceded Kadesh to the Hittites. • In 670 BCE, the Assyrians conquered Egypt.
Weapons	• Hittites used iron-smelting techniques to make iron weapons from large stores of iron ore: swords, spears, lances, shields. • After conquering Babylon in 1000 BCE, the Assyrians adopted the use of the Hittites' iron-smelting weapon-making techniques.	• Used the Hykos technique of fighting in horse-draw chariots and cast-bronze weapons (which were inferior to Hittites' iron weapons), but also compound bows that were easy to carry and very accurate for up to 300 yards, and khopesh swords—slashing weapons used by skilled warriors in close combat.
Military Tactics and Transportation	• The Hittite king was commander-in-chief of armies from 16 or more Hittite provinces; together they made a huge force of horse-drawn chariots (up to 2,500) that led the first offense to create massive destruction, then followed by the second offense of a large infantry made up of two divisions of about 18,000 men to deal with the scattered enemy. • Assyrians created of one of the first well-organized armies—a military machine—with skilled soldiers on horseback and chariot warfare, as well the use of pastoral troops riding camels; brutal tactics practiced on those they conquered.	• The pharaoh was commander-in-chief, with two chief-deputy corps commanders directly below him, and below them, generals who commanded divisions, each consisting of about 5,000 men.

(continued)

Changes in the Empires of Mesopotamia and Egypt: 1567–600 BCE (continued)

	MESOPOTAMIA	EGYPT
Trade and Interactions	• Large-scale trading and interactions with other societies: Hittites controlled copper, silver, and iron deposits. • Around 1200 BCE, large numbers of people of diverse ethnicity, the People of the Sea, began to enter Mesopotamia. • Assyrians acquired metals from Antolia, textiles from Persia, and lumber from western areas in exchange for copper.	• Large-scale trade and interactions; Egypt controlled Syria, Palestine, and Nubia, from which they acquired timber, gold, copper, and myrrh until 1200 BCE, when Egypt lost control of Nubia, a vital part of its trade route to the south. • Around 1200 BCE, large numbers of people of diverse ethnicity, the People of the Sea, began to enter Egypt.
Culture and the Arts	• Mesopotamian political and cultural concepts were adopted by the Hittites and spread widely; the arts flourished; Akkadian was the language of international diplomacy. • Cuneiform writing spread; Mesopotamian artistic style and architecture also spread.	• The Hyksos intermarried with Egyptians and assimilated Egyptian customs; the arts flourished and influenced other cultures.
Religion	• Spread of Sumerian (Mesopotamian) mythology throughout the entire area.	• In the New Kingdom, Amenhotep IV spread a form of monotheism in which the sun-god Aten was worshipped as the exclusive god of Egypt. To emphasize his loyalty to Aten he changed his name from Amenhotep IV to Akhenaten.
Architecture	• Hittites had the best military architecture of the Near East: cyclopean walls with strategic contouring in difficult terrain and sophisticated layout of offensive defense works; also, large temples with architecture with completely asymmetrical ground plans and square piers as supports.	• Pyramids were no longer constructed as in the Old Kingdom, but huge religious temples and statues were built, as well as underground tombs. • Construction of military fortifications.

Time for a quiz
• Review strategies in Chapter 2
• Take Quiz 1 at the REA Study Center
(www.rea.com/studycenter)

Unit II:
Organization and Reorganization of Human Societies,
c. 600 BCE to c. 600 CE

Chapter 6

The Development and Codification of Religious and Cultural Traditions

The time between about 600 BCE and 600 CE is often referred to as the classical period. During this period, states and empires expanded considerably. Interregional networks of trade spread a variety of goods among societies, as well as ideas and many aspects of culture, including religions and belief systems, the arts, and architecture. The intense level of trade and interactions between societies led many of them to adopt some basic, universal beliefs about acceptable human behavior.

Key Terms

Analects	Daoism	shamanism
apostles	diaspora	Siddhartha
Aristotle	empiricism	Socrates
atman	Hinduism	Sutra
Bible	Judaism	Ten Commandments
Brahmanism	Lao Zi	The Way
Buddhism	*Mahabharata*	Torah
Christianity	meritocracy	Vedas
Confucianism	Plato	*wu wei*
Confucius	*Ramayana*	

During the classical period, all of the major religions of the world either emerged or evolved significantly, with the exception of Islam, which would come just after this period. New religious and belief systems formed the basis for communication, common standards of ethics, and trust among people who regularly came in contact with and had business relationships with others from different cultures. However, religions and belief systems were unique to their own cultures; they each provided unique answers to questions about human existence, the nature of society, and the world itself.

Within states and empires, new religions and belief systems influenced internal political systems and social stratification. In addition, in some large states and empires, religious practices were diverse, which created internal conflicts. Religions and belief systems also created conflicts between states and empires. Overall, the emergence and expansion of religions had a tremendous impact on the cultures and events of this period; they have continued to have major influences on the world up to the present time.

TEST TIP

You will not be allowed to use note paper while you are taking the AP World History exam, but you can and should make notes in your exam booklet.

Judaism

The Hebrews had been the first people to develop the concept of monotheism, or a belief in one god, around 2000 BCE, in the Mesopotamian city of Ur. There, they adopted many Mesopotamian cultural traditions, including laws from the Code of Hammurabi. After the Hebrew exodus from Egypt, the Hebrews moved back to what was then known as Palestine, on the Sinai peninsula, which was at the crossroads of trade routes to and from Egypt, Arabia, and the Near East. Politically, the Hebrews were a kingdom only during the forty-year reign of King Solomon in the tenth century BCE. After the death of Solomon in 930 BCE, the unity of the Hebrews disintegrated, and the kingdom split into the state of Israel in the north and the state of Judea in the south. Israel was conquered by the Assyrians in 722 BCE; after the New Babylonian Empire destroyed the Assyrians, it seized Judea in 586 BCE. The Hebrews of Israel scattered throughout the Middle East and Afro-Eurasia in what was known as the **diaspora**, while those in Judah were deported to Babylon. There, they became known as the Jews.

They were allowed to retain their identity, culture, and religion under the Assyrians' rule, and also later, under the conquest of the Persians and the Greeks.

The foundation of Judaism is the **Torah**, which includes the scriptures and the Old Testament of the Bible, which are sets of documents that tell the stories of the founders and early followers of Judaism, and also explains their beliefs. The Torah is believed to have been written by Hebrew leaders over several centuries, beginning in the tenth century BCE, when the Hebrews lived in Palestine.

Judaism involved an abstract concept of God as being limitless, yet also loving and compassionate toward his people, based on the condition that they obeyed the **Ten Commandments**, a set of rules that guided relationships both between people and between people and God. The Jews believed that they were the specially chosen people of God, and they therefore did not try to convert others to their religion. However, Judaism had a huge influence on the development of both Christianity during this period and, later, in the seventh century, on Islam. Judaism's tenets of moral behavior, prayer, and worship would become the tenets of Christianity and Islam, as well as all other monotheistic religions.

Christianity

The Jewish belief in the coming of a Messiah, a leader who would reunite the Jewish people and restore their kingdom, laid the foundation for the emergence of **Christianity**. The founder of Christianity was Jesus, who was born in Bethlehem and raised in Nazareth, in Judea, at the beginning of the first century. At the time, Judea was a province of the Roman Empire. Jesus was raised according to Judaism.

As an adult, Jesus was a prophet and a teacher. He and his apostles wandered throughout Jerusalem and the surrounding countryside preaching a message of religious reform, divine love, and a moral code based on love, charity, and humility. The **apostles** were a group of twelve men who were Jesus' original disciples. Jesus appealed to common people because of his ability to teach lessons of life through his parables, and also because he taught that the soul of every person—no matter what his or her social status was—could be saved. His followers believed that Jesus was the Messiah, the one who would rid Judaism of its elitist priests and ensure that all people who followed his teachings would be rewarded with life after death; they also believed that those who did not follow his teachings would be condemned to eternal hell. The followers of Jesus further came to believe that he was the son of God. The masses embraced Jesus and his teachings, and his apostles were dedicated to converting them all to this new religion. Thus, Christianity spread rapidly throughout the region.

Jewish scholars and priests strongly opposed and even feared Jesus because of his interest in common people and his criticisms of established Jewish society. They viewed him as a rabble-rouser and a threat to their authority. As Jesus' influence grew and his teachings became more widely accepted, the Roman authorities also became alarmed. Like the Jewish elite, the Romans feared that he might cause a revolution that would undermine and even take away their power. Therefore, Jesus was arrested and executed by Roman officials. After his death, his apostles continued to spread Jesus' teachings and the Christian religion. They wrote and gathered the scriptures that form the New Testament of the Christian **Bible**, which also includes the Old Testament of the Jews. Paul, a later convert to Christianity, was instrumental in the success of spreading the Christian religion. He had been born a Jew, but also as a Roman citizen, in a town on the Mediterranean Sea in what is present-day Turkey. Thus, Paul was familiar with Greco-Roman culture and was able to explain the tenets of Christianity in a manner that converted many Greeks and Romans. Paul established numerous Christian churches throughout the eastern Mediterranean, and even some within Rome. Largely as a result of Paul's efforts, Christianity became a widespread religion, crossing many cultural and state boundaries. Paul also developed much of the theology of the early Christian church.

Although Christianity grew steadily throughout the Roman Empire, it continued to create conflicts with the Roman authorities. Christianity was not legal in the Roman Empire and Christians were persecuted and often executed. Early Christians often met in private homes that were owned by women. Phoebe, for example, was one of the most important followers of Paul. They also gathered in the catacombs around Rome. However, in 313 CE, the Roman Emperor Constantine converted to Christianity and established the new capital of Rome in the eastern city of Byzantium, which he renamed Constantinople. Constantine viewed Christianity as the key to solidifying his power in the empire. In many letters and other documents, he claimed that the unity of the Church was crucial to maintaining the unity of the Roman Empire. Christianity therefore continued to expand, west and north from Rome, as well as east from Constantinople. Christianity would later dominate European culture and politics and eventually become the religion with the most followers in the modern world.

DIDYOUKNOW?

In 301 CE, the kingdom of Armenia, at the crossroads of southwestern Asia, the Middle East, and Europe, became the first state to make Christianity its official religion.

Hinduism

The Aryans developed **Hinduism** during the Vedic period in the Indus River Valley and other parts of India. Aryan priests taught values through hymns that were eventually written down in the **Vedas**, the sacred texts of Hinduism. The four castes, or classes, had been in place in Indian society even before the Vedic period: the nobles, the commoners, the Brahmins (priests), and the laborers and serfs. However, during the late Vedic age, which ended in about 500 BCE, many changes in Hinduism and Indian thought occurred; these evolved into new and complex religious and social systems. The changes, collectively called **Brahmanism**, were characterized by the elevation of the Brahmin priests to a position of supreme power and privilege in society, even above the status of rulers and nobles. The priests also sanctioned the caste system as being a religious necessity through the principle that all people must perform the social duties designated to their inherited castes.

In addition, various subcastes emerged within the four main castes. The members of these subcastes each had a particular social, occupational, or religious character. For example, the merchants and artisans who emerged as new types of professionals were subcastes of the caste of commoners. The Untouchables also came into being as a large class of social outcasts. They were so called because their occupations were menial and considered degrading; they were scavengers, handlers of the carcasses of dead animals, and carriers of human and animal wastes, and their very touch was thought to be degrading to those in other castes.

Several classics of Indian literature were created during this period, including epics such as the **Mahabharata**, the world's longest poem and a story about the power struggle of two clans. A subsection of the *Mahabharata* is the Bhagavad Gita, about a discussion between the warrior Arjuna and the god Krishna. In response to Arjuna's concerns about the possibility of killing members of his own clan, Krishna develops the idea of the **atman**, or the eternal self, which has always existed and always will exist; it cannot be destroyed. According to the Hindu concept of reincarnation, the atman lives eternally in innumerable bodies or life forms. The stories of the *Mahabharata* embody important Hindu values that still guide modern-day Indians. The other great epic of the time was the **Ramayana**, which tells about the wanderings of the banished prince Rama and the difficulties of his faithful wife Sita, before they are reunited and Rama is returned to his rightful throne. Over time, priests transformed this simple story into a devotional text in which Rama was the ideal man and the incarnation of the god Vishnu, while Sita was the perfect woman, who was devoted and submissive to her husband.

The following became integral parts of Hinduism's essential beliefs:

The Universal Spirit and Atman.   Hinduism is based on the eternal existence of a universal spirit that guides all forms of life on Earth. The atman, a part of this spirit, is trapped within people and other living things. The atman is constantly drawn to be reunited with the universal spirit, and this guides all aspects of every person's life. When a person dies, his or her atman might be reunited with the universal spirit, but more often, it is born again into a new body.

Reincarnation.   When one person dies, his or her atman is reborn in a different body. Reincarnation has no beginning or end, being part of the universal spirit that encompasses all life.

Dharma.   *Dharma* can be loosely translated as "virtues" or "duties." A person's status in the caste system determines what virtues that person has and thus what duties that person must fulfill. It also governs how close he or she can be to the ultimate reunification with the universal spirit. When a member of a lower caste fulfills his or her dharma, the reward is for his or her atman to be reborn into a higher caste. However, only the atmans of members of the highest caste can ever directly achieve reunification with the universal spirit.

Karma.   Whether or not a person fulfills his or her dharma in one life governs what happens in his or her next life. Thus, karma is the continuing cause and effect of the actions of all individuals in their lives.

The universal spirit is represented by Brahman, a god that has countless forms and unites them all. Two of Brahman's major forms are the gods Vishnu, the Creator, and Shiva, the Destroyer. Because of its principle of a universal spirit and its different manifestations as gods, it is difficult to categorize Hinduism as being either polytheistic or monotheistic.

Buddhism

The Brahmins laid the foundation of classical Hinduism, but their continued emphasis on the sacrifice, rituals, and spells led to the emergence of ascetics and reformers who sought to pursue enlightenment by bypassing these priests and their rituals. These dissenters sought to attain salvation from the cycle of birth and death by meditating about the true nature of human beings as part of the universal spirit. They were indifferent to worldly matters and possessions, focusing only on the achievement of oneness with the underlying essence of all things.

The most important of these dissenters, **Siddhartha**, was the privileged son of a Hindu prince who lived during the sixth century BCE. While still a young man, he became dissatisfied with Hinduism because it offered him no answers to the meaning of life. He left home to become an ascetic, or a person who led a spiritual life of self-discipline and disregard for material things. However, Siddhartha soon came to reject extreme asceticism and found his own way to salvation. It was he who began **Buddhism** in the Ganges River area of India. Siddhartha, who later became known as the Buddha, meaning the "Enlightened One," achieved his own enlightenment while sitting under a tree. The revelations that came to him then form the basic tenets of Buddhism:

The Four Noble Truths.   (1) All of life is suffering; (2) Suffering is caused by desires and cravings for things that do not bring satisfaction; (3) Suffering is cured by removing desires; and (4) Desire is eliminated by following the Eightfold Path of conduct, which is the middle way between worldly pursuits and extreme asceticism.

The Five Moral Rules of Conduct.   (1) Do not kill any living being; (2) Do not take what is not given to you; (3) Do not speak falsely; (4) Do not drink intoxicating drinks; and (5) Do not be unchaste.

The Eightfold Path of Conduct to Enlightenment.   The ultimate goal of Buddhism is for a person to follow the path to nirvana, the state of contentment that is achieved with the unification of the person's soul with the universal spirit. The eight steps of the path are taken one by one in succession, beginning with a change in one's thoughts and intentions, followed by changes in lifestyle and actions, all of which lead to a higher level of thought through the practice of meditation. Ultimately, nirvana is achieved, and the person views life with an entirely new and different level of understanding.

All of these tenets formed the **Sutra**, the text of Buddhism. The Buddha did not believe in the existence of the atman, nor did he believe that people were born into castes; they were only born with the propensity to do good or evil. He also taught against sacrifices to, and forbade his followers from worshipping him as, a god. Life in the sixth century BCE in India was very difficult, and the Buddha's doctrine of nirvana appealed to many for whom the thought of infinite numbers of painful lives was difficult to bear. Like Hinduism, Buddhism emphasized the soul's yearning for enlightened understanding; however, unlike Hinduism, Buddhism embraced the concept that people of all social status could succeed in achieving nirvana. In this way, Buddhism's appeal to ordinary people wanting to be free of the caste system is comparable to the appeal of Christianity to common people who desired to be free of the rigidity of the elite Jewish priests.

During the Buddha's long life, he actively spread his beliefs throughout India. After his death, however, Buddhism faced opposition from Hindus, who viewed it as a threat to India's traditional social and religious structures. Still, Buddhism did have a major impact on Hinduism in that it initiated rejuvenation and some reforms. The Hindu concept of Brahman was able to absorb almost any tradition, and many aspects of Buddhism were absorbed into Hinduism. Hindus explain the Buddha as an incarnation of Krishna, just as they explain the historic Jesus as an incarnation of Krishna. Hindu priests began to place more emphasis on moral conduct as a means of salvation and less emphasis on sacrifices, rituals, and magic.

Buddhism reached its peak in India in the third century BCE, when the great Mauryan emperor Ashoka became a convert and promoted its practice. Ashoka issued his edicts on Rock Pillars throughout India, many marking the path to holy sites associated with the Buddha or celebrating events of his life. Ashoka attempted to spread Buddhism through the conquest of righteousness, without force and with tolerance for diversity. After his death, however, the religion began to decline and eventually disappeared from India.

However, Buddhism survived in the areas where it had spread through the diffusion of cultures via the Silk Road, such as in Southeast Asia, China, and Japan. Trade along the Silk Road often fostered close working relationships and even alliances, and these relationships were the foundation that made the spread of Buddhism possible. Each area adapted Buddhism to its own cultural framework, including architecture and the arts.

The Chinese initially rejected the wandering Buddhist monks. They were also puzzled by the notion of reincarnation, but despite the fact that Buddhist teachings conflicted with Chinese values, especially that of filial piety, Buddhism eventually took root in China. The Chinese translated the Buddhist sutras, and in so doing, fused many of the Buddha's teachings with those of Confucius (who lived after the Buddha) and other important Chinese thinkers. Chinese Buddhists eventually created some of the world's greatest Buddhist art, as seen especially in the caves of Magao along the frontiers of China. There, thousands of caves are adorned with paintings and enormous statues of the Buddha. The Japanese created a unique version of Buddha's teachings known as Zen Buddhism. Zen Buddhists are known for the use of rock gardens to meditate. The rocks are often arranged in groups of three to symbolize heaven, earth, and humanity. The formations are also asymmetrical to symbolize the uneven and imperfect nature of life.

TEST TIP

Look for signal words in multiple-choice questions that suggest that more than one answer seems to be correct, such as *not*, *except*, and *always*. The answer to a question that includes these words is the one that is **both** factually correct and logically consistent.

Confucianism

Confucius was born into a minor noble family in 551 BCE, during the Warring States Period in China, when it was not united. Although he rose to a prominent position in the government of his native province Lu, political intrigue forced Confucius from the government, and he became a wandering teacher. He wrote no texts himself, but his followers collected his sayings and organized them. The most famous collection of the teachings of **Confucianism** is the *Analects*. Confucius taught through parables and short aphorisms, which illustrate concepts rather than attempts to prove them. His teachings form the basis of Chinese culture, and were themselves based on earlier traditions going back to the Zhou dynasty and the Chinese mythology surrounding the Heavenly Emperors. Confucius was not an innovator, but rather a respecter of ancient traditions and customs. For Confucius, the most excellent models of virtue were to be found in the past. He believed that respect for the past would restore balance, harmony, and order to society and to people's own lives.

Confucius also believed that China was in a chaotic state because of the unethical behavior of Chinese rulers and the Chinese people themselves. His teachings centered around the principles of harmony, order, and obedience. Above all, Confucius was concerned with virtue and with the virtuous individual. He did not think of himself as an innovator but rather as a transmitter of excellent models of the past. Significantly, he did not regard himself as an especially brilliant thinker or sage; he taught that the virtuous life is open to and can be followed by all. For Confucius, kindness; his Rules of Propriety, or decency; and filial piety, or the respect of children for their elders—particularly their male elders—were the bases of morality. He taught that strong relationships were the foundation for a strong society in the following hierarchy:

- The emperor must take care of his subjects, and they must obey the emperor.

- A father must take care of a son, and a son must obey his father.

- An older brother must take care of a younger brother, who must obey him.

- A husband must take care of his wife, who must obey him.

- Friends, being equal, must be mutually caring and obedient.

Confucianism thus reinforced the traditional patriarchal social structure of China and the authority and responsibilities of the emperor. It also accepted inequality as being essential for an orderly and harmonious society.

Virtue was not inborn, according to Confucius, but rather was a learned behavior; through watching and imitating the virtuous behavior of one's parents and others in society, particularly the emperor, one learns to be virtuous. So important was inner virtue to Confucius that he taught others to follow **The Way**, or Dao, simply for the sake of the Way rather than for the sake of reward or punishment. These teachings helped to develop a **meritocracy** in China, the idea that government should be run by those whose virtue and learning merited their positions of authority and respect. In other words, heredity was meaningless; only ability and inner virtue determined one's advancement. It was particularly important for government officials to be virtuous. Confucius argued that if one governed people well for several decades or centuries, there would no longer be a need for the death penalty or other harsh punishments: people would submit to virtuous rulers, whereas they would revolt against dishonest ones. Confucianism was a practical form of action that was accessible to all and that sought to create a virtuous society governed by virtuous rulers, a society in which one knew his place and kept it, in which one had respect for those above him and treated those beneath with benevolence.

Although Confucianism was and still is practiced religiously, it is not a religion. It is more of a philosophy—a practical system of ethics designed to produce a well-ordered society and political state. Confucius refused to address questions about the afterlife or the spiritual world, as he believed he had no knowledge of such things. Confucianism eventually formed the basis of Chinese culture and spread to many other parts of Asia, including Japan.

Daoism

Lao Zi, a wandering scholar of the fourth century BCE, is thought to be the founder of Daoism. **Daoism** is a religion based on the Dao, or the Way. However, Lao Zi rejected the Confucian notion that the Rules of Propriety were the path to virtue. He believed that the Dao was not to be equated with filial piety or with any other system of morality or learning, because the Dao itself is limitless and inexpressible. It could not be named or otherwise described, as any attempt to do so would necessarily limit the Dao, which encompassed everything. Lao Zi believed that the Dao was passive, eternal, and unchanging; thus, people must accept it and live in harmony with it and with nature. Lao Zi thought that human strivings, which resisted the Dao, caused chaos in the world.

Daoism emphasizes introspection, a life of simplicity, and an inner journey toward peace and contentment. A major tenet of Daoism is *wu wei*, or noninterference with the natural path of things and detachment from worldly affairs, including government.

Lao Zi believed that any system of rules or laws could capture only a part of the Dao and therefore necessarily would limit a person's entire being.

The Daoist confidence in human nature was boundless; unlike Confucius, who believed that virtue must be learned, Lao Zi believed that following the Way would occur naturally if people were left without interference. Lao Zi rejected the idea of a meritocracy and instead believed that in an ideal state, a ruler could adapt to any circumstances, as he would not hold to any rigid school of thought, nor to any preconceived path of action.

A common misinterpretation of Daoism is to assume that Daoists advocated no action at all; however, the philosophy of nonaction simply meant acting in accordance with the Dao and not interfering with the natural path of things. For Daoists, not interfering with the natural path of humans through artificial laws that could only capture part of the Dao would naturally lead to a harmonious society.

Daoism had many important influences on Chinese culture. Some Daoists pursued the study of alchemy and medicine, and their work was influential in the development of Chinese traditional medicine, including the significant role of herbs, tonics, and good hygiene. Daoist philosophy contributed to the practice of Chinese medicine's consideration of the patient as a whole rather than the disease only, and its fundamental theory that a lack of harmony with nature is a major reason why disorders develop. Daoist breathing practices and Chinese acupuncture share the same theory: energy circulates along numerous paths inside the body.

Comparison of Confucianism and Daoism

Although Confucianism and Daoism both emphasized self-knowledge and acceptance of the ways things were, Confucianism was based on action and extroversion, while Daoism was based on nonaction and introspection. A person could believe in both belief systems, unlike most western religions, which require complete devotion of their followers. Historically, it has often been said that the Chinese are Confucians in their daily lives and Daoists in their private lives. Confucianism helped the Chinese in their daily affairs, while Daoism spoke to their more esoteric and private spiritual desires.

TEST TIP

Turn off the television and radio and study in a quiet place that is free of distractions.

Greek and Roman Beliefs

Although no new religions emerged from the classical civilizations of the Greeks or the Romans, the core ideas of their philosophy had a significant impact on the world during this period. Both civilizations retained their traditional religions, which were based on interrelated gods and goddesses who were thought to govern human life, but offered no real guidance for ethical behavior or answers to persistent questions about the human condition and different ways of approaching the nature of human existence, worship, or communal life. The Greeks and Romans developed models of natural philosophy that were separate and unrelated to religion. Greek philosophers applied logic to develop theories to explain natural and psychological phenomena. To them, there was no contradiction in using reason to understand universal truths about nature and existence and in believing at the same time that the gods fundamentally ruled them.

Ancient Greek philosophers had attempted to identify a single underlying principle of the entire cosmos. Their theories were diverse and reached no conclusions, yet they initiated the quest to investigate the limits and role of reason and sensory faculties, how knowledge is acquired, and what knowledge consists of. Interest in such questions was the basis of the Greek creation of philosophy as "the love of wisdom." Socrates, Plato, and Aristotle were the most influential of the classical Greek philosophers; they were interested more in the role of human beings than in explanations of the material world.

In the fifth century BCE, **Socrates** revolutionized many aspects of Western thought. He analyzed the very nature of knowledge and how people gain knowledge; he developed a philosophy of ethics and advocated a life of good and decent behavior; and he was a strong proponent of democracy, explaining what made laws and governments just. Socrates taught his followers to question conventional wisdom by using rational inquiry. One of his students was **Plato**, who developed his own ideas of philosophy. In his theory of forms, Plato rejected the changeable, deceptive world that we are aware of through our senses, proposing instead his world of ideas, which were constant and true. Plato was a teacher of **Aristotle**, who believed in a realm that was not observable to humans through the five senses. He rejected Plato's assumptions that there was a transcendent or supernatural existence; instead, Aristotle advocated **empiricism**, or a reliance on the senses, as the appropriate method for learning about and understanding the world. Like Confucius, Aristotle taught the importance of moderation and balance in human behavior.

Greek philosophy spread throughout much of the known world, including Asia, during Macedonian Emperor Alexander the Great's conquests between 336 and 323 BCE, as Alexander was particularly interested in Greek culture and philosophy. After Alexander's death and the end of his empire, the people whom he had conquered were still greatly influenced by many aspects of Greek culture, including those relating to philosophy. New perspectives and theories developed in many parts of the world based on the Greek principles of reason and inquiry. When the increasingly powerful Romans conquered the Greeks in 150 BCE, the Romans also adopted many aspects of Greek culture.

After Constantine became the first Christian emperor of Rome in 313 CE, and Christianity was established as the official religion of the Roman Empire in 380 CE, Christianity became increasingly intertwined with Greek philosophy. This merged together the main foundations of the future of Western thought and culture.

Animist Practices, Ancestral Worship, and Shamanism

Each religion had its own basic tenets, but individual societies adapted them to fit their own cultures. Even in places where new beliefs took root, they often merged with ancient animist elements and ancestor worship. Animist beliefs and practices remained as part of the customs of Hinduism and Daoism, and they were not completely displaced by those who converted to Christianity and Buddhism. For example, Christianity still included animist beliefs in magic in the form of miracles and ritual properties of natural objects, such as relics, the bones of saints, and mistletoe. Those who practiced Confucianism, Daoism, and Buddhism continued to revere their ancestors and practice ancestral rites.

It is also important to note that new religious and other belief systems did not extend to Mesoamerica or to societies that were not part of the major civilizations of the classical period. The civilizations of Mesoamerica, as well as many societies in Africa and Asia, continued to practice **shamanism**, in which shamans, or high priests, were revered as healers and as the links between the spiritual world and the natural world.

Religions and Belief Systems as Unifying Factors

The spread of the major religions and philosophies of the classical period was facilitated both by the decline of empires and by the channels of communication that these same empires had developed. Many people in diverse societies shifted away from their previous adherence to the concept of a group of divine spirits or gods and goddesses, and toward belief in a powerful, single divine force, often with the hope of a peaceful afterlife. This shift grew partly out of the needs of many people living in times of political uncertainties. Religions and other belief systems provided comfort, especially to common people, and they also helped to unify societies in which strictly political ties were loosening. Some religious and philosophical belief systems also helped to facilitate long-distance trade because these systems were not localized customs, but rather were based on the overarching concept of an ever-present divine being that imposed order on the world. Trade networks, in turn, helped to spread these new and evolving religions and belief systems. With the decline and fall of empires late in the classical period, religions and other belief systems were major forces in shaping the time to come.

The Development of States and Empires

In their quest for greater wealth and power, the states and empires of the classical period continued to expand their territories and influence. The populations of states grew as well, in both numbers and cultural diversity. Elite classes acquired great wealth and political power at the expense of large numbers of people with lower social status. To manage and organize the people under their control, the rulers and elite classes developed administrative institutions and policies; to protect their borders, they built up powerful military forces. Expansion on too great a scale and over large distances created difficulties over time for some states: it often created conflicts with other states, and it ultimately created cultural, administrative, and political problems that were difficult and sometimes impossible to manage. The exploitation of both subjects and the land also caused difficulties for most of the classical states and empires.

Key Terms

Achaemenid Empire	Huns
Ashoka	Maurya Empire
Athens	Maya
Carthage	Moche
Chandragupta Maurya	Persia
city-states	Punic Wars
corvus	Qin dynasty
Emperor Constantine	Roman Empire
Gupta Empire	Roman Republic
Han dynasty	Sparta
Hellenization	Teotihuacan

Similarities of Classical States and Empires

The political and social structures, cultures, and belief systems of the classical empires differed in many ways, but most also had the following similarities:

- Major cities were the centers of trade and political administration.

- Large, complex governmental and administrative systems imposed unity on the different parts of the empires.

- Economies were complex; they were still largely based on agriculture, and farming was the most common occupation.

- Social hierarchies included elite classes, as well as merchants, artisans, laborers, and slaves.

- Patriarchal family and social structures remained in place.

- Trade continued to expand by both land and sea routes.

Key States and Empires

Carthage

Between the period of 1200 and 900 BCE, there was no major military power in Mesopotamia, and the small state of Phoenicia, on the coast of Syria at the east end of the Mediterranean Sea, prospered. The Phoenicians had excellent seafaring skills, and they came to dominate trade throughout the Mediterranean region. They colonized many areas along the Mediterranean Sea, including the city of Carthage. After Tyre, the main city of Phoenicia, was conquered by the Persians in 575 BCE, Carthage had become the leader of the Phoenician colonies in the west and was a full-fledged empire. It continued to expand and eventually included much of the African coast and parts of present-day Spain and France.

Carthage was immensely wealthy and had a merchant-based economy. It was protected by the strongest navy in the region, and it essentially ruled the Mediterranean Sea. The city and its colonies were all ruled by a small elite class who were mainly ship owners and merchants. All of the Carthaginian colonies paid tributes and taxes to this small group of rulers.

Punic Wars

As the Roman Republic aggressively sought to expand its empire, it inevitably came in conflict with the Carthaginians, starting the **Punic Wars**, which spanned more than a century (264–146 BCE). The Punic Wars began when Rome entered Sicily, where the Phoenicians had a settlement. In the first Punic War, Carthage was confident that its superior navy would defeat the Romans. However, the Romans had built many ships and equipped them each with an ingenious pivotal bridge called a **corvus**, which could be swung out and extended from Roman ships for legions of Roman soldiers to march across and do battle, just as if they had been on land. With this new invention, the Romans defeated the Carthaginians and gained control of Sicily.

In the second Punic War, Carthaginian leader Hannibal won many battles with the Romans. The war was fought on three fronts, with Hannibal eventually leading an army through the Alps and surprising the Romans in northern Italy. However, the Romans cut off his supply route and crossed over to Africa to attack Carthage. Rome again emerged victorious and greatly weakened the Carthaginian Empire. In the third Punic War, the Romans laid siege to the city of Carthage for two years. Although the Carthaginians surrendered, the Romans nevertheless destroyed the city.

In 44 BCE, Roman Emperor Julius Caesar finally reestablished Carthage as a colony, and it went on to become the capital of the Roman province of Africa. Successive Roman emperors gave additional privileges to Carthage. In the third and fourth centuries, Carthage was one of the most important cultural and commercial centers of the Roman Empire.

TEST TIP

Use all of the time provided for taking the exam. If you finish a section of the exam and there is still time left, review your answers or essays.

The Greeks

The rise of classical Greece began around 800 BCE Classical Greece was not a state or an empire, and it had no centralized government. Instead, it was a group of loosely related **city-states**, making Greece unique in its political organization. Most of the Greek city-states consisted of a central city protected by fortifications and surrounded by farmland and villages. Over time, several city-states, most notably Athens and Sparta, grew to have large populations and became highly urbanized centers with thriving societies. Agricultural surpluses and taxes supported the urban populations. The land of Greece could not sustain the cultivation of grain, and the need for this and other resources led both Athens and Sparta to expand their areas of control in the Mediterranean region.

Comparison and Contrast of Athens and Sparta

Although the city-states of Athens and Sparta had some commonalities, they also were different in many ways.

Similarities:

- Neither had a centralized government, but instead the concept of a polis, a fortified city, that formed the center of other smaller city-states and the surrounding land.

- Both developed strong military organizations and established colonies throughout the Mediterranean region.

- Both used diplomacy to negotiate agreements with other societies.

- Both practiced polytheism.

Differences:

- Athens developed the world's first democracy in which all free adult male citizens could participate in politics, whereas Sparta was a military state.

- Athenian society was dominated by wealthy aristocratic landowners and those who were culturally sophisticated, whereas Spartan society promoted equality by not allowing for the accumulation of wealth or land.

- Athens relied heavily on slavery, whereas a great majority of Sparta's population was helots, or agricultural servants, who were neither free citizens nor slaves.

- In Athens, women did not share equality with men, had little freedom, and were not involved in military affairs; in Sparta, women had more equality with men and enjoyed relative freedom, and they were expected to be physically fit because all Spartans, men and women, contributed to the military.

- Spartan boys and men lived separately in military barracks from age 7 to 30.

- Athens was a coastal city and therefore less vulnerable from attacks by land than was Sparta, which was inland; the Athenians had superb seafaring skills and traveled not only around the Aegean Sea, but also the entire Mediterranean Sea.

- Spartan society was focused on military and defensive matters and uninterested in art, whereas Athens developed a rich culture with influences that endure to the present day: they celebrated individual human achievements and the ideal human form; they were interested in logic in philosophy, math, and science; and they created highly sophisticated sculpture, literature, and architecture.

Conquest of Classical Greece

The political decentralization of classical Greece ended when Emperor Phillip II of Macedonia annexed most of the fragmented city-states into his empire. Under Philip II, Macedonia had become a flourishing empire through military aggression and diplomacy. Phillip's son, Alexander the Great, went on to conquer Egypt, the Middle East, and the great Persian Empire, which spread eastward all the way to the Indus River Valley. Alexander the Great was a great admirer of Greek culture, and he initiated **Hellenization**, the intentional spreading of Greek culture. Greek philosophy, political ideas, values, architecture, and science were diffused to many large areas of the world, where they had a great and lasting influence, most immediately in the emerging Roman Empire. However, Greek culture spread as far as Punjab in India, leading to the development of Greco-Buddhist art. Gandharan Buddhist sculptures made in Punjab clearly reflect Greek artistic influences, such as the standing position, the Greco-Roman loose robe that covers both shoulders, the curly hair with a Mediterranean style, the realism of the human form, and even sandals. Greek culture remained intact within Greece, and Athens became one of the great cultural centers of the world.

The Romans

Roman society developed in the Italian peninsula relatively independently of the Greeks; in 509 BCE, the Roman Republic, which was based on the rule of law, was founded. The Republic was highly centralized, with Rome as its political, cultural, and commercial capital.

The Roman Republic

At the top of the Roman Republic's governmental structure were the two consuls, either of which could veto the decrees of other. Citizens elected the consuls from the patricians for a one-year term and the Senate had to approve their election. The consuls were the supreme masters of administration. They brought matters before the Senate for deliberation, carried out decrees of the majority, made preparations for war, and controlled the military during maneuvers.

The most important and powerful governing body in Rome was the Senate, composed of elder statesmen from the patrician class who served for life. The Senate oversaw the treasury; in fact, no money was authorized for the state without the decree of the Senate. The members of the Senate were charged with leading public investigations into treason, conspiracy, and murder. They also served as ambassadors to reconcile warring allies. Nowhere were the powers of the Senate decisively spelled out, which gave it the ability to establish supreme power in Rome.

The third important body in the Roman Republic was the people. The plebeian assembly was the last and final court to decide matters of life and death. The people's assembly met when summoned by the consuls, and later, the office of tribune was established to look after the affairs of the people.

A major difficulty faced by Rome throughout its history was the tension between the patricians, who came from the ancient noble families, and the plebeians. Both were defined as citizens, but they did not enjoy the same rights. The patricians were the aristocracy, and they did not intermarry with the plebeians. They held the highest offices, such as senators and consuls. The plebeians, on the other hand, were citizens who paid taxes and served in the army, but they were barred from holding office in the early Republic. In effect, the history of the Republic was the history of how the patricians and plebeians resolved these tensions so that they could embark on a wave of conquest that would make them masters of the Mediterranean area.

Unlike the Greek city-states, the Roman Republic adopted a policy of aggressive expansion. By 270 BCE, Rome controlled all of Italy. Soon, it also conquered Carthage, Greece, Macedonia, and parts of Asia Minor. This expansion altered the fundamental Roman economy. Aristocrats began to monopolize the land when small farmers could no longer compete with grain imported from conquered territories. They used large numbers of slaves to labor on their lands, as well as to perform many personal and household tasks. Former farmers moved to the cities and remained unemployed. Expansion of the Republic also created a large, permanently underemployed class of urban poor people and, in contrast, a wealthy merchant class that eventually gained a voice in the Senate.

TEST TIP

Study in sessions that are evenly spaced apart and not so long that you become mentally tired or distracted. This will help you understand topics in depth.

The Roman Empire

The demise of the class of free farmers unbalanced Roman society and undermined the republican constitution. The result was class conflict, civil war, and the end of the Roman Republic when Julius Caesar transformed the Republic into a monarchy in 44 CE. During his dictatorship, Caesar implemented some important reforms, such as a unified law code, a new calendar based on the Egyptian calendar, and subsidies for farmers. He ordered Carthage to be rebuilt and offered the impoverished citizens of the Roman Empire a chance to relocate there. Caesar also extended some benefits of citizenship to conquered peoples. However, he had become a dictator who desired absolute power. He began to bring senators from outside of Italy so the Senate would be filled with his supporters. By 44 CE, many powerful patricians had become increasingly alarmed by their alienation and inability to participate in Caesar's decision making; thus, they orchestrated his assassination. After his death, Caesar's grandnephew, Augustus, became emperor and Rome became an empire.

While Augustus was a great patron of the arts and used them to create a grandiose image for himself, he also reformed the military, taking direct command and regulating pay, pensions, and length of service. He mandated that the military's size be permanently fixed at twenty-five legions, and shrunk the borders of the Roman Empire to make them more defensible. Augustus promoted trade, and a great variety of luxury goods, such as silk and fruits from the east, were brought into the empire. During the Pax Romana, or Roman Peace, begun by Augustus, the Roman Empire enjoyed the longest period of unity, peace, and prosperity of its history. Moreover, it was to be the longest period of peace that the coastal civilizations of Western Europe, the Middle East, and North Africa would ever experience.

Augustus's achievements were remarkable and, although most of his successors were corrupt, the Rome he recreated would endure for 500 years in the west and for another 1,500 years in the east. Augustus, like Caesar before him, named a month in his honor,

August, thus giving him divine status. Gone was any semblance of the Republic, and Rome would suffer the consequences of this for many generations to come.

Roman law provided a common system for the entire empire. It focused primarily on property rights and family stability. Roman society was strongly patriarchal, although women were free to go out in public, and some were even educated. Only citizens had access to full protection of the law. Although the Roman Empire was based on the concept of universal law enforced by the military, it did not have a well-coordinated bureaucracy. Local governments were allowed to maintain relative independence. Roman garrisons were posted throughout its empire, with generals often serving as governors of conquered lands, allowing some of them to develop their own power bases.

The Romans did not slaughter or mistreat the people of the states they conquered, but instead treated them fairly, which created strong loyalties to Rome throughout the empire. Rome's conquests were incorporated into the Roman Empire or allowed to remain as independent allies. The conquered people, however, adopted Roman culture, including the Latin language. The empire also provided an arena for the spread of Christianity and the interaction of numerous diverse cultures. Most defeated states were forced to sign a treaty of alliance with Rome, binding them to Rome's foreign policies and requiring them to supply troops for the Roman army. They did not have to pay tributes, and allied states retained their local governments.

The primary role of the state continued to be maintaining order, providing adequate food supplies, and maintaining public works, all of which were funded by taxes. Throughout the first century CE, the Roman Empire continued to expand; however, the huge expense of defending its extensive borders eventually brought an end to further conquests. By 180 CE, the limits of Roman expansion had been reached.

Roman Engineering and Architecture

After the second century BCE, the Romans increasingly adopted Greek culture. The Romans already had a pantheon of gods similar to those of the Greeks, although religion in Rome was characterized by rituals celebrating the authority of the state. Romans adopted much of the philosophy of the Greeks and copied the Greek epic tradition, as well as its styles of statutes and architecture. However, the Romans made many engineering improvements to its buildings that allowed construction on a much more massive scale. Roman buildings were made to last, and their size and grandeur symbolized the power and authority of the Roman Empire.

While the Greeks had perfected the construction of theaters and stadiums, the Romans designed and constructed triumphal arches, baths, basilicas, amphitheaters, and multistoried apartment buildings. One of the most remarkable Roman buildings is the Colosseum, a huge amphitheater that could seat about 45,000 people. It is constructed of three stories of arches embellished with Doric, Ionic, and Corinthian columns.

The Romans also applied their superior engineering techniques to a vast system of paved roads, bridges, and aqueducts. Roman roads were unequalled by those of any other people of the classical period. They were constructed of layers of stone and gravel based on sound engineering principles. The roads were necessary for the military troops and messengers, and they were kept in excellent repair. The earliest main Roman highway was the Appian Way. Running from Rome to the Bay of Naples, it had been built in about 300 BCE to facilitate Rome's southward expansion.

In the design of bridges and aqueducts, Roman engineers placed series of stone arches next to one another to provide mutual support. They sometimes used several tiers of arches, one above the other. In the city of Rome, there were fourteen aqueducts spanning a total of 265 miles, which supplied water to all the inhabitants of the city.

Decline of the Roman Empire

The golden age of Rome ended with the death of Marcus Aurelius in 180 CE. Several factors contributed to the decline and fall of the Roman Empire, including the following:

- The later emperors were weak rulers and were more interested in a life of pleasure than a desire to rule effectively.

- The elite classes also experienced social and moral decay and a lack of interest in politics.

- The vastness of the empire made it difficult to manage, especially without strong rulers.

- Army generals became increasingly powerful and influential in politics.

- Trade declined, and there was a decreasing flow of money into the empire as conquests of new territories ended.

- Taxes became increasingly burdensome.

- The Roman population declined as a result of epidemic diseases.

- There was vastly unequal land distribution, as well as poor harvests.

- Roman dependence on slave labor.

- Non-Romans were recruited into the Roman army and had less loyalty to the empire.

- There were several invasions by nomadic peoples.

Attempts to Save the Roman Empire

Several emperors did try to save the Roman Empire. Emperor Diocletian, who ruled from 284 to 305 CE, imposed strict control and declared himself a god. When the Christians refused to worship him, Diocletian increased the persecution of them. **Emperor Constantine**, who ruled from 312 to 337 CE, established a second Roman capital at the eastern city of Byzantium, which he renamed Constantinople. Constantine converted to Christianity and allowed Christians to practice their faith. The western part of the Roman Empire continued to decline, but the eastern part survived and continued to thrive and maintain its lucrative long-distance trade.

The final blow to the western Roman Empire were large invasions from the north. In the fifth century CE, the nomadic **Huns** from the steppes of Central Asia migrated south and west in search of pastures for their animal herds. The Huns pushed the Germanic tribes who already lived around the borders of the Roman Empire well into its borders. By 425 CE, several Germanic kingdoms were established within the empire, and fifty years later, the last western Roman emperor was replaced by a Germanic ruler from the tribe of the Visigoths.

DIDYOUKNOW?

In 408, King Alaric of the Visigoths exacted a tribute from Rome of between 3,000 and 5,000 pounds of pepper, which was valued both as a medicinal spice and as a disguise for spoiled meat.

The eastern Roman Empire had less pressure from invaders and remained the hub of numerous trade routes. The organization of the eastern Roman Empire ultimately was preserved through the structure of the Roman Catholic Church, and Roman law formed the basis for the Church's corpus of canon law. Nevertheless, although Emperor Justinian, who ruled from 527 to 565, recaptured parts of what was lost in the sixth century CE; and Emperor Charlemagne of the Franks later attempted to reform the old boundaries of Rome in the west, the Roman Empire in the west was lost and, after Justinian, never again would the east and the west be united.

Persia

In 550 BCE, Cyrus the Great ended Persian vassalage to the Medes by overthrowing the Median dynasty. A few years later, Cyrus went on to conquer Anatolia on the coast of Asia Minor. Anatolia gave the Persians access to seaports and thus to trade. Eventually, the access to the sea would bring the Persians into conflicts with the Greek city-states. The Persians then turned to Babylon and captured it in 539 BCE. These conquests were the beginning of the **Achaemenid Empire**. During the reign of Cyrus, Persia expanded into the largest empire of the Near East. Based in the Persian homeland on the northeastern shore of the Persian Gulf, it extended from present-day Pakistan in the east to the Balkan Peninsula in the west and from the Persian Gulf in the south to Central Asia in the north. Never before had such a large area, including so many people of different cultures, been controlled under a single system. Cyrus also ended the exile of the Jews in Babylon.

Although the Persian administrative system was modeled after the Assyrian system, it was much more cosmopolitan, efficient, and humane. The Persian Empire was divided into twenty provinces, called satrapies, each ruled by a governor. To prevent these governors from becoming too powerful or disloyal, Persian emperors sent a secretary and a military official to live in and watch over the affairs of every province.

Persia's next ruler, Darius I (522–486 BCE), conquered Punjab in India and Thrace in Europe. Under Darius I, the Persians lived in peace and prosperity. Darius developed a very efficient system of for his empire. He instituted a sustainable system of taxation on his provinces and a communication network based on efficient communication along the Royal Road, which was 1,600 miles long, stretching from one Persian capital, Susa, to a Greek port. He also established the use of a single language, Aramaic, in government documents throughout the empire, and he firmly controlled his military forces.

Darius also instituted a uniform system of coinage, standard weights and measures, a postal service, a calendar from Egypt, and a legal code. He led expeditions into Eastern Europe all the way to the Danube, into India, and from the Indus River to the Red Sea. At one point, Darius even considered building a canal from the Nile to the Red Sea, which might have made the fifteenth-century CE expeditions of Portugal around the coast of Africa unnecessary. Darius also began a conflict with the Greeks that continued intermittently for more than 100 years, until Phillip II of Macedonia conquered Greece and his son Alexander the Great conquered the Persians.

East Asia

The Qin Dynasty

The Zhou dynasty in China had slowly disintegrated into smaller kingdoms. The time between about 403 and 221 BCE in the region was known as the Warring States period. The period of Warring States ended in 221 BCE when the **Qin dynasty** centralized power and destroyed all opposition in the region. Although it lasted only fourteen years, the Qin made many important changes in Chinese society.

Emperor Qin Shi Huang put an end to feudalism in China, abolishing the system of vassals and landowners. The peasants were no longer loyal to their former aristocratic landlords, but rather to their new emperor, who perpetuated the Mandate of Heaven instituted by the Zhou: the concept that heaven—a spiritual power—grants the right of governance to the person who is most fit to manage earthly matters. Qin Shi Huang further bypassed the aristocracy by establishing a strong bureaucracy, whose members were intensely loyal to the emperor because their positions depended on obedience to the state.

Qin Shi Huang was a harsh ruler who adopted the philosophy of Legalism, which was not concerned with morality, human nature, or spirituality, but instead emphasized the rule of law, which was to be administered objectively, with severe punishments for offenders. As part of his plan to unify China, Qin embarked on several ambitious projects, including the construction of the Great Wall of China. The wall had begun as several small walls that the Warring States had built to fortify their individual areas, but it became the Great Wall under Qin as he ordered the building of a single massive wall that represented the unification of China.

Emperor Qin also undertook the building of roads and bridges throughout China, the standardization of units of weight and measurement, the creation of a standard currency, and a single form of writing. All of this increased trading throughout China and helped unite it economically.

Although the economy thrived during the reign of Qin, the harshness of Legalism created resentment among the people. They had to pay burdensome taxes to fund the emperor's efforts to fortify the military and his construction projects. They were also subject to forced labor and mandatory military service. After Qin died, they revolted and killed many of Qin's officials. However, the positive effects of Qin's unification measures considerably helped the following Han dynasty to become one of the most powerful and wealthy dynasties of early China.

The Han Dynasty

The Han dynasty (206 BCE–220 CE) was established when the Han defeated the imperial army of the Qin as part of the mass rebellion that arose after the death of Emperor Qin. The Han emperors initiated several important innovations that would have a lasting effect on China.

Under Emperor Han Wudi, China officially became a Confucian state, as well as a bureaucratic one. Confucianism was used as an educational tool to prepare large numbers of people to become bureaucrats for the administration of the highly organized Han government. Potential workers had to pass difficult civil service exams that included extensive Confucian content. Thus, the Han bureaucracy was composed of well-educated people who were devotees of Confucianism; they were expected to have complete respect for their superiors and to be models of good behavior for those who worked under them. Confucianism reinforced the chain of authority in the Han government, which perpetuated the concept of the Mandate of Heaven, and also became an essential element of Chinese culture.

Under the Han dynasty, there was a rigid social class structure. Confucianism emphasized a highly patriarchal society, with a strong emphasis on loyalty and obedience within families, which were the basic units of society. A large merchant class emerged; they had a somewhat lower status than the new class of scholar-bureaucrats. There also remained a large lower class of farm laborers in China, who produced agricultural surpluses, which helped to maintain a thriving economy, support the rise of craft industries, and expand China's trade, especially silk and sophisticated iron tools. Technological advances also characterized the period of the Han dynasty. Paper, one of China's major inventions, was invented during this period.

During the reign of the Han dynasty, China was a formidable military power. Emperor Han Wudi expanded the boundaries of China and exerted its political and cultural influence into new areas, including Central Asia, Mongolia, Korea, and Vietnam. To maintain peace with local authorities, the Han established a tribute system. States conquered by the Han were allowed to retain their independent governments in exchange for gifts and goods. Han military forces helped to ensure the caravan trade paths, whose major commodity was silk, through the mountains and valleys across Central Asia and on to the eastern coast of the Mediterranean Sea. These different paths became known as the Silk Road. In 184 CE, as a result of weak rulers and widespread unrest fueled by landlords' exploitation of farmers, the **Yellow Turban Rebellion**, led by Daoists, broke out, beginning a period of revolution and turmoil during which China split into three unstable kingdoms, with the Han dynasty finally ending in 220 CE. The landowning class continued to exist with no governmental control. In addition, the borders of China had grown to be so large under the Han dynasty that the Huns were able to invade it, simply going around the Great Wall of China. At the end of the sixth century CE, the Sui dynasty reunited China.

South Asia

The Maurya Empire

When Alexander the Great conquered the Persian Empire in 326 BCE, he destroyed the small states in Persia's easternmost satrapy in the Indus River Valley, Punjab. Following Alexander's death three years later, the vast empire that he had built so quickly fell apart. However, the trade routes that he had developed between India and Western societies remained open during the Hellenistic era, which continued after Alexander's death.

In the same year of Alexander the Great's death, **Chandragupta Maurya** founded the **Maurya Empire**, which lasted until about 185 BCE. Chandragupta was a great military tactician, first taking control of the state of Magadha in the Ganges River Valley and later expanding his empire to include all of India except the southernmost area. He was the first ruler of the East to conquer a Western state; in 305 BCE, he defeated Seleucus, who had inherited most of Alexander's empire and was attempting to regain Punjab. The conflict between Chandragupta and Seleucus ended amicably; the two emperors established friendly diplomatic relations and sent ambassadors to each other's courts.

The capital city of the Maurya Empire was Pataliputra, which sprawled over an area of eighteen square miles, one of the largest cities in the classical world. The city was surrounded by a fortification of huge wooden walls and a trench that was used for the defense of the city.

The Maurya Empire was very well organized and had an efficient system of administration. The empire was divided into provinces, districts, and villages, all of which had state-appointed rulers, as well as a hierarchal court system that led all the way up to the emperor. In addition to a harsh but extremely efficient bureaucracy, a powerful army and an organization of secret police helped to hold the Mauryan Empire together.

The Mauryan Empire also efficiently controlled its economy. Agriculture continued to be the main source of wealth, with all land essentially being the property of the state, which collected about one-fourth of all agricultural products as taxes. The Mauryan farmers used extensive irrigation systems, as well as crop rotation as a means to maintain fertile soil in the fields. Foreign trade also flourished; the Mauryans exchanged goods with the Gupta in southern India, China, Asia Minor, and Mesopotamia.

Following Emperor Chandragupta's death in 297 BCE, he was succeeded by his son, Bindusara, and then by his only grandson to survive a series of assassinations, **Ashoka**. In his early reign, Emperor Ashoka instituted a number of harsh punishments for even very small crimes against the state. Following his first and only military campaign, Ashoka converted to Buddhism, and became the first Buddhist ruler of India. Throughout his reign, he was much more committed to peace than to war. He was a dedicated propagator of Buddhism, sending Buddhist missionaries to convert people both in India and in many other parts of the world, including Syria and Egypt. The Silk Road also facilitated the spread of Buddhism, as trade often fostered close working relationships and even alliances. Each area adapted Buddhism to its own cultural framework. Ashoka's efforts transformed Buddhism from a small Indian sect to a widespread missionary belief system. He issued his edicts on Rock Pillars throughout India, many marking the path to holy sites associated with the Buddha or celebrating events of his life.

Soon after Ashoka's death in 232 BCE, the Mauryan Empire fell into decline. The last Mauryan emperor was assassinated about 185 BCE in a revolt led by Brahmin priests. For the next five centuries, northern India experienced a period of disorder, with attacks and conquests from various invaders, most notably the Huns from the north.

TEST TIP

Break a multiple-choice question into its stem and the answer choices. First make sure that you understand exactly what the stem means and underline the key terms and any signal words, such as *not*, *always*, and *probably* in the stem. Then review the answer choices.

The Gupta Empire

Early in the fourth century CE, the Gupta state emerged around the Ganges River in eastern India. The Gupta leaders were successful conquerors, extending the boundaries of what originally had been a small state to an empire that included most of northern India. Through most of the fourth and fifth centuries, Gupta emperors ruled over what many historians refer to as India's classical age. They imposed unity on their society and fostered a flourishing of the arts, including great works of Sanskrit literature. The Gupta emperors established a political structure similar to that of the Mauryans, with provincial governors, district officials, and a royal secret police. However, the **Gupta Empire** was never as large, nor as centralized, as the Mauryan Empire had been. It also had a smaller bureaucracy, with the Gupta emperors relying on local authorities to maintain order and to collect tributes.

The Gupta controlled the trade on salt and metals, and also the trade between India, the Middle East, and China. Goods such as cotton, sugar, cinnamon, and pepper flowed out of India in exchange for other goods. Trade with Rome in the last decades of the fourth century brought a great influx of gold and silver into the Gupta Empire. The Gupta economy relied on taxes of one-fourth of all agricultural produce and on forced labor to work on state projects. However, rulers in areas not close to the emperor's administrative center had considerable power, and many were corrupt. As a result, Gupta emperors of this time did not have absolute power over their empires.

The Gupta were tolerant of many religions, though they were themselves Hindus. They patronized the Brahmin priests, who had considerable wealth and prestige. Hinduism evolved, however, through its acceptance of the validity of all forms of religions and by adopting essential Buddhist principles, such as nonviolence and respect for life. In its new form, Hinduism's appeal and popularity grew tremendously and became dominant over Buddhism. Through their promotion of Hinduism, the Gupta emperors gained great loyalty among all the social classes of their subjects. The Gupta Empire collapsed in the fifth century CE, following a massive invasion by the Huns. Much of India fell into a chaotic period characterized by small Warring States.

Mesoamerica

Following the decline of the Olmec, several other cultures arose in Mesoamerica from around 150 to 900 CE. As with other empires of this period, these cultures are known as classical civilizations.

The Teotihuacán

Teotihuacán arose as a major center of Mesoamerican civilization around 300 BCE and flourished until about 800 CE. It was located about thirty miles northeast of modern-day Mexico City, covered about nine square miles, and had a population of about 150,000 people. Teotihuacan was even larger than the cities of classical Egypt and Mesopotamia, and was perhaps second in size only to Rome at its peak during the classical period.

Teotihuacán was the center of important religious functions. It contained more than 5,000 ceremonial structures and was laid out on a north-south and east-west axis. The Pyramids of the Sun and Moon dominated the city. The Pyramid of the Sun had four levels and was over 200 feet high. Each side was 700 feet long. The huge temple pyramids of Teotihuacán rivaled those of ancient Egypt, indicating that the state was highly organized and able to mobilize and manage large numbers of workers. Along with its imposing temples, multistoried apartment buildings, warehouses, workshops, and other structures, Teotihuacán had well-constructed, wide avenues and busy marketplaces, with a wide variety of goods for sale made both by the Teotihuacán and by other societies throughout Mesoamerica.

The city was supported by intensive agriculture and mining in the surrounding regions that it controlled. Teotihuacán had stratified social classes, with the elite living in a special precinct, closest to the most important religious temples; the working classes lived in barrios on the edge of the city; agricultural laborers lived outside of the city's boundaries; and artisans and craftsmen lived and worked in other districts. Teotihuacán exerted powerful influences over other societies, which arose from its wealth, cultural sophistication, and trade connections. The influence of Teotihuacán extended as far to the south as present-day Guatemala, and tribute was likely exacted from many societies that it dominated.

It is unclear whether Teotihuacán was a political empire or a dominant culture that simply spread its influence throughout Central Mexico and even beyond. There were no battle scenes in the art of the Teotihuacán, which suggests that its dominance led to a long period of peace maintained by the authority and power of the great city. Teotihuacan's early structures were primarily religious in nature, whereas its later structures are primarily secular. Since many of the later structures are secular palaces, some historians think that the control of Teotihuacán shifted from religious leaders to civil authorities.

Around 650 CE, invaders from the southwest burned Teotihuacán. Like the Olmec, Teotihuacán influenced later cultures of Mesoamerica. The collapse of Teotihuacán might have contributed to Mayan warfare in the south, as the Maya might have sought control over some of the trade routes formerly dominated by the Teotihuacán.

The Maya

The Maya of Mesoamerica were the heirs of Olmec culture. While Teotihuacán dominated the central plateau of Mexico, the Maya ruled over much of what is today southern Mexico and Central America. There may once have been about 14 million inhabitants in the Mayan cities on the Yucatan peninsula. The largest city was Tikal, with a population of about 100,000. The Maya developed an elaborate system of hieroglyphic writing, a base-20 numerical system unique in its innovation of using zero as a placeholder, and several calendars and other methods of time keeping. Their civilization reached such a degree of sophistication that it has been referred to as the "Greece of the New World."

The Maya did not appear to have a central political center or to be unified as a state or empire. Instead, political organization seems to have been a number of small, city-state-like communities, similar to those of classical Greece, with each one having its own system of power and status. Mayan communities were supported by thriving economies based mainly on agriculture, and to a lesser extent on handicrafts and trade with other societies in Mesoamerica. Mayan farmers maintained the fertility of their soil by building irrigation systems and terraces. They grew squash, peppers, and various other crops, most notably maize, which comprised about 80 percent of their food source.

Mayan social structure was characterized by class distinctions, with each class having specific rights and responsibilities. Slavery was widely practiced; slaves were used for labor in both the agricultural and construction sectors. Peasants were slightly higher in social status. Artisans, craftsmen, and merchants made up a prosperous middles class. The elite governing class of priests and nobles had both political and religious responsibilities, as religion and government were so closely intertwined in Mayan society.

Every classical Mayan polity, or center, was ruled by a hereditary priest-king, who was worshipped as a descendant of the sun-god. A council of priests and nobles helped in the governance of each polity, levying and collecting taxes, administering justice, performing diplomatic functions, and making military decisions. Headmen were appointed to govern the affairs of outlying villages, but only after passing civil service exams. Under the command of the top military officers, these headmen also led their local military forces. Although some centers retained their independence, most belonged to loosely organized leagues that were based on intermarriage, political alliances, or diplomatic agreements.

Nearly all aspects of Mayan social life revolved around religion. Even laws and taxes were viewed as being religious principles and offerings. Education essentially was a training program for priests, who conducted public rituals, sometimes including human. Ritualism permeated Mayan thought; math and astronomy were valued not for the sake of scientific and logical advancements, but instead, because they were necessary for the scheduling of ceremonies honoring the gods who ruled natural events and the all-important agricultural cycles.

The Mayan economy was based mainly on agriculture, but also on handicrafts and long-distance trade. In the fertile soil of the Yucatan peninsula, which the Maya improved by clearing, irrigating, and terracing, they grew maize, peppers, beans, squash, and a variety of fruits. They used raised plots of land and also milpa, created by the burning of forests. The Maya dug holes in the ash and planted maize. After two years, the milpa had to be abandoned for four to seven years to replenish the soil.

The stratification of wealth and status of Mayan culture is evident in the different sizes and elaboration of both residential and public buildings. Larger centers have a common pattern of elaborate aristocratic residences, pyramids, and temples surrounding courts or plazas; these buildings were constructed with cut-stone masonry, sculptures and stucco decorations, stone roofs, and

DID YOU KNOW?

Jade was a precious stone to the Maya, and many jade artifacts have been discovered through Mesoamerica. The Maya used jade for cosmetic dentistry, much like we use gold today. The function of these ancient precious inlays was not to fix cavities or alleviate pain but to beautify the mouth.

paved roads. The elaborate carvings, paintings, and murals that were the hallmarks of classic Mayan art were found in these large civic centers. In contrast, the poor rural settlements had much smaller groupings of crudely constructed, unadorned buildings. In addition to Tikal and Uaxactún in Guatemala, there were numerous other important Maya civic centers, including Palenque and Uxmal in Mexico, and Copán in Honduras.

The Decline of the Maya

The Maya reached their peak from 500 to 800 CE, but began to abandon their cities between 800 and 1000 CE. The reasons for this are not entirely clear, but it is likely that foreign invasions, civil unrest caused by disease, overpopulation, crop failures, administrative problems, natural disasters, and climate change all played a role in the decline of the Maya. Although the Maya had a very sophisticated society, they also fought numerous and bloody wars to expand their territory. The wars devastated the surrounding region, which further contributed to the agricultural problems that developed late in the Mayan Empire.

Andean South America: The Moche

By 300 BCE, the Chavin civilization was in decline, and the cultural and political unity that it spread throughout the Andean region of modern-day Peru was lost. The region was characterized by localized, individual centers with their own cultural and artistic traditions.

By 100 CE, the northern coast of the Andean region and the Moche Valley region gave rise to the **Moche** civilization, which existed until about 700 CE. The Moche had a military state, or a chiefdom, which expanded its control by conquests of other societies in the region. They were often at war with neighboring peoples, sometimes brutally executing their enemies, other times taking them as prisoners to become slaves, and sometimes imposing a harsh administrative rule and extracting tribute from them.

Much of what is known about the Moche is based on their highly sophisticated and extensive artistic works. The Moche apparently did not have a unified written language; no written records have been recovered. It is clear, however, that the Moche were a highly developed civilization, as evidenced by their sophisticated ceramic pottery, pyramids, and metalwork. The Moche artisans produced such realistic and detailed depictions of themselves and their everyday activities that they essentially left behind a pictorial history of their society.

Like many other civilizations of the classical period, the Moche were a wealthy, organized society. Much of their wealth was based on agriculture, including corn, beans, potatoes, squash, peanuts, and fruit-bearing trees, the cultivation of which was supported by an extensive irrigation system that channeled water from rivers to the fields. The Moche had an elite ruling class of nobles and priests, many of whom were also warriors. The Moche are probably best known for their large class of artisans, who created a wide variety of impressive artwork. Some artisans used the precious metals of the area to make detailed copper tools and figurines, as well as intricate gold and silver jewelry and ornaments. Others were expert weavers or mural painters, who depicted daily activities such as hunting, fishing, and worshipping. Still others used clay to produce some of the most extensive and varied shapes and sizes of pottery of any civilization. Their ceramic sculptures were incredibly realistic, including depictions of human heads that were probably portraits of real people. Although the artworks of the Moche were beautifully detailed, they are permeated with images of violence and war.

The Moche had a lower class of farmers and laborers; they also used slaves as laborers for both agriculture and construction. The rulers mobilized great numbers of workers to construct forts and military posts, as well large brick homes, temples, and pyramids, including the Temple of the Sun, a stepped pyramid constructed entirely of unfired bricks that were dried in the sun.

The Moche developed an extremely organized religion. Many pieces of pottery and wall paintings depict complicated religious practices, including ceremonial sacrifices that were often quite violent. The Moche honored and obeyed their priests and warriors. The Pyramid of the Sun and the of the Moon were both used for many religious rites and ceremonies.

The decline and fall of the Moche civilization was likely a result of a series of floods, famine, and possibly climatic change in the sixth century, as well as invasions by the Wari people in the eighth century. Some Moche polities that existed in 650 CE were surrounded by fortifications and other defensive works, suggesting that internal conflict and social unrest resulted from the scarcity of natural resource caused by natural disasters.

The Decline and Fall of the Classical Civilizations

Although the decline and fall of the classical civilizations had many causes in common, they also had unique differences. Throughout history, civilizations seem to rise and fall as part of an inevitable process caused by changes occurring both internally and in their interactions with other cultures. The decline and fall of the classical civilizations certainly did not result in the disappearance of their achievements and contributions to the world; on the contrary, the influences of the classical civilizations on cultures throughout the world continued on into the following eras and persist to this day.

Emergence of Transregional Networks of Communication and Exchange

As empires expanded their boundaries in the classical period, long-distance trade greatly increased. Merchants transported goods such as food, raw materials, and luxury items to distant places, along with technologies and ideas, and, in some cases, diseases. Government ambassadors and educated travelers also traveled long distances; like merchants, they interacted with people in different places, which further facilitated cultural diffusion. Trade routes were the main link between different civilizations in this period. In Eurasia, the Silk Roads linked the Roman Empire in the Mediterranean with the Han Empire in China. In Africa, trans-Saharan roads connected people that lived south of the Sahara to the Mediterranean and the Middle East, while the sub-Saharan trade route linked peoples south of the Sahara with societies on the eastern coast of Africa. In the Americas, localized land-based trade networks were developing into interregional networks that connected people of different cultures, such as the Teotihuacán and the Maya.

Key Terms

Bantu	powered trip hammer
Berbers	Silk Road
bubonic plague	square-pallet chain pump
Indian Ocean trade routes	sub-Saharan trade route
lateen sails	trans-Saharan caravan route
monsoon winds	

The Silk Road

Origin of the Silk Road

The main trade connection between the east and the west was the overland **Silk Road**, so named because silk was China's most sought-after trade item. The Silk Road was actually a series of roads that began to develop across Central Asia around 200 BCE as individual caravan paths for the Han dynasty to collect tribute from its conquests and to facilitate regional trade. In 139 BCE, Han Emperor Wu began a ten-year expedition into Central Asia to try to bring parts of the region under Chinese control and to increase its ability to fend off the nomadic Huns, who were gathering in the northwestern borders of China. The Han government also sought to establish trade connections with other Central Asian peoples; it was especially interested in the horses of nomadic peoples of the steppes. The expedition, however, was essentially a failure. This and later conflicts associated with Chinese expansion into Central Asia between 100 BCE and 100 CE frequently interrupted trade along the Silk Road. Many merchants were unwilling to risk their goods and their lives as Chinese soldiers tried to fend off the hostile nomads who threatened to disrupt trade along the Silk Road.

Spread of Agricultural Innovations within China

Despite the dangers for merchants for those 200 years, the Silk Road did facilitate the spread of new agricultural technologies within China. One such technology was the **powered trip hammer**, a tool used to pound, separate, and polish grain—work that previously had to be done by hand. The Chinese had also invented the **square-pallet chain pump**, which was powered by a waterwheel or an ox pulling a mechanical system of wheels. The chain pump was used by Chinese farmers to channel water to higher elevations as they filled their extensive canal system to irrigate fields of crops. As Chinese farmers developed more efficient agricultural techniques, they grew rice crops twice a year and began to use oxen to plow and fertilize their fields. The sharing of farming techniques among the Chinese via the Silk Road laid the foundations for China to become a major agricultural producer in the world.

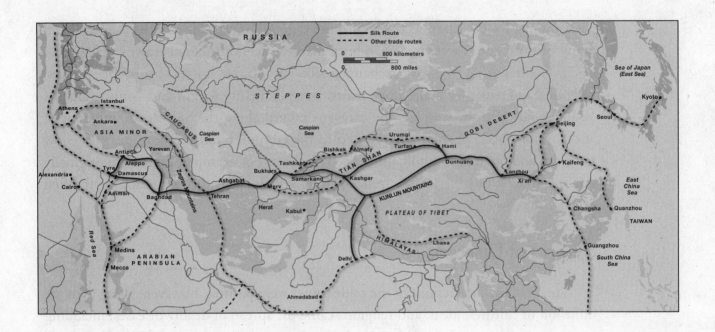

Extent of the Silk Road

By the first century CE, the Han had expanded its empire with the conquests of Central Asia and modern-day Korea and Vietnam. China then had access to the large herds of horses that it had sought more than 200 years earlier from the nomads of Central Asia, along with the stirrups that the nomads had invented. Trade along the Silk Road was thriving, with the constant movement of caravans. The Silk Road extended from western China, across Central Asia, and to cities of the Persian Empire, with connections to the Roman Empire in the Mediterranean and to cities in North Africa. Altogether, the Silk Road spanned 4,000 miles, and most merchants who used it did not traverse it from end to end. It was not a single route but instead consisted of a series of roads with common stops along the way. Both camels and horses were used as

DIDYOUKNOW?

The intense trade along the Silk Road between the East and the West created a huge demand by Romans for Chinese silk in the first century CE. The resulting vast outpouring of gold from the Roman Empire alarmed the Roman senate so much that it issued a series of verdicts—in vain—prohibiting the wearing of silk on the grounds that it was immoral and decadent. Roman senator Seneca the Younger wrote, "I can see clothes of silk, if materials that do not hide the body, nor even one's decency, can be called clothes."

pack animals for the caravans that transported goods on various parts of the road, and many of these goods were traded in busy marketplaces of the oasis towns that sprang up in Central Asia. The east exchanged silk, tea, spices, horses, fruits, rice, spices, ceramics, and paper for grain, nuts, fruits, artwork, luxury goods, and—most valuable of all—gold from the west. As the caravans moved along the Silk Road and stopped at common places, people were exposed to the cultural traditions and ideas of fellow travelers, and often profoundly influenced by them. For example, Buddhism originally was introduced in China from India via the Silk Road in the beginning of the first century CE.

Spread of Diseases

Not all of the interactions of the trade routes were positive, however. Along with the diffusion of cultures, ideas, and religions came the spread of deadly diseases, including measles, smallpox, and the bubonic plague. For example, between 100 and 600 CE, diseases that spread via the Silk Road killed between one-fourth and one-half of China's population, which greatly weakened the Han dynasty. Both the Roman and Gupta Empires experienced similar losses in their populations during this same period as a result of diseases transmitted along the Silk Road. Around 540 CE, the **bubonic plague** originated along the Silk Road in Central Asia, where it quickly spread throughout the long route into the cities of the Persian Empire, and on to the Roman Empire, where the disease came to be known as the Justinian plague, named after Roman Emperor Justinian. The plague further spread throughout the Mediterranean, and to North Africa and the Middle East. The Justinian plague devastated the populations of both the Roman and Persian Empires.

Decline of the Silk Road

During the reign of the powerful Han dynasty, trade was protected by soldiers, allowing goods to move safely and efficiently. However, after the fall of the Han dynasty in 220 CE and the ensuing period of turmoil in China, the caravans that moved along the Silk Road no longer had Chinese military protection, and trade along the Silk Road declined. With the rise of the Tang dynasty in 618 CE, the Silk Road again flourished as a major trade route.

Indian Ocean Trade Routes

Origins of the Indian Ocean Trade Routes

The trade lanes of the western Indian Ocean began to develop at about the same time as the Silk Road. Like the Silk Road, the early trade routes of the Indian Ocean were localized. They were less vulnerable to political conflicts than was the Silk Road and other overland routes, and they were more secure. In addition, boats were able to carry much larger quantities of goods.

By the first century CE, numerous ports along the shores of the Indian Ocean made up a single trade route. This route included connections between Southeast Asia, Southwest Asia, China, East Africa, and India. The early trading ships moved slowly along this long and complex route, staying close to the coastline of the ocean. However, early in the first century CE, at both the eastern and western ends of the Indian Ocean route, political and commercial circumstances resulted in significant changes. The old pattern of ships hugging the coasts in their journeys from one port to the next gave rise to a major maritime route that spanned the entirety of the Indian Ocean between its eastern and western ports.

Expansion of the Indian Ocean Trade Route

During the interruptions in trade along the Silk Road caused by Chinese expansionism between 100 BCE and 100 CE, many merchants sought an alternative means of moving their goods. The Indian Ocean, to the south of the Silk Road, was a safer means for merchants in East Asia and India to exchange goods with their counterparts in West Asia and the Mediterranean. The Roman Empire was then at its peak, and it was able to provide stability and security for ships carrying goods—as well as a huge influx of gold into the eastern empires.

Innovations in Maritime Technology

The shipyards on the Persian Gulf, the Red Sea, and the southern Arabian coastline responded quickly to the growing demand for the rapid movement of large quantities of goods across the Indian Ocean. Their shipbuilders constructed larger ships designed to hold greater amounts of cargo, and they also refined sailing rigs for enhanced speed. For example, the shipbuilders of the Red Sea replaced the square sails that had been

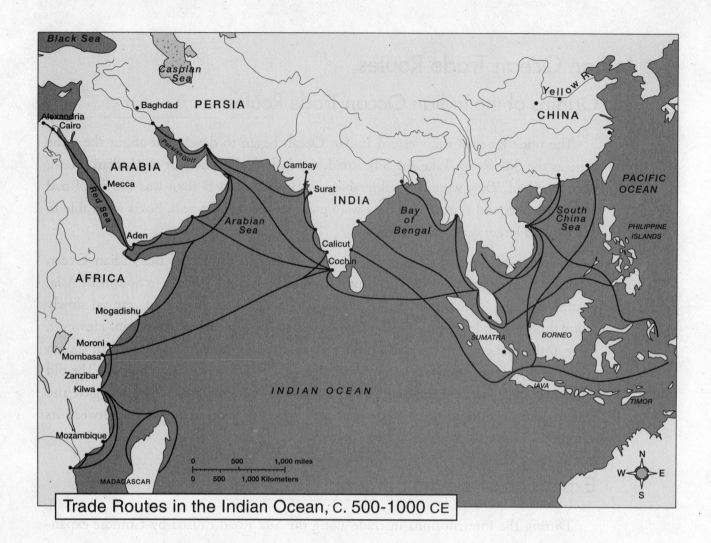

Trade Routes in the Indian Ocean, c. 500-1000 CE

suited to the Mediterranean and the Sea of China with triangular **lateen sails,** which were more effective in waters that were constantly exposed to the contrary monsoon winds, such as the Red Sea and the Indian Ocean. With larger, faster merchant ships that had better maneuverability, along with their familiarity with the steady monsoon winds, the sailors of the Indian Ocean were able to cut the time of their journeys from India to Southwest Arabian ports from four months to just forty days.

The expansion of the Indian Ocean maritime route had a huge impact on transregional trade. From the west, the Romans expanded their shipping down the Red Sea and into the Indian Ocean. The Romans entered into trade agreements with the Indian states, which established pricing guidelines and guaranteed protection of ships carrying Roman goods. Gold flowed into Asia along the Indian Ocean route with the flourishing Roman trade, especially with the Romans' increasing demand for luxury goods from the East.

In India, some ports on the southern coast that engaged in interregional trade had a system of port commissions, each headed by a director of trade who established prices on international goods based on the cost of production, customs duties, shipping costs, warehouse rent, and other expenses. With the development of the maritime route across the Indian Ocean, these Indian ports expanded their trade with Southeast Asia and China, as well as with Africa, to meet an increasing demand for goods to support the growing population of southern India and its economy.

The Indian Ocean route also had a great impact on China, especially on the economies of the southern coastal provinces, which used the route to expand trade as far west as Persia and Egypt. Southeast Asia was also influenced by the long-distance maritime trade from the East to the West. The wealth that the region accumulated from long-distance trade helped regional empires to emerge in a standard pattern of the establishment of governments in Southeast Asia for centuries to come. Southeast Asian ports also served as a link for Chinese trade with Arabia and Africa. Arabian frankincense, a main ingredient in the incense used in Chinese religious ceremonies and medicines, as well as African ivory, was transported to China through the ports of Southeast Asia.

The huge Indian Ocean trade network was an impressive development that resulted from market demands and innovations in maritime technology. By the second century CE, this major route from East to West was beginning to create an interdependent Indian Ocean region.

TEST TIP

The multiple-choice section of the AP World History exam is designed to measure your knowledge and understanding of world history from prehistory to the present. The approximate breakdown of periods is as follows:

Chronological Period	Approximate Percentage
Period 1: Prehistory to c. 600 BCE	5%
Period 2: c. 600 CE to c. 600 CE	15%
Period 3: c. 600 CE to c. 1450	20%
Period 4: c. 1450 to c. 1750	20%
Period 5: c. 1750 to c. 1900	20%
Period 6: c. 1900 to the present	20%

African Trade Routes

The Trans-Saharan Caravan Route

Northern Africa was the far western end of both the Silk Road and the Indian Ocean route. Not only did Africa become involved in the growing commercial interactions from East to West, but it also provided a south to north connection, adding yet another dimension to interregional commercial and cultural interactions. Across the huge African continent, caravan routes had emerged by the second century CE that connected internal African markets and also linked them with the Middle East, Asia, and Europe.

The **trans-Saharan caravan route** established trade relationships between the people who lived in western Africa, south of the vast desert of the Sahara, to the civilizations of the Mediterranean and the Middle East. By about 100 CE, the camel, often called the "ship of the desert," had been introduced to the Berbers of the Sahara from western Asia via Egypt. The **Berbers**, who were nomads of the Sahara, were the most significant facilitators of the Saharan trade route. Their domestication of camels, their invention of the camel saddle, and their use of camels as pack animals in desert caravans were major causes of increased trade by land in Africa—in many ways parallel to the new developments in maritime technology that were also occurring during this time. A single camel could carry a load of up about 550 pounds while crossing the Sahara and go for more than a week without water. Caravans of camels enabled goods to be transported across the desert much more quickly, leading to an inevitable increase in trade. The northbound caravans' most important destination was Cairo, a major trading center that connected many civilizations of the classical period. In Cairo, the merchants that had transported their goods across the Sahara connected with other trade routes, which then transported the goods to other regions. The main goods that were transported out of Africa were salt from the Sahara and gold and palm oil from western Africa. Wheat, olives, and manufactured goods from the Roman Empire were imported into western Africa along the Saharan trade route.

The Sub-Saharan Trade Route

The **sub-Saharan trade route** was also significant in the interregional trade of the late classical period. This route likely emerged from the **Bantu** people, whose language was a unifying factor in the diverse societies in the region south of the Sahara. The

Bantu also developed innovations in iron smelting to make weapons, farming implements, and other tools, which were much valued by other societies. The sub-Saharan trade route linked sub-Saharan peoples with societies in the eastern and southernmost parts of Africa. Food products and iron implements from this region were transported along the Indian Ocean trade routes of the eastern coast of Africa, thereby forming a link between the peoples of sub-Saharan Africa to trade centers in India, as well as Cairo.

Knowledge of the Monsoon Winds

By about 100 CE, the sailors of the trade ships who traveled from the East African coast to destinations throughout the Indian Ocean had become familiar with the **monsoon winds** of the Indian Ocean. The monsoons blow off the east coast of Africa from the southeast between April and October and from the northeast between November and March. This seasonal reversal of direction and timing of the monsoons, and therefore the currents of the Indian Ocean, allowed sailors of merchant ships to complete round-trip journeys from the East African coast to port cities in southern Arabia, the Persian Gulf, and India in just a year.

Trade and Cultural Diffusion

By the first century CE, the East African coast was bustling with continuous overseas trade, which was just as lucrative as trade along the trans-Saharan caravan routes. The port cities of East Africa formed a hub of trade centers that supported the African system of commerce. Goods of all kinds were transported to those cities, to be spread by land caravans throughout the interior of the African continent for local consumption, as well as to be exported to the markets of the Indian Ocean.

The long-distance commercial relations that developed along the large trade centers on the eastern coast of Africa created great prosperity for the societies living there. African merchants welcomed foreign merchants from many different cultures, creating stable relationships and thus a stable economy, as well an increasingly diverse society along the East African coast. A unique culture developed as a result of long-distance trade that had influences from other peoples who participated in Indian Ocean trade, especially the Arabs. The culture was urban, cosmopolitan, and literate. The distinctive African language and culture known as Swahili emerged from the blend of Bantu-speaking and Arabic people who lived in the region. In turn, the Swahili culture spread back to other cultures along the Indian Ocean trade routes, bringing to them such influences as the unique architectural style of coastal and southern Arabia. As was true of many societies involved in the other, major long-distance trade routes of the classical period, the culture of the peoples of East Africa was much enriched by contact with peoples from distant places.

TEST TIP

In addition to your regular study periods, you can study while waiting in a line, in an office while waiting for an appointment or a meeting, or while riding a bus, the train or the subway.

Trade in Central America

In the classical period, the peoples of the Americas remained isolated from the civilizations of Eurasia, the Middle East, and Africa. However, the large civilizations in Mesoamerica had extensive interregional networks of trade within the large territories that they controlled. These civilizations, such as the Teotihuacan and the Mayas, also interacted with one another through widespread exchanges of goods and cultures.

The Teotihuacán

As we mentioned in chapter 7, between about 300 BCE and 800 CE, the Teotihuacán civilization was based in the thriving city of Teotihuacán, which was about 30 miles northeast of present-day Mexico City and had a population greater than that of any other city of the classical period, with the exception of Rome. The large territory that the Teotihuacán dominated included valuable deposits of obsidian, which metalworkers used to make a wide variety of tools and weapons that were extremely valuable to all the cultures in the region. The trade of the Teotihuacán was mainly on obsidian, and also agricultural products and handmade goods. The city of Teotihuacán itself was a major trading center, with an industrial district filled with the workshops of craftsmen whose obsidian tools and weapons, silver and gold jewelry, jade figurines, fine textiles, and ceramic pottery were distributed in an extensive network of trade that linked them to most major Mesoamerican societies, including the Maya. For the most part, goods had to be transported over land using only human labor and without the benefit of horses, other pack animals, or wheeled carts, as these did not exist in Mexico or Central America at that time.

The Maya

During the classical period, the Mayan civilization flourished first in the jungles of present-day Guatemala, then in surrounding regions, and then northwards into the dry scrublands of the Yucatán Peninsula. Like Teotihuacán, the Maya cities of Chichén Itzá, Tikal, and Caracol were major trading centers, which included districts of both warehouses and the workshops of artisans and craftsmen. Religious ceremonies were often held in Mayan cities, and trade fairs were a vital part of these celebrations. Agricultural products such as cocoa and cotton were important parts of trade between various Mayan centers, as were fine textiles, decorative pottery, jaguar and other animal skins; high-quality clay, and minerals used to make dyes, paints, ink; and mirrors, cacao, jade, obsidian, and shells.

The large cities also served as redistribution centers, where merchants bought goods to sell in smaller cities. Tikal was the largest of these; a variety of goods were exchanged there, especially everyday goods such as cotton clothes, chocolate, fruits, vegetables, fish, and meat. Merchants transported their goods along the rivers and waterways and on the roads that linked the Mayan centers. As with other cultures, travel overland was more difficult than via waterways, but this was particularly true in the Mayan world.

Outside of their territories, the Maya traded with the Teotihuacán, as well as with the Zapotec people of the Oaxaca Valley, the Taino people of Cuba, and the Quechua people of South America, introducing all of these cultures to the cocoa bean, which was used to make chocolate. Other important goods involved in the Mayans' trade with other civilizations were salt, obsidian, jade, turquoise, vanilla, and exotic bird feathers. Like the Teotihuacán, the Maya did not have horses, other pack animals, or wheeled vehicles, and wealthy Mayan merchants employed porters to transport their goods for long-distance trade in baskets strapped to their backs.

Transregional Trade Routes Create Permanent Cultural Connections

Although the empires of the classical period declined and ultimately fell, the interactions that were based on trade among the classical civilizations of China, India, the Mediterranean, Africa, and the Middle East created permanent transregional connections. The interregional trading systems in the Americas also created links between different civilizations that would also remain in place, even after empires there eventually collapsed as well. Trade routes that developed in the classical period in all parts of the world laid the foundations for a global trade network.

Time for a quiz
- Review strategies in Chapter 2
- Take Quiz 2 at the REA Study Center
  (www.rea.com/studycenter)

Unit III: Regional and Transregional Interactions, c. 600 CE to c. 1450

Expansion and Intensification of Communication and Exchange Networks

The end of the classical period, with its decline of empires and the emergence of new religions and other belief systems, began a new period. The stage was set for trends that defined 600 to 1450 CE as another time of conquests and migrations, as well as more complex, sophisticated, and intensified cross-cultural interactions and trade patterns. Islam emerged as the last major religion, and its rapid spread to many diverse areas led to the creation of the Muslim Empire by the eighth century.

Key Terms

caliphate	Qur'an
Ghana	shari'a
Grand Canal	Song dynasty
Hanseatic League	Songhay
Islam	Tang dynasty
junks	The Five Pillars of Faith
Mali	umma
Mecca	

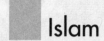

Islam

During the classical period, all the world's major religions had emerged or evolved significantly, except Islam. By the end of the classical period, early in the seventh century, the political disunity that then characterized the Middle East enabled the final great religion—Islam—to emerge. Islam had a major impact on both the dramatic expansion of empires and the continued increase in trade that characterized the period from 600 to 1450 CE. The rapid spread of Islam created a vast new empire that was connected through the Indian Ocean trade routes and the trade lanes of the Mediterranean Sea with Arab sailors, eventually dominating trade along these trade routes. Merchants of the Islamic faith also engaged in trade along the Silk Road from India through China. Islam was very much a part of the cultural diffusion that characterized the cities along all of these trade routes, with mixtures of people of many religions and customs from different parts of the world. Therefore, it is important to understand the nature of Islam before examining the overall expansion of trade networks that occurred during the period between 600 and 1450 CE.

TEST TIP

Be aware of signal words in multiple-choice questions such as *probably, usually, sometimes, rarely,* and *often.* The answer to a question that includes one of these words is often the one that is an exception to the question.

Origins of Islam

Islam emerged in the Arabian Peninsula, just east of Egypt and across the Red Sea, among the Bedouins, nomads who controlled the caravan routes across the vast Arabian desert. At the beginning of the seventh century, the Arabian cities of Mecca and Medina were trade centers for the caravans and formed links along the trade route that extended from the Mediterranean Sea to eastern China. **Mecca** was also a religious center. Many people made pilgrimages to the city to visit a polytheistic temple called the Ka'aba. The temple contained many idols, as well as the Black Stone, which the Jews believed had been put there by Abraham, the founder of Judaism. There was also an annual bazaar and pilgrimage of polytheistic people to Mecca to pay tribute to their gods. Most of the people who lived in Mecca were polytheistic, but both Jews and Christians also inhabited the city.

Islam was founded in Mecca by Muhammad, who had been born there in 570 CE. Muhammad's wife, Khadijah, was a wealthy businesswoman, and through her, Muhammad became a merchant in the caravan trade. However, he became increasingly dissatisfied with the materialistic life of Mecca and with polytheism. At the age of forty, he went up into the mountains around Mecca to a cave on Mt. Hira. There he stayed in prayer, solitude, and meditation for six weeks. During that time he was said to be visited by the archangel Gabriel, who conveyed to him, in the form of a recitation, revelations from Allah (the Arabic word for "lord"), the one true god. These recitations, which Muhammad recited to others, became the **Qur'an**. The Qur'an contains the fundamental beliefs of Islam, expressed in the Five Pillars. It is one of the great works of medieval literature and is written in Foosha, the official dialect of the Arabic language shared by all Muslims.

The Five Pillars of Faith are five duties at the heart of Islam. These practices represent a Muslim's submission to the will of God:

- The first pillar teaches that there is no god but Allah, and Muhammad is his messenger. This pillar emphasizes the belief in only one god. Muslims must recite the Declaration of Faith, "There is no God but Allah, and Muhammad is the Messenger of Allah" many times throughout each day.

- The second pillar demands prayer five times each day, with the person facing Mecca, the place of Muhammad's birth. Prayers can be made in mosques (Islamic houses of worship) or anywhere else.

- The third pillar commands almsgiving through a special tax to other Muslims who are less fortunate.

- The fourth pillar commands fasting for one month a year. This is the month of Ramadan, in which Muslims neither eat nor drink from sunup until sundown. Ramadan commemorates Muhammad's sojourn on Mt. Hira.

- The fifth pillar commands all Muslims, regardless of where they live, to make a pilgrimage to Mecca at least once in a lifetime. All must wear the same white garment to represent their equality before Allah.

The Spread of Islam

After his revelations on Mt. Hira, Muhammad went back to Mecca and began to teach his new religion. His followers became known as Muslims. Muhammad's teachings alarmed the leaders of Mecca, partly because they were afraid that the city would no longer be a center of pilgrimage for polytheist people if most of its inhabitants converted to Muhammad's monotheistic religion. In 622 CE, Muhammad was forced to leave Mecca for fear of his life, and this famous flight to the city of Yathrib became known as the hijrah, the official founding date for Islam. In Yathrib, Muhammad converted many people to Islam, and he renamed the city "Medina," or "city of the Prophet." He called the community the **umma**, a term that came to refer to the entire population of Muslim believers. Muhammad's life was viewed by Muslims as the model for the proper way of life, known as the sunna. Based on the sunna and the Qur'an, Muslims formed a body of law known as **shari'a**, which guided their ethical behavior and family life, as well as their business and community practices. Shari'a was a unifying force for all Muslims.

Muhammad and his followers made a series of raids on Mecca, winning the Battle of Badr in 624 CE. Six years later, they attempted to make the annual pilgrimage to Mecca. As 3,000 of them approached Mecca, the inhabitants assumed that they were making another attack and surrendered peacefully to Muhammad. Muhammad destroyed the idols in the Ka'aba and proclaimed it the holy structure of Allah. The Black Stone came to represent Islam and its belief in one god as the replacement of polytheism.

Muhammad died in 632 CE, only ten years after the hijrah. By that time, however, Islam had spread throughout the Arabian Peninsula. Because Muhammad was believed to be the last prophet, no one else could assume his same role as the leader of Islam. Instead, a form of government was established called a **caliphate**, which was ruled by a caliph (meaning "successor"), who was chosen by the leaders of the umma. The first caliph was Abu Bakr, Muhammad's father-in-law. He and many successive caliphs rapidly extended Dar al-Islam, or the regions where Islam was practiced. Abu Bakr united the Saudi Arabian Bedouin tribes and led a series of raids to expand the religion and domain of the Dar al-Islam. Islam spread west to North Africa and Spain, and Muslim armies had conquered Damascus, Jerusalem, and other cities sacred to Jews and Christians, as well as Syria and the Byzantines, within about 100 years.

Islamic Expansion

By the mid-eighth century, the Muslims controlled a vast area of land stretching from the Atlantic Ocean to the Indus River, extending 6,000 miles from the west to the east. The Islamic world controlled vast trading networks that helped to increase its wealth and aid its spread to other regions. Muslim domination of trade in the Mediterranean area resulted in the final collapse of the last vestiges of the Roman economy and civilization. Muslims traded with the people of southern Europe, transporting goods across the Mediterranean.

Islam in the Middle East

In addition, routes that began in Cairo connected the Islamic world with other parts of the world. In 762 CE, the Abbasid Caliphate established its capital city of Baghdad in modern-day Iran. During the time of the Abbasid caliphate, Baghdad became an important cultural and trade center, and Muslim traders succeeded in restoring trade routes that declined following the fall of the Roman Empire in the west in the fifth century CE, and the collapse of the Han dynasty in China in the third century CE. The creation of the Abbasid caliphate and the Tang and Song dynasties of China provided the stability needed to revive the long-dormant trade routes that once connected Europe, Africa, and Asia. As trade increased, demand for handicrafts and luxury goods also increased, fueling the growth of urban areas.

In 1055 CE, the Seljuk Turks, who had converted to Islam, conquered Baghdad. They allowed the Abbasids to continue to control religion but took over state affairs. Egypt became central to the Islamic world following the collapse of the Abbasid caliphate, and Cairo replaced Baghdad as the main center of trade in the region. Merchants traveled from Cairo south to Aswan along the Nile River, where they then formed caravans to transport their goods by camels to the Red Sea. From there, ships carried the goods down to Aden in southern Saudi Arabia and then via ocean routes east to India. Muslim creativity in technology helped to increase trade. Muslims built larger ships than their European counterparts, using teak obtained in India. To encourage the flow of trade along the Silk Road and other overland trade routes, Muslim money changers set up banks throughout the caliphate so that merchants could easily trade with those at far distances.

Islam in India and Southeast Asia

When pirates from India attacked Arab ships, threatening trade, Muslims conquered the people of the Indus River Valley in the eighth century CE. Thereafter, Muslims increasingly dominated the coastal trade in India, leading to new contacts. The region of the Indus River Valley remained part of the Islamic world for many centuries.

As early as the seventh century CE, Muslim merchants had become active in Southeast Asia. Islam spread to Southeast Asia primarily through port cities, such as Malacca and Java, and early converts were those engaged in trade with Muslims. Southeast Asia had important trading links with China and India, and through India, to the Mediterranean world, fueling the further the spread of Islam. However, Islam spread slowly at first in Southeast Asia because the Shrivijaya Empire, which controlled trade in the area, was strongly Buddhist.

TEST TIP

If your cellphone rings during your AP World History class, it may be a little embarrassing. If your phone rings during the AP World History exam, however, it may be a disaster! Phones, iPods, MP3 players, and all other electronic devices are strongly prohibited in the test room. The test proctor can make you leave the test immediately and cancel your score if he or she sees that you have any of these devices with you. Don't just put your phone on silent; put it in your locker or leave it in your car.

Islam in Africa

By the seventh century CE, followers of Muhammad were spreading their faith and their control westward across the northern shores of Africa and southward along the eastern regions of the continent. Egypt, which had previously been a Byzantine province, quickly became an Arab state in 641 CE. For many of the commoners, life improved, and partially as a result, many Egyptians willingly converted to the new faith of Islam. The Arab conquerors established a new capital at Cairo and used it as a base for further expansion into Africa. By the early eighth century, much of western north Africa was also under Arab control. From there, Arabs spread across the Mediterranean into Spain and southward into Africa across the Sahara. A key result of the Islamic conquest of large portions of Africa was the establishment of a vast trading network. Port cities arose along the east coast and facilitated contact with the Arabian Peninsula and even settlements near the Indian Ocean. Ghana and later Mali in western Africa eventually became linked with this trading network, becoming influential partners through their lucrative gold trade. Moreover, many societies along the trade routes had mostly oral rather than written traditions. The introduction of the written Arabic language, as well as Arabic laws, allowed local rulers greater authority and improved administration over their subjects.

The Effects of Arab Influences on Trading Patterns

Arab armies first swept across North Africa in the seventh century CE. Islam spread to West Africa via the trans-Saharan trade, which was first developed by Berbers between 700 and 900 CE. The trans-Saharan trade brought tons of gold to the European markets and also into Egypt, where eventually it was shipped to India in return for spices and silks. The trans-Saharan trade also helped to develop large cities in West Africa, such as Timbuktu.

Similarly, Islam spread from Egypt south along the Nile and then westward into the East African coast via trade routes. From Saudi Arabia, Islam spread across the Red Sea to the Horn of Africa, and then southward along the coast. Persian and Arab Muslim merchants established large port and trading cities, such as Mogadishu. Gold from the Great Zimbabwe region also flowed into the Muslim cities along the east coast of Africa. The eastern cities of Africa also strengthened sea routes in the fourteenth century. These cities connected southern Africa to the Indian Ocean and to Middle Eastern trade routes. Trade along land routes to China through Persia and Central Asia and to the Persian Gulf declined in this period.

These vast trading routes brought many goods and inventions to the Islamic world. From China, Muslims learned how to make paper, and many Islamic centers, such as Córdoba in Spain, held hundreds of thousands of books. Europeans, in contrast, still produced their books using vellum, and books were consequently much rarer. Muslims traded glass, copper, gold, silver, and textiles for Chinese silk, porcelain, spices, and various other herbal items. Besides the numerous goods exchanged, Arabic traveled as a language of communication along the trade routes. While Muslims did not require those in conquered regions to convert, they did require them to speak in Arabic. The language served as a unifying factor throughout the vast expanse of territory dominated by Muslim rulers.

Trade and Interactions in Africa

Ghana

The kingdoms of West Africa began to grow as a result of their role as intermediaries in the trans-Sahara trade. Kingdoms located in the savanna region traded salt to the forest settlements in exchange for gold, which they then traded with African societies north of the Sahara. **Ghana**, which flourished from 900 to 1100 CE, was a military kingdom of the Soninke people located directly on the trans-Saharan trade routes. It conquered a region approximately the size of Texas in what is today Mali. The name "Ghana" comes from the Soninke name for "war chief," which is what they called their leader. Muslim traders transferred the name to the whole area by the eighth century CE.

Gold from Ghana was the basis of the Mediterranean trade with the East, and its king was known as the "king of gold." According to Al-Bakri, an Arab chronicler, Ghana had an army of 200,000 warriors, and 40,000 of them carried bows and arrows. The king maintained a standing royal guard of 1,000 men. The kingship was hereditary, through the matrilineal line. Income from conquered areas helped to support the extensive administrative apparatus of Ghana. Taxes were also levied on imported goods such as salt, the largest import. Traders from the south, who brought gold, also paid taxes. Social rank in Ghana was based on heredity and on service to the king. The Muslim administrators of Ghana held the highest rank on the social ladder; merchants ranked directly beneath them. Slaves were the lowest class.

The rulers of Ghana were forcibly converted to Islam by the Almoravids, Muslims who lived among the Berbers to the north. In West Africa, Islam was often used to strengthen the native royal cults. The main city of Kumbi Saleh was divided into two cities, one for the king and administrators, and another for merchants and Islamic scholars. Kumbi Saleh housed twelve Islamic mosques, an indication of its size and prosperity. Ironically, the growth of other Islamic movements weakened Ghana. The Almoravids instituted a movement to purify Islam in the eleventh century, and they began to move across the western Sahara and eventually went north into Spain. They also eventually gained control of the gold trade across the Sahara and gradually moved toward Ghana, which they conquered in 1076. Ghana was considerably weakened by the thirteenth century, and several other successor states arose in West Africa.

Mali

One of the successor states to break away from Ghana was Mali, founded by the Mandike people. The Mandike were primarily farmers, but they also benefited from the gold trade. Under the leadership of Sundiata Mali in the thirteenth century and his descendent Mansa Musa in the following century, Mali conquered the warring peoples in the region and established an empire larger in size than that of Ghana. Sundiata divided the kingdom into clans, and assigned to groups of clans certain functions and responsibilities. Mansa Musa strengthened his control over his empire by appointing relatives as provincial governors. He made a historic pilgrimage to Mecca; his entourage carried so much gold with them that the economy of Egypt suffered from inflation for generations and the currency was devalued. Mansa Musa's travels brought many scholars and artists to Africa, and Timbuktu, a city on the Niger River, became a renowned center of Islamic learning and trade. The pilgrimage also opened trade with other Muslim areas and fostered intermarriage between Muslims and African women.

Songhay

By the eleventh century, the rulers of the Songhay had converted to Islam. Their capital was at Gao, and under Sunni Ali in the fifteenth century, the Songhay conquered Timbuktu and Jenne in Ghana and further expanded their territories. Sunni Ali insisted on total obedience, even from the Islamic scholars of Timbuktu, but the Songhay kingdom actually became a mixture of Islamic and native, polytheistic cultures. For example, men and women intermingled in the market places, which often deeply disturbed Muslim travelers. Muslims from Morocco conquered Songhay in the sixteenth century.

> **DID YOU KNOW?**
>
> Under its first emperor, Sonni Ali, the Songhay conquered so many of its neighboring states, including the much-weakened Mali Empire, that the Songhay Empire eventually not only became a major trading state, but also the largest empire in the history of Africa. It covered more than 540,000 square miles of land, greater than the entirety of Western Europe.

Trade and Interactions in Central and East Asia

China

After the final collapse of the Han dynasty in the third century CE, northern and southern China were not united and the north often was invaded by nomadic peoples. During the chaos of this period, Buddhism displaced Confucian influences, and the Chinese worried about foreign influences, especially in the face of increasing invasions by nomadic peoples.

The Sui Dynasty

Yang Jian founded the short-lived **Sui dynasty** in 581 CE and reunited China. He also drove out the nomadic invaders. Yang Jian patronized both Buddhism and Taoism and founded many monasteries. He and his son and successor, Sui Yangdi, built the 1,400-mile-long **Grand Canal** that linked the Yellow and Yangtze Rivers. Yangdi conscripted thousands of peasants to work on lavish palace projects. Rebellions arose after a series of disastrous attempts to subjugate Korea. In 618 CE, a rebel leader named Li Yuan seized the capital city of China, Xi'an, and proclaimed himself the emperor of the Tang dynasty.

The Tang Dynasty

Most of the Chinese people lived in the south, where they produced rice. Those living in the north produced millet. Rivers were the easiest way to transport goods, but they ran from west to east. As in other parts of the world, it was difficult, time consuming, and costly to transport goods over land. The Grand Canal connected the north with the south, and when the south quickly grew to be the most productive in crops, the Grand Canal became essential to move the goods between regions. During the **Tang dynasty**, trade in silkworms and tea flourished as a result of easier access to regions made possible by the Grand Canal. Tea eventually spread to Japan during the ninth century and also to Korea. During the late Tang dynasty, people continued to migrate southward in search of new lands to cultivate.

Culture also flourished in China under the Tang dynasty. During the period of chaos and nomadic raids following the decline of the Han, trade had dwindled along the Silk Road. However, the Tang's success at conquering regions in central Asia led to the revival of trade along the Silk Road. Once again, China transported large amounts of luxury goods, such as silk, paper, and porcelain to Islamic centers along the various routes of the Silk Road. Tang artisans had made innovations in their techniques for producing porcelain that was lighter, thinner, more useful, and more beautiful than it had been. Delicate Chinese porcelain became as sought-after in the West as Chinese silk. Persian rugs and horses were among the commodities imported from the Islamic world.

The Tang also increased trade via sea routes, and they imported spices and woods from Southeast Asia while exporting manufactured goods. Market centers arose in Tang towns, and paper money was first issued in the form of credit vouchers that merchants could carry from one location to another. The Chinese also used checks which allowed the drawing of funds deposited with bankers.

The Song Dynasty

The Kirhgiz people overthrew the Tang, and a new dynasty took their place. The **Song dynasty** ruled China from 960 to 1279 CE. The Grand Canal had encouraged further trade in tea and other goods during the Sui and Tang dynasties. Tea had become such an important crop that the Song established a government monopoly on the tea trade and traded tea for horses from outlying regions, such as Mongolia and Tibet, where tea could not be easily cultivated. The Chinese junk boats made it possible for the Chinese to eventually dominate trade in the East Asian waters.

Chinese Junk Ships

The first Chinese **junks**, which had up to four sails, were designed in the Song dynasty around 960. Because the South China Seas were subject to severe typhoons, the Song shipbuilders constructed each junk with a bulkhead, a partition across the inside of the hull and sometimes along its length, to make the junks' hulls rigid and also to provide watertight compartments, which were very useful in repairing leaks that developed while in the water. Song junk builders also invented the sternpost rudder, a large, heavy board hinged on a post at the bottom of a junk that served as both a keel and a rudder. Other ships of that period were steered by means of long oars projecting from the stern. Large junks, sometimes as long as 492 feet, were used for long-distance trips.

The Mongols

In the thirteenth century, the Mongols had conquered so many regions that there was naturally a great deal of cultural exchange. Mongols often employed the very people they had captured as they assaulted new targets, and often adopted their military tactics. For example, they made use of Chinese catapults until they discovered that the Turks in Afghanistan made better machines. Mongols also borrowed from China projectiles with gunpowder and exploding arrows. China benefited greatly from the presence of Muslim doctors and also from Persian astronomers. Mongols under Kublai Khan employed many Uighur Turks as translators and officials. The Mongols were profoundly interested in other religions, but the religion that benefited the most from Mongol rule was Islam; this made great progress in Chinese Central Asia, for example, which had previously been Buddhist. Many Mongol rulers also converted to Islam.

The Mongols had both a positive and negative impact on trade. Trade was important to them, and Mongol rulers tended to protect trading routes in their realms. It became safer for merchants to travel land routes, and there were routes from the Mediterranean to China. One of the beneficiaries of this increased safety was the well-known adventurer and traveler Marco Polo. On the other hand, the Mongol rulers often were at war with one another, which could just as often disrupt trade. One aspect of trade that was not much affected by the Mongol conquests was the thriving Indian Ocean trade, which was extensively developed during the Islamic period. Mongol conquests did not threaten this trade nor change it in any appreciable way.

TEST TIP

Take a break from studying when you feel that you need one. Take a walk, play a video game, or do another short, relaxing activity.

Trade and Interactions in the Byzantine Empire and Western Europe

The Byzantium capital of Constantinople remained as one of the most important cities in the world, and in the tenth century CE, it was the greatest city in the Christian world. Constantinople, located on the coast of the Mediterranean Sea in what is present-day Istanbul in Turkey, was the center of a vast network of international trading routes.

At about the same time, Western Europe began to revitalize, mainly as a result of the Christian Crusades that exposed Europeans to the more sophisticated Eastern cultures through the long-distance trade routes. Trade between areas also was revived, and cities such as Genoa and Venice, located on the Mediterranean Sea, played an important role. Venetian goods went to Constantinople and many other areas. Italian merchants traded in North Africa in places such as Cairo, Damascus, and even as far away as India and China. Flanders was an important outlet for English wool, and there was a thriving trade between Italian cities and Flanders, in present-day Belgium. Fairs were set up in places along the way from one region to the other, such as France, to sell goods. Leagues of cities were formed, such as the **Hanseatic League** in the north, granting exemptions from tolls and other privileges. Hanseatic member cities had areas in other countries that served as trading bases known as factories. These changes that began in the eleventh century CE were an extremely important commercial revolution that saw the rise of a money economy and the creation of a system of credit and capitalistic enterprise in Europe. The economic changes also elevated the status of many peasants who otherwise would have been doomed to life on a manorial estate. Women also benefited from this shift, as many women engaged in business enterprises. The changes also began a shift away from the landed aristocracy of Europe toward a commercial class.

Continuity and Innovation of State Forms and Their Interactions

Existing states and empires during the period 600 to 1450 CE experienced continuity and diversity, as well as greater complexity. Other new states and empires developed, and for the first time, large empires emerged in West Africa and Mesoamerica. The Muslim Empire and the Mongol Empire of the thirteenth century were even more extensive than any of the empires of the classical period.

Key Terms

Abbasid Caliphate	Franks	Mongols
Aztecs	Funan	Ostrogoths
Baghdad	Genghis Khan	Seljuk Turks
Battle of Tours	Hangzhou	Shi'a
calpulli	Inca	Sunni
Carolingian dynasty	khanates	Taika reforms
Charlemagne	Kublai Khan	Vandals
Constantinople	Lombards	Vikings
Córdoba	Magna Carta	viziers
Crusades	Magyars	Yuan dynasty
Dark Ages	Marco Polo	
Delhi Sultanate	Monasticism	

The Muslim Split between the Sunni and the Shi'a

Long before the emergence of the Muslim Empire, Arab tribes had had numerous conflicts, and Islam could not prevent rifts in its caliphate. All of the four caliphs were killed by rivals, and the assassination in 661 CE of Muhammad's son-in-law Ali sparked a war within the caliphate. The Umayyad family took control, but a fundamental split occurred among Muslims and has lasted to the present day. The split occurred between two main groups:

- The **Sunni**. Most Muslims wanted peace and therefore accepted the Umayyads as their rulers. These Muslims believed that caliphs should continue to be chosen by Muslim leaders. The name *Sunni* means "the followers of tradition."

- The **Shi'a**. These Muslims thought that caliphs should be related to Muhammad, and therefore they took the name *Shi'a*, meaning "partisans of Ali." The Shi'a did not accept the Umayyads as their rulers and sought revenge for Ali's murder.

The caliphate remained intact for several centuries, but the split between the Sunni and Shi'a contributed to its decline as a system that effectively combined political and religious authority. The Muslim Empire eventually fractured into various political states, although Islam remained a unifying force among its conquests. The areas that it conquered remained united by religion, but the tendency to fall apart politically has been a major feature of Muslim lands. Many other splits followed, including the establishment of the Abbasid Caliphate in 750 CE and the Shi'a Fatamid caliphate in Egypt in 973 CE, as well as the formation of the Sufi, who became disenchanted with the materialistic lives of later caliphs and turned to a life of spirituality. The Sufi had many customs in common with Christian and Buddhist monks, such as shunning material possessions, meditating, and chanting.

DID YOU KNOW?

Although Islam was split into the Sunni and Shia branches just 30 years after the death of its founder Muhammad in 632, the repercussions of the split have continued to have a major impact on the world since then. The conflict between the Sunni and the Shia was a driving force behind many tumultuous events in the Middle East during the latter half of the twentieth century, and it is again at the center of the unrest and turmoil that has intensified in the region in the twenty-first century, which continues right up to the present day.

The Abbasid Caliphate

Abu Abbas, a descendant of an uncle of Muhammad, led a revolt against the Umayyads and established the **Abbasid Caliphate**, with Baghdad as its capital, until 1258 CE. During the period of the Abbasid caliphate, the caliphs adopted many Persian ideals of leadership. For example, the Abbasid caliphs relied on **viziers**, or political advisors, to administer their governments. The caliphs progressively withdrew from leading prayers and other public functions and left practical matters of administration to the viziers, a tradition that they adopted from the Persians.

During the Abbasid caliphate, **Baghdad** was an important cultural center. Philosopher **Ibn Rushd** wrote many commentaries on Aristotle, which were eventually transmitted to Western Europe. Ibn Rushd believed in the principle of twofold truth. He argued that philosophy and religion were different kinds of knowledge, each with its own sphere of truth. Religion was for the unlettered masses, and taught through signs and symbols, while philosophy represented truth directly. Teachings in the two areas could conflict with one another, and in that case, philosophy should supersede religion. Ibn Rushd's commentaries on Aristotle created controversy in the Catholic Church, as many of Aristotle's philosophical arguments conflicted with Christian teachings. In contrast to Ibn Rushd's theory of double truth, the scholastic theologians of Europe at that time, such as Thomas Aquinas, sought to harmonize the teachings of religion and philosophy. Ibn Rushd had been born in **Córdoba** in southern Spain, a region that was controlled by Muslims. While under Muslim control, culture in Córdoba flourished, and monuments such as the Alhambra in Granada and the mosque were among the greatest architectural masterpieces in Europe.

In 1055 CE, the **Seljuk Turks** conquered Baghdad. They had been nomads who had migrated to the northern border of the Persian Empire from the Asian steppes, converted to Islam, and unified the Turks of Central Asia. The Seljuk Turks allowed the Abbasids to continue to control Islamic matters, but they took control over state affairs.

The Mongols finally ended the Abbasid rule at Baghdad. Ghengis Khan had conquered the first Islamic kingdom for Mongols, the Khwarazm Empire. His grandson, Hulego, continued a policy of Mongol expansionism and captured Baghdad in 1258 CE. The last Abbasid caliph was executed.

Western Europe

Until the fifth century, most of the European continent was part of the Roman Empire. However, as the push from the Hun migrations from Central Europe caused other groups to move west as well, the Roman armies began to have problems in guarding their borders. As other weaknesses appeared that threatened the empire, Germanic groups such as the Goths, Ostrigoths, and Vandals began to take over, with Rome falling to the invasions in 476 CE. Without the structure of the empire, the groups settled into areas of Europe and retained their own ways of life. The period from about 500 to 1000 CE is referred to as the **Dark Ages** in Europe, as much of Roman civilization was lost, such as written language, innovative architectural and building techniques, organized government, and long-distance trade. The Germanic people could not read or write, and retained the isolated nomadic lifestyles of their ancestors.

When the Roman Empire in the West collapsed, it was the Church that filled the vacuum. The early Church in Europe had been organized along the same lines as the Roman Empire. The dioceses and archdioceses of the Church had been modeled after the same structures in the empire. Christianity was often spread by wandering monks and nuns. **Monasticism** flourished in the age following Constantine's legalization of Christianity, and many foundations arose around the Nile River Valley in Egypt. Monasticism then gradually spread throughout Europe.

By the eleventh century CE, Catholic popes had centralized the Catholic Church, with western popes insisting that the pope in Rome had supremacy over the other patriarchs. This increasing insistence on papal supremacy eventually led the Greek Orthodox Church and the Patriarch of Constantinople to separate from the Roman Catholic Church.

The Franks

Germanic peoples in Europe who migrated into what had once been the Roman Empire largely lived according to tribal and customary law. In 500 CE, Clovis, who had been elected to be king of the **Franks**, became the first Germanic ruler to convert to Catholic Christianity. Clovis's conversion was the beginning of an alliance between the Franks and the other strong power in Europe, the papacy. A few years later he attacked and defeated two Arian Christian groups, the Alemanni and the Visigoths, and Paris became the Frankish capital. The Umayyad Muslims conquered Spain in 711 and advanced into France several years later. In 732, the Franks halted Muslim advances at the **Battle of Tours**, in present-day France. This victory was a turning point in

European history; had the Franks not defeated the Muslims, all of Europe might have been conquered by them. The continuing need of Western Europeans to fight the Muslims was one of the factors that prompted the creation of a feudal society.

When the East Germanic **Lombards** besieged Rome several years later, Christian Pope Steven II turned to the Franks for military aid. In return, Frankish King Pepin was anointed the king of the Franks by a papal legate, clearly suggesting that papal approval could create a king even where there was no legitimate claim through blood. In return for this favor, Pepin carved out a tract of land across central Italy for the pope that would later be known as the Papal States, and which would play a central role in Renaissance politics.

Pepin forged a new dynasty known as the **Carolingian dynasty** after his son, Charlemagne. By the time he died, **Charlemagne** had come close to reestablishing the frontiers of the Roman Empire in the West. Charlemagne continued to support the Church through reform of the educational system for priests; Benedict of Aniane's reform of the monastic life, which mandated the Rule of Benedict for all monasteries; and the forcible conversion of the Saxons in the ninth century. Charlemagne brought the monk Alcuin from Northumbria in England to help him in the reform of the clergy. Alcuin established a school at Aachen that revived the education of the priesthood and so addressed several issues of corruption in the Church. Alcuin and his assistants developed a new style of writing, Carolingian miniscule, that helped preserve the writings of the Greeks and Romans. The revival of learning during Charlemagne's era was known as the Carolingian Renaissance.

Charlemagne united his realm through the use of the *missi dominici*, who were messengers sent to proclaim his laws and report back to him on events throughout the realm. Through his laws, called *capitularies*, Charlemagne enforced military obligations, the *missi dominici* system, and the reform of the Church. Charlemagne would later successfully conquer the Spanish March, a strip of land that he used as a buffer zone between the Kingdom of the Franks and Muslim Spain.

After Frankish nobles, in league with the Lombards, rebelled against Pope Leo III and forced him to leave Rome, Charlemagne restored him to power in 799. The pope then crowned Charlemagne as the Roman emperor the following year, which angered the Byzantines, who refused to recognize a second emperor. However, Charlemagne gave Venice and Dalmatia to Byzantium in 812, and in return, the Byzantine emperor recognized Charlemagne as the emperor at Rome, again supporting the tradition begun with Pepin that the pope anointed the emperor and so created his right to rule.

The **Treaty of Verdun** in 843 CE divided Charlemagne's empire between his three grandsons. While they vied with each other for power, invaders ravaged Europe. Muslims invaded Sicily in 827 CE and controlled it for over a century. The **Magyars** traveled up the Danube River and plundered Bulgaria in 890 CE and then ravaged Saxony, Germany, and other regions, traveling as far inland as Rheims in France. The **Vikings**, however, led by far the most threatening of these invasions from Norway, Denmark, and Sweden. The Vikings invaded many other areas of Western Europe, as well as Russia, in the eighth and ninth centuries, followed by the Magyars, who attacked from the east in the late ninth century.

TEST TIP

The AP World History exam will require you to think about world history in an interpretative way. You will have to analyze, compare, and draw conclusions about the causes and processes of continuity and change within and across the themes of the six historical periods.

France and England

The medieval monarchies emerged during this chaotic period, and many grew out of the settlement of the Treaty of Verdun. The western section of Charlemagne's old territories became the kingdom of France. In 987 CE, the last Carolingian ruler died, and the Frankish nobles selected Hugh Capet as king. The Capetians, however, never had the power of Charlemagne; although they were overlords of Normandy, Brittany, Burgundy, and Aquitaine, in reality they only controlled the small area of land around Paris known as the Ile-de-France. When William, Duke of Normandy, defeated Harold II of England at the Battle of Hastings and became King of England in 1066 CE, the French king was literally overshadowed by his vassal, who was now a king in his own right. William's successors, most notably Henry II of England, gained control of much of the territory surrounding the Ile-de-France. However, his heirs were less successful in maintaining the empire. His son, Richard I, the "Lionheart," spent more time away on the Crusades than he spent at home. Upon his death, his brother John lost territories to the French King Philip II Augustus. During John's war with Philip, the English barons drew up a list of grievances that formed the basis of the **Magna Carta** (1215 CE), an agreement limiting the power of the English monarch and placing him under the rule of law. Several late rulers confirmed the Magna Carta but with modifications, and the document has played an important role in England's constitutional history. In the fourteenth century, the tensions between France and England erupted in the Hundred Years' War.

The Byzantine Empire

While the western Roman Empire collapsed in the fifth century CE, the eastern Roman world remained intact as the Byzantine Empire. While its capital, **Constantinople**, was a major center of long-distance trading routes, merchants did not have high social status in the Byzantine world. Most merchants engaged in trade were Muslim, Jewish, or Italian, while the highest-ranking members of Byzantine society were aristocrats whose basis of wealth was land.

During the sixth century CE, Byzantine Emperor Justinian attempted to reconquer the western Roman world. His general, Belisarius, defeated the **Vandals** in North Africa and soon thereafter defeated the **Ostrogoths**, who had taken the Italian peninsula. By 552 CE, Justinian had reconquered Spain, North Africa, and parts of Italy.

The Crusades

In 1071 CE, the Seljuk Turks defeated the Byzantines at the Battle of Manzikert. By 1095, Byzantine Emperor Alexius was alarmed at the threat posed by the Muslim Turks, whose armies were nearing Constantinople, and he called upon Roman Catholic Pope Urban II in the West for military assistance. Pope Urban II had also been concerned by Muslim invasions and conversions, and he called upon Western Europeans to defend the Christian lands of the Mediterranean region, especially the Holy Lands, against Muslim Turk attacks. This began the first of the four Christian **Crusades**, which lasted for two centuries. The western knights in the First Crusade were successful, partly because of the constant quarrels between various Muslim factions. However, Muslims defeated the Europeans in the following three Crusades; by 1291, they had defeated the last crusader kingdom, with the Christians failing to regain the Middle East. In 1453 CE, Byzantium was dealt a fatal blow when the Ottoman Turks conquered Constantinople, sending a wave of Greek-speaking refugees to Italy, where they helped to fuel the Italian Renaissance.

The Crusades created ill will between Christians and Muslims, and their lasting negative effects are still evident today in the Middle East. On a more positive note, there was a tremendous amount of cultural exchange during this period between Europeans and Muslims. A period of reform, change, trade, and a vast movement of peoples from west to east occurred during the Crusades. In particular, the Christian knights had encountered much wealthier and sophisticated cultures in the Middle East than their own. They learned much about medicine, for example, from Muslims in the Holy Land. The Crusaders also returned home with luxury goods from different parts of the world and created a demand for these goods in Europe. The Crusaders had been transported across the Mediterranean Sea to the Holy Lands in the Middle East from the Italian coastal cities of Genoa and Venice. The Genoans and Venetians transported goods back to Europe on their return voyages, and both cities became major trade centers, acquiring enormous wealth and greater sophistication. This eventually led to dramatic cultural changes in Europe and to the positioning of European kingdoms to gain control of long-distance trade routes during the following era.

India

Following the decline of the Gupta Empire in India, there were several centers of power. In 962 CE, Turkish-speaking slaves took power from the Sasanid Persians. In 997 CE the founder's son, Mahmud Ghazni, became the ruler and began a series of raids in Indian lands. By the time he died in 1030 CE, he had conquered the upper Indus Valley and areas as far south as the Indian Ocean.

By 1200 CE successors to the Ghazni controlled northern India and had established the **Delhi Sultanate**. Under the Delhi Sultanate, Islam spread firmly throughout northern India, but Muslim rulers disapproved of the use of Hindu and Buddhist statues. They destroyed many such religious statues, and were especially intolerant of Buddhism. Nevertheless, Hinduism continued to flourish, and during this period, the caste system was fully defined. People married only within their castes and ate meals with caste members; each caste had a proper function. Muslim rulers essentially remained separate from their Hindu subjects.

Southeast Asia

Indian influence was profoundly important in the development of Southeast Asia. Merchants, wandering Buddhist monks, and Hindu priests traveled the trade routes and encountered many cultures. Of the kingdoms in Southeast Asia, only what is today Vietnam remained immune from Indian influence from around the second through the tenth centuries CE, as the Chinese controlled this region for most of this period until it won its independence in 939 CE. Even after it won independence, Vietnam continued to make use of Chinese bureaucratic structures and a Chinese-style civil service examination system.

Southeast Asians willingly embraced Indian influences, and Ashoka's dream of the "conquest of righteousness" found its fulfillment in the spread of Buddhism, and also of Hinduism and other Indian influences through peaceful trade and wandering monks and priests. Indian travelers traded with the state of **Funan**, whose capital was in what is today as Vietnam. Funan was the first state to arise in this area, and it controlled parts of the Malay Peninsula and Indochina. Hindu religious figures often served in administrative capacities there or as advisors to rulers. Indian merchants succeeded in ferrying goods from ports to points farther inland.

East Asia

Korea

The **Koryo dynasty** arose in the tenth century CE; the name of the dynasty is the origin of the modern word "Korea." In earlier times, previous rulers were strongly tied to Tang China and, although the Koryo were more independent minded than their predecessors, they still copied the Chinese system of civil service examinations and bureaucratic structures. Buddhism had important influences on the Koryo, as it did in China and also in Japan. Slavery was an important aspect of Koryo society, and in this way the Koryo departed from their Chinese models. People could serve in the government only if for eight generations there was no evidence of slavery or lowborn status in their families. The Mongol conquest of the Koryo left long-term effects, as the kings were taken into captivity to Yuan China and intermarried with Mongols. When Mongol rule declined in China, it also weakened in the Koryo realm.

TEST TIP

Study for *every* test in your AP World History class as if you were studying for the AP test.

Japan

In 607 CE, Prince Shotoku Taishi of the **Yamato Kingdom**, in what is present-day Japan, sent ambassadors to Chang'an in China to learn more about Tang-style administration. Shotoku then launched a series of reforms designed to limit the power of the hereditary nobility. In a seventeen-article constitution that was largely based on the ethics of Confucianism despite his proclaimed devotion to Buddhism, he designed a merit system for promotions in the government and created a centralized government. After his death, more reforms were passed, including the Taika, or "great change" reforms of the seventh century CE. The **Taika reforms** established a Grand Council of State and divided Japan into administrative districts based on Chinese Tang dynasty bureaucratic models and philosophical values. The Fujiwara clan rose to prominence after the death of Prince Shotoku. Their position was primarily due to intermarriage with the royal family; while the Yamato emperor ruled in name, the Fujiwara often ruled in fact. In 710 CE, the Japanese built Nara, a capital modeled on the Chinese city Chang'an. In 794 CE, the emperor moved the capital to Heian, where modern Kyoto is located.

China

The Tang Dynasty

Li Yuan, the founder of the Tang dynasty, was of mixed Chinese and nomadic heritage, and he allowed many Turkish nomads to enter the service of China and its armies, especially on the frontiers, where the Tang rebuilt and strengthened the Great Wall of China. The Tang held power in China for over three centuries until it collapsed in 907 CE. China expanded greatly under the Tang, conquered Tibet, and forced the Koreans to pay tribute. The empire of the Tang was even larger than that of the Han dynasty.

The Tang continued the efforts of the second Sui ruler Yangdi to revive Confucianism, and the civil service examination system grew to be even more important. More officials entered government positions through this means than in the Han period. Nevertheless, hereditary connections were still important in the Tang bureaucracy. Although the Tang revived Confucianism, they continued to patronize Buddhists, who had grown in influence. However, in the ninth century, the Chinese began to restrict the influence of Buddhism through a wave of persecutions. The influence of Buddhism gradually waned following this period, though it never ceased to exist.

The Song Dynasty

The Kirghiz people overthrew the Tang, and a new dynasty took their place. The Song dynasty ruled China from 960 to 1279 CE. The Song were never as successful in uniting China as the Tang had been, but they did centralize the government and they continued to strengthen Confucianism and the civil service examination system, at the expense of aristocratic families. The expansion of the bureaucracy created large government expenditures, causing the Song to raise taxes. In protest, peasants rose up in two major rebellions.

At the same time, nomadic migrations continued to pose a threat to the Chinese. The Khitan peoples from Manchuria formed the Liao dynasty in the tenth century in the north, which exacted tribute from the Song. In the eleventh century, a new wave of nomadic peoples, the Jurchen, overthrew the Liao, established the Jin kingdom, and again demanded tribute. The Song moved south and established a new capital at **Hangzhou**, where it survived until the thirteenth century as the Southern Song dynasty. Culture flourished during this period, but again, waves of nomadic conquerors, this time in the form of the Mongols, ultimately defeated the Song.

The Mongols

Two factors contributed to the rise of the **Mongols**, who were a nomadic people from the steppes of Central Asia. First, their pasturelands began to disappear following a drop in the annual temperature in the twelfth century. Second, Temujin finally united the Mongol tribes. The Mongols would eventually form the largest empire in history.

Temujin was born in the 1160s. He was destined to become one of the world's greatest conquerors. Although he spent a portion of his childhood as a refugee in the wilderness following his father's assassination, he won a number of victories against rival Mongol chieftains, and in 1206 he was elected **Genghis Khan**, or "universal ruler," of the Mongol tribes at meeting of all the Mongol chieftains. Genghis borrowed the written script of the Uighur Turks, and the Mongol language was first written down and used to record laws. Ghengis forced the Jurchens of the Central Asia to pay tribute, and then moved on to China in 1212. Again, he sought tribute and quickly moved on to his next conquest, the Islamic Khwarazm Empire of Persia. In 1226, Ghenghis returned to demolish the Tangut state of the Xia, in what is northwest China today.

Genghis Khan's army was not overwhelmingly large, but he and his forces of expert horsemen unleashed terror in the hearts of those who fought them. Mongol warriors wore silk shirts, so that arrows entering their bodies could be easily removed without further tearing of the flesh. They traveled easily because their portable, round felt tents, or yurts, could quickly be disassembled and assembled. They were also expert military tacticians.

After the death of Genghis Khan, his empire was divided among his sons in accordance with his wishes. Various political regions, called **khanates**, were carved from his territory and ruled by the sons of Genghis Khan, including the Chaghadai Khanate in Central Asia, whose capital was Samarkand; the Khanate of Persia with its capital at Baghdad; Khanate of Kipchak, or the Golden Horde, which, under one of Genghis's grandsons, dominated Russia. Ogedai, Genghis Khan's third son, was elected universal Khan, but he was not as able a leader as his father had been. The capital of the Mongol Empire under Genghis Khan and his son Ogedai was Karakorum; today it is located in Outer Mongolia. Under Ogedai, the Mongol Hordes conquered Moscow and Kievan Russia and went deeper into Europe to threaten cities in Poland and Hungary. Following Ogedai's death, his son led the assault on the Islamic world, culminating in the defeat of the Abbasids in Baghdad in 1258 CE. Mongols also conquered Korea, but stopped short of China. Meanwhile, the Delhi Sultanate and the Mamluks had stopped Mongol advances on India and Egypt, respectively.

Kublai Khan, the grandson of Genghis Khan, continued the wave of conquests by attacking the Song dynasty in China beginning in the 1260s. Kublai captured surrounding regions, such as Vietnam, in an effort to cut off the Song, but found it necessary to attack their river cities. The Mongols massacred virtually the entire population of Changzhou and finally defeated the Song in 1276 CE. After conquering China, Kublai twice attempted to invade Japan, and twice failed.

TEST TIP

A multiple-choice question that asks you to choose the *best* answer often includes answer choices that initially seem to be correct. Compare the differences in each answer choice, and then refer each one back to the stem to determine the best answer.

The Yuan Dynasty

Kublai Khan established the **Yuan dynasty**. His capital was Khanbaliq, or the city of the Khan. This city would later be known as Beijing, the northern capital. Kublai Khan extended the Grand Canal of the Sui to the capital city Khanbaliq, which was twenty-four miles in diameter. Italian traveler **Marco Polo** lived there during his visit to Asia and wrote of its magnificence. Kublai Khan was very interested in Marco Polo's stories about his travels and convinced him to become his ambassador to different parts of China. Marco Polo served Kublai Khan in this capacity for seventeen years before returning to Italy, where he was captured by Genoans, who were at war with the Venetians. While he was in prison, Marco Polo entertained his fellow prisoners with tales about the magnificent court of Kublai Khan and his travels throughout China.

One of the prisoners wrote down the stories in a book that became immensely popular in Europe, even though many believed that the stories were too remarkable to be true.

The Yuan dynasty relegated the Chinese to a lower status than Mongols and other non-Chinese foreigners. However, Kublai Khan and successive Mongol rulers respected and adopted Chinese customs and innovations and adopted the customs of many of the people they conquered. While the Mongols did employ some Confucian scholars, they did use the civil service examination system for selecting bureaucrats, which led to the decline in the power of Confucians. The Mongols also increased the status of merchants, which the Confucian bureaucrats further resented.

End of the Mongol Empire

The Mongol Empire was unique in many ways. The Mongols were militaristic and focused on expanding their territories; however, once they used brutal tactics to conquer an area, they only required tributes from conquered peoples and usually permitted them to retain their own customs and religions. The Mongol Empire became so vast that the rulers of the khanates had little contact with each another. The khans not only tolerated the customs and the religions of the people they had conquered, but they also adopted these customs and religions themselves. For example, the khans who ruled in the Middle East converted to Islam and allowed Islamic legal structures, religion, and the Arabic language to prevail over Mongol customs. The Mongol Empire never went into decline or was defeated, as many empires had been; it simply fell apart as the Mongol khans became assimilated into the cultures of the different peoples that they had conquered.

The Americas

The Aztecs

The **Aztecs** wandered for 150 years before settling on the swampy islands of Lake Texcoco, the modern-day location of Mexico City. They worshipped their god Huitzilopochtili in the city there. In 1428, the Aztecs began a policy of expansion. The Aztecs built their empire through warfare. Aztec emperors summoned warriors to duty through the **calpulli**, an organization based on households and kinship. These units rotated service, the length of which was determined by the emperor. The lack of pack animals there, as in the Mayan world, meant that human porters carried the supplies the army needed. Warfare might have strengthened the empire on one level, but over the long run it weakened it. Conquered areas paid tribute to the Aztec emperor, but they were also centers of rebellion. When an area rebelled, the Aztecs would conquer it again with more brutal methods, rule it until it rebelled again, and then conquer it again. This cycle depleted the empire of its population and its military.

The Inca

In the 1980s, archaeologists discovered evidence of great civilizations along the western coast of Peru dating back 5,000 years. These civilizations were older than those of the Maya or Aztecs. For reasons that are not clear, the people of these civilizations moved into the Andes highlands, the highest mountain range in the Western Hemisphere. They became known as the **Inca**, a name taken from a ruling family in the capital city of Cuzco and then applied to all of the societies living in the region. The Inca settled primarily in the valleys of Huaylas, Cuzco, and Titicaca, where they constructed agricultural terraces along the slopes of the steep mountains. The Inca became militaristic between 1438 and 1471 CE, during the reign of Pachacuti Inca, and conquered surrounding peoples. They controlled their population through strong government and unified the language and the religion of their subjects. A well-organized system of roads facilitated the movement of Inca armies and peoples.

Chapter 7

Increased Economic Productive Capacity and Its Consequences

During the period between 600 and 1450 CE, innovations in agricultural techniques and the resulting dramatic increase in food production led to expansions of populations throughout the world, and also to greater urbanization in many empires. By 1000, there were several cities with populations of 300,000 or more, including Hangzhou, Córdoba (Spain), Constantinople, Istanbul, Cairo, Bagdad, and Tenochtitlán. New labor practices, such as slavery and feudalism, as well as changes in social and gender structures, developed in response to increases in populations and the volume of agricultural production. However, later in this period, population growth as well as subsequent declines caused by the widespread bubonic plague decreased the availability of food resources and led to other negative consequences for some empires.

Key Terms

apprenticeship	fiefs	moldboard
Bantu	foot binding	open field system
bubonic plague	guilds	samurai
Champa rice	Hangzhou	shogunate
Chang'an	horse collar	tecuhtli
chinampas	Ibn Battuta	Tenochtitlán
daimyos	Kaifeng	vassals
feudalism	liege homage	
fiefdom	manorial system	

Western Europe

The period between about 900 and 1300 CE, part of what is known as the Middle Ages, was a time of revitalization for Western Europe, including the economy, town life, and trade. To a great extent, this was a result of the Crusades, which had exposed Europeans to more sophisticated eastern cultures through the long-distance trade routes. Up until about 1300, the majority of the population of Europe was peasants, who lived in relative isolation in rural areas. Unlike China, the Middle East, Northern Africa, and the Americas, Europe had few big cities, with the exception of Genoa and Venice.

The agricultural system known as manorialism had been retained in Western Europe from its origins in the western Roman Empire. In the **manorial system**, land was cultivated on vast manorial estates or **fiefs**, which were divided into an area of land reserved for the lord and tracts reserved for peasants. This system of dividing land into two or three units was known as the **open field system**. The open field system was modified to include three fields rather than two by the ninth century CE. Whereas 50 percent of the land in earlier times went uncultivated, during this period much of that land became productive again. Crops were rotated on the cultivated land, and one-third of the land lay fallow every year to allow it to recover needed nutrients. Also in the ninth century CE, the introduction of a better iron plow known as the **moldboard** improved farming, as it allowed for deeper cultivation of fields. In addition, large new areas of land were cleared for farming. Whereas the Roman Empire was centered on the city of Rome, the heart of Europe during this time was the manorial estate.

By the eleventh century, an agricultural revolution occurred in Western Europe, leading to increased production. The use of the **horse collar**, which was padded, contributed to more efficient agriculture, as horses could pull more weight than oxen. The use of horses in farming became more widespread after the twelfth century, and by the thirteenth century horses were used to take goods to markets. Combined with the open field system of agriculture, innovations in agricultural techniques caused agricultural yields to increase markedly between the ninth and thirteenth centuries CE.

Increases in agricultural production contributed to a rise in population, and eventually, city life was revived. Many of the first new cities had at one point been important Roman towns. These cities became centers for trade, as well as for craftsmen and specialized laborers. As trade grew exponentially, Western Europe returned to a money economy. In addition, a new class of artisans arose, mainly from peasant stock. Peasants who migrated to cities and lived there for one year and one day could earn their freedom from feudal restrictions. By the twelfth century, artisans organized themselves into **guilds**, which regulated their activities.

TEST TIP

In your studies for the exam, begin by learning the basic facts, events, and quotes of each era and its topics. Once you understand the facts and events, put them together into themes and trends.

China

The Tang

An equal-field system was also used in China, when Tang emperors first allocated farmland to individuals and families with the goal of ensuring that the distribution of farmland was equitable. Peasants were given land to farm in return for paying taxes. In addition, the equal-field system allowed the Tang to maintain some control over the amount of land that influential Chinese families could acquire, which had been a serious threat to the Han dynasty. The equal-field system flourished until the ninth century, when the powerful families of China were again able to accumulate large parcels of land.

The Tang also completed construction of the Grand Canal, which led to greater trade within China. The capital city, **Chang'an**, was a cosmopolitan urban center with a population that may have exceeded a million people by about 640 CE. Foreign ambassadors and merchants from the Byzantine and Muslim Empires frequently visited Chang'an. However, higher taxes imposed by the Tang created tension among the farmers, which led to rebellions by the peasants, the abdication of the emperor in 907 CE, more independent regional governance, and the decline of the city of Chang'an.

The Song

When the Song reestablished centralized control over China in 960 CE, they introduced many new developments, including the cultivation of rice from Champa (present-day Vietnam). The Song began to use Champa's new strains of fast-ripening rice, which could produce both a summer and winter crop each year. The result was a huge increase in the yields of rice in the empire. The production of the **Champa rice** was extremely successful and became a valuable commodity that was traded along the

Silk Road and Indian Ocean trade routes, in addition to allowing other farmers to turn to the cultivation of luxury fruits and vegetables to sell in China's urban marketplaces. Agricultural products also were traded along the Grand Canal, which connected the northern and southern regions of China. Other innovations in agriculture under the Song included the use of heavy iron plows in the northern fields and water buffaloes in the southern farmlands. They constructed extensive irrigation systems as well, allowing agricultural production to extend farther away from the rivers.

With its much greater agricultural yields, China's population continued to increase dramatically, with the northern capital of **Kaifeng** becoming not only a major urban trade center, but also a manufacturing center for cannons, movable-type printing presses, looms, and water-powered mills. The Song's southern capital, **Hangzhou**, remained a large trading city with an ever-growing population as well.

The Bantu of Africa

The **Bantu** people were enormously important in the history of Africa, as they were the first to introduce the smelting of iron and the use of iron tools. While the iron age may have started in Africa as early as the first millennium BCE, iron making did not spread across Africa until after the first century CE. The Bantu people originated near the area where modern Nigeria is located in West Africa. Starting in the second millennium BCE, they moved into the rain-forest zones south and to the east, and then to the savanna regions straddling the Congo River. The Congo and other rivers were an important path of migration. However, it took another 1,500 years for the Bantu to migrate throughout the savanna region. During this period they began to adopt agriculture, and the growth in their populations led to a series of other migrations.

Throughout the first 1,500 years CE, the Bantu migrated to eastern and southern Africa. Agriculture prompted the series of migrations, as successful cultivation of crops such as bananas created more and larger villages and the need for more territory. The Zambezi River was an important path for the Bantu as they moved to the south. Thus, the Bantu migrations resulted in not only the spread of iron making but also the spread of agriculture.

DIDYOUKNOW?

The Bantu migration spread outward throughout Africa and eventually led to the settlement of most of the African continent, which is why many African languages are very similar. The Bantu eventually became a language group rather than an ethnic group. Currently, Bantu is the native language of more than 60 million Africans.

The Aztecs of Mesoamerica

By the mid-fifteenth century, the Aztecs inhabited virtually all of Mesoamerica. The capital city of **Tenochtitlán** was built on a raised island in Lake Texcoco and included about 60,000 households, with the city's population being somewhere around 500,000. The total population in the Aztec Empire was over 5 million. To support their large population, the Aztecs used several different agricultural techniques. They developed unique agriculture fields called **chinampas**, or floating gardens, to grow crops. Chinampas were raised fields that the Aztecs constructed in swampy areas and in shallow water. To build a chinampa, the Aztecs would stake out a large area, build a fence around it, and then fill in the area with sediment and vegetation to bring it above the water level. The chinampas were separated by channels of water to allow canoes to pass through and allow Aztec farmers access to the fields. The Aztecs grew maize, beans, squash, tomatoes, chilies, and even flowers on the chinampas, which yielded about two-thirds of the food consumed by the people who lived in Tenochtitlán.

The Bubonic Plague

By the fourteenth century, the numerous interactions that had been taking place between people throughout the Eastern Hemisphere had fatal consequences. As people from different cultures traveled long distances for the purposes of trade, military activities, and diplomacy, they also spread disease. The deadly **bubonic plague**—or the Black Death, as it came to be known—most likely originated in southwestern China. Victims of the bubonic plague developed black swellings on their bodies caused by buboes, or internal hemorrhages. The Mongols spread the plague throughout China during their military campaigns, and merchants engaged in long-distance trade spread it westward. As the Mongols rode through desert areas, such as the Gobi Desert, they came into contact with rodents, which carried the fleas that also carried the plague. When the Mongols laid siege to the Black Sea port of Kaffa and threw infected bodies over the walls with their catapults, the Genoese sailors there fled, and then took the plague with them to Italian cities on the Mediterranean, from whence it spread throughout Western Europe by 1346. From the Red Sea, the plague reached Syria, Mesopotamia, Persia, and Egypt. From China, the plague spread to India.

Once the plague entered a town or city, it typically killed 70 percent of the population or more. About 25 percent of the population in Western Europe died from the plague. The populations of both China and Egypt also suffered severe losses. Many once-thriving cities were devastated by the plague in the fourteenth century, as well as farmers in surrounding areas. Trade nearly came to a standstill, and shortages of labor created social unrest, leading to rebellions in many areas affected by the plague. Peasants' revolts occurred throughout Europe, the most famous being the Peasants' Revolt in England in 1381 and the Revolt of the Jacquerie in France in 1356.

Trends in Labor Management

Europe

During the reign of Charlemagne, a system of landholding and obligations began to develop in Europe called **feudalism**, a term that includes the complex social, economic, and political relationships that characterized much of Europe from the ninth century through the French Revolution, which began in 1789. Feudal society developed out of a need for kings and other powerful landowners to have the support of an army. Feudalism developed to provide a system of armed retainers for those who wanted to gain and retain power.

Feudal society was based upon private contracts and had three main characteristics:

- Political and public power was held by private individuals.

- Political power was fragmented.

- Armed forces were necessary to obtain and maintain power.

Land was the basis of the feudal economy; with enough land, a man could support himself, a household, and retainers to protect his holdings. Although there were coins and other forms of currency minted during the Middle Ages, the economy was not based primarily on monetary exchange but rather on barter. In order to survive in a world based on warfare, a king or lord needed **vassals,** or knights. In order to be a vassal, a man had to be wealthy. The training of vassals was lengthy and costly, and the suits of armor that they wore were also very costly. Further, the necessary battle horses were expensive to acquire, feed, and train.

Thus, to obtain vassals, a lord had to supply them with the means to maintain their profession; in the Middle Ages, that was only possible through the gift of a plot of land known as a **fiefdom**. A vassal or knight was invested with his fiefdom, in return for which he pledged homage to his lord. A vassal was required to fight when his lord demanded it and to ransom his lord if he was captured on the battlefield. The length of service varied, but by the twelfth century CE in many parts of Europe, a vassal only had to serve his lord for forty days a year. Because vassals became powerful in their own right, they had to seek the permission of their lords before their daughters could marry or before they, themselves could enter into such a contract. Marriage was often used as a tool to gain political, social, and economic power; hence, the right marriage could propel a vassal to a greater status than his lord.

The agreement between lord and vassal was of a personal nature, and it often resulted in conflicts within the feudal system. For example, a vassal might have more than one lord and those two lords might wage war on one another, both demanding the services of the vassal. Such situations eventually created **liege homage**, whereby a vassal pledged homage to a particular lord above all others. A vassal of a lord might also divide the fiefdom that he had received and thus create his own vassals.

TEST TIP

Be aware of superlatives, such as *always, never,* and *only* in both multiple-choice questions and answer choices. Keep in mind that superlatives usually describe a definite fact and therefore they are very limiting and difficult to defend.

Japan

In 1192, the Japanese emperor gave a clan leader named Minamoto Yoritomo the power to establish the first Japanese **shogunate**, a feudal system government that would last for seven centuries. Although the emperor remained the supreme ruler of Japan, the shogun had immense power as the supreme military administrator. Yoritomo did not live in Kyoto, the imperial capital of Japan, but instead set up his own centralized field quarters outside of the city and commanded the Japanese military from there.

The Japanese system of feudalism was similar to the European system in that Japanese vassals, or **daimyos**, were granted tracts of land and protection in return for military service and agricultural compensation. However, Yoritomo did not demand oaths of loyalty from the daimyos in return for fiefdoms and therefore they were more independent from the shogun. The Japanese feudal system was based on a code of honor and on mutual political and social obligations and loyalties. Japanese daimyos had a high social status, and each had a group of **samurai**, or professional warriors, who swore an oath of loyalty to them. The name samurai means "to serve," which described the samurai's social status as military servants. The samurai lived by the Confucian ideals of personal honor and individual loyalty to their master. They did not receive land in return for their military services, but instead were paid fees by their daimyos.

As in Europe, Japanese peasants formed a lower social class and worked on the lands of the lords to support the agricultural needs of the fiefdoms. However, many Japanese peasants willingly worked the land so as to avoid the high property taxes in Japan. Japanese peasants had greater freedom than did European serfs in that some could actually own land.

Africa and the Muslim World

Slavery was widespread in the empires of Ghana, Mali, and Songhay, and the exports of slaves supplemented the exports of gold. The thriving gold trade also increased the slave trade across the Sahara because of the need for workers in the mines. Slaves in the African kingdoms were both African and white men and women who were used for a variety of purposes, including agricultural workers, servants, soldiers, and government officials. Muslims also took African slaves for their armies and as servants for Muslim households. Many of these slaves had been captured by the Muslims in military campaigns.

Slavery was a feature of life in many parts of the Islamic world outside of Africa. As Islam expanded rapidly, it acquired an increasing supply of slaves. Slavery in the Islamic world was not tied to any particular sort of economy, such as an agricultural economy. Slaves served many functions in the business world, in the home, and in the armies of the Muslims. Slaves of Muslims were not of a specific ethnicity or race. The Qur'an commanded Muslims to treat their slaves fairly, and although it encouraged masters to free their slaves, slavery continued to grow in the Islamic world in proportion to its expansion.

The Aztecs

As was the case with the early Olmec society, the Aztec social structure changed over time from an egalitarian society to a hierarchical society. After the emperor, who was elected by important nobles, priests were also of high status in Aztec society. Regions paid tribute to sustain some of the famous Aztec temples. The next-highest ranking members of Aztec society were the **tecuhtli,** a group of nobles who had won distinction as warriors. They served as judges, governors of provinces, or as generals. Warriors who captured four prisoners or killed four enemies became part of the **tequiua,** nobles who were given a portion of the plunder of war. A warrior who failed in such a task was relegated to the class of workers, or **maceualtin**. In the Aztec capital, the maceualtin had land that they held for life. They also paid taxes and were required to work on imperial projects. A landless class of workers were the **tlalmaitl**, who were also required to perform military service. Aztecs also had slaves, who could intermarry with free people and thereby have children who would be free. Aztec slaves could also own goods and land, and they could buy their freedom. In addition, an escaped slave would earn his freedom if he managed to reach the king's palace.

The Inca

The Inca were organized in clans who worked plots of land in return for tribute paid to a provincial governor and for their service on state building projects. A rotation system determined when state duties were required. Members of clans owed their allegiance to curacas, a class of men who were the sons of the leaders of peoples whom the Inca had conquered and taught them to rule the Inca way. However, during the reign of Pachacuti Inca (1438–1471), the Inca became more militaristic, and this allegiance was transferred to the Inca ruler rather than to the curacas. Under Pachacuti, a system of colonization deported the populations of newly conquered regions and replaced them with a more servile and docile group of people who had previously been conquered. Pachacuti controlled the population of his empire through a strong central government and unified the language and the religion of his subjects.

Gender Relations and Social Structures

Europe

Although European society during the Middles Ages was largely patriarchal, women ran the households. Peasant women were active as laborers on manorial estates, many of which were managed by aristocratic women whose husbands were off fighting campaigns. With the revitalization of trade in the eleventh century, women benefited, as many women engaged in business enterprises. Middle-class women who lived in towns and cities maintained their households, and also helped their husbands in their businesses, either by helping them with their craft or trade or by practicing one of their own. To learn a skill or trade, both men and women had to serve an **apprenticeship**. An apprenticeship agreement was made between two families and required a legal document called an indenture. Widows and other single women who practiced trades were often allowed to join the guilds, although they could not achieve leadership positions in them.

TEST TIP

Each multiple-choice question on the AP World History exam now has four answer choices, (A) through (D), instead of the five choices it featured before 2011.

The Muslim World

Muslim society was also patriarchal, but Muslim women could engage in business, inherit property, and divorce their husbands. Women could also keep their dowries as wives, and female infanticide was prohibited. According to the Qur'an, women had equal status with men before Allah. However, the Qur'an and the shari'a recognized descent only through male bloodlines, and the social and sexual lives of Muslim women were strictly controlled to ensure the legitimacy of heirs. Muslim men were allowed to follow Muhammad's example and have as many as four wives, while women could have only one husband. Muslims also adopted the earlier Mesopotamian and Persian custom of making women wear veils and leaving their homes only when they were accompanied by servants or chaperones.

China

During the Tang dynasty, upper-class women could own property, move about in public, and remarry. Women also could inherit property in the absence of male heirs. However, marriages were arranged within the social classes.

As agricultural productivity and wealth increased during the Song dynasty, the patriarchal social structure became more rigid. Members of the upper class ensured the purity of their bloodlines by confining women to their homes. However, women could keep their dowries and were allowed to engage in business and trade. During the late Tang dynasty, **foot binding** had been introduced and became a common practice for upper-class women during the Song dynasty, when it was viewed as a sign of wealth and status. Foot binding was a painful process that involved breaking the bones of the feet and then binding the feet to ensure that they did not grow to normal adult proportions. Foot binding restricted the ability of women to walk or to work, and therefore led them to greater subservience to their husbands and confinement to the household, especially for upper-class women. The lower classes, who had to work to survive, did not practice foot binding.

The Mongols

Mongol women were kept strictly separate from the Chinese, and Mongol women also often fought on horseback. In addition, Mongol women had rights to their property and control within their own households. The Mongols did not adopt the practice of foot binding, which limited the roles of Chinese women. The wife of Kublai Khan had tremendous influence and power; on two separate occasions Empress Dowagers ruled the Mongol Empire during interims between the death of the Great Khan and the time when the next Great Khan was selected. Mongol women were often seen in public. Muslim travelers, such as the great fourteenth-century Moroccan historian **Ibn Battuta**, who wrote a comprehensive history of the Eastern Hemisphere, were often alarmed at the high status of women in the Mongol world.

India

Muslim rulers adopted many Hindu practices in the Delhi Sultanate that weakened the status of women. During this period, Hindu practices contributed to the loss of status for women. Girls were married before the onset of their menstrual periods to protect their virginity, and many Muslims adopted this practice. Further, women could no longer own or inherit property, in contrast to earlier practices in the Vedic period. Women were confined to their households, and when they were widowed, only their children saw them. Hindus expected women to live very ascetic lives, wearing plain clothes, rarely eating, sleeping on the hard ground, and often shaving their heads. While the Qur'an taught greater equality for women, Muslim conquerors were profoundly affected by these Hindu customs. The status of women declined in this period both for Hindus and their Muslim conquerors.

The Aztecs

The Aztecs had a patriarchal society, but it was not overly rigid. Aztec women had some rights, such as owning and inheriting property. However, in political and social life, women were subordinate to men, though some served as priestesses and mothers were honored for giving birth to warrior sons. Aztec women who were skillful weavers were highly regarded. The mature women of the calpulli were responsible for training young upper-class girls, and their marriages were often arranged between lineages. Peasant women worked in the fields and also maintained their households. In the maize-based economy of the Aztecs, peasant women typically spent about six hours a day grinding the maize by hand to prepare food for their households. Without the use of wheels or animals to help perform work, peasant women had to work between thirty and forty hours a week simply to prepare food.

The Inca

In Inca society, women and men were theoretically viewed as having a complementary status, but the emphasis on military virtues reinforced the superiority of men. Like the Aztecs, Inca peasant women worked in the fields, wove cloth, and took care of the household. Inca women were required to weave high-quality cloth for the nobility and for religious ceremonies. Some women were made to be concubines for the nobility, while others, called the "Virgins of the Sun," were servants at religious temples. The Aztecs recognized parallel descent of property, so property among the nobility was inherited through both the male and female bloodlines. Women left their property to their daughters, while men left their property to their sons.

Time for a quiz
- Review strategies in Chapter 2
- Take Quiz 3 at the REA Study Center
  (www.rea.com/studycenter)

Take Mini-Test 1
on Chapters 3–11
Go to the REA Study Center
(www.rea.com/studycenter)

Unit IV:
Global Interactions,
c. 1450 to c. 1750

Chapter 12

Globalizing Networks of Communication and Exchange

Between the tenth and fifteenth centuries, several concurrent movements had led to transoceanic interconnections between the Eastern and Western hemispheres. During the Crusades era, beginning in the eleventh century, Europeans were introduced to desirable products from East Asia: spices such as pepper, cinnamon, ginger, nutmeg, and cloves; tropical foods such as figs, rice, and oranges; and luxury goods including perfumes, silk, cotton, dyes, and precious stones. The complicated trade routes involved tariffs at many ports of entry as products went overland to Constantinople, through the Mediterranean on Venetian sailing vessels, and ultimately to Western European ports. This trade was costly not only because of the number of handlers, but also because every ruler whose land Arab caravans crossed exacted a tax on the goods. The balance of trade

Key Terms

Amerigo Vespucci	Francisco Pizarro	Medici
astrolabe	Henry the Navigator	Pedro Cabral
Bartholomew Diaz	Henry VIII	Reformation
caravel	Hernando Cortés	Renaissance
Christopher Columbus	indulgences	Sikhism
Columbian Exchange	John Cabot	Treaty of Tordesillas
compass	Magellan	Vasco da Gama
Ferdinand and Isabella	Martin Luther	Zheng He

was unfavorable from the standpoint of the European countries; the necessity to cut out the middlemen was crucial. The exploration of the Americas and of new sea routes to the East by Europeans between 1450 and 1750 created a new global economy that forever transformed Europe, Africa, and the Americas.

European Explorations

Technological Advances

A number of technological tools of European, Asian, and Arabic origins were important in the fifteenth-century explorations. By 1350 the Europeans had perfected the cannon, capable of firing iron or stone balls, which, when mounted on a seagoing vessel, was a formidable force. A new sailing vessel, the **caravel**, replaced the old galleys that had relied on rowers for motion. Although slower than the galleys, the caravel relied on wind power and was designed to carry larger cargoes. The lateen sail, which then supplemented the ancient square sail widely used in the Mediterranean region during earlier periods, made it possible for ships to sail into the wind through a movement known as tacking. When combined with square-rigged sails, the lateen sails gave caravels increased maneuverability on the seas. Other inventions used in navigation during the Age of Exploration included the **compass**, perfected by the Chinese many centuries earlier. The compass pointed north, which was an important means of location for ships traveling east to west. The **astrolabe**, a tool developed by the Arabs, was also important. It allowed sailors to determine the altitude of the sun and thereby to plot latitude. Improvements in European cartography gave navigators more exact information on distances, sea depth, and geography.

TEST TIP

Change an answer to a question that you were fairly sure was correct the first time only if you find information somewhere else in the exam indicating that your first choice is wrong. The first answer that you choose is more likely to be correct.

Portuguese Voyages

The Portuguese were the first Europeans to become involved in the voyages of exploration. Following the lead of their king, **Prince Henry the Navigator**, they set sail down the west coast of Africa in search of a sea route to the Spice Islands of the East Indies.

Henry had established a school for navigators that produced some of the most skillful navigators of the time. Two of his students finally discovered the southern tip of Africa. In 1488, **Bartholomew Diaz** reached the tip of South Africa, and **Vasco da Gama** rounded the southern tip of Africa and sailed east to reach India. The Portuguese had limited success in their conquest of Africa, however, due to the difficulty of penetrating the continent's harsh terrain, and also because of the strength of the African monarchies.

King Manuel I of Portugal was impressed by the goods brought from India by Vasco da Gama and sent an expedition, in 1500, under the leadership of **Pedro Cabral** to set up trading posts in India. Following what he thought was da Gama's path, Cabral headed for India. The fleet was blown off course, however, and Cabral sighted Brazil and claimed it for the Portuguese crown. After spending a few days on the east coast of South America, Cabral and his crew continued on to India, arriving in 1501. From that point on, ships were sent from Lisbon each March headed for India and the Spice Islands. The harbor of Lisbon, the capital of Portugal, became the entry point for goods from the East.

Spanish Voyages by Christopher Columbus

While the Portuguese were attempting to reach the East by sailing around the tip of Africa, the Spanish turned to another route suggested by **Christopher Columbus**. Columbus was an Italian from Genoa who had studied the ancient maps of Ptolemy, a second-century geographer whose works were still highly regarded. Ptolemy's map of the ancient Mediterranean area was very accurate, and scholars had always assumed, without proof, that his other geographical works were equally accurate. Ptolemy, however, had overestimated the landmass from Europe to Asia and extended Asia much farther to the east than it actually was; he also underestimated the amount of water on Earth. According to his map, the measurements of the known world were about 4,580 miles from north to south and 8,250 miles from east to west. All of these factors led Columbus to conclude that he could more easily reach the East by sailing west across the seemingly limited expanse of ocean that separated Asia from the western coast of Europe than the Portuguese could reach it by sailing around the enormous continent of Africa. Of course, Columbus had no idea that the Americas separated Europe from Asia.

In 1485, Christopher Columbus approached **King Ferdinand and Queen Isabella** of Spain with his plan of sailing west to reach the East. Although the Spanish were at first disinterested in Columbus's ideas, Spain was newly unified and eager to counter the rising power of the Portuguese that resulted from their initial voyages around Africa. It was Queen Isabella who was converted first to Columbus's plan; in 1492, she promised Columbus everything he had asked for and he set off on his first voyage. In October of that year he reached the Caribbean, believing that he had attained his goal of sailing west to reach the East. In all, Columbus made four journeys to the islands of the Caribbean, embarking in 1492, 1493, 1498, and 1502. Although he was convinced that he had reached the East Indies and called the natives he encountered Indians, he failed as governor of Hispaniola, the Spanish name given to the Caribbean.

Other European Voyages

In 1499 and 1500, **Amerigo Vespucci** took part in an expedition led by Spanish explorer Alonso de Ojeda. In the course of this trip, Vespucci wrote at length about the "New World" reached by the Europeans. Because of his descriptions and his realization that the Europeans had not, in fact, reached the Indies, but instead continents previously unknown, other European states also financed exploratory voyages.

John Cabot, a native of Italy, born Giovanni Caboto, sailed under the English crown in 1497 and became the first English representative to reach North America. He, like Columbus, da Gama, and Cabral, was interested in a shorter route to India and chose a more northerly path. Embarking in 1487, he reached land, probably either Newfoundland or Cape Breton, an island off the coast of present-day Nova Scotia. Cabot made a second voyage in 1498. His voyages gave England claim to the North American mainland; they would lead to future English colonization. However, the next English expedition did not take place until the late sixteenth century.

Magellan, a Portuguese student of astronomy and navigation, further developed some of Columbus's pioneering ideas. He believed that a shorter route to India was possible, if, instead of sailing around the tip of Africa, ships sailed west and rounded the tip of South America. The Portuguese king would not support his request for ships, men, and money, so Magellan turned to the Spanish King, Charles I. Magellan set sail in 1519 and became the first European to circumnavigate the globe. Magellan's route took him from Europe, around the tip of South America, through the Pacific Ocean, the Philippines, the Indian Ocean, around the Cape of Good Hope (which Bartholomew Diaz had first sighted in 1488) of southeastern Africa, and back to Spain. He set out with a fleet of five ships and returned home three years later with one ship and only seventeen of the original crew.

Dividing the Portuguese and Spanish Conquests

The early success of both the Portuguese and the Spanish in exploration led to many disputes. In 1493, Pope Alexander VI attempted to adjudicate the controversy. Essentially, he established an imaginary line running north and south through the mid-Atlantic Ocean, 100 leagues (480 km) from the Cape Verde Islands in the mid-Atlantic. Spain would have possession of any unclaimed territories to the west of the line and Portugal would have possession of any unclaimed territory to the east of the line. In 1494, the **Treaty of Tordesillas** redrew the line at 370 leagues (1,770 km) west of the Cape Verde Islands. Portugal lost much in the Americas, as it received only Brazil. The Spanish became the beneficiaries of the vast wealth of the Americas.

Chinese Voyages

The Yongle Emperor of the Ming dynasty in China began a series of naval expeditions that began in 1405 and continued until 1435 under his successors. The Yongle Emperor liked exotic goods and also wanted to expand trade, so he commissioned seven expeditions led by Admiral **Zheng He** to such places as Ceylon, Calcutta, South Vietnam, and Africa. Zheng He commanded 60 vessels with 500 troops. His ships were 400 feet long and weighed 500 tons, far bigger and faster than those of the Portuguese. The expeditions brought back zebras, ostriches, and tributes from other kings. In 1391, over 50 million trees had been planted in Nanjing to prepare for maritime exploration, and during this period, the Ming had the most powerful maritime empire in the world. The Yongle Emperor's empire was bigger than all of Europe in size, and his expeditions were far larger. The maritime expeditions led to great commercial success, and those involved became very wealthy.

DID YOU KNOW?

Admiral Zheng He's seven expeditions remain unrivaled in world history. Zheng He's enormous fleet, made up of 60 huge treasure ships and 200 smaller ships, carrying more than 25,000 men, sailed from China to India, to the Persian Gulf, and to Africa, visiting the rulers of more than thirty states, eighty years before the first Portuguese expeditions. For political and economic reasons, China ended its brief age of exploration after Zheng He's last voyage and entered a period of isolation. Many historians have speculated whether China, rather than Europe, would have gone on to dominate the world had China continued its expeditions.

The Spanish in the Americas

Just as technological advances spurred exploration, they also aided the Spanish in their conquest of the natives of Mesoamerica and South America. By this time, Europeans had adapted the Chinese invention of explosives to make not only cannons, but also guns. The guns had limited accuracy, but their power to intimidate people who had never seen anything like them gave the Spanish, as well as Europeans in other colonies, the means to conquer any societies that did not possess guns.

Cortés

The Aztecs of Central America and the Incas of Peru had well-established empires by the end of the fifteenth century. Nevertheless, in less than two years, **Hernando Cortés** destroyed the monarchy, took possession of Tenochtitlán, and defeated most of the Aztecs.

Cortés was a notary and farmer in Hispaniola in the early years of the Spanish discovery of the Americas. In 1511 he accompanied Diego Velazquez in his conquest of present-day Cuba. Cortés later became clerk under Velazquez. For his service, Cortés received a gift of land and native slaves. In 1518, Cortés was put in charge of an expedition to establish a colony on the mainland. He sailed for the Yucatan Coast in present-day Mexico with 11 ships, 508 soldiers, and 16 horses. Cortés captured a native slave, Malinche, who spoke both Mayan and the Aztec languages. She was known as the "tongue" of Cortés and was eventually baptized as Doña Marina. Doña Marina was likely one of the reasons Cortés was initially able to charm the Aztec Emperor Montezuma. Through his interpreter Doña Marina, Cortés learned of unrest among the subjects of the Aztecs. He swayed more than 20,000 of the Aztec subjects to his side and marched to Tenochtitlán. At first, Montezuma welcomed Cortés, as he identified him with Quetzalcóatl, the legendary god of the Aztecs who had, by coincidence, promised to return that very year. Although Cortés enjoyed momentary success in Tenochtitlán, Spanish explorer Narvaez attacked him in 1520. While Narvaez distracted Cortés, the Aztecs, who had become increasingly resentful of the Spaniard's greed for gold, finally revolted and attacked the Spaniards. In 1520, the Aztecs drove Cortés and his men out of Tenochtitlán. Cortés then laid siege to the city, which finally surrendered.

Pizarro

The Incas met a similar fate in 1532 at the hands of 175 Spanish troops led by **Francisco Pizarro**. He first traveled to the New World in 1510 on an expedition to what is modern-day Colombia. In 1513 he accompanied Balboa on the expedition on which Spaniards first sighted the Pacific. From 1519 to 1523, he served as mayor of Panama. In 1523, Pizarro left on the expedition that would discover the empire of the Incas.

From 1524 to 1527, Pizarro journeyed to the south, and his men endured many hardships. Upon finding traces of civilization, Pizarro sent for reinforcements from

Panama. The governor told him to return, whereupon Pizarro drew a line across the ground asking those who desired wealth and glory to cross it. Thirteen men crossed the line, and Pizarro continued south. He named the land Peru, which he derived from the name of the river Viru. In 1529, the king of Spain made him governor of the region called New Castile, which extended 600 miles south from Panama along the coast. In 1530 he and his crew of about 180 men set sail for Peru, where they made their first contact with the Inca Emperor Atahualpa. Pizarro attempted to convert the Inca king to Christianity, but Atahualpa adamantly refused. Pizarro attacked and quickly defeated the Incas. Pizarro ordered Atahualpa to be put to death and then took Cuzco, the Inca capital, without a struggle. Pizarro founded Lima, Peru, in 1535.

Reasons for the Success of the Spanish Conquest

The superstitious conviction of many natives that the Spanish were somehow divine, combined with European technology, contributed to the defeat of the Native American populations. Aztec and Inca warfare was no match for the well-trained Spanish troops, their ships, and their guns. Frightened and then defeated by European technology, the Mesoamerican and South American peoples fell prey to the Spanish conquistadores. Their civilizations were devastated by the policies of the Spanish overlords and the devastation caused by European diseases, some of which were carried by rats aboard the Spanish ships. With exposure to such European diseases as smallpox, measles, and influenza, Native Americans died in droves. Some historians believe that in Peru alone, the population of Native Americans fell from 1.3 million in 1570 to 600,000 in 1620. In Central America, of the 25.3 million Native Americans living there at the time of the arrival of Cortes in 1519, only 1.3 million remained by 1620.

The Creation of a Global Economy
The Columbian Exchange

The European voyages of exploration created a global economy through the sea trade called the **Columbian Exchange.** The routes of the Columbian Exchange linked the continents of North America, South America, Europe, and Africa, and they also connected with the existing sea trade routes that had been established in earlier times.

The Columbian Exchange transported many agricultural products that increased the variety of food and enhanced the nutrition of the diets of people in many parts of the world. Agricultural products and domesticated animals flowed through the Columbian Exchange in the following ways:

- From Europe to the Americas, domesticated animals such as horses, pigs, and cows were transported. Crops such as wheat, melons, and grapes also followed this path.

- From Africa and from Asia via Africa to the Americas, chickens and goats were transported, as well as foods such as sugar cane, bananas, and coffee.

- From the Americas to Europe and Africa, agricultural products such as maize, potatoes, tomatoes, beans, squash, peppers, chocolate, and tobacco were transported.

The Atlantic routes of the Columbia Exchange were circular, and they were larger and more complex than earlier trade routes had been. Most trade ships stopped at several ports along their journeys. For example, Portuguese trade ships first stopped in India and then went on to Japan and China. Their merchants brought back spices to Lisbon and often paid for these goods with textiles from India and gold and ivory from East Africa. From the Portuguese outpost at Macao, they took Chinese silk to Japan and the Philippines. There, they traded silk for Spanish silver. The Portuguese also took horses to India from Mesopotamia and copper from Arabia, and they carried hawks and peacocks from India to China and Japan.

In addition, the Portuguese traded in African slaves. On Portuguese plantations in Brazil, African slave labor produced the sugar, which had been brought to Brazil from Africa and went on to form the bulk of Europe's sugar supply by the sixteenth and seventeenth centuries. The Portuguese also transported potatoes from Peru to Europe, with potatoes eventually becoming a staple food for the poor in many parts of Europe. Similarly, Portuguese ships transported maize and cassava (a starchy root plant) from Brazil to southwest Africa. Africans there cultivated these plants, which adapted well to the dry land. Portuguese became the language of trade in East Africa and in the Asian trade.

The Spanish took control over the Philippine Islands, and its capital city, Manila, linked Spanish trade in the Americas with the eastern trade. The Portuguese took silk to the Philippines, and the Spanish carried it to the Americas, where it was exported to Spain. The silk trade transmitted huge amounts of silver bouillon from the New World to Manila.

Thus, the Age of Exploration brought Europe into contact with not only the Americas, but with the Asian trade market. It forever changed the worldview of the Europeans and created the first global economy. Nevertheless, many parts of the world were not fully a part of the new global economy or played an unequal role in it. Russia, for example, was largely left out of the new economy. Other areas continued to focus on their own internal developments, and although they did trade in certain areas with Westerners, their economies were not transformed. Still other areas, such as China and Japan, sought to limit trade and contact with the West.

TEST TIP

The AP World History exam no longer penalizes you for wrong answers, so make sure to not leave any questions blank.

Changes in World Trading Patterns

The European explorations did not entirely obliterate the old trading networks. Prior to the European Age of Exploration, the Islamic world dominated the trade networks west of India, linking Africa, the Middle East, and parts of Asia to the Indian Ocean trade. On the eastern side of India, China dominated trade, linking India, Southeast Asia, and Central and Eastern Asia over the vast network of the Silk Road. China also controlled sea routes after the thirteenth century. India was the central link between these various powers and both their sea and land routes. The arrival of the Europeans did not disrupt the old trade routes nor make it impossible for Arab and Asian merchants to continue trade. Asian merchants continued to dominate trade in the seas connecting China to India, while Arabs continued to trade between the east coast of Africa and other parts of the Islamic world. However, Europeans gradually began to dominate shipping on some of these sea routes.

When the first Portuguese traders and explorers arrived in Calicut under da Gama, they brought little to trade beyond crude European iron pots, textiles, and coral beads. Merchants in the Indian markets were not interested in these goods, but rather in the exotic silks of China, its porcelain, and its paper. Indians also were not interested in European cloths, as India excelled in the production of cotton cloth. The one commodity that Europeans brought that did interest merchants in Calicut was silver from the newly developing Spanish empire in the Americas.

Aside from the silver and gold they brought, Europeans were also helped by the fact that in the areas where these trading routes converged, such as the Straits of Malacca, in Southeast Asia, and the Persian Gulf and Red Sea in the Islamic world, there was little in the way of centralized control over trade. Further, Muslims were deeply divided politically.

The rise of competing sects within the Islamic world, even in the early years following the death of Muhammad, contributed to deep political divisions. Lack of interest in European products by those in the East and European unwillingness to sacrifice all their supply of silver on trade for highly desired items made Europeans willing to use force to obtain their desired end. The Portuguese, for example, attacked ports along the African and Indian coasts, eventually controlling trade from places such as Malacca. Their ships were more heavily armed and larger than the ships of other traders, except for the Chinese. The Portuguese attempted to establish a trading monopoly in regions they conquered, and later, so too did the Dutch East India Company and other private companies.

Europeans had less success as they attempted to move away from the port cities and farther inland. Although in some cases they were able to subjugate native peoples and establish a tributary system, in general, their primary success was in the coastal regions. In places such as China and Japan, isolationism kept European merchants from making great strides inland, and in both cases, Europeans had special places to reside, from which they could trade, such as Nagasaki, Japan, where Dutch merchants lived in a special section. Lack of interest in European goods in China also kept trade from progressing further. China really had no need of imported goods, except that it did find trade for silver beneficial.

Impact of the New Economy on European Countries

Increased revenue from colonies in the Americas flooded European markets with silver and other wealth, which increased manufacturing in some parts of Europe. In Portugal, however, increased bullion was traded to other European nations, such as England, for goods, and in fact, ultimately discouraged manufacturing production in Portugal. Although the flow of silver into Spain from the New World was vital to the Spanish economy, it also had a negative effect, as the Spanish kept borrowing more and more money to fund their wars on the basis of expected silver shipments. By the eighteenth century, Spain's revenues from the Americas could no longer keep up with escalating debt, and other powers, such as England, rose to take its place.

Changes in Religions

New interactions between the Eastern and Western hemispheres, as well as shifts in political divisions and intensification of interactions within the two hemispheres, both helped to spread and reform several religions during the period between 1450 and 1750.

The Ottoman, the Safavid, and the Mughal empires arose in this period, and, despite their military conflicts, these three Turkish empires helped to spread Islam even further than in previous years.

- The rulers of the Ottoman Empire were Sunni Muslims, and as their empire expanded, Islam spread to new areas. However, as the Ottomans conquered regions in Europe and other areas of the world, they incorporated people from many religious traditions, including Christianity, into the empire. The various religious groups were known as millets (meaning "nations" or communities") and each had a patriarch that reported to the sultan. Each millet administered its own form of law and collected taxes for the government.

- In the Safavid Empire of Persia, there was an intensification of the split between the Sunni and Shi'a Muslims. The population had originally been Sunni, but sixteenth-century ruler Ismā'īl rigidly enforced Shi'a traditions and laws and forced the Sunni to convert to Shi'a.

- The Mughals spread Islam to their conquests of present-day Pakistan and Afghanistan, and also to the northern part of India. The Hindu people of India, however, were resentful of Muslim rule, and there was much tension between Muslims and Hindus.

Also in India, a new faith called **Sikhism** emerged around 1500 CE. The word Sikh means "disciple," and the Sikhs were disciples of the Guru. The Sikh religion taught that God was one with and present in all creation. The Sikhs believed that God could be directly apprehended by the human mind and thus, there was no need for churches, rites, or other practices. Since all humans had God within them, there were no castes. The Guru, the leader of the movement, revealed to his followers the Name of God, through which they could experience unity. In the eighteenth century, the Guru Gobind Singh transformed the Sikhs into a radical brotherhood, and the Mughal rulers regarded the Sikhs as heretics.

The Renaissance

The **Renaissance**, or "rebirth," is considered by many historians to be the beginning of the modern era. The Renaissance began in Italy, in part due to its unique economic position throughout the Middle Ages. After the collapse of the Roman Empire in the West, urban life virtually ceased to exist in Western Europe. The Italian city-states, however, survived, and had developed apart from many of the restrictions of feudal society.

Many merchant and banking families not of the hereditary nobility amassed great wealth, and this wealth helped to fuel the artistic Renaissance. Of these, the **Medici** family in Florence came to power after one of many peasant revolts in the wake of the Black Death. They were the bankers for the papacy, and they did business with merchants from England, France, and Flanders. They also had banking branches in Lyon, London, and Antwerp. The Medici lent money at exorbitant interest rates for wars or other endeavors to various European heads of state. With the revenues, they bought English wool, had it shipped to Florence, and exported the fabrics created with a large profit. The Florentine gold florin became the monetary standard for much of Europe. While the medieval Catholic Church taught that usury, or the making of a profit from interest, was a sin, the Renaissance redefined the role of money and profitable businesses.

The Medici were patrons of Michelangelo, Donatello, Botticelli, and many other artists. The explosion of artistic genius during the Renaissance was partly due to the fact that for the first time, artists were supported by wealthy patrons and had the time and financial resources to devote themselves to their art. The Italian Renaissance was in large part characterized by its fascination with the culture of Greco-Roman antiquity. The rediscovery of many ancient Greco-Roman scholarly manuscripts opened a new world to the humanists, as many ideas contained in them departed from those of the medieval Catholic Church. The humanists of the Renaissance found inspiration in the Greco-Roman interest in the human condition and in their belief in the power of human reason. The Renaissance zeal for Greco-Roman antiquity was one source of the humanist interest in individual achievement.

TEST TIP

Make a list or flashcards with important vocabulary words and brief definitions, such as *migration*, *imperialism*, and *socialism*.

The Protestant Reformation

The **Reformation** was, in many ways, an outgrowth of the Renaissance. It was also an outgrowth of centuries of general problems in the Catholic Church, dating back to the Babylonian Captivity of the fourteenth century and the Great Schism that followed. The corruption evident in the Catholic Church during these periods had sparked a great deal of dissent and literature of protest, despite the dominance of the Catholic Church in many aspects of society other than religion, including politics, art, and science.

In addition, the Catholic Church had become immensely wealthy by 1450. Many popes in previous years had come from rich Italian merchant families, and Catholic officials owned many valuable lands throughout Europe, which gave the Catholic Church widespread political power that caused resentment on the part of European kings. The Renaissance helped to create more criticism of the papacy and of the Catholic Church in general.

Between 1450 and 1750, the power of the Catholic Church dramatically declined. The rising power of European kings caused a decline in the pope's political power, and scientists, philosophers, and others wrote about ideas that challenged the Catholic Church. Starting in the early sixteenth century, the church's religious authority was seriously weakened by the Protestant Reformation, a movement led by **Martin Luther**, a German monk, believed that the Church was corrupt and needed to be reformed. Luther was incensed by the sale of **indulgences**, or payments to the Church that Catholics believed would ensure their eternal salvation in heaven. Luther disagreed with the Church's view that one could achieve true forgiveness and purity through acts of penance. Rather, he believed that no amount of outer penance could affect inner repentance, and that humans could never do enough good to earn salvation.

In 1517, Luther openly defied the Catholic Church by posting his Ninety-Five Theses on the door of the Church at Wittenberg. At the time, the pope was calling for indulgences to raise money for improvements to St. Peter's Church in Rome. Luther asked the Church to consider ninety-five points of dispute, among them the claim that the pope had no power at all to forgive sins. Luther believed that only God had this power. In his treatise, Luther also denied the value of Holy Orders or the validity of the priesthood. Luther argued that all Christians were able to be their own priests and to interpret the Scriptures for themselves.

Luther's writings initiated a massive social rebellion that would ultimately fragment the Holy Roman Empire. Many historians debate whether the Reformation would have happened or unfolded with the conflicts it did without the complicated set of social, political, and economic conditions that were evolving at the time in Europe. Luther's beliefs came to be known as Protestantism, and it became widely accepted in Germany.

Other Protestant movements emerged in France, and then in Switzerland, where John Calvin began a different type of Protestantism. Calvin believed that the Church should control the state, and, as Luther did, that the laity should control church affairs. Calvin advocated the idea of the calling, the notion of doing God's work as a holy endeavor. Calvinism spread to Scotland and then to England.

The Catholic Church was further weakened when King **Henry VIII** of England separated the English Church from Rome when the pope refused to grant him an annulment from his first wife, Catherine of Aragon. Holy Roman Emperor Charles V had invaded Italy in order to prevent the pope from annulling the marriage. In 1534, Henry proclaimed himself the head of the Church of England. He confiscated Church property, dissolved the Roman Catholic monasteries and took their land and other possessions, but everything else about the religion remained the same. The Church of England retained bishops, archbishops, and essentially the rest of the structure of the Roman Church without the pope.

By the end of the sixteenth century, the Roman Catholic Church had lost authority in many areas of Europe, including Germany and Britain. Although the Catholic Church fought the growing threat of Protestantism in a movement known as the Counter-Reformation, Europe remained deeply divided between Protestants and Catholics, which fueled numerous conflicts between European states.

New Forms of Social Organization and Modes of Production

During the period 1450 to 1750, agriculture again expanded dramatically and the demand for agricultural laborers increased proportionately. The thriving trade that was intensified by the Columbian Exchange also created a demand for workers to extract raw materials and produce finished goods in large quantities. Labor systems were transformed in many parts of the world, with an extensive slave trade between Africa and the Americas being a major economic factor of this era. Powerful gunpowder states emerged in Africa as a result of the thriving African slave trade.

Key Terms

Ashante	Dahomey	Ming dynasty
Benin	encomienda	mita
chattel	gun and slave cycle	mulatto
Confucian scholar gentry	indentured servitude	peninsulares
cottage industry	mestizo	Qing dynasty
creoles		

Agricultural Production and Manufacturing in China

The Ming Dynasty

The **Ming dynasty** (1368–1644) was the last native dynasty to rule China. Under the Ming, China experienced a great social and economic revolution. The Ming were also the first dynasty to interact with Europeans on a large scale.

Before the Ming, the Mongol conquest of China had left the border areas of China virtual deserts. In order to reclaim useless land, the Ming transferred a segment of their population to deserted regions. Irrigation pumps allowed peasants to introduce fish into the rice paddies. The fish fertilized the paddies and also removed mosquitoes, which often brought disease. The Chinese had learned to cultivate Champa rice, which could resist the effects of drought and could be harvested more quickly than traditional rice. Agricultural output rose dramatically, and from around 1550, so did the population of China. However, the greater output of crops did not mean higher income for the people. In fact, it was the greater use of peasants for labor that helped to fuel the growth of production. The expanding population increased the number of market towns, as people began to cluster together in towns. Greater population density in towns led to greater demand for goods. Consequently, trade and industrial development increased, despite the general disdain that the Confucian scholars had for merchants. Nanjing, for example, became an important center for textile production, and several other urban manufacturing centers evolved during the Ming dynasty.

The Ming created a functional division of the population, whereby anyone born a peasant, soldier, or craftsperson remained in that station throughout life. The system of taxation led to the need for a census, and the population was divided into groups of ten families responsible for levying taxes equitably among their members and for maintaining order. The poor of China often became dependent on the gentry. Taxes were paid in rice. Unlike the absolutist governments that were developing in Europe, though, the Ming failed to establish a central ministry responsible for taxation, and lack of centralization in this respect weakened the Ming government.

The Qing Dynasty

The **Qing dynasty** replaced the Ming in 1644 after devastating famine and plague created mass unrest in the countryside. Under the Qing, the population exploded; between 1650 and 1750, China's population tripled. China became the most populous region in the world, and included 30 percent of the world's population by 1750. The need to feed such a large population led to massive intensification of peasant labor in the agricultural sector. A huge part of Chinese land was devoted to agriculture, with farming being by far the main occupation. In addition, agricultural taxes contributed huge amounts of money to the government's coffers. Not only were peasants able to own land, but also, the government provided them with incentives to do so. Peasant farmers who were willing to relocate to outlying areas were given financial aid, farming tools, and seeds. Peasants who owned land were motivated to produce greater yields by using more efficient farming techniques and better crop varieties, such as fast-ripening rice, and also by growing maize and sweet potatoes, which were introduced in China by the Columbian Exchange.

TEST TIP

Make a timeline of the most important events for each era. As you study for the exam, go back to the timeline and review everything you know about each event on the timeline.

The Confucian Scholar Gentry

The Ming and the Qing retained the Confucian system of bureaucracy and placed great emphasis on the **Confucian scholar gentry**. Those who acquired wealth used it to educate themselves so as to acquire the status of a Confucian scholar. This class of scholars was known as the gentry. The importance of the gentry, however, was a contributing factor to China's failure to develop a large manufacturing sector. Although the Chinese were highly inventive, they focused their efforts during both the Ming and Qing dynasties on the Confucian literary classics, as opposed to the sciences. Further, the wealthy used their resources for education, rather than investing in business and manufacturing interests. According to Confucianism, merchants were parasites who did not produce anything useful for society. Confucians generally distrusted trade because it encouraged change.

Textile Production in India

By 1580, under the reign of the Mughals, India had developed a commercial economy based on capitalist enterprises. Manufacturing industries were present and were supported through a money economy. The chief export of India was cotton cloth made by artisans who worked at home, known as India's **cottage industry**. In this system, brokers provided materials and money to the artisans in return for finished cloth products. Women contributed to the success of India's cloth industry and wove the cloth in their homes. The cotton industry grew to such proportions that new road systems became necessary. Cloth was exported across the Indian Ocean to East Africa and from there across land to West Africa, across the Red Sea to the Mediterranean, up the Volga River to Russian cities, through the Persian Gulf to Persia, and also to China, Japan, and many other areas. The Indian trade, in fact, extended over a wider area of territory than did trade conducted by the Medici family in Renaissance Italy.

Goods were so much in demand from India that in 1695, English merchants asked their government to stop the importation of Indian cloth, still reflected in some modern English names for cloth, such as calico (derived from the name of the port city of Calicut) and muslin. The success of the Indian cloth industry created an imbalance of trade between India and the West. Their great affluence helped many Indian merchants to transcend earlier caste restrictions and to distribute wealth to groups outside of the traditional elite.

Slavery and the Merchant Class in Europe

The Renaissance humanistic veneration of the individual did not have an impact on slavery in European societies, where slaves served in the households of the elite. However, slaves generally were not used for labor in Europe, because by this time, most farms were small and family owned. Many slaves of this period came from Eastern Europe and were captured during wars. Venice was an important port through which many Slavic and Eastern Europeans entered Europe as slaves. The voyages of the Age of Exploration, which began during the Renaissance in the fifteenth century, brought many African slaves to Europe. Although most were concentrated in Spain and Portugal to serve the gentry, Italians also owned African slaves, and Genoa was an important port through which Portuguese traders often brought their African slaves. Despite the condemnation by the Catholic Church of the African slave trade and the lofty ideals of the humanists, Europeans had no apparent aversion to slavery in this period.

Many European merchants, such as the Medici in Venice, became enormously wealthy through long-distance trade with the Americas and the East. Because of their wealth, these merchants became elite members of society. They were able to increase their profits by commissioning the production of goods, allowing them to control the costs of the finished products and thereby also to control their internal markets.

Labor Systems in the Americas

Early Spanish conquerors in Mesoamerica and South America were mainly interested in the large deposits of gold and silver. They adopted the Inca system of forced labor called **mita** to obtain workers for the gold and silver mines. The Inca rulers had given men plots of land to work on in exchange for taxes and a rotation system of work on construction projects and other services. Usually, these men worked for the rulers for several months a year and then returned to their farms. The Spanish adopted the mita system by forcing Native Americans to work in the silver and gold mines. However, so many Native Americans died as a result of the harsh working conditions in the mines, and the diseases that they had contracted from the Spanish, that there were not enough of them to sustain the mita system.

The Spanish as well as the Portuguese also used Native Americans as forced laborers on large sugar cane and banana plantations in the colonies that they established in the Americas, for the Spanish, in Mexico and Peru; and for the Portuguese, in Brazil. The labor system that they used was called **encomienda**. Spanish conquistadors and Portuguese colonists with large land grants believed that they owned the native people who lived there. They forced native people to work on the plantations and also extracted tribute from them. As with the forced laborers in the Spanish mines, so many native people died as a result of grueling working conditions and disease that the encomienda system lasted only during the sixteenth century.

Slave Labor in the Americas

The development of colonies in the Americas by Europeans fueled the demand for workers after Native Americans died in large numbers from European diseases and mistreatment. Once Europeans had established colonies and plantations, there was an economic need to import large numbers of workers, both slaves and indentured servants. By the end of the seventeenth century, slaves made up fully one-half of Brazil's population, with most of those slaves having been brought from Africa.

Different forms of forced labor had long existed in Africa, the Middle East, and India. Some workers were peasants who worked to pay off debts, but most were slaves, who were bought and sold as **chattel**, or property. Many African kingdoms themselves had institutionalized slavery long before the arrival of the Europeans. These African kingdoms were eager to trade slaves for goods with Europeans when the demand for slaves arose. Sub-Saharan African economies were transformed by the prosperous slave trade and entered the new global economy. Trade with Europeans brought a new focus on transatlantic trade routes as opposed to earlier focus on the trans-Saharan trade. However, Arabs continued to dominate the slave trade across the Sahara, along the eastern coast of

DIDYOUKNOW?

The word *slave* is derived from the Greek word *sklabos*, the Greeks' name for all Slavic peoples. The word evolved around 580 BCE, when the Vikings began to capture Slavic people to sell to the Romans as slaves. Before then, the Latin word *servus* was used to refer to all kinds of servants, whether or not they were actually enslaved.

Africa, the Middle East, and India. These slaves were typically either porters who worked in the caravan trade, or women, who became part of the households of the Muslim men who bought them.

After the demise of the encomienda system in Brazil and the Spanish colonies, most African slaves were taken to work on sugar plantations in the Americas. European demand for sugar, especially by the English, continued to grow, and by about 1650, the Spanish had established additional plantations in present-day Jamaica, Cuba, and Puerto Rico. The British also established sugar cane plantations in Barbados, the Dutch in the Guyanas, and the French in Martinique and present-day Haiti. Each plantation typically had hundreds of acres of sugar cane fields, as well as a mill to process the raw sugar cane into sugar. For all of this grueling work on plantations in the Caribbean, thousands of slaves were transported there.

The French also established sugar plantations in present-day Louisiana in the eighteenth century. The growing demand for tobacco in England led to the development of large tobacco plantations in Virginia. Plantations with fields of tobacco and other crops, particularly cotton, spread throughout the southern colonies in North America, which required an ever-increasing number of slaves to work in the fields, as well as to serve in the households of wealthy plantation owners.

On the plantations of the Americas, the demand for male slaves was far greater than the demand for female slaves for females because of their strength needed for the arduous labor. The disproportionate number of male slaves meant that there were few African families. Also, in Brazil and the Caribbean, many slaves died from dysentery caused by contaminated water and malaria. Thus, the slave populations in most parts of the Americas did not grow but instead continued to decline, leading to a continuing need for more slaves. The southern plantations in North America were an exception; both female and male slaves were used in the fields, as well as in various household positions, and thus the slave population there had a positive growth rate.

Indentured Servants in North America

The English colonists in North America typically had small family farms, but trade in the cities was thriving. However, shopkeepers, craftsmen, and merchants had difficulty finding free workers. Instead of using slaves, they employed a labor system of **indentured servitude**, a legal agreement whereby they paid for the ship passages of young men and women, primarily from England and Germany, but also from Ireland and Scotland. These immigrants agreed to work for an indentured period of several years to pay their employers for the cost of their passages. Employers provided indentured servants with lodging, food, and training, but no wages. When these workers' period of indenture ended, they were free to leave their employers and pursue other opportunities. In the seventeenth century, about two-thirds of English immigrants to the colonies were indentured servants.

Race and Ethnicity in the Americas

In colonized areas of the Americas, racial and ethnic classifications changed radically as Europeans intermarried with natives. In the Spanish colonies in the Americas, for example, Europeans were considered to be of the highest status in the social structure, while slaves from Africa and Native Americans had the lowest status. In between, a whole new class of people arose who were of mixed ancestry, and these people primarily became farmers and shopkeepers. The designation for those of mixed European and Native American ancestry was **mestizo**, and the designation for those of mixed European and African ancestry was **mulatto**. This group of mixed people, made up of both the mestizo and the mulatto people, was called the castas. Although those of European heritage who were born in the Americas, called **creoles**, had a high social status, Europeans who were originally from the continent, called **peninsulares**, were the elite class.

Impact of the Slave Trade on Africa

The long-standing practice of slavery in Africa and the existing slave trade with Muslims and other peoples of the Middle East helped the Europeans to quickly obtain large numbers of African slaves. The rulers of African kingdoms were eager to supply slaves to the Europeans in exchange for goods. African rulers typically did not enslave their own people, but instead led raids and captured Africans from groups other than their own. They would then take them to trading ports on the eastern coast for European ships to transport them to the Americas. In the sixteenth century, the slave trade was concentrated along the west coast of Africa. In the seventeenth century, it shifted to West Central Africa. Later, areas of southwestern Africa, known as the Gold Coast and the Slave Coast, were important suppliers of slaves.

The impact of the slave trade on many African societies was profound, and its expansion, spurred by the Europeans, transformed many African states and societies. The region of western Africa, in particular, was very unstable at the beginning of this period. There were frequent wars resulting from relatively small states seeking to expand their territories and consolidate their military power. These ongoing wars and the great profits to be made from the slave trade became part of the politics of the states of West and Central Africa. The states that were most involved in the capture and enslavement of millions of their neighbors became increasingly centralized and developed more hierarchal societies, with warriors rising to great social status. Rulers of these states typically used rituals to reinforce their authority and they established elaborate courts. In contrast, the societies that suffered from slave raids became anti-authoritarian and self-sufficient.

Several large kingdoms developed or grew more powerful in Africa during the era of the European slave trade. With increasing access to European firearms, horses, and iron, West and Central African kingdoms began to expand their influence toward the western coast. The desire to control the slave trade continued to fuel wars among many African kingdoms and cause the disruption of societies as the search for slaves pushed ever farther into the interior. The link between firearms and increased trading in slaves, leading to further acquisition of firearms and the renewal of the cycle, has been called the **gun and slave cycle**.

The **Ashante** of the Gold Coast rose to prominence in the seventeenth century as a result of the slave trade, especially after acquiring firearms. The Ashante were members of the Akan people who lived between the Atlantic coast and the northern trade centers. The Akan had about twenty small, loosely knit clans, but, after obtaining guns around

1650, they came together and became centralized. They created the position of the **asantehene**, who established unity among the diverse clans and became their supreme political ruler and religious leader. The supreme ruler was advised by a council, and he instituted a series of military reforms to facilitate more conquests in the region. The Ashante controlled large gold deposits in the region and became the dominant supplier of slaves on the Gold Coast, both of which they traded for firearms in the gun and slave cycle. By the end of the seventeenth century, about two-thirds of the Ashante's trade was based on the sale of slaves.

TEST TIP

For each essay question, be prepared to develop an in-depth, convincing, and solid critical analysis of the topics about which you're writing. It is more effective to accomplish this by using the third-person point of view and the active voice to show confidence in your position. Avoid the use of such timid phrases as "My opinion would be . . . ." or "I think that it might . . . ."

On the Slave Coast, east of the Gold Coast, **Benin** was a strong kingdom when the slave trade with the Europeans began. However, in the beginning of the sixteenth century, the king of Benin limited the slave trade, preferring instead to trade in goods. However, by the eighteenth century, the desire of the nobility in Benin to acquire more wealth, along with pressure from European traders, led to Benin becoming prominent in the slave trade on the Slave Coast. Even so, slavery was never the primary focus of Benin's trade economy or its politics.

The kingdom of **Dahomey**, about seventy miles west of the Gold Coast, emerged in the seventeenth century by dealing in the slave trade. Like other African states that rose to power during this time, Dahomey used profits from the slave trade to obtain more and more guns, which it used to conquer smaller states and thereby expand its kingdom. Dahomey was the most highly centralized state in Africa at the time, with its kings being absolute monarchs. The kings directly controlled trade and the armies that made conquests and went on slave raids. A regiment of women was part of the Dahomey army; they later became the personal guards of the kings. When the Dahomey conquered other kingdoms, they eliminated their royal families and customs, imposing Dahomey traditions on them. As a result, the Dahomey territories became a unified kingdom that was able to retain power for several centuries.

Some historians have estimated that between 1450 and 1750, about 10 million West and Central Africans were transported across the Atlantic as slaves, with more than

1 million dying during the long and difficult journey. In part, the increasing number of slaves transported over the centuries was due to their huge mortality rate, both from the inhumane conditions on the slave ships and the difficult working conditions at their destinations. Further, since many more men than women were transported, the proportion of women to men was inflated in West and Central Africa. The transatlantic trade did bring the benefit of new crops, such as maize, to those areas depopulated through the slave trade, which provided a new food supply and helped those areas to recover from population losses.

State Consolidation and Imperial Expansion

During the period between 1450 and 1750, empires and states in both the Western and Eastern hemispheres became more centralized as rulers sought to consolidate their power. Many states limited the power of the nobility and established systems of taxation that placed a great burden on peasants, which sometimes led to peasant revolts. The expansion of European empires was facilitated by the use of cannons, guns, and

Key Terms

Abbas I	Kremlin	samurai
absolutism	Magna Carta	Spanish Armada
boyars	Manchu	Sufi
constitutionalism	Mughals	Suleiman the Great
Cossacks	Ottomans	Taj Mahal
daimyo	Ottoman-Safavid conflicts	Tokugawa Shogunate
devshirme	Peter the Great	viziers
gunpowder empires	Safavids	
Janissaries		

domination of maritime trade routes. Land-based empires that emerged in the East also relied on the use of guns obtained from Europeans to expand their territories; these were called the gunpowder empires.

Centralization of European Maritime Empires

Between 1450 and 1750, the European feudal kingdoms of Portugal, Spain, France, England, and the Netherlands had become wealthy and powerful enough to sponsor the maritime voyages of exploration that led to colonization of the Americas. Portugal was the first European kingdom to explore distant lands, partly because of its geographical location on the Atlantic Ocean and its long seacoast with good harbors. However, during the sixteenth century, the Portuguese slowly faded as a power while Spain claimed and kept more and more land in the Western Hemisphere. In addition to Spain, France and England rose to become the most powerful European kingdoms with strong centralized governments, powerful armies, and various policies that limited the power the nobility. The kings and queens of these kingdoms financed their expeditions with various taxes and fines; in England, King Henry VIII amassed even greater wealth when he split England apart from the Catholic Church and confiscated its property.

The Dominance of Spain

The marriage of Ferdinand and Isabella in 1469 united Aragon and Castille and created a strong new Spain. The wealth generated from the Spanish colonization of the Americas and the trade that it generated greatly strengthened the Spanish monarchy. The power of Spain also propelled it to leadership of the Catholic world.

The Hapsburgs had first become rulers of Austria in 1278, and also ruled Spain, large parts of the Holy Roman Empire in Central Europe, and the Netherlands. The Austrian Hapsburgs ruled over a tremendously diverse group of people, making it very difficult to achieve any kind of unity. At its height, the empire contained most of the territory of modern Germany, Austria, Slovenia, Switzerland, Belgium, the Netherlands, Luxembourg, and the Czech Republic. It also contained parts of eastern France, northern Italy, and western Poland. Emperor Charles V, the grandson of Ferdinand and Isabella, eventually became unable to control the various territories of the empire and their rulers. Charles was forced to defend his eastern territories from the invasion of the Ottoman Turks into Hungary and the siege of Vienna in 1529. Charles defeated the Ottomans, but they continued to threaten parts of European for many years thereafter.

However, Charles abdicated his throne in 1556. Consequently, the Hapsburg holdings were divided between an Austrian and a Spanish line. To his brother Ferdinand in Austria, Charles ceded the Holy Roman Empire, while to his son Philip II, he ceded his personal kingdom of Spain. Philip also encountered threats from the Ottomans, but in the Mediterranean rather than in the east. In 1571, the combined navies of Spain, the Vatican, and Venice defeated the Ottoman navy on the coast of Greece at the Battle of Lepanto, slowing the Ottomans' advances to the west and denying them access to the Atlantic Ocean and the Americas. However, the Ottomans continued to dominate much of the land bordering the Mediterranean.

The intense orthodox Catholicism of the Spanish monarchs attracted the attention of the Catholic queen Mary of England. Mary was a staunch opponent of her father Henry VIII's break with the Catholic Church. She married Philip to restore Catholicism to England. When she died, Philip launched the **Spanish Armada**, the largest naval fleet ever assembled, against her Protestant half-sister Queen Elizabeth I of England. In 1588, the small but fast ships of England grounded the legendary Spanish Armada before it could attack, thus assuring the success of the Protestant reformation in England. Despite this defeat, the Spanish retained great power and wealth at the close of the sixteenth century.

Absolute and Constitutional Monarchies

Spain and France

Spain, as well as some other powerful new European kingdoms, including France, had become an absolute monarchy, with the king or queen having supreme power. Such rule was called **absolutism**, which was reinforced by the belief in the divine right, or the god-given authority, of the monarchs to rule. Kings and queens were thought to be God's rulers on Earth, with the divine right to rule absolutely and alone, with no one else having the right to share the power to make decisions with them, including the nobility.

France developed a strong monarch in the 1460s under King Louis XI, who gained control of the taille, an annual tax on land and property. He used the funds from this tax to strengthen his control over troublesome provinces such as Maine, Anjou, and Provence. However, absolutism was firmly established in France in the early seventeenth century by Cardinal Richelieu, King Louis XIII's chief minister. Richelieu severely curbed the power of the nobility by burning their castles and quashing all attempts to conspire against Louis XIII. He also established a bureaucracy that collected taxes and looked out for the interests of the king. Louis XIV was a later absolutist French king, whose reign lasted for seventy-two years and ended with his death in 1715. Louis XIV believed that all things revolved around him and called himself the Sun King, often saying, "I am the state," to impress upon others his absolute authority. To limit the ambitions of the French nobility, Louis XIV invited them to stay for long periods at his magnificent palace at Versailles, where they enjoyed a life of luxury. While the nobility remained occupied at Versailles, they were under the watchful eye of the king, away from their castles, and unable to start any conflicts with him.

TEST TIP

Most multiple-choice questions on the AP World History exam are not "recall" questions that simply require you to select a one-word or one-phrase answer; the questions require you to think and reason in a deeper way and apply your knowledge.

England and the Netherlands

England and the Netherlands developed **constitutionalism** rather than absolutism. Although neither state had a written constitution, they each placed limitations on the power of the monarchs. The nobility in England had the right to confer with the king or queen before he or she imposed new taxes, which had begun in the eleventh century under William the Conqueror. England had a long tradition of representative government going back to 1215, when English barons made King John sign the **Magna Carta**. The Magna Carta established the concept that the king, just like everyone else in society, was subject to the law, and it also listed the rights of the nobility. These rights developed in the English governmental body of Parliament, which entered into the English Civil War with King Charles I in the 1640s. Parliament won the war, thereby reinforcing the limitations of the monarchy in favor of a constitutional government. Merchants participated in the government because their wealth was essential to the English economy.

When Philip II of Spain suppressed political liberties and the growing Protestant movement in the Netherlands, William of Orange led a revolt against him in 1568. Under the **Union of Utrecht**, signed in 1579, the seven northern provinces of the Netherlands became the United Provinces of the Netherlands and agreed to support each other against aggression by Spain. In 1588, the provinces became a republic. The new constitutional government was limited to protecting life and property. There was no monarch; instead, merchants were prominent in the government councils that were established, and disputes were settled peacefully for the most part.

The centralization of governments in Europe in both absolute and constitutional monarchies was essential in their departure from feudalism and the building of powerful states and, eventually, the empires that arose from colonialism.

Land-Based Gunpowder Empires

In most of the Eastern Hemisphere, land-based empires remained dominant between 1450 and 1750, in contrast to the maritime empires of Europe. In the era between 1450 and 1750, some of these land-based empires, called **gunpowder empires**, increased dramatically in size, largely because of their immense armies and their use of guns. The gunpowder empires included the Ming and Qing in China, the Ottoman Turks and the Safavids in Southwest Asia, the Mughals in India, Japan, and the new Russian Empire. All had large land armies armed with guns. These empires developed relatively independently from Western influence, and to some extent they counterbalanced the growth of European power and colonization.

Gunpowder Empires in China

The Ming Dynasty

Hong Wu, the first emperor of the Ming dynasty (1368–1644), was himself a peasant and had led a successful peasant revolt against the Yuan dynasty of the Mongols. The peasants had resented the Mongols for giving the most important official positions to Mongols, and they also believed that the Mongols had lost the Mandate of Heaven.

Hong Wu instituted an absolute monarchy, comparable to that established by Louis XIV. He was very conscious of his peasant origins and so distrusted the nobles and scholars. He forced the nobles to live at his court and to participate in many elaborate rituals designed to establish the court as divine and all-powerful.

The Ming revived the civil service system of exams and created a three-part exam that was held at the district, provincial, and imperial levels. These extensive examinations were very difficult to pass; only about ninety scholars a year passed them. The exams supported the Confucian ideal that advancement should be on the basis of competence as opposed to high social standing. They also emphasized the importance of an orderly hierarchy of authority, with respect due to one's superiors. The Ming emperors did not tolerate dissent, and only those who abided by Ming philosophies passed the exams.

The maritime voyages started by the third Ming emperor ended in 1435. Although the voyages of Admiral Zheng He had generated tremendous wealth for those involved, resentment on the part of the Confucian scholarly gentry likely led to the renewed emphasis on agriculture, in keeping with the first Ming emperor's style of government. The Chinese also developed a policy of isolationism from the West and allowed their once-renowned navy to decline.

The European voyages also had a major impact on China's economy. Plants from the Americas led to agricultural reform in China, as maize and sweet potatoes became staples of the Chinese diet. These products could flourish in poorly irrigated areas. Silver mined in the Americas also made its way across the globe, and about one-half of it ended up in China. Goods from China's various craft industries, such as silk and lacquerware, were in great demand in other parts of the world, and China received a disproportionate share of American silver. Merchants from Europe began to trade in the Chinese cities of Macao and Canton. The influx of silver from the Americas made it possible for the Ming to take thirty or forty different types of taxes and reduce them to a single one payable in silver. This was known as the **Single Whip Reform**. So much silver came into China, however, that by 1620, its value had dropped by over two-thirds. The previous Ming emperors' practice of issuing more and more paper money had lowered its value to one-fortieth of its original worth and caused economic inflation. The country's financial base was seriously weakened.

Ming emperors spent great amounts of money supporting the aristocracy with maintenance payments. Some had as many as ninety-four heirs and relatives. Many expeditions against the Mongols had forced the Ming to levy higher and higher taxes. They built lavish tombs while the peasantry suffered. Later Ming rulers did not handle the demands of the bureaucracy well, and they also had to contend with pirate raids along the coast from the Japanese as well as Mongol attacks.

The Qing Dynasty

In 1644, the **Manchu**, members of the Jurchen dynasty of Manchuria, overthrew the Ming. The Manchu looted Beijing and set up a civil administration, whereby a Manchurian prince administered each ministry, or board. Each prince had five assistants, including at least one Mongol and one Chinese. The Manchu renamed themselves the Qing, meaning "pure," to avoid the negative associations with the third century BCE Qin Empire. However, with the dominance of the Manchurians and the presence of Mongols in the government, the Qing dynasty was far from "pure" from the Chinese point of view. The Manchu adopted the Ming system of the bureaucracy and its civil examinations, and a large number of the Chinese scholar-gentry held positions in the

Manchu government. The Manchu also retained the court ceremonies and much of the political system of the Ming, but they became more directly involved in appointing local officials.

The Manchu tried to quell the prevailing peasant unrest and hardship by lowering the taxes and labor requirements. They also attempted to limit the amount of land that the nobility could acquire, and they repaired roads and irrigation systems. However, the Manchu were largely unsuccessful in many of these efforts, as the population continued to expand rapidly while available land to accommodate them did not. The gap between the landowning nobility and the peasants continued to widen.

At the same time, urbanization and commerce expanded during the first centuries under the Manchu dynasty. Silver continued to flow into China in exchange for Chinese goods. Under Emperor Qianlong (1736–1796), China had become a land-based gunpowder empire that controlled the largest expanse of territory in its history, including Mongolia, Tibet, Nepal, Taiwan, and portions of Central Asia.

Qianlong also sponsored a compilation of the Confucian Classics called the Five Classics, a standard of Chinese learning. Literature flourished during the Qing period, including China's greatest novel, *The Dream of the Red*. The Qing interest in learning earned the loyalty of the literati, who had opposed the Ming as repressive.

The Muslim Gunpowder Empires

Three powerful Muslim gunpowder empires, the Ottomans, the Safavids, and the Mughals, arose from their nomadic Turkish roots with military conquests based on the effective use of guns and coerced, but highly trained, warriors. Once they came to power, all three empires had absolute monarchs who modeled their courts on those of earlier Islamic dynasties and spread Islam to new areas through their religious zeal.

The Ottoman Empire

The **Ottomans** were a Turkish dynasty of the Sunni branch of Islam that rose to prominence when Mehmed, the Turkish name for Mohammad, conquered Constantinople in 1453. Mehmed's success was largely due to huge cannons, developed for his forces by a Hungarian engineer. One cannon was 26 feet long and 8 inches in diameter and could fire a 1,200-pound ball as far as 1 mile. Mehmed attacked the walls of Constantinople from the west, the only part of the city not protected by water.

Under the next two rulers, called sultans, the Ottomans became an Asian as well as a European militaristic power. After conquering Mecca and Medina, Sultan Selim took the title of caliph, or successor of Muhammad. This title had not been used since the Mongols captured the capital of the Abbasid caliphate, Baghdad, in the thirteenth century.

The further conquests of Selim's successor, Sultan **Suleiman the Great**, earned him the title of the "protector of the sacred places," which were Mecca and Medina. Suleiman extended the Ottoman Empire to Mesopotamia (in modern Iraq) and parts of present-day central eastern Europe. He captured Belgrade in 1521, and in 1526 the Ottoman Turks defeated the Hungarians. Suleiman besieged Vienna from 1526 to 1529, and although he failed to take the city from Holy Roman Emperor Charles V, the Ottomans remained a continuous threat to the Western European states. Suleiman's presence in Eastern Europe contributed to the ferocity of the wars of religion, as he aided Protestant nations in an effort to destabilize Europe.

Suleiman built magnificent walls around Jerusalem which still surround the Old City today. Under Suleiman, the Ottoman Empire reached its high point, encompassing the area from Hungary to Yemen on the Saudi Arabian Peninsula and Persia, including dominance of the Mediterranean Sea and the Black Sea, which is bounded by Eastern Europe, Central Asia, and Turkey, with an outlet to the Mediterranean.

The Ottoman Military and Government

Suleiman controlled the aristocracy by creating the **devshirme**, a system of conscripting Christian boys from the provinces, raising them as Muslims, and using them as soldiers. Although many improved their lot in life through the devshirme and families often competed for the honor, these boys were essentially conscripted slave soldiers. As the system evolved, it became highly selective.

The Christian slave soldiers came to be the elite force of Ottoman infantry soldiers known as the **Janissaries**. Members of the Janissaries could not wear beards, as free Muslims did, and could not marry until 1566. Their chief loyalty was to the empire, and they were taught to consider the sultan their father. Since the empire controlled their property, there were no claims

DID YOU KNOW?

The Ottomans expanded their empire into Europe through the use of a mobile cavalry composed of highly skilled mounted archers called *gazis*, whose tactics were to rapidly attack and retreat on horseback. However, the gazis were tribal Turkish Seljuks, and they were often unwilling and unequipped to go on lengthy military campaigns and to set up permanent military stations in the Balkans to control Ottoman conquests. The Ottomans then supplemented the gazi cavalry with a permanent infantry that included the Janissaries.

based on heredity from members of their families. One of the most famous boys who began their careers through the devshirme was the architect Sinan, who built more than 400 beautiful buildings and mosques, including the Suleymaniye Mosque, which blended Islamic and Byzantine architectural features.

The Janissaries' control of artillery and firearms gave them great power. Starting in 1449, they led revolts against the government and demanded higher wages and other rewards. By 1683, the Janissaries had become so successful that the sultan abolished the devshirme, allowing Turkish boys to enter the elite ranks. Through palace coups, the Janissaries succeeded in controlling the sultanate. The conservatism of the Janissaries helped to isolate the Ottomans from cultural influences of the West.

Suleiman also restructured the Ottoman legal system. He codified a system of laws dealing with cases not covered by the Islamic Shari'a, and created a military state, in which the school of study of Islamic law was a part of the government. The Ottomans used **beys**, or provincial governors, who collected taxes from the tribal chiefs and who had both administrative and military control. Muslim laws did not supersede tribal laws in the Ottoman Empire; when the Ottomans conquered Byzantium, they adapted their leadership to Byzantine customs. The sultan became more powerful at the expense of tribal leaders, and his position was a hereditary one. The administration was centralized at the imperial palace. The sultan's orders were channeled through the imperial court, led by his chief minister, the **vizier**. Often a vizier rose to power through the devshirme system. Many bureaucrats under the vizier were also drawn from the devshirme. Merit played an important role in advancement.

Provinces and districts continued to be run in much the same way as when the old tribal leaders controlled them. The sultan granted land as fiefdoms in exchange for military support to the most important leaders in the provinces, who were often descendants of the tribal beys. These leaders, in turn, divided their lands among their own military leaders, whose salaries came from taxes collected from peasants.

The Safavid Empire

The **Safavid** rulers of Persia were descendants of **Sufi** mystics, who rejected all worldly pleasures and possessions in favor of a life of complete dedication to and worship of Allah. In the early fourteenth century, they fought to purify Islam and spread it throughout the Turkish people. In 1501, Safavid leader Shah Ismā'īl I led his army, which was equipped with guns, to defeat the Turkish ruler of Iran. The population of Iran had originally been Sunni, but Ismā'īl did not tolerate the Sunni form of Islam and rigidly enforced Shi'a traditions and laws.

Safavid-Ottoman Conflicts

The Safavids had ongoing wars with the Ottomans known as the **Ottoman-Safavid conflicts**. The Ottomans defeated Ismāʻīl and his forces at the Battle of Chaldiran in northwestern Iran in 1514, largely because of the Ottomans' greater arsenal of guns. This was a huge loss to the Safavids in that Shi'ism was prevented from advancing farther westward. Under **Abbas I** (1587–1629), the Safavid Empire regained the strength it had lost after the death of Ismāʻīl. Abbas I consulted with English advisors to help him reorganize and train his army in the use of guns and cannons. He also established a centralized administration and treasury for the organization, training, and funding of the army. With his professional forces, Abbas I drove out the Ottomans where they had invaded Safavid territories and conquered most of Persia, defeating the Ottomans in Iraq and Azerbaijan, largely with the use of guns and the help of British mercenaries. There, Abbas I continued Ismāʻīl's efforts to eradicate the Sunni sect of Islam and forced his conquests to convert to Shi'ism. The Ottoman-Safavid conflicts were a major influence in defining some of the boundaries and Islamic divisions in the Middle East that still exist today. For example, the border of Turkey and Iran was determined, as was the border of Iran and Iraq.

The Safavdis controlled the Turkish warrior-leaders and granted them fiefdoms with peasants who labored in agriculture fields and paid tribute. Some of these Turkish leaders attained important positions in the government and posed a constant threat to the shahs. To counterbalance their influence, the shahs brought Persians into the bureaucracy. Like the Ottomans, the Safavids captured young men and trained them to serve in the military and the bureaucracy. These slaves often rose to high positions in the government and the army.

Under Abbas I, the Safavid Empire was at its peak. The capital of the empire was Isfahan, one of the most architecturally renowned cities in the world, with its impressive mosques, expansive courtyards, and detailed decorations. Many of its buildings were constructed during the reign of his great-grandson, Abbas II. Later, the severity of the rule of Shah Hussein led to revolt among Sunni Afghans, who forced the abdication of the shah in 1722. After a brief period of Afghani rule, Tahmasp II recovered the empire for the Safavids. General Nadir Khouli (1736–1747), who had recovered much territory that had earlier been lost to the Ottomans, eventually became the shah and abandoned Shi'ism as the official religion of the empire. Persian became the common language in Safavid lands. The art of the Safavid kingdom reflected Chinese and other Asian influences.

The Mughal Empire

The **Mughals** were descendants of the Mongols from Turkestan, and they brought further Persian influences to India, especially that of Sufi mysticism. The Mughals were not the first Muslim power in India, as southeastern India was ruled by the Delhi sultanate, whose ruler was an Islamic Turk. The Mughal leader Babur, a descendant of Genghis Khan, rose to power in 1483 and conquered Afghanistan and the Delhi sultanate. Babur's Mughal Empire was also a gunpowder empire, and his success may be attributed in part to the arrival of the Portuguese in 1510, who greatly weakened the Delhi sultanate. Although Babur's army was small, its firearms more than made up for their numbers.

Shah Akbar continued the wave of conquests started by Babur. By the time of his death, he had conquered most of northern India and Afghanistan. His empire was larger than Babur's, and he believed that any empire not expanding must be in decline. Akbar's empire, like that of Babur's, was a gunpowder empire, as much of his success was a result of his use of heavy artillery. Negotiations and other military tactics also contributed to his success, as well as skill at leadership and religious zeal. Akbar's rule was benevolent, as he canceled the poll tax on non-Muslims and was tolerant of all faiths. He stopped the pilgrimage tax on Hindus, and so earned their support. Many Hindus served in his bureaucracy, and he allowed Hindus to be governed by their own law as opposed to the Muslim Shari'a code of law.

Shah Jahan continued Akbar's wave of conquests, capturing parts of the Deccan Plateau in southern India and turning back the Portuguese intrusion at Bengal. He moved the capital from Agra to Delhi and built a magnificent palace for himself within the famous Red Fort. His peacock throne symbolized the success of the Mughals, and some have estimated that it cost as much as $5 million in today's money. Shah Jahan's most famous project was the **Taj Mahal**, built to commemorate the memory of his wife and to display the wealth and power of the Mughal Empire. It took more than 20,000 people to build the monument, which was intended to be representative of paradise. Shah Jahan's military conquests and the expense of the lavish tomb, however, caused him to raise taxes from the one-third of the crop value paid under Akbar to over one-half of the crop value. The heavy tax was a burden for poor Hindus.

Japan

In 1467, there were almost 260 feudal houses, or **daimyo**, in Japan. Each daimyo was independent and maintained its own separate army. This period is commonly called Warring States in Japan. Powerful warlords arose, such as Nobunaga, who tried to remedy this situation by taking strong control of the daimyo. He destroyed the Buddhist monastery on Mt. Hiei, as the monks there had often been involved in Japan's political and military struggles. To further thwart the influence of Buddhism, Nobunaga encouraged Christianity and was especially interested in the teachings of the Jesuits. He also embraced the use of Western firearms and retrained his army to accommodate new weapons, built stone forts, and became the first Japanese leader to clad his ships in iron. Nobunaga, however, never managed to eradicate the warring lords, and he was assassinated by two of his generals in 1582.

Hideyoshi was the son of a peasant who became the complete master of Japan by 1590. Hideyoshi, like the Hong Wu emperor of Ming China, was concerned about the ability of people from lower classes, such as himself, to rise to power. Consequently, he froze the social classes, making class status permanent for people and their children. In 1586 he ordered farmers to stay on their land. Hideyoshi gave the **samurai**, who had helped to create the chaos of the Warring States and who were the professional soldiers of Japan, special status. In 1587, Hideyoshi decreed that only the samurai could carry their famous long swords and wear armor and only the samurai had last names; others in Japan were simply known by their functions. Hideyoshi invaded Korea in 1592 and 1597 in order to prepare for an eventual invasion of China. However, he died without accomplishing this goal.

In 1600, Ieyasu Tokugawa began a process that would eventually create a centralized government and unite Japan as another gunpowder empire, the only one that was not land-based. The emperor gave Ieyasu the title of shogun, or chief military leader. The **Tokugawa Shogunate** relied upon the domain system, and the shogun became the most important leader in Japan. Under the Tokugawa shoguns, the emperor lived in Kyoto, while the shoguns resided in Edo, a city that later became known as Tokyo. The emperor became a mere figurehead, and the daimyo became vassals of the shogun.

Various methods of controlling the daimyo were developed, such as the requirement to march to the shogun's court in Edo every year. At the court, they were forbidden to draw weapons, and along the way, daimyo stopped at inns of the shoguns, thus generating revenue for the shogunate and keeping the daimyo under control as they marched.

Their absence from their territories further contributed to their inability to wage wars with one another or revolts against the shogun.

The Forty-Seven Samurai Revolt

There were about 2 million samurai during the Tokugawa period out of the 30 million of Japan's total population. One of the most famous events of the period is that of Lord Asano and his forty-seven samurai. Lord Asano was angered by Lord Kira while at the shogun's court and drew his sword against him. He was ordered to commit seppuku (self-disembowelment while still alive). According to the samurai code of honor, this was the only way to restore honor when a samurai disagreed with and then morally protested an order of the shogun. Asano's samurai believed that he had been treated unjustly by Kira and the shogun, and so plotted their revenge. For two years they gave the appearance of accepting the verdict and watched Asano's estate dismembered while they lived as unemployed samurai. Two years later, they stormed Kira's palace and killed him. Because they had violated the shogun's codes, they too committed seppuku. The forty-seven samurai remain the greatest heroes of Japanese literature.

Japan and the West

During the Tokugawa period, Dutch traders appeared in Japan. They were restricted to the port of Dejima in Nagasaki. Jesuits also were in Japan, but while Hideyoshi had allowed them to teach to thwart the influence of Buddhism, Ieyasu ordered them expelled in 1616. Those who failed to leave were killed, and converts to the faith were executed or forced to recant. The shogunate adopted an increasingly isolationist strategy and expelled all Westerners after 1638. The Tokugawa forbade Japanese to travel abroad. Japanese isolationism resulted in the development of an interest in Japanese culture. A branch of scholarship called kokugaku, which means "native studies," became prominent in this period. Since the Japanese had long been greatly influenced by China, it had always been difficult for them to separate out their native traditions, such as Shinto.

TEST TIP

Make sure that you carefully read all parts of the essay questions and follow the directions as closely as possible. Quickly review the essay question a few times as you are writing your response and when you finish writing to be certain that you've addressed everything in the question.

The Russian Empire

Before the fifteenth century, Russia, with its Byzantine-influenced culture, had few interactions with other parts of the world. However, during the period between 1450 and 1750, Russia formed new connections with the West while retaining its unique culture.

Russia had a history of autocracy beginning with Tsar Ivan III, who annexed other Russian principalities and defeated the Mongols in 1480. Ivan III ruled with a military focus, and he used nationalism and the Orthodox Christian religion to unify the large independent Russian state. Tsar Ivan IV continued his father's policy of expansion, conquering the Tartars and establishing a kingdom that went all the way east to the Urals and west to Poland and Sweden. He greatly increased his power as tsar by killing many of the, **boyars**, or nobility, based on charges of conspiracy, which earned him the name of Ivan the Terrible.

Both Ivan the Terrible and his father were well aware of their cultural and economic inferiority to the Europeans under Mongol rule, so they began to initiate contacts with the West. Ivan III began a series of diplomatic missions to European states, and Ivan the Terrible established trade with English merchants. The two tsars invited Italian artists to collaborate with Russian architects to build Byzantine churches and the **Kremlin**, a huge complex that included the palaces of the tsar, the governmental administrative center, and other monuments. These buildings, which had a distinct and majestic style of architecture, were a public display of the tsars' power.

The Russian tsars continued to expand into Central Asia, advancing to the Caspian Sea, the Ural Mountains, and western Siberia. To conquer and occupy new lands, the Russians recruited **Cossacks**, nomadic descendants of peasants who had fled the taxes and other obligations of feudalism, and who had acquired great military prowess and horsemanship. As the Russians acquired new agricultural regions and labor sources in their new territories, they gave land grants to loyal boyars and bureaucrats, who used both peasants and slaves for labor. Russian expansion, as well as Ottoman expansion to the south, eliminated Central Asia as a threat by nomadic invasions and enabled Russia to establish trade with Asian empires. With the diversity of cultures in the lands it conquered, Russia became multicultural and tolerant of different cultures, and it did not force the large Muslim population that it then controlled to adopt Russian culture.

Following the death of Ivan the Terrible, there was chaos during the "time of troubles," which lasted from 1604 to 1613. The boyars became more powerful and elected Michael Romanov as tsar, since he was not a member of any faction. Michael restored order to Russia, drove out Polish and Swedish invaders, and continued the expansion of Russia.

Michael's son, **Peter the Great**, continued the policies of his father, but he wanted to revolutionize Russia's mainly agricultural economy and its culture by adapting Western systems. Peter was well aware of Russia's need to have access to warm-water seaports on the Baltic Sea, as well as the inferiority of the Russian army against European forces. In his youth, Peter was exposed to Western scholars. While traveling incognito in Europe, he became interested in shipbuilding and navigation, as well as other forms of technology and science. He brought 1,000 Western experts to Russia to bring it in line with Western technological advances. This was the first time in history that a society had deliberately attempted to Westernize. However, Peter was an autocratic ruler and brutally suppressed all revolts against him. He solidified his power by recruiting bureaucrats who were not aristocrats and used secret police to guard against dissent. Peter also reorganized his army and modeled it after Western armies. He implemented the use of European officers and Western uniforms, drew soldiers from each territory, and armed his regiments with Western guns and cannons, so that by 1704, Peter led his forces to victory against the Swedes. This gave Russia Estonia, Livonia, and part of Finland, and most importantly, his long-sought presence on the warm waters of the Baltic Sea, which enabled Russia to become a major force in the diplomatic and military affairs of Europe. To facilitate this, Peter established his new capital, St. Petersburg, on the Baltic coast.

The Modernization of Russia

St. Petersburg was known as the "window to the West," and it symbolized a revolution in Russian society and the Westernization of Russian belief systems. It was a new city facing Europe, and Peter gave very favorable terms to foreign merchants. He also secularized the Russian Orthodox Church and created the Holy Synod, headed by the Procurator, who was a government official and directly controlled by the tsar.

To limit the power of the boyars, Peter created the Table of Ranks, according to which a person's rank was independent of his or her noble status. Rank in society was equated with rank in Peter's bureaucracy, and he required service to the state. The new government was organized into ten territorial governments. There were no heads of departments, but rather committees to run affairs of state. Peter supported his new, Westernized state with taxes on almost everything, including a tax on each person, which Russians pejoratively referred to as the soul tax. Previously, taxation had been by household, and it had been possible for many people to avoid paying taxes.

Peter brought new industries to Russia, which had been primarily a backward agricultural land, and introduced to Russia the concept of conscripted labor utilizing peasants. His reforms, however, further distanced the aristocracy from the rest of the population. The boyars spoke Western languages, while the peasants spoke Russian. The condition of the serfs was worse than ever before, and Peter regarded them as brutes for their lack of the new Western culture and exploited them as a supply of cheap labor. Peter the Great was one of the most hated rulers during his time in world history. The Russian Orthodox Church deeply resented his reforms, and those dedicated to Russian culture were in open revolt. Nevertheless, Peter is justifiably credited for dragging Russia "kicking and screaming" into the modern age.

Time for a quiz
- Review strategies in Chapter 2
- Take Quiz 4 at the REA Study Center
  (www.rea.com/studycenter)

Unit V: Industrialization and Global Integration, c. 1750 to c. 1900

Chapter 15

Industrialism and Global Capitalism

Europe dominated the world during the period between 1750 and 1900, in part because of its expanding control of maritime trade and its colonization of other parts of the world. While the large, Asian land-based empires retained influence in their own geographical region, the European countries came to have significant control over the Eastern Hemisphere as well as the Western Hemisphere. The collective series of events that led to European hegemony was the Industrial Revolution.

Key Terms

Banana Republics	internal combustion engine	second Industrial Revolution
bourgeoisie	limited liability system	spinning jenny
communism	Marxist socialism	steam engine
cotton gin	Meiji reforms	Suez Canal
Crimean War	mercantilism	textile manufacturing
factory system	Mitsubishi Company	Tsar Alexander II
first Industrial Revolution	Panama Canal	United Fruit Company
Hong Kong and Shanghai Banking Company	power loom	upper-middle class
insurance companies	proletariat	water frame

The First Industrial Revolution Begins in Britain

The **first Industrial Revolution** began in the late eighteenth century in Britain and later spread to other parts of Europe, such as France, Belgium, Germany, and eventually to the United States. There were reasons why this revolution occurred in Britain: it had many natural resources, such as good water supplies for mills and steam power, harbors for ships, rivers for the inland transportation of goods; and raw materials needed to produce goods, such as coal and iron. The geographic location of Britain, for the most part, protected it from invasion, and it enjoyed internal political stability and peace between 1750 and 1900. It also did not have the constraints of an absolute monarchy; by 1750, Parliament was more powerful than the monarchy, and it enacted laws that encouraged the development of capitalistic enterprises. In addition, economic structures and systems were in place, including banks that loaned money to businessmen; and the growing middle class was very much involved with the manufacturing and trading of goods.

England was also the dominant power in maritime trade in the eighteenth century. After a series of wars with the Dutch, Great Britain went on to win victories against the French in the War of the Spanish Succession and the Seven Years' War (also called the French and Indian War) in North America. The success of Britain in these wars helped to build its vast network for trade, and Britain's colonies provided yet another outlet for trade. The stage was thus set for the Industrial Revolution, which occurred in two phases.

The Textile Industry

The Industrial Revolution began in the area of **textile manufacturing**, Britain's chief industry. The British had long been in search of newer and cheaper ways to make cotton. In 1733, John Kay invented the **fly shuttle**, a machine that was able to weave thread together better than a one-person loom. It performed the work of two weavers and increased the speed of weaving, as the shuttle was passed mechanically across the warp threads. Prior to this invention, a person could not weave a piece of cloth wider than the human body, as the shuttle had to be passed from hand to hand. The fly shuttle cut in half the cost of labor, and in 1753, weavers sacked Kay's house in protest. In 1760, James Hargreaves invented the **spinning jenny**, a device named for his wife. The jenny could spin eight spindles of thread at once and later was expanded to a sixteen-spindle device. This was the first machine to improve on the spinning wheel. In 1769, Richard Arkwright became the father of the Industrial Revolution when he produced the first power-driven spinning mill, the **water frame**. It took six spinners to keep a weaver busy, and although the spinning jenny helped that situation, it had to be operated by highly skilled laborers. Arkwright's invention eliminated that difficulty and produced stronger warp thread. It also enabled the rise of the **factory system**.

The first factories were very small in comparison to modern factories. In the early eighteenth century, most manufacturing was done in homes in the countryside. The system of sending out raw materials and farming out manufacturing work to country homes was known as the cottage industry. The invention of the spinning jenny and other devices made work in cottage industries more efficient, and eventually, other inventions, such as Edmund Cartwright's **power loom** and Eli Whitney's **cotton gin** (1793), helped to fuel the growth of factories. The cotton gin mechanically removed the seeds from raw cotton, which was a laborious process by hand. It caused the demand for and supply of cotton to increase dramatically, thus contributing significantly to the use of slavery in the Americas. The manufacture of cotton in England increased fivefold after 1793. By 1820, cotton made up one-half of all its exports.

As the Industrial Revolution progressed, more and bigger factories that produced diverse finished products were established, requiring workers to leave their homes and go to work in centralized locations. Many workers became specialized in the type of work that they did.

DIDYOUKNOW?

Eli Whitney and his busines partner, Phineas Miller, produced as many cotton gins as possible and distributed them throughout the South. Instead of selling the machines outright, since they were essentially doing the ginning for the farmers, the partners chose to charge farmers two-fifths of the profits. Farmers resented having to go to Whitney's gins and having to pay an exorbitant fee, so copies of Whitney's gin, what were dubbed as "new" inventions, began to surface. Because Whitney had patented his invention in 1794, costly lawsuits followed. However, due to a loophole in the wording of the 1793 patent law, Whitney and Miller did not win any of these lawsuits until 1800 when the patent law was changed. Deep in debt due to continuing lawsuits, Whitney's cotton gin company went out of business in 1797. To view Whitney's 8-page request in 1812 to renew the patent on his cotton gin, go to the National Archives (www.archives.gov) and search on ARC Identifier 306631.

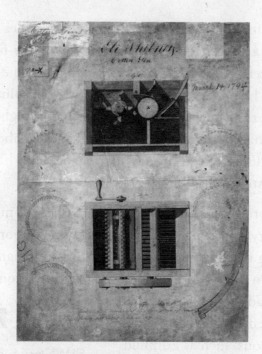

Figure 15.1. Eli Whitney's 1794 patent request for the cotton gin (numbered X-72).

The Steam Engine

During the 1700s, there was a severe wood shortage in England that led to the search for other sources of fuel, such as coal. Coal, however, was deep in the ground and demanded new techniques to get it out of deep shafts and to pump out the water that inevitably filled the shafts. Thomas Newcomen invented the first **steam engine** in 1702, and James Watt further perfected it in 1763. The steam engine transformed the iron industry in Britain, and the production of coal also rose dramatically. The steam engine created a revolution in transportation when Robert Fulton used it in his riverboats in 1807, and in 1829, George Stephenson invented the Rocket, which used the steam engine to power a locomotive. The Rocket traveled at 16 miles per hour from Liverpool to Manchester. The steam engine on boats and locomotives made travel much more efficient between various parts of England—and later other parts of the world. It also increased trade and contributed to the expansion of the economy.

The Industrial Revolution did spread to other parts of Europe, but not all areas industrialized at the same speed or in the same way. In fact, by 1815, the gap between Britain and continental Europe was even wider than it had been in the early phases of the Industrial Revolution. Unstable political conditions in continental Europe and the expense and skill required to implement Britain's increasingly complex technology made it difficult for other European countries to keep up with advances in Britain. This was true in areas outside of Europe as well. European colonies were generally not as industrialized as the countries that controlled them; Britain, for example, exported manufactured goods to India and attempted to confine the Indian economy to the production of raw materials for export to Britain.

The Second Industrial Revolution

The development of more efficient ways to produce iron with the steam engine in the first Industrial Revolution fueled a **second Industrial Revolution,** which began in 1870, also in Britain. Greater availability of iron encouraged the building of railroads. In the nineteenth century, railroads expanded virtually across the world. Although they brought many benefits, the railroads also contributed to the decline of Native American lifestyles in the American West and of tribal cultures in Africa, and they negatively impacted the indigenous cottage industries of India. Steel made possible the production of lighter and smaller machinery, and the Industrial Revolution of the nineteenth century was centered on the production of steel to produce railroad tracks. New industries, such as the electrical industry, arose to meet demands for new sources of power. Hydroelectric power industrialized Italy, which had never had adequate supplies of coal to compete with Britain in the early phases of the Industrial Revolution. The development of the **internal combustion engine** led to the rise of the automobile industry in the early twentieth century.

During the second phase of the Industrial Revolution, Germany overtook Britain as the industrial leader of Europe. The United States became another leading manufacturer, particularly in the steel industry. After the American Civil War (1861–1865) ended, the construction of the transcontinental railroad was completed, allowing travel and the transport of goods from the east coast to the west coast of North America. The United States had an abundance of natural resources necessary for industrialization, including vast coal and iron deposits, as well as many rivers to supply power to mills and steam engines. In the late nineteenth century a wave of millions of immigrants from Europe and Asia provided a large pool of cheap labor.

The gaps between industrialized nations and the areas that technology had not yet reached became even larger during the second phase of the Industrial Revolution. Southern and Eastern Europe remained well behind Britain, Germany, Belgium, the Netherlands, and northern Italy. Russia, Spain, Portugal, the Balkans, and most of the

Austro-Hungarian Empire continued to have an agricultural economy, and they served to produce the raw materials and basic food supply for the industrialized nations.

Industrialized Countries' Consolidation of a Global Economy

The industrialized countries were those that had wealth, natural resources, and the support of their governments. The countries that were industrialized became the economic powers of the world, as well as the military and political powers. Throughout the world, an inequity in the wealth and quality of life of industrialized versus unindustrialized countries resulted, as did a worldwide division of labor. The workers in unindustrialized countries, which were often European colonies or former colonies, supplied the raw materials needed for the production of manufactured goods, and the workers in industrialized countries produced the finished goods. Increasing industrialization created a demand for more and more raw materials, such as coal, iron, and cotton. In particular, the British Empire took advantage of industrialization to expand and meet the growing demand for raw materials, as well as to develop outlets for its manufactured products.

Growth of the British Empire

Mercantilism

British colonial rule was based on the economic philosophy of **mercantilism**, a theory articulated in detail by Scottish economist Adam Smith in his 1776 book *An Inquiry into the Nature and Causes of the Wealth of Nations*. According to mercantilism, colonies supplied raw materials for the mother country and also could be subjected to taxes and other economic policies. Smith's philosophy also inspired the development of capitalism in the period of industrialization; he believed that self-interest and competition would lead to economic prosperity; he justified the use of free markets, and explained how the division of labor begins the process of economic growth and the accumulation of capital keeps it going. Britain expanded its use of financial instruments to facilitate its industrial production.

Britain quickly stepped into the vacuum that was left when the Latin American countries gained their independence from Spain and Portugal. Britain became the dominant economic power through the sale of manufactured goods to the Latin American countries, especially in Brazil. Latin American countries grew more and more dependent on foreign imports until around 1850, when their economies revived as the Industrial

Revolution in Europe and the United States resulted in demand for more and more raw materials. The economies of Latin American countries, as well as India and parts of Asia and Africa, became dependent on the production of a single raw crop, especially bananas, cotton, rubber, sugar, and palm oil. Those countries that were exploited by industrialized countries—and whose economies were controlled by industrialized countries—for a single agricultural crop were called **Banana Republics**.

The economic vitality in Latin American countries after 1850, however, had negative consequences for the people who lived there. In Brazil, for example, owners of large tracts of land increased their holdings to meet the demands for increased exports, dispossessing poor farmers from their lands. Most of the plantations and mines that produced the crops and raw materials in Latin America were owned by foreign investors, who reaped the profits of their exportation. The vast majority of Latin Americans were poor laborers or farmers with little money to spend, and therefore, internal market economies did not develop there.

The American Civil War's disruption of the American cotton trade prompted the British to search for a new source of cotton in India, so Indian cotton began to be produced for export rather than for internal use. Simultaneously, the British imported textiles, and these imports undermined the native Indian market for finished cloth. India had once been the principal producer of cotton cloth, but it was transformed into a consumer of British imports and Britain's chief supplier of raw cotton. English goods produced by machine weakened the market for the traditional Indian village artisans. Poverty increased and Indian agriculture collapsed. A serious drought in the 1870s created widespread famine throughout India.

A new means of exploitation by the British came with the discovery of diamonds and gold in 1866 and 1867, respectively, in South Africa. In 1889, British businessman Cecil Rhodes founded the South Africa Chartered Company to mine the diamonds in the Zambezi Valley, and other mining companies soon followed. The production of diamonds dramatically increased, and a once extremely rare material became available to Western society, with its growing wealth. Within a decade, 90 percent of the world's diamonds were being mined by British and Dutch companies in South Africa.

TEST TIP

Always include dates in your essays. This will help demonstrate the precision and richness of your knowledge.

Developments in Transportation, Communication, and Financial Institutions

The advancements in financing, transportation, and communications that occurred during the nineteenth century revolutionized commerce worldwide. New transnational banking practices enabled investors to access and dominate markets throughout the world, and these investors and their companies became extremely wealthy and politically powerful. Steam-powered boats made previously inaccessible regions more accessible, and new canals enabled steamships to travel to remote parts of the world more quickly. The **Suez Canal,** built between 1859 and 1869 in Egypt between the Mediterranean Sea and the Gulf of Suez, a northern part of the Red Sea; and later, the **Panama Canal,** built between 1904 and 1914 across Panama between the Atlantic and Pacific Oceans, linked oceans and seas and made trade between industrialized countries and their less-industrialized markets and sources of raw materials more profitable. Communication was also revolutionized by the development of undersea telegraph cables, which were capable of transmitting messages, for example, from Britain to India in about five hours. Railroads also greatly contributed to the ease and efficiency of moving large quantities of goods for long distances overland, and also to port cities, where goods could then be shipped by sea.

Financial Institutions and Instruments

England had had a long-standing and close relationship with Holland since about 1730, although it had also been competing with the Dutch in world trade markets. The Dutch were one of the prominent colonial states in Europe in the Age of Exploration, with trade centers in the Americas, Asia, and the Pacific. The Dutch had developed new financial mechanisms to handle both the risks and market opportunities of their trade networks. They had created a system that spread the risks of a company, enabling businessmen to invest in the company and earn profits while not having to face the possible loss of the entirety of their investments. This was the **limited liability system**, whereby investors were responsible for a company's debts and losses only to the extent to which they invested in the company. If the company were to lose everything, the investors would lose only the amount of money that they invested in the company. The limited liability system greatly decreased the risk of investment ventures, especially for overseas trade, which had become inherently risky. The system greatly encouraged investment and the growth and expansion of businesses. To further reduce the risks of business enterprises and make it easier to invest in companies, the Dutch had also established a stock exchange, a central bank, and the first **insurance companies**, which covered losses resulting from both long-distance and internal trade, thereby reducing the risks involved in establishing and operating business ventures.

The English learned about these innovative financial instruments through their close association with Holland, and they gradually introduced them into England. These financial instruments and the economic stability of Britain created an ideal situation for the buildup of capital, the creation of businesses, and eventually, large-scale manufacturing in Britain. The British also developed their own financial innovations and laws to become the leading competitor for international trade and the expansion of their colonial empire. One of the first of these was the Limited Liability Act of 1855, which was intended to encourage investment during the Industrial Revolution. Under the act, a company with more than 25 shareholders and shares valued at 10 pounds or more was granted limited liability upon registering with the Registrar of Joint Stock Companies.

Transnational Companies

The Hong Kong and Shanghai Banking Company

After the British acquired Hong Kong as a colony in 1842, European merchants doing business found that they needed a local bank to finance the heavy transnational trade between China and Europe. In 1865, the **Hong Kong and Shanghai Banking Company** was established, with one center in Hong Kong and another center in Shanghai. The bank was incorporated in Hong Kong by a special dispensation from Britain's Treasury Department. The Hong Kong and Shanghai Banking Company issued its own local denomination of bank notes, and, in 1874, it made the first public loan in China and afterwards handled most others. Under the British Parliament's Hong Kong and Shanghai Bank Ordinance of 1866, a new branch of the bank opened in Japan.

The United Fruit Company

Large-scale global trade also led to the development of the U.S.-based United Fruit Company. An American, originally from a business family in New York, named Minor Keith left his cattle ranch in Texas when his uncle offered him a contract to help build a railroad in Costa Rica in 1871. The railroad was to extend from the Costa Rican city of San Jose to the coastal port city of Limon. As he was working on the construction of the railroad, Keith planted banana trees on the land beside the tracks. When the railroad was finally completed, the banana trees were flourishing: Keith owned three banana companies, and the railroad conveniently offered a means to transport the bananas to

Limon, where they were exported to the United States and Europe. Keith organized the Tropical Trading and Transport Company, with the help of British banks, to transport his increasing banana shipments to the United States. The new company also controlled the internal banana market of Costa Rica. In 1899, Keith joined with Lorenzo Baker and Andrew Preston of the Boston Fruit Company, which was his main business rival, to form the **United Fruit Company**, thereby creating the biggest banana company in the world. The United Fruit Company dominated the banana trade, and owned plantations in Costa Rica, Colombia, Nicaragua, Panama, Santo Domingo, Cuba, and Jamaica. It also owned a fleet of steamships, called the Great White Fleet, as well as more than 100 miles of railroad track that connected the plantations to port cities.

Responses to Global Capitalism

While factory owners and other businessmen from industrialized countries were becoming quite wealthy, the lives of the working class were often miserable. Millions of people labored in factories under dismal working conditions and still made barely enough money to survive. Many workers who were resentful of the way in which capitalism exploited them while their labor helped others to become rich organized themselves to try to gain better working conditions and higher wages. Some thinkers of the time, particularly Karl Marx, shared the workers' opposition to the capitalistic exploitation of their labor, and developed new ways of thinking about capitalism and society.

Marxism

Marxist socialism arose following the publication of Marx's *The Communist Manifesto* in 1848, in which he advocated the interests of the working class, or **proletariat**. Marx believed that capitalism exploited workers and widened the gap between the rich and the poor. Further, he envisioned that the conditions of the working class in capitalist countries would eventually become so intolerable that workers would join together in a revolution against the industrialists who controlled the "means of production," whom he called the **bourgeoisie.** Marx believed that after this revolution there would be no social classes because ownership of private property would not be permitted; there would be no cause for greed or strife, and therefore no need for a government. This would lead to true **communism,** a society of equality and cooperation. Marx's view of history relied upon the notion that class conflicts over economic issues drove the events of history. Marxist ideas that workers had the right to organize and negotiate for better wages and working conditions took root in several European countries, although communism did not become the foundation of any governments in Europe. However, Marxist communism would later be reinterpreted and implemented in Russia and China in the twentieth century.

TEST TIP

To help prepare for the AP exam, make a list of people who had important roles in world history, such as rulers who made significant changes in their states or empires, thinkers whose ideas affected society, and people who led major revolutions.

European Revolutions

In 1848, revolutions spread across Europe, largely because of the economic hardships caused by rapid industrialization. Factory workers protested working conditions, women demanded greater rights, and workers skilled in traditional crafts worried about the loss of the market for their labor. Social movements such as nationalism, liberalism, and socialism brought diverse groups together, all striving to better their society. The revolutionaries of this time were primarily bourgeoisie, wealthy members of society who controlled the means of production. The bourgeoisie protested their conservative, reactionary governments. Romanticism encouraged further innovative thinking, as literati and artists broke out of the cultural confines of classicism. Revolts occurred throughout Europe that affected France, Italy, and Germany, and the Austrian Empire. For example, the people of Paris revolted in February, forcing King Louis Philippe to abdicate. He abdicated in favor of his grandson, but the people would not accept another king. A provisional republic was declared and the Second Republic was born. This first French revolution was interested in social reform and reform of the government and working conditions. It freed colonial slaves, abolished the death penalty, and recognized rights for the working classes. Only England and Russia were spared from the revolutions of 1848. By the end of 1849, the revolutions had failed, but the idea of revolutionary social change would live on.

The Industrialization of Russia and Japan in the Nineteenth Century

In response to growing concern about the inequities caused by capitalism, some governments implemented various types of reforms. In a few countries where industrialization was not developing, such as Russia and Japan, governments took matters into their own hands and initiated state-sponsored policies to bring their countries into the age of industrialism.

Russia

The Crimean War served as a motivating force for change in Russia and forced its leaders to realize that Russia was a barely industrialized, agricultural backwater compared to the rest of Europe. During the **Crimean War,** Russia had fought and lost against the much more technologically sophisticated forces of France and Britain for control of the territories of the crumbling Ottoman Empire. If Russia was to keep up with the industrialized world, great changes would have to be undertaken, and so, in the latter half of the nineteenth century, **Tsar Alexander II's** government embarked on a program of social reforms and modernization schemes.

In 1861, Alexander freed the serfs. No longer tied to the land by servitude, they were allowed to own land. This was a major step forward for Russia, but it was not as revolutionary as it might have been, for while the serfs were free to own the land, they could not own it outright as individuals. They had to own it as part of their local community or village. The serfs were free, but yet still bound if they could not buy their land. They remained in a state of temporary obligation, but the tsar did implement legal reforms abolishing traditional punishments for serfs.

Reforms also implemented changes in local government, as local councils regulated roads and made other decisions instead of the aristocrats who had formerly owned the serfs. However, the local councils had no say in Russia's national policies and thus political life in Russia remained largely unchanged. Alexander II had seen the need for reform, but the measures his government enacted did not go far enough to suit everyone. In 1881 he was assassinated when a bomb was tossed into his carriage.

Tsar Alexander III was naturally affected by his father's violent death and remained steadfastly opposed to political reforms. He was not blind to economic realities, however, and so it was in his reign in the 1890s that Russia truly joined the industrial revolution. Alexander initiated construction of railroads to link places within the vast reaches of Russia. The Trans-Siberian railroad track was built between 1891 and 1904, connecting the capital city of Moscow to Vladivostok, a port city on the Pacific Ocean, and thereby greatly facilitating trade. The railroads also created access to Russia's numerous coal and iron deposits. By 1900, Russia ranked fourth in worldwide steel production. In just forty years, Russia advanced from being a static, agricultural nation to being a world leader in the production of steel and oil. Missing from the newly industrialized

Russia, however, was a middle class of professionals, such as those that developed in Western Europe following the Industrial Revolution there. Despite the reforms, Russia remained backward in terms of agricultural techniques and consequently was still largely a peasant society. Also, foreign investments resulted in Russia becoming a debtor nation. Further, heavy taxes on imports had still not enabled Russia to export more products than it imported.

Japan

The Japanese government also instituted profound economic changes. Beginning in 1868, the Meiji emperor fought against the growing impact of Western imperialism in Asia by purchasing Western interests in businesses and discouraging foreign investments in Japan. Under other **Meiji reforms**, trade rules favored exportation rather than imports. Foreign loans were repaid and no more were taken out. The Meiji regime raised revenue through a new agricultural tax of 3 percent and formerly private domains were ceded to those who worked the land. The new tax raised needed revenue, but often proved disastrous to the farmers.

Much of this revenue was channeled into industrial development, and government banks provided capital to promote industries, such as shipbuilding, chemicals, and weaponry. The government implemented improvements in transportation and communication, and subsidized industries with financial grants. A system of state education was developed to provide training in areas beneficial to industry, such as science. Exports of tea and silk generated tremendous revenue. Some samurai went into industry, such as Iwasaki Yataro, who founded the **Mitsubishi Company**, which was to become a transnational corporation. Mitsubishi received many government contracts, as did other Japanese companies.

Western models were often imitated, especially in the educational system. Japanese students traveled, were educated abroad, and brought back Western ideas. Other aspects of Western culture, such as art and architecture, also influenced the Japanese during this period. Although tensions erupted in Japanese society over new Western influences, the government retained control of the industrialization process through the Ministry of Industry, created in 1870, and channeled other tensions into nationalistic pride. Farmers who lost their lands because of their inability to pay the new agricultural taxes migrated to urban areas, where they provided a source of cheap labor. Conditions in Japanese factories were as bad if not worse than many of those in Europe during the Industrial Revolution. Workers who attempted to escape their miserable plights were often shot.

By 1900, Japan was the most industrialized country in Asia. While Europeans had industrialized over the course of more than a century, the Meiji regime industrialized Japan in less than forty years. Some historians point out that Japan adapted more readily than China to Western models because Japan had been accustomed to borrowing from other cultures, as it had from China.

Social Changes

Urban Life

City life increased dramatically as a result of the Industrial Revolution. The population of the cities expanded in industrialized countries; for example, the industrial city of Manchester, England, increased in population from 25,000 in 1772 to 455,000 in 1851. By the mid-nineteenth century half of the English population lived in cities, whereas before the Industrial Revolution most lived in the country. A similar trend occurred in the late nineteenth century in North America; following the second Industrial Revolution, great numbers of people began to move from rural areas to urban areas. Such a rapid rate of expansion naturally led to problems in urban areas, such as unsanitary conditions and overcrowding. Slums developed in the factory cities, and whole families lived in single rooms or on the streets.

Urban planning became important, especially after 1850. In Paris, for example, urban planners such as Georges Haussmann built wider streets and tore down many of the slums. Better housing districts arose complete with city parks. Paris also established an improved water supply. During the second phase of the Industrial Revolution, other urban centers began to implement similar renewal projects.

TEST TIP

Approximately ten to fifteen of the seventy multiple-choice questions on the AP World History exam will require you to read a passage or interpret an image, map, or chart.

Working Conditions

During the first Industrial Revolution, working conditions in the factories were, for the most part, squalid. Because workers in the cottage industries were often unwilling to work in the conditions of the new factories, many factory workers were paupers and abandoned children. Even after Britain banned the use of pauper children as apprentices in factories in 1802, child labor and long hours were common. Workers had few or no rights in the early factories and received no workers' compensation for injuries, which were frequent; no minimum wage, no breaks, or other rights.

In 1833, Britain restricted the hours that children could work, and this may have helped create a new division of labor not previously present in European society. The cottage industry was run by families, and families went together to the new factories. When children could no longer completely share the parents' work schedule, it became difficult for women to work at the same jobs as men. Factory life was regulated in a way that life in the country was not, and it was often much more difficult for a woman to work in a factory and raise a child. Men were paid more than women, and those women who did work outside the home generally came from the lowest classes. In general, women could not make enough to support themselves.

However, whereas the first Industrial Revolution disrupted gender roles and family life, the second Industrial Revolution provided a more stable context. The distinction between gender roles for women and men continued to grow wider in the late nineteenth century. When middle-class women's work again became more restricted to the home, women gained a great deal of autonomy over the running of their homes and the raising of their children. There was more attachment between children and their mothers. Women also generally had fewer children, and the birth rate dropped. The roles of women had changed dramatically from what they had been just a few decades earlier.

Class Structure

The class structure of Europe and other industrialized areas, such as the United States, became more complex in the nineteenth century. While the average level of income increased in the Industrial Revolution, the gap between the rich and the poor segments of society persisted. The working classes, which included agricultural laborers and accounted for as much as 80 percent of the population, collectively earned less than the wealthy elite and the middle class together. The Industrial Revolution created a new group of people in the middle class, and this group was extremely diverse. New industries created a demand for highly skilled workers, and each of these groups of workers were largely separated from the others by competing interests and lifestyles.

A new **upper-middle class** also emerged; it consisted of the most successful industrial business families. After the revolutions of 1848 failed, many of these people had moved away from their radical leanings of earlier years and more toward the aristocracy.

Gradually, they developed a lifestyle similar to the old aristocracy that was financed by their new wealth. Below them were less-successful merchants without the great wealth of the industrialists, but nevertheless, they were successful and secure. This group included professionals in law, medicine, and other areas.

Small-business owners formed another diverse subclass of the middle class, and as industrialization created demands for new products, a larger array of these businesses continued to develop. Those working in areas that demanded specialization, such as engineering, were another subclass. Highly skilled workers became almost a new kind of aristocracy within the working classes. A new class of white-collar workers also emerged in businesses and distinguished themselves from those who worked with their hands.

Industrialization also created new opportunities for leisure activities, as subways and streetcars enabled people to travel for recreation. Organized team sports became popular. Mass events such as fairs also became a significant aspect of life in urban areas. Finally, industrialization created a greater need for educated workers. Compulsory education became common in the West. A drive for voter's rights also contributed to the need for education. Daily life changed greatly in the eighteenth and nineteenth centuries, because industrialization resulted in dramatic changes in gender roles, the structure of the family, and working conditions.

Chapter 16

Imperialism and Nation-State Formation

Europeans had established colonies in other parts of the world since the Age of Exploration. Thus, in the late nineteenth century there was really nothing new about Europe extending its control and power over other parts of the world. Europeans first used the word **imperialism**, however, in the mid-nineteenth century to describe the web of transoceanic colonial empires that they had built beginning in 1870. The word refers to the European domination of other nations and cultures, such as those in Africa and eastern Asia, the only parts of the world not already dominated by Europeans. However, other nations besides those in Europe also became imperialistic in the late nineteenth century. In Asia, Japan developed into an imperialistic power and expanded its holdings;

Key Terms

Afrikaners	imperialism	scientific racism
Belgian Congo	Louisiana Purchase	Sepoy Mutiny
Berlin Conference	manifest destiny	social Darwinism
colonization	Meiji Restoration	South African Republic
East India Tea Company	Muhammad Ali	Tanzimat
French Equatorial Africa	Opium Wars	The Monroe Doctrine
French Indochina	Pan-Slavic movement	Treaty of Nanjing
French West Africa	Russo-Turkish Wars	viceroy

in North America, the United States developed an expansionist philosophy and acquired large new territories.

In this era, the word **colonization** took on a new meaning that referred to the political, economic, and social structures created by Europeans in foreign lands that supported their efforts to dominate native cultures. Many political leaders viewed imperialism as the only way to preserve national security, and they also saw new colonies as a possible outlet for the population explosion brought on by the advances of the Industrial Revolution. Further, industrialization had created a need for raw materials to support European manufacturing. Colonies provided a means of obtaining raw materials, as well as an outlet for manufactured goods. Parts of Europe were greatly overpopulated, and another motivation for imperialist expansion was to create opportunities for Europeans elsewhere.

Consolidation of Imperialist Power

Imperialism in Africa, India, and parts of Asia created a system whereby these continents were economically, politically, and socially subjugated to European powers. The long-term effects of imperialism lingered even after the Western powers lost their colonies as a result of the global wars of the twentieth century.

Perhaps the most frightening tools of the imperialist age were accurate rifles and machine guns. The power of these weapons is illustrated by events in 1898 near Khartoum, when a British force with only 20 machine guns killed a force of 11,000 Sudanese men. The British were fighting for their lives against the Mahdi, who led a massive insurrection against Turkish rule in Egypt, but the Sudanese were no match for machine guns. They eventually established a regime in the Sudan, but not before the Mahdi defeated British General Gordon Pasha in a shocking victory at the Sudanese capital of Khartoum in 1885. The Mahdi died shortly thereafter, with shock waves still emanating through the British Empire. Four years later, the British, under Lord Kitchener, led a combined force of British and Egyptians to Khartoum and recaptured it. In 1889, they did eventually succeed in gaining control of the Sudan and continued to do so until the Sudanese won their independence in 1956.

TEST TIP

Remember that you need to sign up for the AP exam at least several weeks before the test date, so be sure to talk to your AP teacher or your school's AP coordinator about taking the exam well before the scheduled exam time. If you are home schooled or if your school does not offer AP programs, you can still take the exam. However, you will need to contact AP Services directly to learn how to register. Usually, you need to do this by the beginning of March to take the exam in mid-May.

The British in India

By the 1850s, the British had established rule in India. As a result of the Industrial Revolution, their continuing need for raw materials and outlets for their manufactured goods prompted further expansionistic tendencies. Intense rivalry with France in the eighteenth century also played a role in British expansion. British imperialism was motivated by a desire to protect its national security and to develop outlets for its goods, especially after the loss of the North American colonies as a result of the American Revolution. Following these events, its colony in India took on special significance.

After the British established factories at Bombay, Madras, and Calcutta in the seventeenth century during the Mughal period, the **East India Tea Company** expanded to the interior of India and bit by bit won rights to govern areas there. Robert Clive defeated the army of the ruler of Bengal in 1757. He bribed the ruler's soldiers and his chief rival, and thus began the British Raj domination of India and the transformation of the East India Tea Company from traders to the rulers of Bengal, and eventually to all of India.

In the 1760s, the British defeated their French rivals for India, thus paving the way for complete domination. In 1765, the East India Tea Company acquired the right to collect revenue in the name of the Mughal emperors in the Bengal region. British rule in India would last nearly two hundred years. In 1803, British General Wellesley, who was governor-general of British India, continued to expand British control when he defeated the Maratha chieftains. He began to build an empire in India through conquering the forces of several native rulers or making treaties with them.

The Sepoy Mutiny

The British controlled their conquests with British forces, supplemented by larger numbers of Indian troops called sepoys. Rebellions against the British culminated in the

1857 **Sepoy Mutiny**. The chief cause of this revolt was the refusal of the Hindu troops to use animal grease on the cartridges of their Enfield rifles. Soldiers had to bite off the ends of the cartridges to load the rifles, which violated both Islamic and Hindu beliefs. Muslims worried that the fat might be from pigs, which were prohibited animals under their dietary laws; while Hindus feared it was from cows, which were prohibited by their beliefs. By June, nearly 90,000 troops—about 70 percent of the Bengal army's sepoy force—were involved in the mutiny. The sepoys defeated the British in several battles, but the British army, helped by their Sikh and Gurkha forces, eventually stopped the rebellion. This marked the final defeat of the Mughal Empire. The British Parliament then replaced the East India Tea Company with a **Secretary of State for India**, who was directly responsible to the British Cabinet. In 1858, British Queen Victoria gave the governor-general of India the title of **viceroy**.

The British in Egypt

Britain's presence in Egypt grew out of events following the revolt of **Muhammad Ali** (1769–1849), who was pasha of Egypt under the Ottomans. He fought for the Ottomans in the Balkan Wars against Greece until he revolted against his overlords for their failure to establish him as governor of Syria. Only the failure of his European allies to support him kept him from toppling the Ottomans, and Muhammad Ali never successfully established Egypt as a power that could withstand European pressures. Although he attempted to implement Westernized reforms in Egypt, competition from Western goods ultimately brought about the failure of his attempts to industrialize Egypt. Muhammad Ali had insisted that Egypt attempt to increase its production of goods such as cotton for export, leaving it vulnerable in the area of food production and dependent on its cotton exports for survival.

After the construction of the Suez Canal transformed Egypt into a strategic location, competition among European powers for influence in Egypt became intense. In 1882, the British occupied Egypt to ensure their access to the Suez Canal, which they essentially stole from the French by becoming the major stockholders. To the south, in the Sudan, rebellions emerged against both the corrupt Egyptian rulers and their British allies. The most significant of these was led by Muhammad Achmad, who in 1881 called himself the Mahdi, or "deliverer." He claimed to be appointed by Allah to lead the rebellion against the British intruders and the corrupt Egyptian version of Islam. Although the Mahdi died, it was not until a decade later that the British put down the revolt continued by the Mahdi's followers. Following the British victory over the Mahdists in 1898, the way was clear for British domination of Africa.

The French in Asia

Christianity began to spread in Vietnam during the nineteenth century. The ruling powers believed that Christianity posed a threat to their Confucian values and outlawed Christianity. When Christianity continued to spread, the Vietnamese began executing missionaries. France retaliated by taking Saigon and three other provinces in the south of Vietnam between 1859 and 1860. In 1884 and 1885, the French succeeded in conquering the rest of Vietnam. By 1887, **French Indochina** included Vietnam, Laos, and Cambodia. At that time, the only area of Southeast Asia that was not ruled by Europeans was Siam (present-day Thailand).

The Opium Wars

The Qing in China also had to manage issues related to an increased European presence in Asia. The Qing initially only allowed the Europeans into Canton. In 1793, the Europeans asked for more privileges, but the Chinese were not interested and forbade the importation of opium in 1800, a highly addictive drug commonly used by many Chinese for recreational purposes. By the 1830s, the Chinese were no longer masters of the trade market; rather, Europeans had the advantage and they wanted fewer taxes on their goods and the right to trade opium. At this point, more than 30,000 chests of opium, each of which held about 150 pounds of the extract, were flowing into China each year. Some historians have suggested that the loss of Chinese supremacy in trade was the result of the opium trade.

By 1839, the Chinese were desperate to stop the trade, as it was damaging the health of their citizens and bringing in unwanted foreign intrusions. They burned several tons of opium in Canton, which started the **Opium Wars.** The British reacted by surrounding Canton, and in 1842 the British defeated the Chinese. In the **Treaty of Nanjing**, the Chinese lost Hong Kong to the British, who held it until the late twentieth century, when it reverted to China. The treaty forced the Chinese to open other ports to the British, and by 1844 the French and Americans had a trading presence in China as well. The French joined with the British to fight a second opium war, which led once again to the defeat of China in 1856. The Treaty of Tientsin (1858) opened new ports to trading and allowed foreigners with passports to travel in the interior of China. The Chinese granted Christians the right to spread their faith and to own property, and in separate treaties, the United States and Russia received similar privileges.

The Scramble for Africa

The Belgians in the Congo

The scramble for Africa officially began when British explorer Henry Stanley claimed the Congo River Valley for Belgium in 1879. King Leopold II of Belgium, in essence, created a personal colony there, with Stanley opening the region to trade by overseeing the construction of roads and using forced labor on both the roads and the rubber plantations. Leopold essentially thrust out the Portuguese, who had established a colony in the Congo in the fifteenth century. He declared the Congo a free trade area, but his legacy of repressive rule there eventually forced the government of Belgium to take control of the colony in 1908. It then became the **Belgian Congo**.

The British and the Dutch in South Africa

The British had established a presence in South Africa well before their occupation of Egypt in 1882. In 1652, the Dutch East India Company had founded Cape Town as a supply station on the route to Asia. Company employees settled there as well as other Europeans, and they were known as Boers. Later, they were called **Afrikaners**, from the Dutch word for "African." In 1806, the British took over the Cape of Good Hope and drove the Afrikaners farther inland. The British abolished one of the key features of Afrikaner life, slavery, which prompted the movement of Afrikaners northward. Another group moved to the east, and this eastward movement led to conflict between the Afrikaners and the native populations. These Afrikaners eventually defeated the Zulu and other groups and created the Republic of Natal, the Orange Free State, and the **South African Republic**.

The French in West Africa

As early as 1659, the French had established a trade port on the West African coast at St. Louis in present-day Senegal. Unlike other European powers following the Age of Discovery, France never played a major role in the slave trade, but instead was primarily interested in Africa for trade. During the wave of imperialist expansion in the nineteenth century, the French at first began to move eastward into the savanna regions of western Africa. Military troops usually led this expansion. By the twentieth century France controlled much of present-day Senegal, Mali, Burkina Faso, Benin, Guinea, the Ivory Coast, and Niger. France also controlled Algeria, Morocco, and Dahomey (part of present-day Benin). Out of various territories in West Africa, France created **French West Africa**. Their base remained St. Louis in Senegal, and only there did they allow the native populations any voice in the government. The French attempted to rule 9 million West Africans with a force of only 3,600 men.

France also conquered the region on the north bank of the Congo and created **French Equatorial Africa**. On the east coast, France claimed part of Somaliland, and by 1896, France had also conquered the island of Madagascar. The leader of Germany at that time, Otto von Bismarck, cooperated with the French to counter British influence.

The Berlin Conference

At the **Berlin Conference** of 1884–1885, fourteen European nations and the United States determined that any European nation could found a colony

> # DIDYOUKNOW?
>
> Before the imperialist colonization of Africa, there were about 10,000 different African states and independent groups, ranging from small family hunter–gatherer clans to large kingdoms. Only two states in the entire continent of Africa were never colonized or controlled by the Europeans: Liberia, which was founded as a colony in 1822 by American slaves who had been freed and became an independent nation in 1847, and Ethiopia, which adopted Christianity as its state religion in the 4th century CE.

in unclaimed territory if it notified the other nations of its intentions. Effective occupation of an area was to take the place of historic precedent, and Portugal was officially thrust out of the Congo. The Conference awarded Mozambique, Angola, and Guinea to Portugal. Not one African attended the conference.

Other Imperialist Colonies in Africa

Imperialist governments, for the most part, granted monopoly rights to the various companies formed to develop regions of Africa. The British Royal Niger Company, for example, colonized Nigeria. Germany established German Southwest Africa and German East Africa with the development of the region by the German East Africa Company. By 1914, Germany had acquired new territories of 1 million square miles and as many as 13 million people. Italy had formed the Italian East African Empire in Eritrea by 1885 and appropriated Asmara and the southern coastal strip of Somaliland in 1889. The Italian Benadir Company developed Somaliland. Italy attempted to form a protectorate in the African kingdom of Abyssinia, but the Abyssinians defeated it in 1896.

The Impact of European Imperialism: Comparative Patterns in Africa and Asia

Western colonization of Africa and Asia brought mixed results. In India, the availability of Western education created a new middle class of educated professionals, opening new job opportunities for native peoples. These professionals, however, were usually paid less than Europeans who were performing similar tasks in government or industry. Western ideas also provided a common foundation for those who were colonized. Often, many different ethnicities or tribal alliances were engaged in conflicts with one another before the arrival of the Europeans, and Western culture and education created commonalities among these diverse societies. In some places, such as in Africa, Europeans sometimes forced societies at war with one another to combine into single tribes. The newly educated class of colonized peoples in such places as India often felt separated from those who still followed a traditional way of life. Western education created in them a new mind-set that distanced them from others not given such opportunities. Further, in India, those who received Western education were exactly those who later led rebellions against the British presence in India. Partly because of the difficulties in India and also largely because of racist assumptions about black Africans, colonizers in Africa did not provide as many opportunities for Africans to receive a Western-style education. In Africa, introduction to Western education was largely the work of Christian missionaries. Even so, few Africans were admitted to the priesthood of the Roman Catholic Church. As Europeans became more convinced of their racial supremacy in the late nineteenth century, the gulf between European colonizers and native peoples continued to widen.

European colonization also brought dramatic changes to the daily lives of many native peoples. While Europeans brought with them consumer goods, in general the native peoples were used to produce raw materials or crops needed in Europe. In the Belgian Congo, villagers who could not meet their expected production quotas were beaten and, in some cases, killed. Taxes were imposed that could be paid in crops needed for transport to Europe. Uncultivated areas of land were used to produce cocoa, hemp, rubber, and other items destined for export. Even fields that had been under cultivation for food crops were transformed into producers of export commodities. While native peoples were used to work these lands, the profits went to European manufacturers and so did the manufactured goods. In Africa and India, especially, the economies were dependent on the global market for their resources, and this market was dominated and controlled by Europeans.

European Imperialism in the Pacific

Australia

In 1770, English Captain James Cook landed in Botany Bay, Australia. This and subsequent voyages of Captain Cook opened up Australia to European colonization. In 1788, a group of migrants who were mostly convicted criminals settled in the colony of New South Wales. The British argued that Australia was *terra nullius*, or land belonging to no one, that could be seized and used at will. By 1900 their settlers had pushed the native aboriginal population into reservations in regions that were largely deserts.

New Zealand

When Europeans colonized the New World during the Age of Exploration, they brought smallpox and other diseases that devastated the native populations. This was also true in New Zealand, where the native Maori population dropped from about 200,000 to 45,000 within a century, following the arrival of European timber traders in New Zealand in 1790. European firearms also created more tension among the warlike Maori people of New Zealand. The arrival and settlement of British farmers and herders in the mid-nineteenth century eventually culminated in a series of wars from 1860 to 1864, after which the British forced the Maori onto reservations. Western education, however, gave some Maori the ability to fight for their rights, and the Maori continued to survive despite their near extermination.

Other Islands

The European powers that colonized Africa wasted no time in competing for the Pacific Islands. France had created colonial governments by 1880 in Tahiti and New Caledonia, while Britain took Fiji, and Germany took most of the Marshall Islands. The Berlin Conference of 1884–1885 also divided up the Pacific Islands, with the United States and Germany dividing Samoa.

TEST TIP

You may only work on each section of the test during the stated time period. Looking ahead at the essays or trying to go back to check your multiple-choice answers when you're supposed to be working on something else can result in having your test scores canceled.

Expansion, Contraction, and Emergence of States Caused by Imperialism

The imperialism of the industrialized countries created inequalities among regions throughout the world. The power and wealth of these countries influenced not only the extent of their dominance, but also the formation of new states and the decline of others.

The United States Emerges as an Imperial Power

Nationalism played an important role in the development of the United States in the nineteenth century, and the new country expanded rapidly in the years following its Revolutionary War. Britain ceded to the United States the area west of the Appalachian Mountains to the Mississippi River, almost doubling the size of the territory occupied by the thirteen original colonies. In 1803, French general and ruler Napoleon knew that he could not defend French territories from the Mississippi River to the Rocky Mountains, and so he chose instead to gain the revenue from their sale. The **Louisiana Purchase** again doubled the size of the United States. Meriwether Lewis and William Clark then mapped the new territory from 1804 to 1806. In 1845, Texas entered the Union, forcing a war between Mexico and the United States from 1845 to 1848. According to the **Treaty of Hidalgo,** the United States paid Mexico $15 million for Texas, California, and New Mexico.

The nineteenth century became the era of **manifest destiny** for Americans, who believed that it was their clear and obvious right to control all of North America; some even discussed an American presence in Canada, Cuba, Latin America, and South America. Manifest destiny assumed that the democratic experiment in America was a superior form of civilization, and that the white people who brought it westward were superior to those people and cultures that they replaced.

At the same time, although historically the United States had pursued a policy of isolationism going back to its founding, in the nineteenth century it became a world power that intruded often into international affairs. **The Monroe Doctrine** in 1823 effectively put the Western Hemisphere under U.S. domination, as President Monroe warned European nations against imperialist activity in the Western Hemisphere.

In 1867, the purchase of Alaska again greatly increased U.S. territory in North America, while in 1875, Hawaii became a U.S. protectorate. In 1893, a group of white planters overthrew the last Hawaiian queen, Lili'uokalani, with the help of the U.S. Minister to Hawaii, John Stevens, and a contingent of marines from the warship USS *Boston*. Acting without the permission of the U.S. State Department, Stevens declared that Hawaii was a U.S. protectorate. Most native Hawaiians strongly opposed this action. Although the next U.S. president, Grover Cleveland, strongly criticized Stevens and the overthrow of Queen Lili'uokalani, Hawaii became a republic in 1894. When rebellion erupted, many natives were arrested along with Queen Lili'uokalani. The United States annexed the islands in 1898.

Those who subscribed to the U.S. doctrine of manifest destiny had always hinted at the desire to annex Cuba, one of the last remaining bastions of Spanish power. When the U.S. battleship *Maine* exploded in Havana Harbor in 1898, the United States accused Spain of treachery and the Spanish-American War began. In 1899, the United States defeated Spain, taking Cuba and Puerto Rico; soon thereafter, the United States took the Philippines and Guam from Spain.

Japan

U.S. Influence in Japan

In 1853, Commodore Matthew Perry arrived in Japan with a fleet of warships and a letter to the shogun from American President Millard Fillmore requesting that trade be established between Japan and the United States. A few months later, when Perry returned to Japan, the shogun agreed to a treaty. Rebellions erupted in the southern regions of Japan, particularly in Satsuma and Choshu. After Western ships fired on the rebels, the rebels strengthened their forces and their opposition to the Western presence, leading to the demise of the Tokugawa Shogunate and the emergence of Meiji Japan.

In 1866, Saigo Takamori, the leader of the Satsuma domain, and Kido Takayoshi, the leader of the Choshu domain, formed the Sat-Cho Alliance. Its purpose was the overthrow of the Tokugawa Shogunate so as to restore the emperor to power. The armies of Choshu and Satsuma defeated the Tokugawa army in 1869.

The Meiji Restoration

The fourteen-year-old heir to the imperial throne, Mutsuhito, became emperor and took the title **Meiji**, meaning "enlightened ruler." Shortly thereafter, he signed the Five Charter Oath, according to which the feudal order was abolished, the Tokugawa freezing of classes was abandoned, the isolationism of Japan ended, and the formation of a governmental assembly was promised. In 1871, the daimyo were stripped of their hereditary titles to their land. Similarly, samurai were forbidden to wear the symbols of their hereditary status, their swords. An imperial army was formed to replace the old feudal structures. Important positions in the new government were given to the elder samurai from the Sat-Cho Alliance. The Meiji Constitution of 1890 created a Parliament with an upper house that was appointed and a lower house that was elected, called the Diet. The Diet could pass laws provided that both houses agreed, but in the end it served merely in an advisory capacity. Only 5 percent of Japanese males owned enough property to elect representatives to the Diet. The Diet also was subordinate to the executive branch, which directly controlled the military and handpicked its cabinet.

The Meiji Restoration was accomplished without violence, and so it was not a revolution in the typical sense of the word, but it wrought many changes in Japanese society, and these changes were revolutionary. It accomplished these changes, however, entirely in a top-down, dictatorial manner. For this reason it has been called a "revolution from above." While a centralized group of elite people restructured Japan but managed to leave their former power intact, they also combined their efforts with those of a new order, such as people with capitalistic interests who formerly were not highly placed in the government. The despotism of the Meiji leadership arose out of the feudal precedents of the Tokugawa period, yet they combined these tactics with Western capitalistic enterprises. Some historians have referred to the Meiji regime as a form of "Asian fascism" and argue that this unique combination of despotism and capitalistic interests drove the Japanese to fixate on nationalism, power, and wealth. What followed was a wave of imperialist expansion on the part of Japan, which was only stopped in the mid-twentieth century.

The Rise of Japan as an Imperial Power

The industrial transformation of Japan during the Meiji period also inspired expansionist tendencies. Japan began to expand in the Pacific in the 1870s, when it encouraged Japanese settlers to live on Hokkaido and the Kurile Islands in an effort to block Russian expansion. By 1879, Japan had hegemony over Okinawa and the Ryukyu Islands, and it also controlled the islands to the south and north of the four islands of Japan.

In 1876, Japan expanded control over Korean trade through an unequal treaty similar to others imposed on China and Hong Kong by the Western powers after the Opium Wars. In 1894, the Koreans began a series of protests over foreign intrusion, leading the Chinese to send a force to restore order there and to reassert their authority. Later that year, the Meiji government in Japan declared war on China. In a five-hour battle, the Japanese defeated the Qing navy on the Yellow Sea and within only a few months took control of Korea. China recognized Korea as being independent and ceded Taiwan, the Pescadores Islands, and the Laiodong Peninsula to Japan. Japan also gained unequal rights in China that paralleled those of the United States and Europe following the Opium Wars.

These gains created tension with Russia, who desired much of the territory controlled by Japan, in particular Korea and the Liaodong Peninsula. Manchuria was also a common interest. The Japanese escalated their military buildup, and in 1904 the Russo-Japanese War broke out. The Russian Baltic fleet sailed halfway around the world to meet the Japanese, but the Japanese quickly routed them and won control of Sakhalin Island and a railroad in Manchuria. The Russo-Japanese War firmly established worldwide acceptance of Korea as a colonial territory of Japan.

Like the Europeans, the Japanese often justified their brutal imperialist regimes on the basis of their alleged racial superiority. Just as European imperialism has been condemned on this basis, so too have the Japanese racist views that emerged as they became one of the major world imperial powers.

Russia, Eastern Europe, and Nationalism

The rise of nationalist movements in the early nineteenth century that helped to fuel imperialist expansion also led to the establishment of new states and the decline of others. Like Meiji Japan and the United States, Russia continued its attempts to extend its influence over neighboring territories in the vast regions of Eastern Europe and Asia.

The **Russo-Turkish Wars,** one of the longest conflicts in world history, continued sporadically throughout the nineteenth century as Russia fought with the Ottoman Empire in an ongoing attempt to dominate territories in the Balkans, the Crimea, and the Caucasus. After the Russo-Turkish War of 1877–1878, Bulgaria emerged as an independent state, after 500 years of domination by the Ottoman Turks. Montenegro, Serbia, and Romania also gained independence, inspiring feelings of nationalism in the various Slavic peoples throughout the region. Serbia in particular was at the center of nationalist aspirations, as the Serbs led the **Pan-Slavic movement,** whose goal was to unite the Slavic peoples who were under the control of the Austro-Hungarian Empire. Polish, Czech, Croatian, and Slovakian peoples struggled to form their own independent states in a series of rebellions. Russia strongly supported the Pan-Slavic movement, not because it supported nationalism of these neighboring regions, but because it hoped to eventually annex them into the Russian Empire. Another result of the 1877–1878 war was that Russia gained southern Bessarabia and part of Armenia, the Austro-Hungarian Empire acquired Bosnia and Herzogovina, and the Ottoman Empire continued to weaken.

TEST TIP

Whether you're taking the AP exam in your regular classroom, your school library, or a high school you've never visited before, dress for the unexpected. Wear layers and bring a sweatshirt or light sweater so you can be comfortable, even if the room is warmer or cooler than you might have thought.

The Decline of the Ottoman Empire

Beginning in 1839, a series of reforms called the **Tanzimat** attempted to Westernize the Ottoman world. First, the Ottomans granted equality to non-Muslims and allowed the importation of foreign goods. Western education, especially in mathematics and the sciences, and other Western customs were also adopted. The Ottoman reformers built railroads and created a state postal system. Military officers and bureaucrats became increasingly Westernized. The Tanzimat, however, did not succeed in stopping the decline of the Ottomans. Granting equality to non-Muslims contributed to the growing nationalism among them and created further tensions within the conservative elements of Ottoman society. Further, the massive importation of goods, especially from Britain, threatened the livelihood of the Ottoman artisans. The removal of the tariffs and other trading barriers also removed the protections that the Ottoman merchants had from competition with the West.

A continuing string of military and political defeats, including losing the Crimea to Russia in 1856 and being forced into unequal treaties with Britain and France, also contributed to the decline of the Ottomans. Another factor that contributed to the Ottoman decline was financial instability. In 1875, the Ottomans declared a state of near-bankruptcy and European creditors gained a strong foothold over Ottoman finances. Sultan Abdul Hamid realized the threat that Western influences posed to his bureaucracy and military. Westernized officers increasingly saw the sultan himself as the biggest barrier to reform, and Abdul Hamid attempted to thwart their influence by restricting freedom of the press and other civil liberties, and eventually by nullifying the constitution. Nevertheless, he continued to Westernize the military and to promote the foundation of Western-style educational institutions. In 1908, Abdul Hamid was removed as sultan in a coup engineered by the Young Turks, who wished to see the Tanzimat reforms restored. Later, World War I would undercut their efforts and bring the final collapse of the empire, which officially ended in 1922 when Turkey became a Republic.

Scientific Racism and Social Darwinism

During the late 1800s, conservatives in industrialized countries used two related schools of political thought to justify and facilitate the many inequalities created by imperialism. Contributing to conservatives' justification that imperialistic expansions were actually missions to civilize other societies were new, allegedly scientific views. One such view was **scientific racism,** which was developed by Count Joseph Arthur de

Gobineau, a French noble who divided humanity into four basic races. In his *Essay on the Inequality of the Human Races*, Gobineau argued that Europeans were superior to the other races. Scientific racism was based on the belief that basic differences existed among the races that made black people inherently inferior to whites. This school of thought was an attempt to justify the inferior positions of black people in societies and economies.

Gobineau's views, combined with Charles Darwin's thesis concerning the survival of the fittest, evolved into **social Darwinism.** Pure Darwinism, however, did not justify racial differences, but it was made out to justify differences between the poor and the rich. Darwinism was based on Darwin's scientific theory of natural selection. (Animals that are best adapted to their environments will find a way to survive, while the less fit or less well adapted will not survive.) It was used to explain why some people became wealthy while others remained poor. Social Darwinists went further, however, and argued that stronger and more capable individuals competed better and so became more successful; therefore, white domination of less-well-developed cultures was a natural and just situation.

Many modern historians reject social Darwinism and the idea of imperialism as being "civilizing missions" made by Europeans. While modern academics are making a strong effort to recover the indigenous histories and cultural contributions of those areas of the world colonized by European and American powers, it is difficult to counter the legacy of ill will created by European beliefs in their cultural supremacy, especially in those areas where native cultures were denigrated and even destroyed. Further, imperialism created a huge gulf between industrialized nations and those that were not industrialized, a chasm that remains even today.

Nationalism, Revolution, and Reform

The eighteenth century was a period of revolutionary changes in many aspects of societies and governments throughout the world. Political revolutions arose against long-established governments, and colonists rebelled and fought for independence from the imperialist governments that ruled them. Many of these revolutions and rebellions were inspired by the ideas of enlightened thinkers. Some revolutions resulted in the formation of new states with democratic forms of government, and these newly formed states were uniquely viewed by their people more as nations than as states.

Key Terms

Articles of Confederation

Benito Juárez

Bill of Rights

Boxer Rebellion

Camillo Benso di Cavour

Constitution of the
   United States

Declaration of Independence

Declaration of the Rights
   of Man

Elizabeth Cady Stanton

Enlightenment

Francois Dominique
   Toussaint

Giuseppe Garibaldi

Gran Colombia

Haiti

Jean-Jacques Rousseau

John Locke

Letter from Jamaica

Liberalism

maroons

Mary Wollstonecraft

Montesquieu

National Assembly

Nationalism

Olympe de Gouges

Otto von Bismarck

Radicalism

Self-Strengthening
   Movement

Seven Years' War

Simón Bolívar

Socialism

storming of the Bastille

Susan B. Anthony

Taiping Rebellion

Thomas Jefferson

Thomas Paine

Voltaire

The Enlightenment

The 1700s are also known as the Age of Enlightenment in Europe, as many thinkers began to question the authority of absolute governments and other accepted traditions, and to focus on the rights of individuals. The **Enlightenment** was a result of the many changes brought about by the Renaissance, the Scientific Revolution, and the Protestant Reformation, all of which had swept through Western Europe between 1450 and 1750. The most basic feature of Enlightenment thought was reliance on reason above all else. Enlightenment thought began in France and quickly spread to Germany, England, and other parts of Europe.

Thinkers of the Enlightenment insisted on the public use of reason, meaning that past authorities had made assertions without proof and merely expected others to follow. All thought now was to be subjected to public scrutiny, and there would be no repositories of mysterious wisdom, such as the Christian Church. Eventually, the widespread questioning of nearly all aspects of life that began in this period would lead to revolutions against many governments in European countries, Latin America, and in the United States.

John Locke

John Locke (1632–1704) was an English philosopher who pushed the Newtonian worldview to its logical conclusions. In *Two Treatises of Government*, Locke developed a natural rights theory of government, according to which the laws of government and of society were embedded in nature itself. Newton had proven the universe to be mechanical, and Locke insisted that according to nature itself, humans had the rights of life, liberty, and property, and that these rights were to be respected and protected by their governments. He pushed to its logical conclusion Newton's third law of motion relating to cause and effect by arguing that there should be checks and balances in an efficient and acceptable system of government. Locke wrote that when the government did not respect the natural rights of man, people had a right and even a duty to rebel. Much to Britain's chagrin, Locke's ideas became part of the basis for the American Revolution in 1776.

Voltaire

Voltaire was a prolific French writer and political activist who played an important role in the Enlightenment. He wrote many satiric plays, stories, and poems that were philosophical and political in nature. Voltaire was influenced by the ideas of John

Locke, who believed that a ruler's authority should be based on the will of the people. Locke had also promoted the idea of a social contract, in which subjects had the right to replace a bad or unjust ruler. Voltaire's ideas incorporated those of Locke and went even further. In the *Philosophical Dictionary* (1764), he attacked religion as fanaticism and superstition. In *Candide* (1759), Voltaire advocated governmental and social reform, and he suggested that government was the only thing in life that people might be able to control. Voltaire criticized the monarchies of Europe for their elaborate institutions, their need for power, and their control of the economy. He believed in the rights of individuals and the importance of ideas, knowledge, and rational thought. Voltaire also was a strong advocate of the value of the careful observations of the natural world through science as a means of understanding the world. Another French writer, **Jean-Jacques Rousseau** argued, in his famous treatise *Emile*, or *On Education*, that education should be left to nature, and that only when a person returns to nature can he or she truly learn.

Thomas Paine

Similarly, **Thomas Paine** (1731–1814) rejected institutionalized religion. In the *Age of Reason*, Paine argued against Christian doctrines and also advocated the importance of the use of reason and freethinking. Paine was also a well-known revolutionary; he moved from England to America, where his pamphlet *Common Sense* made the case for American independence from Britain. Later, he went to France and became very involved in supporting the French Revolution.

Montesquieu

The Baron de **Montesquieu** applied the scientific methodology of the seventeenth century to the idea of natural law. In *The Spirit of the Laws*, Montesquieu dissected various kinds of government, and in particular focused on the parliamentary system of England and its checks and balances. Montesquieu believed that England's government allowed the greatest amount of freedom for its people; his theories had a profound impact in the United States, where they influenced the drafting of the Constitution.

DIDYOUKNOW?

The enlightened despots had much in common with the absolute monarchs, but they were influenced by the ideals of the Enlightenment and enacted reforms in education and other areas. Along with Frederick the Great of Prussia and Catherine the Great of Russia, Maria Theresa of the Austrian Hapsburg Empire was an enlightened despot who ruled firmly but still implemented reforms based on Enlightenment thought. During her reign and those of her successors, Vienna became a renowned center of culture, a city where Enlightened musicians such as Haydn, Mozart, and Beethoven created some of their finest compositions.

The Declaration of Independence

Thomas Paine first raised the issue of American independence in his 1775 pamphlet *Common Sense*, but it was not until 1776 that independence was formally declared. The Second Continental Congress, representing the colonial governments, adopted the **Declaration of Independence** in July 1776. **Thomas Jefferson** drafted the document, but the declaration was influenced greatly by John Locke's *Two Treatises on Government*. The Declaration opened with a statement of principles and concluded with a list of the "injuries and usurpations" of the British monarch. Because many of the ideas articulated by Jefferson had, in fact, been the basis of the Glorious Revolution of the 1640s, whereby the British Parliament gained more power than the monarchy, the document presented a reasonable argument for independence. Jefferson had a flair for writing, and while Locke had said that the rights of life, liberty, and property were inalienable, Jefferson changed "property" to the "pursuit of happiness."

Bolívar's Jamaica Letter

In South America, a Venezuelan Creole named **Simón Bolívar** worked to create an independent and unified Latin America. In 1810, Bolívar, a young military officer, joined with a group that later instigated revolts against the Spanish rulers in Venezuela. In 1813, Bolívar was given a military command in present-day Columbia, but later that year he and his group seized the Venezuelan capital of Caracas and declared independence from Spain. However, the new republic was overthrown by Spanish troops in 1814. Bolívar went into exile in Jamaica for about a year. While there, he wrote the **Letter from Jamaica**, in which he advocated his ideas for a republican government and the unification of Latin America. In the letter, Bolívar expressed his ideas using the language of Enlightenment thinkers such as Locke, Rousseau, and Montesquieu. He explained his belief that the revolutionary movement in Latin America was a continuation of the French Revolution of 1789 and the American Revolution of 1776. Like the thinkers of the Enlightenment, Bolívar advocated the idea that human freedom and rights are inalienable and natural. He further justified the violence in Latin America as being necessary for the revolutionaries to reclaim their natural rights.

Nationalism

Many revolutions that occurred between 1750 and the early twentieth century were inspired by nationalism as well as Enlightenment thought. Both the American Revolution and the revolution in South America were based not only on Enlightenment ideas, but also on a strong sense of nationalism. **Nationalism** was based on the belief in cultural unity based on a common language, history, region, and ethnicity. Nationalists created nations based on the common identity of groups of people, and these nations' survival was not based on the success or survival of individual leaders. These nations' political boundaries were still based on military victories and defense, but what held them together as nations was this sense of belonging to a common group—their nation, a feeling that continues to dominate world politics.

Unification of Italy

Italy entered the nineteenth century not as one single country, but rather as a collection of small kingdoms that had evolved from the city-states of the Middle Ages. Count **Camillo Benso di Cavour** was the leading figure in Sardinian politics from 1850 to 1861. Cavour was the chief minister of King Victor Emmanuel. Cavour's original aim was to unite northern and some of central Italy into a state dominated by Sardinia. Cavour worked on strengthening the infrastructure of Sardinia, supporting civil liberties, and opposing the privileged status of the Church. He also built highways and railroads, which brought benefits to northern Italy and increased support for Sardinian rule. Increased revenues also made it possible for Cavour to assemble and train an army.

In other parts of Italy, particularly in central Italy, nationalists rose in successful revolt and called for a united Italy, demanding that their particular regions be joined to Sardinia. Cavour returned in 1860 to control most of Italy in the name of Sardinia. **Giuseppe Garibaldi** had been active in the fight for Italian unity and in the fight to liberate parts of Italy from foreign control since the 1830s. As the Italian states began to unify, Cavour and Garibaldi joined together, and Italy became a unified nation under King Vittore Immanuele II. In 1870, Rome became the capital of a united Italy.

Unification of Germany

Prussia and Austria were the two strongest Germanic states; they controlled the German Confederation that was created by the Congress of Vienna in 1815. Each wished to dominate a unified Germany, and each feared the results if the other succeeded. In 1848, major rebellions broke out within the German Confederation, led by nationalists who wanted a German nation ruled by a parliamentary government. By 1853 the economy had also become a factor in forming a united Germany.

The revolts in Italy in 1859 had caused Austria numerous problems, and Prussia had learned important lessons. Prussia was now under the rule of William I, who was well aware of the potential for war and greatly concerned that Prussia was not prepared as well as it should be. The energetic and militaristic William I set about making military reforms. His goal was to restructure the Prussian army and double its size. To do this, he needed a larger defense budget, which meant higher taxes.

William I was, however, a constitutional monarch, not an absolute monarch. He could not simply raise taxes, no matter how just the reason. The Prussian Assembly had been formed in 1848 and had some power. The liberal members of the Assembly, mostly wealthy and middle class, wanted to increase their power and make the Assembly more powerful than the king. There was no enthusiastic support for increasing the military, since Prussians did not want to live in a military state and there was no obvious, undeniable military threat to Prussia's borders to sway the people to William I's position. The Assembly rejected William I's proposed military budget in 1862.

William I responded by creating a new ministry and appointing **Otto von Bismarck** as its head. Bismarck, an aristocrat, was devoted to Prussia and its king, and also to Prussian supremacy in Germany. Bismarck became the true controlling power of Prussia. He provoked wars with Denmark, Austria, and France, and then he appealed to German nationalism to create a strong German nation. Bismarck first formed a new North German Confederation from the Protestant German states north of the Main River; Prussia, as the largest state, dominated the Confederation. In 1870 the southern German states joined with the North German Confederation to form the new German Empire, with King William I of Prussia as Emperor William of Germany. In less than ten years, Bismarck had united the people of Germany and transformed Prussia into the major power of Central Europe.

TEST TIP

Do not include unsupported or very general statements that simply make your essays longer. The strength, not the length, of your essay is most important.

Revolutions and Reform Movements

A combination of economic changes, enlightenment movements, and increasing resentment of imperial governments on the part of colonists, slaves, and other oppressed peoples caused the wave of revolutions and reform movements in the late 1700s. Growing nationalism and, at the other extreme, resistance to the dominance of new cultures, also inspired rebellions. These continued into the mid-nineteenth century. The revolutions began in the American colonies and shortly thereafter in France, later spreading to Latin America and other parts of the world.

The American Revolution

The British colonists who went to the Americas often made the assumption that they would have the full rights of British subjects. Many colonies had representative houses, such as the Virginia House of Burgesses, and in colonies such as Massachusetts Bay, a large percentage of the male population was able to vote. For many years the British had allowed the colonists to live virtually unaffected by taxation, and when taxation became an issue following the Seven Years' War, the American colonists demanded the right to participate in the decision-making process.

The **Seven Years' War** (1756–1763), also known as the French and Indian War, drastically affected England's financial situation. Also in the Seven Years' War, the British defeated the French and pushed them off the continent, except for two small islands off the coast of Newfoundland. Britain acquired all French possessions, including Canada, in the Treaty of Paris (1763). The British were in debt and needed to raise revenue. Moreover, they needed to defend their new territories won in the war. The American colonies posed a special problem for the British, as the colonists represented one-quarter of the population of the empire, yet they paid only one one-hundredth of the cost to maintain the colonies. The perception that the colonists were not contributing to the cost of protecting them led the British to impose a series of restrictive policies and taxes. Continued rebellions spread from Boston throughout the rest of the colonies as the American colonists expressed intense opposition to taxation without representation.

During the first year of the rebellions, the colonists continued to hope that the British would address their grievances. In July of 1775, the Continental Congress drafted the Olive Branch Petition, which attempted to reconcile the colonists to the monarchy. It was addressed directly to King George III and asked for his help. The king refused to look at the petition and, instead, declared the colonists to be in a state of rebellion.

By this time, George Washington had assumed command of the Continental Army, and the Continental Congress drafted the *Declaration on the Causes and Necessity of Taking Up Arms*, explaining their reasons for continuing to fight and "die as free men" rather than to live "as slaves." King George III then closed the colonies to trade. The war for independence had begun.

The colonies, which then became states, had no central system of government, inadequate military forces, and no European ally. What they did have, however, was a common national experience as Americans and a common determination to escape from the system of "tyranny" imposed on them by the British. Those colonists who remained loyal to Britain were mostly wealthy landowners with moderate political beliefs, and they returned to Britain during the Revolutionary War.

During the first year of the war, from the spring of 1775 to summer 1776, there was inconclusive action as the British tried to figure out whether they were indeed engaged in a war or simply caught up in the irritating plots of a group of colonists. At first the war was a struggle that was localized in and around the city of Boston. Following the Declaration of Independence in 1776, the conflict spread. The American victory at Saratoga, New York, resulted in more than just a defeat for the British in New York; it convinced the French, and their new king Louis XVI, that the new American states might actually win the conflict. In 1778, the French government extended official recognition to the United States. A military alliance and military aid were forthcoming. The French were also driven by the bitterness of their loss in the Seven Years' War. The final phase of the Revolutionary War took place in the South. With the surrender of Cornwallis at Yorktown, Virginia, in 1893, the war for independence ended.

In November 1777, the Continental Congress had proposed the **Articles of Confederation**, which created a national system so weak that it barely had more power than the Congress itself. The conflict between those who wanted to emphasize the rights of the states as opposed to the rights of the whole (the Federalists) dominated American history until the Civil War. The thirteen states ratified the Articles of Confederation in 1781; they were in effect until 1789. Under the Articles of Confederation, the first national laws were passed; these laws addressed the issue of lands west of the Appalachian Mountains.

The Constitution of 1789

Delegates to a constitutional convention met in 1789 to address the weaknesses of the Articles of Confederation. They expected to revise the Articles of Confederation, but instead created a radically new kind of government for the new nation based on the ideas of French philosopher Montesquieu. Montesquieu had discussed the need for a strong central government comprised of branches empowered to check each other. In the new **Constitution of the United States**, the government's powers were divided among three branches: the legislative, judicial, and executive. The legislative branch was to be bicameral, following the model of the British Parliament. There were checks and balances established to prevent any one branch from controlling the government. The Great Compromise resolved disputes between large and small states about representation by having representation in the lower house in proportion to population and equal for every state in the upper house. In 1791, the **Bill of Rights** was added to the Constitution, guaranteeing individual rights. The Bill of Rights represents the first ten amendments to the U.S. Constitution.

The French Revolution

Discontent with the absolutist government created by French King Louis XIV boiled over in the eighteenth century. The financial crisis following the Seven Years' War contributed to the rise of revolutionary sentiment. Fully half of the royal budget went toward interest payments on the royal debt, and although the nobility had great wealth, they found numerous ways to escape the payment of mandated taxes. Louis's ministers attempted to stabilize French finances, but to no avail. When the government attempted to reform the tax system so that the nobility paid the taxes they were intended to pay, King Louis XVI was forced to call together a meeting of the Estates General, the old parliamentary structure, for the first time in 160 years.

Although there was great hope among the common people surrounding the first meeting of the Estates General in 1789, that hope was quickly dashed. The Estates General voted by body, that is, one vote per estate. The three estates were the clergy, the nobility, and the commoners. The first two could and did always outvote the Third Estate, which represented the majority of the French population. The famous pamphlet by Abbe Sieyes, *What Is the Third Estate?* pointed out the folly of this process when he argued that the answer to the question was "Everything." The Third Estate, he pointed out, performed most of the work in France and paid most of the taxes, and, therefore, was entitled to more rights. When the Estates General met for the first time, the first two estates marched in together and sat in their traditional locations dressed in their finery. The Third Estate soon realized that nothing would change for them through this process.

The National Assembly

The Third Estate left the Estates General and then invited the clergy and the nobles to join them. By June 17 of 1789, they had declared themselves the **National Assembly**. On June 20, they took the Tennis Court Oath, promising not to disband until the Assembly had created a new constitution. The majority of the clergy and a large number of nobles joined with them. The French Revolution was the first movement in which the masses participated. The role of the people became intense about the time the National Assembly began its work. In 1788 there had been a widespread famine, leading to bread riots in 1789. The royal family had little or no understanding of the needs of the masses.

The Storming of the Bastille

The bread riots alarmed the monarchy, which already had many troops stationed in Paris because of the revolutionary activities of the Third Estate. The masses became further agitated when Louis dismissed his minister, Necker, whom the people saw as their champion against the aristocracy. This volatile situation erupted on July 14, 1789, and culminated in the **storming of the Bastille**, a fortress prison where the monarchy traditionally kept dissenters. The rioters killed troops and released seven prisoners and formed a new municipal government, the commune. The situation became progressively more volatile as the so-called Great Fear swept through France. Fear of an aristocratic conspiracy to overthrow the Third Estate in the National Assembly, desperate needs in time of famine, and long-standing anger over feudal dues brought about violent protest against ancient manorial privileges. Peasants still paid fees for the use of village mills and other privileges. They also paid rent for land.

Declaration of the Rights of Man

On August 4, 1789, while the nobility was absent, the National Assembly abolished feudal society in France, outlawed the dues and tithes to the Church, and mandated that jobs be made open to all. Three weeks later, the Assembly issued the **Declaration of the Rights of Man**, by which everyone in France was considered born free and equal in rights, especially those of life, liberty, property, security, and resistance to oppression. Although the document contained many lofty sentiments, including freedom of the press, the delegates' use of the word "man" clearly left women out of the equation. Mary Wollstonecraft would later write a rebuttal of the assumptions that women were not equal to men in her *Vindication of the Rights of Women*. The ideals of the Declaration of the Rights of Man, however, later led to a wave of abolitionism throughout Europe.

The Haitian Revolution

On the island of Hispaniola in the Caribbean, the ideas of the French and American revolutions were embraced by the oppressed people there. Hispaniola had both French and Spanish colonies, with the French colony of Saint-Domingue being one of the most productive of all European colonies in the Caribbean. During the American Revolution, French support had meant that many *gens de couleur*, or free people of color, had been sent to aid the American colonists. The white colonists in Saint-Domingue took advantage of the opportunity created by the French Revolution to establish their own government, but they did not concede any rights to the *gens de couleur* nor to any of the large slave population.

In 1791, Boukman, a Voudoo priest, led a slave revolt that ignited the struggle into a full-scale civil war. Many former or escaped slaves, known as **maroons**, joined in the revolt. Boukman died, but his revolt did not. **François Dominique Toussaint** then rose to lead the slave revolt. By 1797 he controlled most of the island, and by 1801 he had created a constitution that granted equality and citizenship to all residents of the colony. Although Toussaint did not declare independence from France, in 1803 his successors did. On January 1, 1804, the new nation of **Haiti** became the second independent republic in the Western Hemisphere. As for Toussaint, invading French forces took him in 1802, and he died in a French jail in 1803. Nevertheless, his name is synonymous with slave revolts, and with the fight for human rights among repressed peoples everywhere.

TEST TIP

When you take practice tests, create an environment as much like the actual testing environment as possible. Sit at a quiet table free of distractions. Make sure to time yourself, breaking the test down by sections.

Revolutions in Latin America

A struggle for independence in Latin American countries also followed in the wake of the French Revolution. France invaded Spain and Portugal in 1807, which weakened French power and inspired revolution in their colonies. The revolutions of the early nineteenth century, however, did not bring independence to the common people, but instead succeeded in strengthening the white, Creole elite, as well as their European traditions of Roman Catholicism and slavery.

Gran Columbia

After his stay in Jamaica, Simón Bolívar continued his attempts to unify Latin America. He moved to Haiti, and then, with the help of Haitian soldiers, to whom Bolívar promised that he would abolish slavery there, Bolívar seized Angostura in Venezuela. He went on to lead victorious revolutions for independence in Colombia and Ecuador. In 1821 the republic of **Gran Colombia** was formed, including Venezuela, present-day Colombia, Ecuador, Panama, and northern Peru, with Bolívar as the president. He then fully liberated Peru, and in 1824, the Peruvian congress named him dictator of Peru. The following year, the Republic of Bolivia was created, named after Bolívar. However, Bolívar was ultimately unable to maintain control of the large region that Gran Colombia included. By 1826, internal divisions and differences sparked dissent throughout the nation, and regional uprisings erupted. Bolívar's vision of creating a federation among all the newly independent Latin American republics modeled after the United States, with a government that recognized and upheld the rights of individual citizens, ultimately failed. In 1830, Bolívar resigned as president of Gran Colombia, and it broke apart.

Mexico

In Mexico, Miguel de Hidalgo led a rebellion against the Spanish in 1810. The white inhabitants of European ancestry, the Creoles, executed Hidalgo. Later, a Creole general, Augustin de Iturbide, conquered the capital and named himself emperor. Although he declared Mexico's independence, other Creoles deposed him later and declared a republic. Shortly thereafter, the southern regions of the Spanish Empire in Mexico declared independence and formed the Central American Federation. In 1838, the Federation split into Guatemala, El Salvador, Honduras, Nicaragua, and Costa Rica. **Benito Juárez** attempted to curtail the influence of the Church and of the military in Mexico. In the Constitution of 1857, Juárez limited the privileges of priests and other elite members of society. Church properties were confiscated, and Mexicans gained such civil liberties as freedom of speech and universal manhood suffrage. Juárez was a native Mexican, not a Creole, and he intended his reforms to benefit the native Mexicans. However, Creoles bought much of the confiscated Church lands, and more than 95 percent of Mexican peasants remained landless.

Brazil

The French invasion of Portugal in 1807 had driven the royal family into exile in Brazil. Portuguese King Dom João VI lived in Brazil, which became the center of royal power. Although the king returned to Portugal in 1821, his son Pedro stayed behind as regent. Revolution erupted only one year later. Pedro disobeyed his father's command to return home, and eventually revolutionaries established him as Emperor Pedro I. Of the Latin American countries, Brazil alone remained under the control of a monarchy.

Argentina

Creole leaders continued to exploit and oppress native populations in Argentina, where regional military leader Juan Manuelde Rosas (1835–1852) put down rebellions through brutal means. Rosas ruled as a despot, but he did succeed in establishing a centralized government in Argentina.

Rebellions and Reform in China

The Taiping Rebellion

Hong Xiuquan, the son of a poor farmer near Canton, led the **Taiping Rebellion** in China. He had failed the civil service examinations twice, then studied with a Baptist minister, and then formed a new Christian sect, the God Worshipers. He believed that the overthrow of the Manchu Qing dynasty would bring about the Kingdom of Heaven. The famines of the 1840s likely contributed to revolts such as this one, as peasants looked for new ways and groups to provide for them. In the 1840s, Hong Xiuquan's followers began to amass weapons and develop a military structure, and in the 1850s the government saw them as a big enough threat to attack them. Hong Xiuquan followers successfully repulsed the attack, and in 1851, Hong Xiuquan declared that the Kingdom of Heavenly Peace had been founded, and that the Chinese were in the era of Taiping, or peace, with Hong Xiuquan as the Heavenly King. Taiping was to be a classless society with all wealth distributed equally, and with women equal to men. The generals of the movement claimed to receive visions from God, and the "Heavenly King" himself tolerated no dissent. However, the movement failed to maintain authority in the areas it conquered, and Hong withdrew from public life. In 1864, faced with the desertion of his most important general, Hong committed suicide, and the twenty-year-long Taiping Rebellion was over.

The Self-Strengthening Movement

In response to the loss of the Opium Wars in 1842, unequal treaties with Western countries, and internal rebellions, the **Self-Strengthening Movement** arose in China. The movement was advocated by scholar-administrators such as Li Hongzhang and Zuo Zongtang, who had fought on the side of the government in the Taiping Rebellion. Although she had previously opposed reforms, Dowager Empress Tz'u Hsi became the first imperial ruler of China to agree that China could learn much from the West, and she also supported the Self-Strengthening Movement. Beginning in the early 1860s and continuing until the end of the century, leaders of the Self-Strengthening Movement established modern institutions in China, including capitalistic practices, and modernized the military, industries, communications, and transportation based on Western models. Students studied Western science and languages; special schools were opened in the cities; and students were sent to study in Western countries by the government, in the belief that the restoration of China could be accomplished with the application of Western practices. Despite some accomplishments, the Self-Strengthening Movement ultimately was not successful. The Chinese failed to understand the significance of the differences between Western experiences and China's own history, and the importance of the political structures and social movements that had facilitated Western innovations and prosperity. The modernization of China at this time was further thwarted by the continued influences of Neo-Confucianism on the bureaucracy, as well as the ongoing European and American economic encroachments that continued to weaken China.

The Boxer Rebellion

The increasing influence of Western countries in the Chinese economy and resistance to Western customs led to a mass outpouring of antiforeign sentiment and Chinese nationalism. This culminated in the **Boxer Rebellion**, led by the Society of Harmonious Fists, which first arose in Shandong province. The name of the rebellion came from the fact that members of the society practiced shadow boxing, which they believed made them impervious to bullets. In 1900, the Boxers invaded Beijing, with the complete support of Dowager Empress Tz'u Hsi, who was the de facto ruler of the Qing dynasty from 1861 to 1908. At that time, fearing further encroachment from Western nations, she fully supported the Boxers. In Beijing, the Boxers attacked foreign embassies, including those of Britain, Germany, Japan, Russia, and the United States, while Chinese troops watched the events. The foreign ambassadors survived the assaults for two months before an international relief force came, known as the Eight Power Allied Forces. They occupied Beijing and put down the rebellion, and U.S Foreign Secretary John Hay formulated the Open Door Policy, allowing all nations access to Chinese markets.

TEST TIP

Leave your AP World History textbook and review materials at home or in your locker during the exam. You are not allowed to refer to any potential sources of information during the break period between test sections. If the test proctor thinks you are trying to study during the exam period, you may be forced to leave the exam and have your score canceled.

Ideologies of the Nineteenth Century

The revolutions that occurred in the United States, France, and Latin America resulted not only in dramatic changes in the governments, but also in the reshaping of Western views of politics and the nature of social orders. The revolutions inspired a feeling of solidarity among many people with others who shared their views—both within their own countries and in other parts of the world—and gave them hope for a truly democratic society that valued equality, freedom, and justice. Some ideologies, however, went further than others in terms of just how drastic social and political changes should be.

Liberalism

Liberalism was based on the ideals of liberty and equality. Liberalists advocated representative government, equality before the law, freedom of speech, freedom of assembly, freedom of the press, and freedom from arbitrary arrest. Liberalism also promoted free enterprise and lack of governmental control of the economy, also known as the *laissez faire* approach or classical liberalism. After 1815, advocates of liberalism were largely from the middle class. Their interests collided with those of the lower classes; for example, they often wished to limit such things as the right to vote to those who owned property.

Socialism

Socialism first emerged in France. One of the most influential early advocates of socialism was Count Henri de Saint-Simon. He welcomed industrialization but advocated government control of the economy with the industrialists in charge. Socialists such as Saint-Simon advocated help for the poor, government control to ensure economic equality between the rich and poor, and the regulation or abolition of private property.

Radicalism, as its name implies, proposed drastic changes to existing governments and mainly advocated the narrowing of the gap between the rich and the poor. There were several branches of radicalism, with some advocating the elimination of titles of nobility and the redistribution of property, but all believed in some means of achieving social equality among the existing elites and the rest of society. During the French Revolution, for example, the Jacobin radicals opposed all forms of counterrevolution and wished to limit the power of the king and institute a republic. The Marxists, who became influential thinkers in the mid-nineteenth century, were also radicals, as well as socialists.

Women's Rights

Many women believed that the values of equality, liberty, and democracy that inspired the revolutions of the time should apply to them as well as to men. Movements that demanded rights for women emerged in France, Britain, and the United States.

In France, many women assumed that the revolution would grant them rights equal to those of men, such as the right of citizenship and the rights to vote and to participate in politics. However, these rights were not granted to women following the French Revolution. In 1791, French playwright **Olympe de Gouges** wrote the *Declaration of the Rights of Woman and of the Citizen*, which was modeled on the 1879 *Declaration of the Rights of Man* issued by the National Assembly after the success of the French Revolution. The *Declaration of the Rights of Man* had declared that everyone in France was considered born free and equal in rights, especially those of life, liberty, property, security, and of resistance to oppression. Although the document contained many lofty sentiments, including freedom of the press, the delegates' use of the word "man" clearly left "women" out of the equation. The *Declaration of the Rights of Woman and of the Citizen* echoed the ideas of the *Declaration of the Rights of Man* but extended these ideas as applying to women as well.

Mary Wollstonecraft, an English writer, also wrote a rebuttal of the assumptions that women were not equal to men in her 1792 *Vindication of the Rights of Women*, in which she argued that women deserved all of the rights that men had achieved in the French Revolution, including the right to equal education and participation in politics. Wollstonecraft also argued that women were rational thinkers apart from their husbands and that equality should extend to women. *A Vindication of the Rights of Women* was translated into French and circulated throughout France, Britain, and the United States. By 1882 women in England had gained property rights in marriage. Women's groups began to fight for the right to vote and for rights for working-class women. Around the turn of the twentieth century, the fight for women's rights created a new ideal, that of the "new woman" who broke with tradition and worked in a profession outside of the home.

In the United States, **Elizabeth Cady Stanton** and **Susan B. Anthony** organized movements based on women's suffrage, or the right to vote. At a convention at Seneca Falls, New York, in 1848, a resolution was passed that justified women's rights to suffrage, and to equal rights in the areas of education, professional occupations, and politics. Similarly to de Gouges and Wollstonecraft, Stanton composed the *Declaration of Sentiments*, modeled on the *Declaration of Independence*, in which she set forth the rights of women. However, the women's movement in the United States would not receive popular support until the twentieth century.

Global Migration

Chapter 18

The rise of imperialism and colonization, as well as the global capitalist economy that followed the Industrial Revolution, dramatically changed migration patterns worldwide in the nineteenth century. In industrialized nations, people moved close to the factories where they worked, causing the population of cities to grow, and generally resulting in mass migrations from rural areas to cities. There were also large-scale immigrations from Europe and Asia into the Americas. People migrated for a variety of reasons, and while some benefited economically in their new societies, others endured both physical and economic hardships as laborers in their new countries. In areas with large new immigrant populations, there were various reactions to the introduction of foreign peoples and their cultures.

Changes in Population and Agriculture

During the eighteenth century, the population of Europe grew dramatically. In 1700, the European population was around 120 million; by 1800, it was 200 million; and by 1850, it had reached 266 million. This population explosion created a ready supply of labor for the Industrial Revolution. Contributing factors to the population growth included improved medical practices and increased immunity to the plague and other diseases that had cycled throughout Europe since the Middle Ages. In addition, crops from the Americas, such as potatoes and maize, combined with new agricultural

Key Terms

Chinese Exclusion Act

convict laborers

Emancipation Proclamation

Enclosure

indentured workers

Pacific Island Laborers Act

upper-middle class

White Australia policy

techniques, increased the food supply and the nutrition of the poor, and therefore diminished the mortality rate and increased life spans.

Continuous rotation of crops replaced the open-field system that had dominated European agriculture since the Middle Ages. Under the open-field system, some fields had been allowed to lie fallow while others were cultivated, and there had been land reserved for common use. Under the new system, common rights were lost as wealthy landowners enclosed common fields and a variety of crops were cultivated there on a continuous basis. **Enclosure** was already underway in England before the eighteenth century, but the enforcement of enclosure laws by the English Parliament in the last half of the eighteenth century consolidated the gains that the landowning classes had made. The enclosure system displaced many peasants from the countryside, and they flocked to the developing cities, providing a cheap supply of labor for factories and other businesses.

TEST TIP

You will not have time to write drafts for the essay questions on the AP World History exam, but you can write notes or make a brief outline for each essay in the space provided in the exam booklet.

Social Changes

The class structure of Europe and other industrialized areas, such as the United States, became more complex in the nineteenth century. While the average level of income increased during the Industrial Revolutions, the gap between the rich and the poor segments of society persisted. The working classes, including agricultural laborers, accounted for as much as 80 percent of the population but collectively earned less than the wealthy elite and the middle classes put together. The Industrial Revolutions created a new group of people in the middle classes, and this group was extremely diverse. New industries created a demand for newly trained and highly skilled workers, with each of these groups being somewhat separate from others by different and sometimes competing interests and lifestyles.

A new **upper-middle class** developed in the form of the most successful industrial business families. After the political revolutions of 1848 failed, many of these people had moved away from their radical leanings of earlier years and more toward the views of the aristocracy. Gradually, they developed a lifestyle similar to the old aristocracy.

Below this new upper-middle class was a middle class that included less-successful merchants without the great wealth of the industrialists, but nevertheless successful and secure. The middle class also included professionals in law, medicine, and other specialized areas. Merchants and especially professionals of the middle class had the freedom to move to different cities and even different countries, as their services were valuable nearly wherever they chose to go.

Small-business owners formed another diverse subclass of the middle class, and as industrialization created demands for new products, a vaster array of these businesses continued to develop. Those working in areas that demanded specialization, such as engineering, were another subclass. Highly skilled workers became almost a new kind of aristocracy within the working classes. A new class of "white collar" workers emerged in the offices of businesses and distinguished themselves from those who worked with their hands. Like lawyers, doctors, and other professionals, these specialized, highly skilled, and experienced office workers often chose to move to bigger cities to take advantage of better opportunities.

Imperialism and the Labor Force: Migration Patterns

In the nineteenth century, approximately 56 million Europeans left Europe and migrated to other areas in search of work. The poor of southern and eastern Europe migrated to the United States in the late nineteenth century, whereas earlier in the century, many people from Britain, Ireland, Germany, and Scandinavia had immigrated to the United States. Their labor helped to support the U.S. move toward industrialization in the late nineteenth century, such as in the steel and railroad industries. Other migrants from Europe went to Latin American countries and became seasonal agricultural workers; others went to newly formed parts of the British Empire, such as Australia and New Zealand, where they often became herders or cultivators.

While many immigrants envisioned the beginning of new and better lives in new countries and planned to stay permanently, others expected to work in other countries only long enough to return home with enough savings to improve their lives in their homelands. For example, beginning in the 1850s, men from Italy migrated in great numbers to Argentina as industrialization created the means for Argentina to export greater quantities of beef and other goods. Argentina appealed to Italians, who endured harsh economic conditions at home. They were drawn by the prospects of working in agricultural and factory jobs for fair wages and by the adventure of living in the New World. Many of these Italian immigrants intended to stay only until they had saved enough money to buy land in Italy and reunite with their families. Working conditions in Argentina often turned out to be harsh, and tensions between workers and their employers resulted in a series of strikes, which eventually led the government to clamp down on the workers. Industrial development in Argentina also turned out to be relatively slow, and about half of the Italian immigrants eventually left Argentina and returned home. While other European immigrants also returned to their homelands after some period of working, the rate of Italians returning to Italy from Argentina was especially high.

Slavery

Early in the nineteenth century, several Western European countries abolished the slave trade. Britain was the first to do so, in 1807, followed by France in 1808, and the Netherlands in 1817. Even the American colonies abolished the slave trade in 1808, years before Spain did, in 1845. Nevertheless, slavery itself continued to be practiced throughout the Americas, especially on plantations, as long as it was profitable.

Thinkers of the Enlightenment criticized slavery, leading to emancipation and abolition movements in Europe and in the Americas. The American and French revolutions, which had been based on the values of equality and liberty, also fueled opposition to slavery. Britain abolished slavery in its colonies in 1833, and the first French Revolution of 1848 freed French colonial slaves. In the United States, the northern states bitterly disagreed with the southern states over slavery, as well as the issue of states' rights as opposed to the power of the federal government. The rift between the northern and southern states led to the American Civil War, which lasted from 1861 to 1865. During the Civil War, President Abraham Lincoln issued the **Emancipation Proclamation** of 1863, which freed all slaves in the United States. Brazil was the last country in the Americas to abolish slavery, in 1888.

Indentured Workers

Indian Indentured Workers

After slavery was abolished by the European colonial powers and the trans-Atlantic trade in slaves ended, workers were in great demand in the colonies, especially in the agricultural sector, such as on sugar and rubber plantations. To meet this demand, Britain, France, and the Netherlands implemented a temporary system of **indentured labor** whereby they transported poor Indian peasants to their colonies in the Caribbean, East and South Africa, and the South Pacific island of Fiji. In most cases, Indian peasants were under contract to work for five years in a colony. Most of them renewed their contracts, and many eventually chose to stay in the colonies permanently, in which case they were paid or given a small piece of land instead of being transported back to India. The Indian immigrant workers were almost all men who were isolated from the local populations. They lived together in squalid barracks, and their lives were entirely regulated by their employers, who treated them harshly, very much as if they were slaves.

TEST TIP

If you have a hard time understanding a question, try circling or underlining key words and ideas from the question stem. Then focus on defining or restating those parts in your own words to help you figure out the purpose of the question overall.

Asian, African, and Pacific Islander Indentured Workers

There was also a mass migration of Asians, Africans, and Pacific Islanders to different parts of the world in the nineteenth century. Most of these migrants sold their services as indentured laborers. Once slavery had been abolished by the Western imperialist powers, owners of plantations in colonies needed another large labor force and turned to indentured servitude as a solution. Indentured workers got free passage and food and shelter in exchange for their labor. They pledged to work from five to seven years in most cases. Most indentured laborers were from India and China, but there were also indentured laborers from Japan, Africa, the Pacific Islands, and Java. While the European migrants usually went to areas with temperate climates, these indentured laborers went to tropical and subtropical areas in the Americas, Africa, the Caribbean, and Oceania. After the Opium Wars, many Chinese were transported to sugar plantations in Cuba and Hawaii, mines in various parts of the world, and railroad construction sites in the United States and other parts of the Americas. The indentured migrants often were treated badly and were sometimes worse off than they had been in their home countries. Although many of these migrants became permanent settlers, others eventually returned home.

Convict Labor

Britain and Australia

In nineteenth-century Britain, persons who were convicted of crimes routinely served hard labor as part of their sentences. Most **convict laborers** were leased to private companies in England under government contracts. The penal colonies that the British first established in Australia in 1788 also made extensive use of convict labor throughout the nineteenth century. More than 150,000 convicts were expelled from Britain and sent to live in the Australian penal colonies during this time. The great majority of these convict laborers had been convicted of theft or minor offenses by British courts. The convicts typically served sentences of seven or ten years, or life sentences, and were treated harshly as prisoners and laborers. They worked either in government works programs, such as building roads, or on farms. Even after these convict laborers had served their sentences, many were never allowed to return to Britain.

The United States

The use of prisoners as laborers was also common in the United States in the nineteenth century, especially in the South. Prisoners were leased to private contractors to labor on plantations, in coal mines, on railroads, and in other industries. Prisons that leased convicts were self-supporting; further, state governments reaped profits by making the contractors responsible for providing shelter, food, and other necessities for the convicts. This resulted in very harsh working and living conditions for the convicts, many of whom were literally worked to death.

Even though contractors were responsible for the care of convict laborers, they were still a cheaper source of labor than paid workers. The leasing of convict labors was strongly opposed by workers in the areas of the United States where this practice was used, as many of these workers were displaced from jobs. For example, in the Coal Creek Rebellion of 1891, the Tennessee Coal, Iron, and Railroad Company dismissed its paid miners and replaced them with leased convict workers. In response, the miners threatened company employees and set fire to some of the company's buildings, eventually taking over the prison from which the convicts had been leased and freeing hundreds of them. When the company responded by simply leasing other prisoners, the miners burned down the prison. Although hundreds of miners were arrested, the state's use of prison laborers remained controversial and was especially opposed by companies that lost work to prison contractors as well as by free workers who had lost or could not get jobs. In 1896, the Tennessee state government did not renew its convict lease contracts with private companies, and Tennessee became one of the first Southern states to end the practice of leased convict labor.

Immigrant Experiences

The waves of migrations changed the makeup of societies in many parts of the world. Millions of men left their families and former lives behind in search of work, hoping to earn enough money to eventually reunite with their families either in their new countries or their home countries. The women who were left in their home countries were forced to take on more responsibility for their children and other family members. In many other cases, entire families left their home countries to escape from famine and extreme poverty.

Immigration of the Poor to the United States

The poor who immigrated to the United States often had difficult journeys where they were packed into ships with deplorable conditions. Once they arrived, these families had little or no money and were forced to settle in the port cities where they landed, such as New York City and Boston on the East Coast and San Francisco on the West Coast. Whole families often lived in single rented rooms in rat-infested slum buildings with no running water or indoor plumbing. Sewage remained uncollected and diseases were rampant in the slums of cities on the East Coast, causing the deaths of many immigrant babies and young children. Competition for jobs was intense, and many who did get jobs barely made enough money for their families to live, even in the most squalid conditions. Immigrants from the same country tended to settle together in their own areas in cities, forming ethnic communities that provided some support in the midst of new, often-hostile societies. As the ethnic makeup of various areas became more diverse and complex, tensions often erupted. Eventually, government efforts were made to stop the flow of foreign migrations from certain areas, especially those from Asia.

TEST TIP

Waiting by the mailbox for your AP exam score? Expect your score report to arrive around mid-July, about two months after you take the exam.

Immigration of the Chinese to California

In 1848, gold was discovered in California, which would attract thousands of Chinese miners and contract laborers over the next several decades. By 1860, nearly 37,000 Chinese had immigrated to California, with about 95 percent of them being men. Even though few Chinese women initially immigrated to either California or other parts of the United States, Chinese women at home bore much of the cost of subsidizing Chinese immigrant men's labor. Employers in the United States paid Chinese workers lower wages than they paid white workers—in many cases barely enough for them to survive. As a result, Chinese women at home bore the costs of raising their children and taking care of older members of their families.

In the mining towns that sprang up in California, some enterprising Chinese men left the mines and began to sell food and perform menial services, work that had traditionally been done by women. Small restaurants and laundries established by Chinese men often became flourishing businesses. Many Chinese men also went to work on the Transcontinental Railroad, which was completed in 1888. They agreed to accept lower wages than the white workers received, and they often worked under the most dangerous conditions. The Chinese were largely responsible for constructing the railways in the American West.

However, the Chinese faced decades of discrimination in California. Especially as the gold rush subsided and the economy of California weakened, many white workers viewed the Chinese laborers as a threat to their own jobs. The Chinese had always been willing to work for lower wages, and racial discrimination and repressive legislation against the Chinese led many of them to congregate in their own communities, apart from Americans. In San Francisco the Chinese formed a community in a neighborhood that became known as Chinatown. There, they developed a support network for themselves and for new Chinese immigrants.

1882 The Chinese Exclusion Act

Between 1850 and 1882, more than 300,000 Chinese had immigrated to the United States, many of them to California. In support of the widespread anti-Chinese sentiments of the population, the U.S. Congress passed the **Chinese Exclusion Act** of 1882. The new law was a significant event in U.S. history. Whereas the United States had previously welcomed immigrants from all over the world, the Chinese Exclusion Act made the Chinese the only ethnic group in U.S. history to be specifically denied entry into the country. Chinese people were also prohibited by law from becoming U.S. citizens, testifying in court, owning property, voting, and having their families from China join them in the United States. This repressive act further alienated the Chinese from mainstream society by preventing them from assimilating into society as other immigrants had successfully done. They retreated further into their own communities and retained their own culture.

Nevertheless, the Chinese population in the United States continued to grow in the years immediately following 1882 and peaked in 1890, but then began to steadily decline, partly as a result of the restriction of new immigrants, but also because of the disproportionate number of Chinese men. Many returned to China to reunite with their families.

Immigration of the Japanese to the West Coast of the United States

The Japanese who immigrated to the western United States in the nineteenth century were similar to the Chinese in that they were not easily accepted into American society. Japanese people began to immigrate to the United States as a result of the changes that occurred during the Meiji Reformation. Following the Chinese Exclusion Act, manufacturers and agricultural businesses supplemented the Chinese labor force with Japanese workers. Most Japanese immigrants worked as contract seasonal agricultural workers, on the railroads, and in canneries. Similar to what the Chinese had experienced, working conditions for the Japanese were harsh, wages were low, and they faced racial discrimination. They were not allowed to work in factories or offices. Also similar to the Chinese, many Japanese immigrants set up small businesses such as restaurants to serve their own communities, while others became vegetable farmers. Later, in the twentieth century, the Japanese would face even more discrimination and harsher treatment by the U.S. government than the Chinese had.

DIDYOUKNOW?

Immigrants were not the only ones to suffer as the United States expanded. Numerous conflicts arose, and many Native American cultures were virtually wiped out as European settlers encountered Native Americans. In 1830, the Indian Removal Act forced Native Americans east of the Mississippi into reservations in Oklahoma. The Seminoles, the Cherokee, and other Native Americans in southeastern North America also endured great suffering as they were forced westward on the Trail of Tears in the 1830s. By 1837, approximately 46,000 Native Americans from this region were forcibly removed from their homelands by the U.S. government. Conflicts continued; in 1890, U.S. soldiers at Wounded Knee killed more than 200 Sioux who were performing the Ghost Dance, which expressed beliefs in a world free of white people.

Chinese and Pacific Islander Immigration to Australia

Similar to the situation in California, the Australian colonies of New South Wales and Victoria experienced a gold rush between 1851 and 1860. More than 300,000 immigrants flocked to the colonies in the hopes of finding gold, many of them from China. White miners resented the Chinese miners because of both their industriousness and their cultural differences, resulting in discrimination, conflicts, and even violence against the Chinese. Chinese immigrants were forced to leave many towns that they had settled in beginning in the 1860s. In response to the conflicts, the Commonwealth (Australia) government instituted a **White Australia policy**, which restricted Chinese immigration and established poll taxes and other anti-Chinese policies.

Between 1863 and 1904, more than 60,000 people from the Pacific island of Vanuatu and the Solomon Islands were forced to migrate to work as indentured laborers on the sugar plantations of the Queensland colony in Australia. Some of these laborers might have voluntarily entered into contracts, but for the most part they were essentially kidnapped from their islands and forced to work under slave-like working and living conditions on the plantations, and were therefore not accepted members of society. The Australian government ended these practices with the **Pacific Island Laborers Act** of 1901, which went into effect in 1904. The act specified that the Pacific Islanders be returned their homelands but that they could choose to stay in the colonies if they had lived there for twenty years or longer.

Time for a quiz
- Review strategies in Chapter 2
- Take Quiz 5 at the REA Study Center
  (www.rea.com/studycenter)

Unit VI:
Accelerating Global Change and Realignments,
c. 1900 to the Present

Science and the Environment

Throughout the twentieth century and into the twenty-first century, scientific understanding of the principles of the natural world has grown and deepened in unprecedented ways, which has resulted in technological advances in many fields, including communication and transportation. Along with these advances has come an explosion in global population growth, which has had—and continues to have—a dramatic effect on the environment in many different places on Earth, and on the planet itself and its surrounding atmosphere.

Key Terms

AIDS

antibiotics

atomic bomb

BP oil spill

DDT

deforestation

extinction

firebombing

Fukushima Daiichi

global warming

Green Revolution

greenhouse gases

Hiroshima

HIV

id

Internet

lifestyle diseases

long-range artillery

machine guns

malaria

Nagasaki

nonrenewable energy
   sources

nuclear power plants

penicillin

quantum mechanics

sexual revolution

smart phones

smog

strip-mining

theory of relativity

trench warfare

Type 2 diabetes

uncertainty principle

vaccine

Scientific and Technological Advances

Transportation and Communication

The technological innovations of the Industrial Revolution continued to develop during the twentieth and twenty-first centuries. The internal combustion engine, invented in the late nineteenth century, led to the rise of the automobile industry in the early twentieth century and later to the development of the airline industry. As the twentieth century progressed, researchers, engineers, and scientists designed bigger, faster, and increasingly more sophisticated vehicles of all kinds, including airplanes, trains, and trucks, giving rise to national and international airports, major urban train stations, and national highway systems. Travel from almost any place in the world became quicker and less expensive.

Similarly, continued advancements in communications began to tie together the world's communities. Television, radios, telephones, and other communication devices made it easier than ever for people to communicate locally and globally. Since its development in 1990, the rise of the **Internet** as a global means of instant and frequent communication has furthered the interconnections between individuals and among groups and societies to an incredible extent, as have cell phones, particularly **smart phones**, social networking sites such as Facebook, and video-sharing networks such as YouTube.

Satellites that orbit the earth can transmit voices, images, text, and other data almost immediately across all distances. Smart phones enable people everywhere to make live videos of events, both public and private, that national and international broadcasting companies and even governments do not have access to—and in some cases, do not want to be recorded and transmitted—and then post them on video networking sites, where they can be viewed by virtually anyone in the world who has access to the Internet.

Scientific Paradigms

Throughout the past eras of history and across the globe, religions have significantly influenced societies in such aspects as family life, traditions, government, and politics. As the trend of nonreligious Enlightenment ideals such as liberalism, socialism, communism, and the importance of scientific observations continued, many people and groups in the twentieth century came to rely less on religion and its explanations of the natural world to guide their lives. Instead, there was a greater interest in newly emerging scientific explanations for the nature of human existence, society, the world, and even the universe, especially in Western cultures.

Physics

The scientific theories of both Albert Einstein and Werner Heisenberg are examples of revolutionary scientific paradigms that transformed scientists' and others' fundamental understanding of the nature of the world. According to Einstein's **theory of relativity**, published in 1915, space and time are relative to the person measuring them; this introduced the extraordinary idea that all the absolutes of past ages did not exist, and that reality or truth are merely mental constructs.

In 1925, Werner Heisenberg developed **quantum mechanics**, a physics theory that mathematically describes the interactions of matter and energy. Quantum mechanics made possible an understanding of phenomena that could not be described by previously accepted mathematical and scientific ideas and systems; these phenomena included the properties of materials such as semiconductors; superconductivity; and nuclear and chemical reactions. Heisenberg's work on the foundations of quantum mechanics led to his theory of **the uncertainty principle**, according to which it is impossible to specify simultaneously the position and velocity of a subatomic particle; the more accurate the statement of a particle's position is, the less accurate the determination of the particle's velocity. Heisenberg's theory, which suggested that one cannot accurately observe electrons because the very act of observation interferes with them, undermined the basic human assumption that humans can be objective only if they rely on their powers of observation.

Psychology

German psychiatrist Sigmund Freud, whose psychological theories created much interest among those in the social sciences and intellectuals from 1899 to the 1930s, also undercut ideas that most people had always taken for granted. Freud developed a new view of the self whereby much of a person's inner life was relegated to the realm of the subconscious. He introduced the idea of the **id**, the hidden, disorganized aspect of personality made up of desires that are not conscious but that often dictate human behavior. Freud's theory was that inner forces over which people have no control—and in fact are not even aware of—determine how they think and act, which diminished people's sense of having any real personal freedom or control of their destinies.

The Green Revolution

The global population continued to grow rapidly in the twentieth century. Between 1913 and 1960, the number of people in the world increased from about 1.8 billion to 3 billion, despite the great number of deaths resulting from genocide, war, and diseases.

During this time, population growth was relatively slow in Europe, India, and China, while rates of growth in Africa, Latin America, and other regions in Asia were high. Population growth in these traditionally poor regions created the necessity of providing food for millions of people.

In the 1940s, U.S. scientist Norman Borlaug began the **Green Revolution** with his agricultural research in Mexico, which at that time was importing about half of the wheat that its people needed. Borlaug developed high-yield varieties of wheat that were highly resistant to diseases. Using new mechanical agricultural technologies and Borlaug's wheat varieties, Mexico was producing enough wheat for its own people by the 1950s; by the 1960s, it had surpluses of wheat and was exporting it to other countries.

With Mexico's success, the Green Revolution spread worldwide; the United States, for example, experienced nearly the same results with wheat as Mexico did. In 1963, the U.S.-based Rockefeller Foundation and Ford Foundation, along with government agencies throughout the world, provided funds to establish the International Maize and Wheat Improvement Center in Mexico. It continued the research that Borlaug had begun and used the technologies of the Green Revolution to greatly increase the supply of food needed for the growing global population. Many other countries throughout the world were greatly helped by the Green Revolution. For example, since implementing Green Revolution technologies, the highly populated countries of India and China have not experienced any periods of widespread famine, as they had in the past.

Medical Advances

The dramatic increase in food supplies resulting from the Green Revolution was partly responsible for the continuing overall rise in the human population in the latter half of the twentieth century. Another major factor was greater understanding of medicine—notably, the discovery of antibiotics and the polio vaccine.

Antibiotics

Before the discovery of **antibiotics** in the 1940s, there was no protection against any type of bacterial infection. Even a minor cut could be fatal if it became infected with bacteria. In fact, during World War I, more troops died from infections in their wounds than from the wounds themselves. In 1928, Scottish biologist Alexander Fleming discovered that *Penicillium,* a mold that he had been studying, produced a substance that could kill disease-causing bacteria without damaging healthy cells. Fleming called this substance **penicillin**. By 1945, pharmaceutical companies were producing the antibiotic for mass distribution. Penicillin soon became known as the "wonder drug" because it successfully treated not only minor bacterial diseases but also a variety of virulent bacterial diseases, including bacterial pneumonia, scarlet fever, gonorrhea, and syphilis. During the 1940s and 1950s, scientists discovered other antibiotics, including strepto-mycin, which was successfully used to combat tuberculosis, a deadly bacterial infection of the lungs. Antibiotics saved millions of lives throughout the world and eradicated some diseases that had previously been untreatable and incurable.

Vaccines

At the beginning of the twentieth century, polio was one of the most dreaded viral diseases by parents of young children, especially in industrialized countries. Children were particularly susceptible to polio, a disease that spread mainly during the summer and caused muscle weakness, paralysis, and even death. In 1916, a polio epidemic in the United States killed about 6,000 people and paralyzed about 27,000 others, heightening concern about the disease and sparking intensive research into how it was spread and how it could be prevented. In 1955, American Dr. Jonas Salk developed the first polio **vaccine.** Unlike antibiotics, which are used to treat bacterial diseases once they have been contracted, the polio vaccine prevented people from getting the polio virus. Salk's vaccine was a polio virus that had been killed; it worked by immunizing people against polio without actually infecting them with the disease. Polio vaccines were soon made widely available in the United States and other countries. By the late 1960s, polio was essentially eradicated in those countries. Vaccines for smallpox, measles, mumps, rubella, diphtheria, and other viral diseases soon followed, and efforts by national and international organizations to distribute vaccines transformed terrifying epidemics of these diseases into rare outbreaks within a few decades.

By 1950, more than 50 percent of people in industrialized countries lived in cities. For centuries before then, human death rates had been significantly higher in cities than in rural areas. With the development of antibiotics and vaccines that successfully treated or eliminated epidemic diseases, combined with improved sanitation in cities, urban death rates became lower than rural death rates, and have remained so since that time.

TEST TIP

Keep track of your practice test scores. This will help you gauge your progress and discover any general weaknesses that you have in particular areas. Carefully study and review material that covers areas with which you have difficulty.

Energy Technologies

Oil

During the twentieth century, increasing amounts of coal were used to supply fuel for huge electric power plants in industrialized countries. However, the use of the internal combustion engine in automobiles, which were mass-produced in the first decade of the twentieth century, gave rise to oil as the prominent energy source in these countries. Oil made possible all modern forms of transportation of both people and goods throughout the world. The production of oil, including gasoline, rose to incredible levels to fuel the engines of cars, trucks, tanks, airplanes, and other vehicles. Oil, or petroleum, was also the main component of hundreds of manufactured goods, including tires and plastic. When the use of petroleum as an energy source and its products became widespread—and skyrocketed beginning in the 1960s—factories in the United States, Japan, and much of Europe experienced exponentially higher rates of the production of finished goods.

Nuclear Power

After nuclear power was harnessed by scientists working in the United States to make atomic bombs during World War II, the governments of the United States, Britain, Canada, and the Soviet Union supported research in the late 1940s and into the 1950s to develop ways of using nuclear energy for peaceful purposes. Because nuclear power had been shown to be used for incredibly destructive military weapons, these governments strictly controlled all nuclear research and restricted access to information about it. In 1956, Calder Hall, in England, became the first operational nuclear power station capable of generating enough electricity for commercial use. By 1960, seventeen **nuclear power plants** were generating electricity for commercial use in Britain, the United States, the Soviet Union, and France, and several other countries were in the process of developing nuclear power plants.

Throughout the 1960s, nuclear power was accepted as a relatively inexpensive, environmentally clean, and safe source of electricity. Nuclear-powered electricity became widespread, with 90 power plants operating in 15 countries by 1970 and more than 250 plants operating in 22 countries by 1980. All-electric heating systems were installed in buildings around the world to take advantage of nuclear-generated electricity. Like oil, nuclear energy became an energy source that boosted productivity and manufacturing production to even higher levels.

In the mid-1980s, the growth of nuclear energy slowed as a result of public concerns about the safety of reactors, following a disastrous accident at the Chernobyl nuclear power plant in Ukraine in 1986. There were also concerns about the disposal of highly radioactive nuclear waste and the effect of nuclear power plants on the environment. Nevertheless, by 2010, there were about 440 nuclear power reactors operating in 31 countries, and nuclear power accounted for about 14 percent of the worldwide use of electricity.

In 2011, an earthquake with an enormous magnitude of 8.9 and a huge tsunami hit the coast of Japan and traveled more than three miles inland, creating an unprecedented disaster at the **Fukushima Daiichi** nuclear power plant. The earthquake and tsunami disabled the nuclear reactor's cooling systems, led to nuclear radiation leaks, and killed more than 12,000 people, with another 15,000 people going missing. The disaster at the Fukushima Daiichi nuclear power plant caused government leaders worldwide to reconsider the use of nuclear energy, with Germany, for example, deciding to eventually close all of its nuclear-power reactors by 2022.

Human Effects on the Environment

Since the mid-twentieth century, the explosion in population growth and the widespread use of new technologies has had detrimental impacts on natural environments, with varying consequences in different parts of the world. With the increase in the population of the world from 2.5 billion in 1950 to almost 7 billion in 2011, individuals, corporations, governments, and other organizations have competed for the Earth's natural resources at an unprecedented rate. While some natural resources, such as water, are renewable, others, such as fossil fuels, are not. Thus, some environmental damage caused by human consumption of natural resources has or can still be repaired, but damage to some parts of the Earth's environment might be irreversible.

Deforestation and Extinction

The tremendous growth in the human population has had numerous negative effects on environments throughout the world. Large areas of forests, including rain forests, have been cut down in the process of **deforestation**; pastures and fields have been cleared; waterways have been diverted; and swamplands have been destroyed—all to make room for more people and the buildings, factories, and other structures that people desire. The effects of population growth have been especially devastating to less-developed countries, which do not have the resources to limit the damage to their environments. Millions of people in various parts of Africa and the Southern Hemisphere, including Brazil, Haiti, and southern Asia, continue to deforest the land, as they still rely on wood fires for cooking and heating.

The expansion of human populations into previously untouched environments has caused the **extinction** of countless species of plants and animals and has threatened many others. In 1996, scientists estimated that as many as 20 percent of all species of vertebrates on Earth likely were in danger of extinction. In 2004, research by the Natural Environment Research Council Conservationists indicated that for the first time since the extinction of dinosaurs, humans were driving species of animals and plants to extinction faster than new species could evolve, as the result of the destruction of natural habitats, hunting, the introduction of alien predators into new environments, and climate change. It further concluded that the rate of extinction was approaching the rates of the five natural mass extinctions that had occurred on Earth in the past several hundred million years.

Fossil Fuels

Industrialized countries have progressively become heavily dependent on nonrenewable sources of energy, especially coal and oil, for transportation, electricity, manufacturing, and heating. **Nonrenewable energy sources** are so named because they either cannot be replaced at all or they cannot be renewed quickly enough to keep pace with their consumption.

Coal

The most abundant fossil fuel in the world is coal, which accounted for more than half of all the energy used worldwide in 1950. The use of coal began to decline in the 1960s as nuclear power plant construction was on the rise. By 1990, coal represented only 20 percent of the global energy consumption, but it currently accounts for about 41 percent of total usage, which is partly a result of fewer plans to build nuclear power plants and partly the result of the rapid industrialization in China, parts of eastern Europe, and other regions that have occurred over the past several decades. In addition, many poor and rural people in both industrialized and less-developed countries use coal fires for heating and cooking.

Although there are still billions of tons of coal reserves—enough to possibly last for another 200 years if world consumption continues at the current rate—the use of coal as an energy resource has created significant environmental problems in regions of the world where it has been mined. Coal has been intensively mined from deposits near the Earth's surface in the process of **strip-mining**, which destroys the natural habitat of the entire area and leaves huge gaping holes surrounded by waste rock. Areas that have been strip-mined are essentially wastelands, and they cannot recover unless the land is restored. Although some industrialized countries, such as the United States, have enacted laws since the 1970s that require reclamation of land that has been strip-mined, many other countries have not.

Oil

The use of oil to generate electricity began to increase in the 1920s and reached its peak in the 1970s, with oil accounting for about 23 percent of electric power worldwide. However, oil prices rose sharply at the time because of political tensions centered in the Middle East, and by 2001, oil use for electric power had declined to 7 percent. However, since the late 1940s, oil has continued to be the most important energy resource in the world because of its use in transportation. In 1950, slightly less than 2 million barrels of oil were used to fuel vehicles. By 1986, that number had skyrocketed to 28 million barrels per day. Oil now accounts for almost half of the total energy used worldwide every year.

More than 50 percent of the oil reserves on Earth are located in the Middle East, with most of the once-considerable reserves in the southwestern United States having already been used up. The majority of the oil reserves in the world that have been discovered are being used, and oil is being consumed at rates that far exceed the likelihood of the discovery of new reserves. Many experts estimate that if the consumption of oil continues to increase at present rates, the world's oil supplies may be exhausted in about thirty years.

Like coal, the use of oil creates problems for the environment and can be dangerous for workers. Outside the Middle East, a significant amount of the world's oil reserves must be extracted by erecting platforms over the ocean and drilling into the ocean floor. Accidental oil spills involving offshore drilling can severely damage the surrounding environment, killing marine plants, animals, and birds. For example, the 2010 explosion and oil spill on a BP oil rig in the Gulf of Mexico killed 11 men and injured 17 others working on the oil rig. The **BP oil spill** was the biggest marine oil spill in history, releasing an estimated 5 million barrels of crude oil into the water. The spill killed and damaged marine organisms within at least a 4,200-square-mile area of the Gulf's water and caused further damage to wildlife habitats along more than 300 miles of the Gulf Coast. The devastation to the environment was so great that its extent may never be fully known.

Other oil reserves, such as those in northern Alaska, are located in the wilderness. Wildlife in such areas suffer when their environment is disrupted by the building of roads and pipelines to extract oil from the ground.

Air Pollution and Global Warming

The burning of both coal and oil releases pollutants into the atmosphere. When coal or oil is burned, the toxic gases sulfur dioxide, nitrogen oxides, and carbon dioxide are emitted. Burning coal also emits heavy metals. The emissions from coal-fired power plants result in acid rain, which can kill trees and other organisms and also corrode metal structures, such as bridges, buildings, and statues. Acid rain accumulates in rivers and streams as well, and it has left lakes and ponds virtually without life in parts of eastern North America and northern Europe.

With increased public concern about the threats to the environment caused by the burning of coal and oil beginning in the 1980s, many coal-fired power plants in industrialized countries were required by law (or voluntarily) to install scrubbers and electrostatic precipitators in their smokestacks, which reduce but do not eliminate the harmful emissions. In addition, the millions of vehicles in the world that burn oil-based fuels, particularly gasoline, continue to release toxic gases into the air every minute of every day. These gases pollute the air near the surface of the Earth and sometimes form toxic smog in big cities. In the twentieth century there were several instances when the **smog** enveloping big cities became so dense and toxic that it caused the deaths of many people and harmed many more, such as the noxious black smog that covered London in 1952. The smog was so thick that there was zero visibility in London and people were trapped in the city for four days. The smog caused the deaths of about 4,000 people, most of whom of were elderly, very young, or had respiratory or coronary diseases. This event led to England's Clean Air Act of 1956.

DIDYOUKNOW?

In the 1990s, government reports confirmed that the white marble of the Taj Mahal, one of the world's most famous buildings, was turning yellow and being damaged by air and water pollution. The Indian government committed more than $100 million in 1998 to a program that would restore the monument and prevent further damage. However, in 2010, a new report found that the efforts of the program were not sufficient to keep up with increased levels of pollution caused by the growth of the population, industries, and vehicles in Agra, a manufacturing center where the Taj Mahal is located. In addition, the new report found that the population increase in Agra had created such a high demand for water that the underground water table had dropped by about 12 feet within several years, creating concerns about the Taj Mahal's foundations. Both the city's water supply and the Yamuna River, which flows alongside the Taj Mahal, were found to be heavily polluted by the discharge of industrial waste and clogged sewage pipes. It remains unknown whether one of the world's most magnificent structures will ultimately be irreparably damaged by water and air pollution.

Currently, there is a virtually unanimous consensus among scientists and other experts in the world that the toxic gases that have been emitted into the atmosphere by the burning of fossil fuels for more than a century are contributing to **global warming**. While there are opponents to this mainstream scientific belief, no scientific organization in the world disputes it. The scientific community and many others believe that the enormous amount of carbon dioxide, fluorocarbons, and other **greenhouse gases** that have risen into the ozone layer of the atmosphere have damaged it to the extent that average surface temperatures on Earth have risen and will continue to do so. If the rate of greenhouse gas emissions remains unchecked, scientists expect that global weather patterns will be disrupted and that some environmental regions on Earth will be devastated; as huge Arctic glaciers continue to melt, sea levels will rise and low-lying regions will likely be permanently flooded. Climates throughout the world will change, with results of varying severity.

Water Pollution

In the twentieth century, manufacturing industries began to use synthetic materials, including plastics and inorganic pesticides, most notably DDT. These materials turned out to be toxic to the environment, as they are not biodegradable but instead accumulate in the ground and in rivers, streams, and other water sources. Although water pollution had become widespread as the Industrial Revolution of the nineteenth century progressed and factories simply dumped their wastes into the nearest river or lake, water pollution became a major crisis in the twentieth century.

Rivers, streams, and lakes continued to be used as dumps for wastes and sewage in industrialized countries. However, the industrial wastes that were dumped in bodies of freshwater were becoming more and more toxic—so toxic, in fact, that the Cuyahoga River in Ohio, which flows into Lake Erie, burst into flames several times between 1936 and 1969 as a result of oil slicks and flammable industrial waste floating on its surface. The media attention to the fire in 1969, as well as increased awareness of the widespread contamination of bodies of water throughout the United States, led to the enactment of the U.S. Clean Water Act of 1972. The act prohibited the dumping of any wastes of any amount into waterways, and the water quality of freshwater sources soon showed considerable improvement.

In areas close to freshwater sources where industrial waste had been dumped or pesticides had been used, there were unusually high rates of physical birth defects, babies born with low IQs, cancers, and other health problems. In 1962, U.S. scientist Rachel Carson's book *Silent Spring* became the driving force of the newly emerging environmental movement both in the United States and around the world. Carson's book exposed the dangers that pesticides, especially **DDT**, posed to both humans and to the environment. Soon after the publication of *Silent Spring* and the intense public concern that it generated, the use of DDT was banned in many countries.

Demographic Shifts

Dramatic demographic shifts occurred in the twentieth and twenty-first centuries resulting from advances in medicine, the development of birth control, social movements, different types of emergent diseases, and military conflicts. Although tens of millions of people from industrialized countries died in World Wars I and II, the number of births balanced the number of people that had died, and the populations of these countries became relatively stable. The numerous advances made in medicine throughout the twentieth and twenty-first centuries have saved millions of lives, particularly in industrialized counties, while diseases in poorer countries continue to ravage their populations.

Birth Control

Human reproductive and sexual patterns changed significantly in the mid-twentieth century. Birth control pills were first developed in the late 1950s, and by the 1960s they were widely available. Birth rates declined in industrialized countries, largely because of birth control pills and other contraceptives. In addition, more women began to work outside of the home and go to college, and couples tended to marry at later ages. Death rates also declined, as advancements in medicine and overall improvements in health led to increased longevity.

The freedom that birth control pills gave women allowed them to determine when they became pregnant and gave many of them a sense of having control over their own destinies. Contraceptives also had a great influence on the women's rights movement of the 1960s and the **sexual revolution**, which began in the late 1960s in the United States and spread to Europe and other Western countries. The sexual revolution challenged traditional attitudes toward sexuality and resulted in greater acceptance of sexual freedom, including sexual relationships outside of marriage. Continuing into the 1980s, the sexual revolution also led to an acknowledgment and some acceptance of homosexuality and the legalization of abortion in many countries.

Diseases

AIDS/HIV

Although great strides were made in health care and medicine in the twentieth and twenty-first centuries, there also was a rise in epidemic diseases, such as **AIDS** (acquired immunodeficiency syndrome), caused by **HIV** (human immunodeficiency virus), that particularly threaten underdeveloped regions such as Africa. In 2005, a staggering 22.5 million of the 33.3 million people worldwide who had HIV were living in sub-Saharan Africa, where 1.3 million of the total 1.8 AIDS-related deaths worldwide also occurred. In some parts of Africa, two of three children are orphans as a result of the ravages of AIDS. As Johanna McGeary stated in her 2001 *Time* magazine article "Death Stalks a Continent," "Barely a single family remains untouched."

The high-quality health care and effective but expensive drugs that developed countries can provide are not available to the poor of Africa. Thus, some experts predict that the ravages of HIV/AIDS in Africa will continue to rise, with the vast majority of deaths being adults. Those who live with HIV infection and AIDS are eventually unable to work. This has already led to a rise in child labor in parts of Africa and could eventually cause the collapse of economies there.

Poverty remains a significant problem in the twenty-first century. Although every nation in the world has some people who live in poverty, the majority of impoverished people live in Central Asia, sub-Saharan Africa, and South America. The AIDS crisis in Africa, which is a direct result of poverty, also threatens to dramatically raise the level of poverty on the continent.

Malaria

Malaria is an infectious disease that is also associated with poverty. It is caused by parasites that are transmitted to humans from female mosquito bites. Although malaria has existed throughout human history, it has persisted in tropical and subtropical regions of the world. Malaria can be successfully treated within about 48 hours; however, when it is left untreated, as it often is for the poor, it can be fatal. Malaria is prevalent in the poorest tropical and subtropical areas of the world, particularly in Africa, Central America, South America, and southern Asia.

Since the mid-1980s, the incidence of malaria has more than doubled, and it has become the fifth-leading cause of death among infectious diseases worldwide. In Africa, it is the second-leading cause of death, after AIDS. In 2009 there were an estimated

225 million cases of malaria worldwide and about 781,000 deaths resulting from the disease. Ninety percent of these deaths occurred in sub-Saharan Africa, with most being young children.

Untreated cases of malaria and resulting deaths are not only caused by poverty; they also perpetuate the cycle of poverty and hinder economic development in places where it is widespread. In Africa alone, billions of dollars are spent every year trying to control malaria, but even this has resulted in little or no success in curbing the spread of this deadly disease. Because there is limited access to health education programs and medicine that is widely available in wealthier societies, malaria remains a disease of poverty.

Lifestyle Diseases

While societies in the poorest regions of the world are afflicted with endemic diseases, and diseases that are curable but remain rampant because of poverty, for several decades the most industrialized Western countries have been experiencing high incidences of preventable diseases associated with lifestyles. However, these **lifestyle diseases** are no longer confined to the industrialized countries of the West, as millions of people in other countries are adopting Westernized lifestyles and are developing diseases related to lifestyle choices. Obesity, smoking, and alcohol abuse are among the lifestyle choices that most contribute to the development of noncommunicable diseases, such as diabetes, heart disease, and cancer. The World Health Organization reported that in 2008, noncommunicable diseases were responsible for the deaths of about 36 million people out of a total of 57 million deaths worldwide, and that many of these deaths were preventable.

Type 2 diabetes is one noncommunicable disease that has reached epidemic proportions and is growing at an alarming rate worldwide. Type 2 diabetes is associated with obesity; it is easily preventable by the adoption of a healthy lifestyle, including a nutritional and well-balanced diet along with regular physical activity. However, millions of people throughout the world have busy lifestyles that include overconsumption of high-calorie fast foods, which are laden with unhealthy fats and sugars and often lead to obesity.

In 2008, more that 38 percent of adults and 17 percent of children in the United States were significantly overweight or obese, with many other industrialized countries having similar rates. However, obesity and associated diseases such as Type 2 diabetes are no longer a problem that exists only in wealthy Western countries; obesity and diseases that result from this disease are also dramatically increasing in developing and less-developed countries. In 2010, more than 250 million people in the world had

Type 2 diabetes, with the World Health Organization projecting that by 2025 this number will rise to more than 380 million people, with developing countries bearing the brunt of this epidemic.

Wartime Casualties

The military weapons and tactics developed for both World War I (1914–1918) and World War II (1939–1945) gave the industrialized nations the power to cause massive destruction. The advanced weaponry used in both wars caused unprecedented human casualties. Throughout World War I, military leaders successfully sought ways to develop more mobile, accurate, and destructive weapons. These weapons and the tactics with which to use them were further refined after World War I and laid the groundwork for the even deadlier weapons that were used in World War II.

World War I

Machine guns, with their ability to fire rapidly and continuously, dominated and even came to symbolize World War I. At the beginning of the war, machine guns were very heavy; they had to be mounted on tripods and required several men to operate them, and thus were not very portable. However, over the course of the war, lighter, one-man machine guns were developed. The use of machine guns ultimately led to the horrors of **trench warfare**. The armies of the French, British, and Belgians and their German enemies dug lines of narrow trenches on Europe's Western Front. The area between the opposing trench lines was fully exposed to artillery fire from both sides. Within this narrow area, the combatant forces attacked enemy trenches, only to be gunned down. The opposing armies continued to fire machine guns back and forth, gaining a few miles here and there, only to lose them again, with neither side able to achieve victory. For much of the war, the opposing armies remained stalled in the trenches along the Western Front. More than 200,000 soldiers died in the trenches. Most died from gunshot wounds, but many died from the diseases and infections cause by unsanitary conditions.

During World War I, machine guns were adapted for use on newly invented armored tanks, which were used to transport troops to strategic locations. Tanks could then simultaneously fire artillery at the opposing army. Airplanes were also used for the first time to drop bombs, although these bombs were small and not very accurate. Chemical weapons in the form of tear gas and mustard gas were widely used as tactics to confuse and render opposing forces helpless for short periods of time.

Altogether, about 17 million people died as a result of World War I, including 7 million civilians. Another 20 million people were wounded, making World War I the deadliest conflict in human history—until World War II.

TEST TIP

You can edit each essay as you write by crossing out and inserting words, phrases, and sentences, and by indicating that these and even entire paragraphs should be moved to a different part of the essay. Save some time to review each essay and make your revisions.

World War II

The tanks used during World War II were much more advanced than those used in World War I. Unlike the slow, unwieldy tanks that were primarily used to transport troops and fire machine guns, the new tanks were fast, low to the ground, and outfitted with much more powerful and accurate machine guns and **long-range artillery**, including rocket launchers, such as bazookas and anti-aircraft ballistic missiles. Tanks were used tactically for offensive action to spearhead swift surprise attacks.

Airplanes were also much more advanced, and they were used for both strategic and tactical warfare. Heavy bomber planes conducted long-range strategic air raids to drop bombs on cities and industrial targets. Fighter planes were faster and highly maneuverable, but they also were heavily armed, not only with bombs, but also with heavy machine guns, automatic cannons, and air-to-ground rockets. Fighter planes made accurate, tactical strikes on battlefields without a great risk of heavy losses of troops. They could make steep dives and rapidly attack the enemy low to the ground, often engaging in ground fire.

During the final stages of World War II, a bomber plane was used to unleash the most destructive weapon in history: the **atomic bomb**. In 1945, U.S. President Harry Truman authorized the first use of the atomic bomb against the opposing forces of Japan. A U.S. bomber plane dropped an atomic bomb on the city of **Hiroshima**, Japan, but Japan still did not surrender. Three days after the Hiroshima bombing, the United States dropped a second atomic bomb on **Nagasaki**, Japan. The world had never seen a weapon with such destructive force. The cities of Hiroshima and Nagasaki were annihilated in an instant. In Hiroshima, about 75,000 people were killed on the day of the bombing, and about 75,000 more died from radiation, burns, and other horrible injuries within months. Similarly, in Nagasaki, about 40,000 people died in the bombing itself, with the same number of people dying over the course of two to four months. The magnitude of the loss of life and devastation shocked the world; even the two days of **firebombing** by U.S. planes on Tokyo, which had occurred earlier in the year, paled in comparison. One hundred thousand people died in the firebombing of Tokyo, but it took two days and hundreds of tons of bombs to accomplish what the two atomic bombs did in a split second.

Atomic bombs have never been used since the bombings of Hiroshima and Nagasaki. Their use completely changed the nature of warfare by proving to the world that in the face of such massively destructive weapons, all other military weapons are essentially useless. Atomic bombs by themselves, if used, would be the only deciding factor in the outcome of a war.

Global Conflicts and Their Consequences

Chapter 20

At the beginning of the twentieth century, the politics of the world were dominated by European nations. Although the influence of the United States, Russia, and Japan was rising in the European-led political world order, both Britain and France still held large empires with territories scattered throughout the world. Following the unification of Germany in 1871, and its subsequent emergence as one of the leading industrialized nations, the centuries-old struggle for power among the European nations intensified.

Key Terms

9/11

38th parallel

Adolph Hitler

Allies

al-Qaeda

anti-Semitism

appeasement

Balfour Declaration

Bay of Pigs

Benito Mussolini

Black Hand

Bolsheviks

Central Powers

Chinese Communist Party

Civil Rights Movement

Cold War

Comintern

containment

Cuban Missile Crisis

D-Day

demilitarized zone

détente

domino theory

Duma

Eastern Front

Fascists/Fascism

Fidel Castro

Franklin D. Roosevelt

Gestapo

glasnost

Government of
India Act

Guernica

Holocaust

Irish Republican
Army (IRA)

Iron Curtain

James Bond

Jawaharlal Nehru

(continued)

John F. Kennedy

Joseph Stalin

Juan Perón

kamikaze

Mao Zedong

Marshall Plan

Martin Luther King Jr.

Mein Kampf

Miracle of Chile

Mohandas Gandhi

Muhammad Ali Jinnah

Muslim League

Mustafa Kemal

national socialism

Nationalist People's Party

Nazi Party

Neville Chamberlain

North Atlantic Treaty Organization (NATO)

Osama bin Laden

Pakistan

Palestine Liberation Organization (PLO)

Pan-Africanism

Pan-Arabism

Paris Peace Accords

Pearl Harbor

People's Republic of China

perestroika

Petrograd Soviet

Poland

Raul Prebisch

reparations

Rome-Berlin Axis Agreement

Russian Revolution of 1917

SALT treaties

Salvador Allende

Schlieffen Plan

SS

Strategic Defense Initiative

Sun Yat-sen

Taliban

terrorism

Treaty of Versailles

Triple Alliance

Triple Entente

Truman Doctrine

Vichy government

Vietnam War

Vladimir Lenin

Warsaw Pact

Western Front

Winston Churchill

World War I

From the latter half of the nineteenth century up to 1914, the nations of Europe entered into numerous alliances that were intended to prevent war between them. Instead, they formed an inescapable web, so that what affected one European nation affected all of them. European nations would bring numerous other countries into their disagreements and conflicts, giving rise first to World War I and then, later, to World War II. In their quest to retain power and avoid war, the European nations ended up accomplishing the very opposite. They not only caused the two biggest and only global wars in history, but they also lost their dominant position in the world.

By the end of the twentieth century, a new world order had been established. Few nations retained the same type of government that they had had at the beginning of the century. Democratic governments or authoritarian regimes replaced monarchies in areas throughout the world, and many colonies gained independence. In the latter part of the twentieth century and the early part of the twenty-first, tyrannical regimes were overthrown so as to establish democratic forms of government, which often struggled with their own difficulties, especially in countries that tried to apply Western democratic models that were ill-suited to their cultural, economic, and political traditions.

The Collapse of Land-Based Empires

At the beginning of the twentieth century, the centuries-old and far-reaching, land-based empires had become unmanageable. Their militaries experienced continuous defeats in trying to defend their large borders, their economies were weak, and they could not control the social and political unrest of the diverse people who had been their conquests. The Chinese and Russian empires both faced a collapse that likely was inevitable, even without the pressures of World War I, while the Ottoman Empire's demise—while also perhaps inevitable—was precipitated by World War I.

China

By the late nineteenth century, China was seriously weakened by the increasing presence of the Europeans and the unequal treaties that European nations and the United States had forced upon it. This foreign presence also led to the decline of the Confucian scholar-bureaucrats. In 1911, the Yangtze River flooded and killed about 100,000 people. The Qing government failed to respond quickly, and many Chinese people believed that the Qing dynasty had lost the mandate of heaven. Revolts began throughout China, and soldiers from the Qing army joined in a rebellion. The Qing emperor abdicated, and the leaders of the rebellion formed the first Chinese republic, with **Sun Yat-sen** becoming the provisional president. However, China soon fell into a period that was fraught with internal fighting. When World War I began, China was so divided and weak that it declared neutrality.

Russia

Despite the reforms of Tsar Alexander III that had industrialized Russia in the late nineteenth century, there was no middle class of professionals, such as those that developed in Western Europe following the Industrial Revolution. Russia remained backward in terms of agricultural techniques and consequently was still largely a peasant society. Also, foreign investments resulted in Russia becoming a debtor nation, and heavy taxes on imports had still not enabled it to export more products than it imported.

The October Revolution of 1905

The surging Russian economy, however, spurred an interest in imperialistic expansion, with the Far East as the target. However, Imperialist Japan defeated Russia in the conclusion of the Russo-Japanese War in 1905, resulting in a peaceful protest in St. Petersburg. Russian troops opened fire on the protestors, and the resulting massacre turned the people against Tsar Nicholas II. Revolutionary political groups became openly active and organized revolts throughout the summer of 1905. The opposition to the government became so great that a general strike was carried out, effectively shutting down the country. Nicholas II responded with the October Manifesto, which promised civil rights for the people and free elections for the newly created representative body, the **Duma**. In reality, the elections for the Duma did not constitute direct representative government. The tsar still chose and controlled his ministers, and the ministers ran the government, not the Duma. The Duma did have the power to make laws, but the tsar had the power to veto any legislation the Duma passed. The tsar also held ultimate control over the Duma, and was able to dismiss it as he pleased.

When the Duma failed to support Nicholas's views, he dismissed it in 1906. New elections in 1907 brought in even more members opposed to the tsar's government. Again the tsar dissolved the Duma. The tsar's ministers then took steps to see that the tsar's supporters would gain the majority in the Duma by altering the election laws. They were successful, and the next election, also held in 1907, yielded the results the tsar had sought. However, all was not lost for the revolutionaries. The new leader of the Duma, Peter Stolypin, a supporter of the tsar, recognized the need for real reform. He rewrote agricultural policies to make it easier for the peasants to truly own the land they farmed. Although these and other reforms did much to modernize Russia, they failed to end the hardships of the common people, which soon sparked a much more powerful revolution.

The Revolution of 1917

Long-standing social unrest in Russia was brought to a boil by World War I. In 1914, Russia entered war with Germany with the same patriotic fervor that swept the rest of Europe. War seemed to be an opportunity for the various factions of Russian politics to make gains, and thus the war had widespread support in Russia. However, Russia was not prepared for an all-out, extended military campaign. The Russian army was ill-equipped and soon ran short of weapons and munitions; it suffered 2 million casualties in 1915 alone.

Tsar Nicholas II failed to provide effective leadership or work with the Duma. By 1915, factions in the Duma were openly critical of the tsar and of each other. Distrusting the Duma and dissatisfied with the progress of the war, Nicholas again dissolved the Duma and headed to the battlefront, leaving his wife, Tsarina Alexandra, in charge in his absence. The situation in Russia rapidly deteriorated and social unrest exploded into open revolt. Continued bad news from the war front and shortages of food in the cities created widespread resentment among the common people. Bread riots broke out in St. Petersburg in 1917. The tsar ordered his troops to restore order, but they joined the revolt instead. The Duma declared a provisional government and the tsar abdicated, ending centuries of Romanov imperialist rule. Alexander Kerensky, an advocate of the rights of commoners in the Duma, became the new leader of the provisional government.

The **Russian Revolution of 1917** was a revolt against the Russian monarchy and the Russian government as it then existed. The revolutionaries were diverse groups with differing goals, values, and ideals. Once their common goal of removing the tsar was achieved, they then turned against each other, each determined to realize their vision for a new Russia. The government formed after the abdication of the tsar was still pro-war, including Kerensky. It granted freedoms to the people, but it did not engage in the social reforms that the more radical revolutionary groups sought. St. Petersburg, renamed Petrograd, was under the control of the **Petrograd Soviet**, a collective group of workers and soldiers who were determined to give political power to the people. By the summer of 1917, Russia was in turmoil, and the government faced a total breakdown.

The Ottoman Empire

At the beginning of the twentieth century, the Ottoman Empire was near the end of its long decline. Centuries of military defeats that had begun as early as the late seventeenth century, continuing wars and loss of territories, financial bankruptcy, and increasing Western control of the economy had irreparably weakened the once-great and powerful empire. The 1908 coup of the Young Turks, who desired greater Westernization, was undercut by World War I, which brought about the final demise of the Ottoman Empire. It ceased to exist when Turkey became a Republic in 1922.

Unprecedented Global Military Conflicts
World War I

World War I was the first war to encompass more than half of the world. It was also known as The Great War and "the war to end all wars" until World War II usurped that distinction. Some historians suggest that the First World War is more properly thought of as the first phase of a 30-year-long war that began with World War I and ended in 1945 with the termination of hostilities in World War II.

In World War I, twenty-eight nations, the **Allies** and their Associated Powers, fought four other nations or empires known as the **Central Powers**: Germany, Austria-Hungary, Bulgaria, and the Ottoman Empire. World War I was the first total war in history, as those involved used every resource available for the war effort. For the first time, people referred to the **home front**, meaning the mobilization of resources for the military front within countries at war. Mobilization at home drained countries of their males who were old enough to fight, creating a vacuum in the workforce. Many women, particularly in Britain and the United States, went to work in factories to make war supplies. The poor in the United States and Europe benefited from mobilization, as new jobs provided more money for their basic needs.

World War I brought about not only the end of the Ottoman Empire and the Russian Empire, but also the German Empire and the Austro-Hungarian Empire. It also resulted in the creation of nine new nations and ended the global supremacy that Europe had enjoyed for centuries.

TEST TIP

Leave your AP World History textbook and review materials at home or in your locker during the exam. You are not allowed to refer to any potential sources of information during the break period between test sections.

Nationalism

The rise of nationalist movements in the nineteenth century culminated in World War I. Independence movements had erupted in the early nineteenth century and threatened the Ottoman Empire, with its territories of Greece, Montenegro, Serbia, and Romania all having gained independence by the latter part of the century. The Austro-Hungarian Empire's control of Bosnia and Herzegovina, which had large populations of Serbs, Croats, and also Muslims, created further tension between Serbia and Austria. Serbia, along with Greece and Bulgaria, fought the Ottoman Empire in the First Balkan War, leading to Austria-Hungary's attempts to control Serbian expansion. From 1912 to 1913, the Balkan states of Bulgaria, Greece, Montenegro, Serbia, and Romania fought two wars over territories held in Europe by the Ottomans.

Imperialism

The nineteenth-century colonial empires of Britain, France, Russia, and Germany had created tensions and military actions throughout the world. Starting in 1905, there erupted a series of conflicts over colonial possessions, laying the foundation for World War I. Although Germany was rather late in joining the imperialist colonization of Africa, it often conflicted with Britain and France over its aspirations in Africa. In Morocco, for example, the Germans supported the movement for independence against France. Britain had several disputes with other powers, such as France, as a result of its expanding presence as a colonial empire, leading to the creation of a series of treaties. While these treaties resolved some of the tensions in the nineteenth century, they created a system of alliances that quickly came into play during the early phases of World War I.

Alliance Building

In the latter half of the nineteenth century, the nations of Europe participated in alliance building on a grand scale. The purpose was to form alliances for mutual defense, alliances to isolate potential enemies, and alliances to negate the potential of nations to engage in wars that would threaten the security of other nations. The great German statesman Otto von Bismarck led the way, making his Prussian-dominated Germany a great power in Central Europe through treaties that he hoped would keep Germany's enemies weak and its neighbors at peace.

Major Treaties that Created the System of Alliances

1873: Three Emperors' League: An alliance of Germany, Austria-Hungary, and Russia

1879–1918: Austrian-German Alliance (Dual Alliance)

1881–1887: Alliance of the Three Emperors: An alliance of Germany, Austria-Hungary, and Russia

1882–1914: The Triple Alliance: An alliance of Germany, Austria-Hungary, and Italy

1887–1890: Russian-German Reinsurance Treaty, whereby Germany and Russia pledged neutrality in the event of an attack by a third party, provided that Russia did not attack Austria nor did Germany attack France

1894: Franco-Russian Alliance

1902–1915: Anglo-Japanese Alliance

1904: Anglo-French Entente

1907: Anglo-Russian Entente

1907–1914: Triple Entente: An agreement among Russia, France, and Great Britain

By 1914, Europe's major powers were the **Triple Alliance** and the **Triple Entente**. The Triple Alliance became the Central Powers of World War I and had grown out of the Dual Alliance of the treaty of 1879, formed for mutual protection against Russia. In 1882, Italy joined this alliance, creating the Triple Alliance. This alliance was tenuous at best, as Italy threatened German relations with the Ottomans and Austria-Hungary's possessions in the Balkans. During the Franco-Prussian War of the nineteenth century, France had suffered a humiliating defeat; it was determined to contain the Germans.

Russia feared the German and Austrian-Hungarian Alliance, while Britain still feared events such as those that had happened in the Napoleonic Wars and tried to preserve the balance of power. Britain, France, and Russia, then, together formed the Triple Entente, or the Allies, of World War I. Between 1904 and 1914, Britain and France also signed a treaty (Anglo-French Entente) and so did Britain and Russia (Anglo-Russian Entente) over their colonial possessions.

The Event that Sparked World War I

On June 28, 1914, a Serbian revolutionary and member of the radical **Black Hand** group, Gavrilo Princip, assassinated Archduke Franz Ferdinand of Austria-Hungary and his wife Sophie in Sarajevo, which was the administrative center of Bosnia. The Black Hand wanted the unification of all Yugoslavs within Serbia. Austria-Hungary was determined to punish the Serbs for this event. As a result of a treaty of alliance, Germany supported its neighbor Austria-Hungary, while Russia supported its ethnic kinsmen the Serbians and their bid for independence, setting the stage for war in Eastern Europe. The Austrians issued an ultimatum to Serbia, demanding the right to participate in the investigation of the assassination. The Serbians refused, and the Austrians declared war on Serbia. Austria-Hungary immediately declared war on Russia, as Russia was mobilizing to defend the Serbians. Then Germany responded by declaring war on Russia, followed by a declaration of war on France. Russia had been allied with France since the Dual Alliance between Russia and France in 1894, and in the Triple Entente, which included England. Therefore, Germany would have expected the French to join in the hostilities.

War Strategies

The alliances and plans for military mobilization based on projected points of conflict ensured that war could not be confined to one region. Austria moved against Belgrade, the capital of Serbia, while Russia mobilized and prepared to attack both Austria and Germany. The French based their maneuvers on offensive attacks without concern for their opponents' strategies, which accounted for many of the massive casualties in the war. The Germans wanted to avoid a war on two fronts, as this might mean that Germany would be surrounded. They relied on the **Schlieffen Plan,** developed by Count Alfred von Schlieffen in 1905, which directed their first assaults on France and then focused on defending Germany from Russian attacks. Germany believed it would take a few weeks to mobilize the Russian forces, which would give the German army the necessary time to knock the French out of the conflict.

The German Advance

Germany, confident in its military, had its army march west rather than east so as to eliminate France from the war. Standing between Germany and its target, France, was the neutral country of Belgium. Belgium's neutrality in such conflicts had been recognized and supported by its more aggressive neighbors since 1839. However, victory for Germany in France depended on its ability to invade swiftly, and the German army would have to enter France through Belgium. Belgium refused to grant Germany permission to pass its borders. Germany refused to be denied and attacked Belgium in 1914. Germany failed to achieve the expected swift victory; its offensive stalled short of Paris. The two combatants flanked each other in a series of moves known as the "race to the sea." Paris was the objective of the German push. With the capture of Paris, France would fall and the Western Front of the war would be under German control. The German army drove hard into France, pushing the allied forces before it. The year ended with the two sides digging into a line of trenches, marking the **Western Front.**

The German plan failed in part because Germany had expected Belgium to either allow the German army to pass or to offer minimal resistance. Instead, the Belgian army fought well against the overwhelmingly superior German forces, and withdrew in orderly fashion to the Allies in France rather than breaking and running. Their efforts delayed the progress of the German army, allowing the British forces time to join with the French. German fear of a potential French invasion across the border between Germany and France had prompted them to leave behind some of their forces to protect the homeland, and so they sent a smaller number of troops into France than mandated by the Schlieffen Plan. Consequently, the Germans were unable to counter the unexpected resistance of the Belgians, especially after they were reinforced by the French.

Germany Is Stopped on the Western Front

Later in 1914, a gap in the German lines gave the French the opportunity to counterattack. The Battle of the Marne halted the German advance and forced the Germans back, but the Allies were not able to mount an offensive strong enough to drive the Germans out of France. In 1916, the Germans attempted to break out of the trenches with an assault on Verdun, a French fortress. The French succeeded in stopping the Germans, but the loss of life was frightening. At the Battle of the Somme, British forces attacked the Germans to help relieve pressure on Verdun. By November, the British had advanced only a few yards at a tremendous cost of life. By 1916, neither side had managed to gain a strategic advantage.

The loss of life was on a scale difficult to imagine. In 1916, more than 1.8 million men were killed or wounded in just two battles; there were 1.1 million combined casualties in the Battle of the Somme and 700,000 casualties in the longest battle of the war at Verdun. Those who did survive war on the Western Front were forever transformed by the carnage.

The Eastern Front

The **Eastern Front**, with Germany and Austria-Hungary opposing Russia, was a different type of war. The Russian army mobilized and moved into eastern Germany, where it faced stiff opposition from the German forces, who drove the Russians back in 1914. They would not be able to mount another major offensive against Germany for the rest of the war. In the Austro-Hungarian campaign, the Russians fared little better. Unable to make any progress against the Austro-Hungarian forces, they were soundly repulsed when the Germans were able to join the campaign. By 1915, the Russians had been driven back to their own territory, with 2.5 million men lost, captured, injured, or killed.

Other nations then joined in the war. In 1914, Italy had declared itself neutral but reversed its position and joined the Triple Entente of Great Britain, France, and Russia in 1915 in the hope of making territorial gains at the expense of Austria. Bulgaria was neutral in 1914 but followed the Ottoman Empire in joining the Central Powers of Germany and Austria in 1915, lured by the possibility of defeating Serbia.

The Ottoman Empire

The entry of the Ottoman Empire into the war was perhaps most significant because it moved the conflict from the confines of Europe and spread it to the Middle East. In 1915, the British launched an attack on Ottoman territory in the Dardanelles, a strait through which supplies could be shipped to Russia, in an effort to distract the Germans. A heavy force of Ottoman troops defended the straits, with the Allies suffering more than 250,000 casualties in the Battle of Gallipoli. Although the British led the campaign, many of the troops were from British colonies. Following the war, the resentment of the Canadian, Australian, and New Zealander soldiers was a factor in the weakening of the British Empire.

The commander of the Ottoman forces at the Battle of Gallipoli was **Mustafa Kemal,** whose success made him a hero in Turkey, his homeland. By the end of World War I, the Young Turks' government had collapsed, with most of their leaders having fled from Turkey. General Kemal led a nationalist movement against the division of Turkey by the Allies, formed the Turkish Republic, and became known as Ataturk, "father of the Turks." He became Turkey's first president in 1924 and served until 1938. Lawrence of Arabia, a British colonel, also took advantage of the weakness of the Ottoman Empire and helped the Arab revolt of Ibn Ali Hussein, sheriff of Mecca and king of the Hejaz, against the Ottoman Turks in 1917. The Ottoman Empire came to an end in 1918 as a result of defeat by the British, who employed troops drawn from the far reaches of the British Empire.

Conflicts over Colonial Territories

The colonial territories of the warring European nations played significant parts in the war. British and French colonies remained loyal, providing food and supplies to the war effort and helping to take control of German colonies, thus removing Germany's ability to draw on its colonial resources. In Africa, the British and French gradually took the four colonies that Germany held. Many Africans fought in the trenches of World War I in Europe and also provided labor for the Allies. Meanwhile, the Japanese, allies of the British, moved against German possessions in the Pacific and in China. Japan captured the Shandong Peninsula and several islands possessed by Germany. The captured German island possessions later became the basis of Japan's line of defense in the Pacific during World War II. Japanese aggression also added to the tension existing between China and Japan.

The United States Enters the War

Early in 1917, the U.S. ambassador to the United Kingdom obtained a copy of the Zimmermann Telegram, which helped to thrust the United States into World War I. In the telegram, which was sent by Germany to Mexico, the Germans offered to return the southwestern portion of the United States to Mexico if Mexico would declare war on the United States. The unrestricted submarine warfare also contributed to the U.S.

decision to enter the war. The sinking of the passenger liner *Lusitania* in 1915 with 139 Americans on board had outraged the United States. Germany then quickly changed its policy for submarine warfare from one of total blockade, in which any ship was a legitimate target, to a more relaxed stance, thus avoiding war with the United States. By 1917, however, Germany felt that the possibility of starving Britain was worth risking the enmity of the United States and went back to a policy of unrestricted warfare. U.S. president Woodrow Wilson declared Germany's new stance to be "warfare against mankind." The United States entered the war on the side of the Triple Alliance in April of 1917.

Russia Makes Peace with Germany

The Russian Revolution crippled the already failing effort of the Russian army to combat Germany. In February of 1918, Russia accepted Germany's peace terms, leaving Germany free to turn its attention back to the Western Front. Germany then launched a new offensive in France, attempting once again to reach Paris. One-hundred-forty-thousand American troops joined the exhausted Allies in stopping the German advance. By August, the United States had committed 2 million men to the war effort. This influx of the fresh troops into the lines of the war-weary Allies proved to be the deciding factor in the war. By October of 1918, the Allies had pushed the Germans back, and they were prepared to accept peace terms.

The Treaty of Versailles

In 1919, the victorious powers met in Paris at the Paris Peace Conference to negotiate the fate of many nations. U.S. president Wilson went to Versailles with high hopes of crafting a lasting peace. He presented his **Fourteen Points**, advocating open treaties, free navigation of the seas, and equality of trading conditions. Chief among the Fourteen Points was his call for the creation of "a general association of nations," which later became the League of Nations. Other Allies had different priorities, specifically, the punishment of Germany. French president Clemenceau was particularly determined to see Germany punished and permanently crippled so that it could never again threaten France. British prime minister Lloyd George was not as strident, but he had to consider the opinion of the British people, who, having had their lives forever changed by the war, were still angry and wanted retribution.

With the **Treaty of Versailles**, Wilson was able to deny France's most punishing demands with the support of the personally moderate Lloyd George. Clemenceau did not achieve the secure buffer zone he sought for France but gained the promise from Britain and the United States that each would come to the aid of France should France be attacked again. Germany lost little territory within Europe, but all of its colonial holdings were divided among the victorious Allies. Germany was allowed to maintain an army, but its size was limited to no more than 100,000 troops. Germany also was allowed to keep the Rhineland but was not allowed to place military installations there, and Germany returned Alsace-Lorraine to France. A part of northeastern Germany that was inhabited largely by Polish people was given to the newly created **Poland**, an action in line with the national self-determination beliefs espoused by Wilson and others.

Wilson could not block the demand for **reparations**. The Allies insisted that the blame for the war be laid squarely on Germany and Austria. Further, Germany would have to pay an undetermined amount of reparations for the destruction resulting from the war. Germany protested the terms of the treaty, but as it too suffered from the devastation wrought by the war, it had no choice but to sign the treaty.

World War II

The harsh terms of the treaty that ended Word War I had the unintended, but not altogether unpredictable, effect of galvanizing nationalistic feelings in the German people. The very measures designed to keep Germany down in fact primed it to rise to the call of a strong leader and helped to fuel the rise of the Nazi Party in Germany.

The Rise of Hitler in Germany

In 1919, **Adolf Hitler** became a member of the German Worker's Party, which was small and radical in its beliefs. It was anti-Semitic, anti-Marxist, anti-democratic, and anti-capitalistic. It advocated **national socialism,** building Germany into one large community of Germanic, and only Germanic, people. The party grew, and Hitler's power within the party grew as well. In 1921 he took control and kept the party moving forward and growing with radical propaganda and mass meetings at which he delivered mesmerizing speeches railing against the government of Germany, the Weimar Republic.

By 1923 the Weimar Republic was clearly becoming unstable. Hitler seized the opportunity to launch a revolt in Munich. Hitler's revolt failed and he was arrested. He turned this defeat into something of a victory, using his trial as a platform to expound his ideals and gaining increased notoriety and exposure. He served less than a year in prison, just long enough to become a near-martyr to his supporters and to write *Mein Kampf,* which articulated the fundamental ideas of the Nazis. This defeat and imprisonment also gave Hitler time to rethink his tactics. He decided that rather than attempting to overthrow the Weimar Republic by open rebellion, he would do better to use his ever-growing base of support to take over the government by political means.

Hitler's party, then the National Socialist German Workers' Party, or **Nazi Party,** continued its growth, reaching a membership of 100,000 by 1928. These members were dedicated, disciplined, and devoted to the Nazi cause. In 1929 the Great Depression gripped Germany, as it did the rest of the industrialized world. As the economy of Germany entered a severe downswing, the Nazis had the opening they needed to find an issue to appeal to the masses. By 1932, 43 percent of German workers were unemployed. The government could not contain the economic crisis, and in desperation, German president General Hindenburg enacted emergency measures. However, these essentially failed to do anything other than increase popular support for Hitler's ideas.

Hitler altered his speeches to appeal directly to those most affected by the failing economy. The middle and lower classes had traditionally supported the conservatives and moderates. In the face of economic disaster, the Communist Party was rising in power. Reacting to the threat of Communism, the danger of personal financial ruin, and the promise by Hitler that the Nazi Party, if given the chance, would turn the economy around and stamp out Communism as well, the middle- and lower-class voters supported the Nazis.

Meanwhile, Hitler sought the support of big business by promising to bring back the profits it had enjoyed, even sacrificing workers' wages if need be. To the army leadership he promised that if given the opportunity, he would overturn the Treaty of Versailles with its punitive conditions and rearm the German military. To the youth of Germany he promised a chance to make a difference, to build a better Germany and to be leaders in the new Germany. German nationalism appealed to the young. They flocked to the Nazi Party in droves. No other political party in Germany could compete with the Nazis for their appeal to German youth. In 1932 the work of Hitler and his party paid off. They won 14.5 million votes and took control of the Reichstag as the largest single party represented there.

Hitler demanded to join the government as the chancellor. The conservatives believed that as they held the majority of government posts, they could control Hitler, even if he were the chancellor. They agreed to his demand, and in 1933, President Hindenburg appointed Hitler as chancellor of Germany. Hitler moved quickly with his new power to end opposition to the Nazi Party. The Nazi Party became the only party in Germany. After the death of Hindenburg in 1934, Hitler abolished the presidency and became Führer. He banned strikes and established the Nazi Labor Front to replace the labor unions. No independent organizations were allowed in Germany. Only those related to the Nazis could exist.

Books and art that did not fit the Nazi mold were banned. In fact, anything that did not fit the Nazi mold was banned. The Nazis controlled virtually every aspect of German public life by 1934, with Hitler's most trusted security guards, the **SS (Schutzstaffel)**, having increasing power along with the **Gestapo,** which became a dreaded organization with few limits on its power.

As Hitler had made clear in *Mein Kampf,* he believed in the superiority of the German race and, because of its superiority, its right to take whatever it needed to expand and fulfill its destiny. Those nations opposed to such expansion simply did not know how to handle Hitler. They tried appeasement and failed, and they did not understand that Hitler's ambitions for expansion would not be limited to what other nations were willing to give up.

Hitler's Aggression Meets with British Appeasement

In 1935, Hitler issued a general draft and fulfilled his promise to the army by declaring that Germany would no longer be bound by the Treaty of Versailles. He announced his intention to rearm Germany in violation of the treaty. Italy, France, and Great Britain protested, but the protest was weak and an alliance of the three nations failed to form.

Instead, Britain tried **appeasement**, first with the Anglo-German naval agreement, then in other ways. In 1936 the German army occupied the Rhineland in direct violation of the Treaty of Versailles. France had specifically demanded that the Rhineland be a de-militarized buffer zone as a defensive area to protect France from German aggression and was alarmed by this aggression. However, without support from the British, the French were afraid to act. There were several reasons why the British tried appeasement. First, the memory of the overwhelming loss of life in World War I was still fresh in the minds of the British. They did not want to enter another devastating war. Also, the British felt that Germany had been harshly punished for World War I and therefore it understood some of Hitler's demands, such as rebuilding the army and moving into the Rhineland. Further, Russia, which had by then become the dominant part of the Soviet Union, and the brutality of Soviet leader Josef Stalin's brand of Communism, had been the foremost threat in the minds of the British. They did not believe that Hitler was as dangerous as Stalin. Hitler was something of a champion against the spread of Communism, as he had stamped it out in Germany. This made Hitler at least somewhat sympathetic in the eyes of the British. As long as Hitler did not do anything that could not be excused or ignored, the British did not intend to move against him.

TEST TIP

On the day of the exam, wake up early enough so that you do not have to rush. Eat a good breakfast and dress comfortably, so that you are not distracted by being too hot or too cold while taking the exam. Also plan to arrive at the test center early. This will allow you to collect your thoughts and relax before the exam, and it will also spare you the anxiety that comes with being late.

The Rise of Mussolini in Italy

In Italy, **Benito Mussolini** was organizing war veterans into a new group, the **Fascists**. Mussolini's early ideology was a blend of nationalism and socialism. He advocated territorial expansion and land reform, both of which had been promised by the Italian government but never delivered. He also wanted benefits for the working class. Because many of his ideas were also the ideas of the socialists, Mussolini had difficulty in attracting people to his party. By 1920, however, he had discovered that by attacking the socialists he could draw conservatives to his cause. He had found a winning formula and his party grew.

Mussolini organized unemployed war veterans into armed, terroristic squads known as Black Shirts. In 1922 the government of Italy broke down, partly because of the activities of Mussolini's supporters. Mussolini demanded that the current government resign, and that he, Mussolini, be appointed by the king to form a new government. His supporters marched on Rome to make their demands clear, and Italian king Victor Emmanuel III agreed. Mussolini was made dictator for a year and changed the election laws so that, in 1924, his party was able to gain a clear majority in the government. Then the socialist leader Giacomo Matteotti was kidnapped and murdered by Mussolini supporters; this created a political crisis and opposing parties demanded that Mussolini disband his Black Shirts. Mussolini responded by declaring Italy a Fascist nation. He enacted restrictive laws, abolished independent unions, abolished freedom of the press, put the schools under the control of Fascists, and created Fascist unions, organizations, and a youth movement. Mussolini summed it up in 1926: "Everything in the state, nothing outside the state, nothing against the state."

Mussolini Attacks Ethiopia

In 1935, Germany was not alone in its military aggression. Mussolini decided to attack Ethiopia, an independent African nation on the eastern coast. Italy had colonies in East Africa and used these to launch the attack. The reason for the attack had nothing to do with Ethiopia beyond its convenience as a target; Mussolini, like Hitler, felt that expansion was an important part of his doctrine. While he could not expand in Europe without engaging in a war he could not win, Africa provided opportunities for colonial expansion with little risk of an all-out war. Publicly, Hitler supported Mussolini; privately he supplied arms to Ethiopia. Thankful for Hitler's public support, and apparently unaware of his private dealings with Ethiopia, Mussolini signed the **Rome-Berlin Axis Agreement** with Hitler. By 1940, Japan would also join the Axis.

Hitler Invades the Sudetenland and Czechoslovakia

In 1938, Hitler, by threatening an invasion, convinced the Austrian chancellor to give control of the government to the Nazis. Hitler then invaded anyway and divided Austria into two provinces, absorbing both into Germany. Hitler then demanded that the Sudetenland, an area of Czechoslovakia with some German-speaking citizens, be given to Germany. Czechoslovakia did not want to cooperate. Its position was strengthened by its alliance with France and by France's agreement with the Soviet Union. If Germany attacked Czechoslovakia, France was obligated to declare war on Germany and the Soviet Union was pledged to come to the defense of France. **Neville Chamberlain**, prime minister of Great Britain, negotiated feverishly with Hitler to avert the almost-certain war. Chamberlain and France agreed to Germany's immediate annexation of the Sudetenland. The Czechoslovakians had no choice, since they were unable to stand alone in the face of the German army. Chamberlain proclaimed that he had achieved "peace with honor" and "peace for our time." Seeing this betrayal of Czechoslovakia as a sign of weakness, Hitler then used his army to occupy the remainder of Czechoslovakia in 1939. The British and French finally realized that appeasement would not work.

Germany's Nonaggression Pact with Stalin

Hitler next turned his attention to Poland, but did not move until he secured a nonaggression pact with Soviet leader Stalin. Germany and the Soviet Union each pledged to remain neutral if the other country became involved in a war. The agreement included a secret plan for the division of Eastern Europe between Germany and the Soviet Union. Britain and France had hoped to make Stalin their ally and trap Germany into a potential two-front war, but Stalin had never trusted the West and although he did not trust Hitler either, an alliance with Hitler offered territorial gains, while one with the Allies did not.

World War II Officially Begins with Germany's Invasion of Poland

In August of 1939, Hitler invaded Poland, but contrary to his expectations, Britain and France did not back down and instead declared war on Germany. World War II officially began. Chamberlain was replaced as British prime minister by **Winston**

Churchill, who had long warned of the dangers posed by Hitler. Poland was able to fight against the German invasion for just four weeks. The German military used its blitzkrieg ("lightning war") tactic of hitting hard and fast in an attempt to so overwhelm the enemy that it could not form a significant defense. Germany then turned its attention west, launching another blitzkrieg through Denmark, Norway, and Holland, then moving through Belgium, the Netherlands, and finally into France. The French and British forces dug in to defend France, but Hitler's surprising movements through Luxembourg and the Ardennes forest divided the British from the French and trapped the British on the coast at Dunkirk. In a famous rescue effort, the British employed practically anything that would float, be it military or civilian, to save its army. The soldiers were brought home, but the loss of equipment and supplies was huge.

The Vichy Government in France

German forces took control of France, with Marshal Henri-Philippe Pétain of France, a hero of World War I, forming the **Vichy government** and accepting defeat. With the defeat of France, Germany occupied most of continental Europe, and the rest was in the hands of nations friendly to Germany. In 1940, Hitler controlled northern Europe from the Atlantic to eastern Poland. Italy was firmly in the hands of Mussolini and his Fascists; Spain was in the hands of Franco's Fascists; and the Soviets were neutral. The only European power opposed to Hitler lay across the English Channel. The new British prime minister, Winston Churchill, would prove to be an unyielding enemy of Hitler's Germany.

The Battle of Britain

Britain refused to surrender to German assaults. Hitler was savvy enough to realize that an invasion of Britain across the English Channel would fail if the British could attack the Germans from the air. Germany therefore launched an air attack with its Luftwaffe in the Battle of Britain. German forces hoped to cripple Britain's ability to defend itself or to launch a counterattack through massive air assaults on British military targets, rendering Britain unable to interfere with German forces on the continent. Both sides sustained heavy losses, but the British held on. Hitler then made the mistake of ordering the attack to strike civilian targets as well as military ones. He hoped to break the morale of the British people. Instead, this change of tactics steeled the British against the German aggressors. The British people pitched in and pulled together. Factories increased production. British pilots flew as if their world depended on them, which in fact it did. By October of 1940, German losses in the air outnumbered British losses three to one. The East End of London became a symbol of British defiance, and that defiance became a source of national pride. The air war against Britain had failed.

Germany Begins the Two-Front War

Instead of trying another means to invade Britain, Hitler turned his armies east, to the Soviet Union, based on his belief that support from the Soviets enabled the British to stay in the war. The attack on Russia that began in 1941 was a dangerous move that ultimately put Germany in a two-front war. Britain had survived the German air onslaught and was steadily building up its forces. Its supply lines had not been cut. The Soviet Union was not as susceptible to the strategy of blitzkrieg as the rest of Europe. The logistics of launching such an attack successfully over the vast distances required to be effective against the Soviet forces made it a long shot at best. However, after protecting his army in the Balkans and taking Greece and Yugoslavia, Hitler attacked the Soviet Union along a front that was 1,800 miles long. At first the momentum was with the Germans; within five months they were threatening Leningrad and Moscow and had taken much of Ukraine. The Soviets held on, and the winter caught the Germans unprepared. The unforgiving Russian winter punished the Germans and stopped them in their tracks.

The War in the Pacific and the U.S. Declaration of War on Japan

Hitler's string of victories in 1940 had prompted the Japanese to join the Axis, especially as it had hopes of taking advantage of European colonial empires in Southeast Asia. Soon after joining the Axis, Japan invaded French Indochina. The Japanese invasion sent a dangerous signal to the United States, which immediately demanded that Japan withdraw from China, where, since 1937, Japanese forces had moved up the Yangtze River Valley in pursuit of nationalist leader Chiang Kai-shek. The Japanese had long been worried that Chiang Kai-shek would unite China and threaten their presence in Manchuria, which had been established in the 1905 Japanese victory over Russia. While fear of public opinion against involvement had kept U.S. president **Franklin D. Roosevelt** from taking strong action when Japan initially invaded China, he was now no longer willing to tolerate the situation in China and decided to act quickly against the latest wave of Japanese aggression in Southeast Asia. The United States imposed quarantine, cutting off its sales

DID YOU KNOW?

The ships that were in Pearl Harbor when the Japanese attacked were all damaged or destroyed, including the *Arizona*, which was left where it sank in the harbor as a memorial to the servicemen who lost their lives in that fateful attack. President Franklin D. Roosevelt called December 7, 1941, a "date which will live in infamy."

of rubber, iron, oil, and aviation fuel to Japan. In 1941, Japan replied with the devastating attack on the U.S. fleet at anchor in **Pearl Harbor**. The Japanese attack practically destroyed the naval base.

Allied Strategy

Britain, the United States, and the Soviet Union then found themselves bound together as allies by their common enemies, the Axis Powers. The United States agreed to join with Britain and the Soviet Union in fighting Germany first, with Japan remaining as the secondary target. The United States became the "arsenal of democracy," giving roughly $50 billion in military aid to its allies. Britain continued to stand firm, and soon U.S. troops and equipment were pouring into the country as Britain and the United States prepared to push against Hitler's Western Front.

On the Eastern Front, the Soviets had regrouped from Germany's initial push into Soviet territory. The Nazi invasion had helped spark feelings of nationalism in the Russian people. They responded to the call of their country with great determination and personal sacrifice. The supply lines to the Soviet army were kept at a steady flow and, unlike the Germans, who were suffering in the cold, the Soviets were in better shape with each passing day. There was resistance to Hitler both within the German-occupied territories and within Germany itself. An underground resistance network was formed, and governments in exile from the countries under German control operated in London, bringing together information to aid the Allied Forces.

War in North Africa

War raged in North Africa as well, but the tide was turning against the Germans. At the Battle of El Alamein in 1942, the British defeated the German and Italian desert forces. The British also launched attacks in Egypt, and the British and Americans landed in Morocco and Algeria. These were French possessions in Africa and they went willingly over to the side of the Allies. By the spring of 1943, the Axis Powers were out of Africa.

The Surrender of the German Sixth Army

As the Allies were fighting their way to victory in Africa, in 1942, the Soviets were launching their first major offensive of the war, a counterattack against Germany. Facing Romanian and Italian troops, the Soviets dealt with them and quickly positioned themselves to trap the German Sixth Army. When the Sixth finally surrendered in January of 1943, only 123,000 of its original 300,000 troops were left standing. The Soviets had been able to successfully encircle the German Sixth Army because Hitler had refused to allow the army to retreat. The defeat was a hard blow to the Germans. The Soviets had the momentum and were on the offensive. They defeated the Germans at the Battle of Kursk in 1943, and then moved on to retake Ukraine. Soon thereafter, the Soviets freed Leningrad.

The Fall of Mussolini

With the Axis Powers out of Africa, the Allies could concentrate on Europe. They launched an invasion through Sicily in 1943 and deposed Mussolini. The new Italian government surrendered unconditionally in September of 1943. The allied victory was short-lived, however, as the Germans launched a counteroffensive, rescued Mussolini, captured Rome and northern Italy, and continued the fighting in 1944, when the Allies entered Rome. Mussolini was later killed by Italians, many of whom had come to despise his dictatorship.

D-Day

In June of 1944, the Allies launched a massive invasion of Normandy, France, known as **D-Day**. This offensive, launched from Britain, was the beginning of the liberation of France and Western Europe. American and British forces hit the beaches and marched inland, steadily pushing back the Germans. General Dwight D. Eisenhower served as supreme commander of the Americans and the British. His plan was not to go straight for Berlin, but rather to roll the Germans back all along the front, liberating Europe as the Allies progressed. His forces crossed the Rhine in March 1945. As the Allies moved forward, the Soviets entered Warsaw and then turned south, clearing out German forces from Romania, Hungary, and Yugoslavia.

The Surrender of Germany

The British firebombing raid on Dresden in February of 1945 was the culmination of two years of bombing of German industrial targets. Meanwhile, the Soviets had continued their offensive on the Eastern Front. The Soviets and Americans met at the Elbe River, and the Soviets broke into Berlin. Hitler was not captured but chose to commit suicide just two days after Mussolini was murdered. His aides burned his body to ash. The Germans surrendered on May 7, 1945.

The Battle for the Pacific

Despite Germany's surrender, the war in the Pacific continued. While the Allies were fighting the Axis Powers in North African and Europe, other events were taking place in the Pacific, where the United States had renewed its fleet. The United States stopped the Japanese advance at several fierce battles in 1942. In the Battle of Midway, the Japanese navy suffered a devastating blow that marked the turning point in the war in the Pacific. The United States had managed to break the Japanese code in an operation known as "Magic" and it knew of Japanese plans to attack Midway. All four of the Japanese aircraft carriers involved in the battle were sunk. The United States, rather than Japan, then had the superior navy in the Pacific. In August of 1942, land troops finally entered the war in the Pacific. U.S. Marines landed on Guadalcanal in one of the most hard-fought battles of the war. The Americans and their Australian allies pushed on and forced Japan into fighting a defensive war, using the strategy of "island-hopping," taking one island at a time. Midway had been the last island in the Pacific controlled by the United States, but the Americans also fought bitter battles closer to Japan on Iwo Jima and Okinawa.

Fighting continued on Okinawa for two months, and the Japanese introduced **kamikaze** pilots, who flew their planes loaded with just enough fuel to reach allied ships and then made suicide dives straight into them. The Japanese flew more than 1,900 kamikaze suicide missions and many Okinawans also died in the battle, convincing the United States that victory over Japan would not come quickly or easily. Saipan fell in July 1944, thus bringing the islands of Japan itself closer to the reach of U.S. bombers. This unleashed a wave of napalm firebombs over Tokyo in March of 1945, destroying 25 percent of the city's buildings and killing more than 100,000 people.

Nevertheless, the war in the Pacific did not look promising for the Allies. There remained significant territory to take back from the Japanese, who were still fighting with determination. U.S. president Harry Truman believed that the circumstances justified drastic measures. A crucial consideration was to prevent greater loss of life through months or even years of continued fighting, although some historians have made the controversial suggestion that Truman wished to test the atomic bomb, which had been developed through the efforts of the Manhattan Project. At any rate, he authorized the atomic bombing of Hiroshima and Nagasaki, Japan. Japan finally surrendered. World War II formally ended on September 2, 1945, when Japan signed the terms of surrender aboard the battleship *Missouri*.

Aftermath of World War II

Approximately 60 million people died in World War II. The Soviet Union lost more than 20 million people, only one-third of whom were soldiers. China lost 15 million people, who were primarily civilians. Germany lost 4 million, while Japan lost 2 million. Great Britain lost 400,000 and the United States lost 300,000. The Poles suffered the loss of 6 million inhabitants, and 6 million European Jews died as well, the victims of state-sponsored killing by Nazi Germany and its collaborators. Historians estimate that Nazi persecutions also resulted in the deaths of 1 million other people from minority groups, including gypsies, homosexuals, Serbs, anti-Nazi political dissidents, and those with mental illnesses.

World War II left virtually no one untouched. The war devastated Europe and left it in need of reconstruction. Millions of refugees from devastated areas migrated across Europe, and over 13 million of them settled in post–World War II Germany. The Germans lost territory to Poland, and the Soviet border expanded to the west. Germany was divided into three occupation zones controlled by the United States, Britain, and the Soviet Union. The agreements made by the Allies during and after the war concerning the fate of Europe eventually led to the Cold War and the creation of a bipolar world split between the world's democratic superpower and the world's Communist superpower. While Western European nations, such as France, Italy, and West Germany, recovered from the war and reestablished republics, Eastern Europe came progressively under Soviet influence and control. Independence movements also swept through the Middle East and Africa as Western imperialism was weakened during and after the war.

The Cold War

The **Cold War** refers to the ideological conflict between the Communist nations of Eastern Europe, led by the Soviet Union, and the Western democracies, led by the United States. Although the United States and the Soviet Union were allies during World War II and united to fight Nazi Germany, the two new superpowers of the world had opposing ideologies and a deep-seated mistrust of each other. During the Cold War, the United States sought to contain the spread of Communism, while Soviet leaders often sought to spread Communism to other countries, particularly those of Eastern Europe.

In 1943, Soviet, American, and British leaders had agreed on the strategy that eventually defeated Hitler. According to this strategy, however, the Soviets were to liberate Eastern Europe. In 1945, the Big Three, as Soviet, American, and British leaders came to be known, met again at Yalta, in southern Russia. By that time, Soviet forces controlled Poland, Bulgaria, Hungary, Romania, as well as parts of Czechoslovakia, Yugoslavia, and Germany, while the forces of Britain and the United States were still struggling to get out of France. At Yalta, the parties agreed that when victory came, they would divide Germany into zones under the control of the Big Three, and Germany would pay reparations to Russia. Free elections for all the Eastern European countries under Soviet control were guaranteed, but those countries had to remain friendly to the Soviet Union. In return, Soviet dictator Josef Stalin promised to declare war on Japan after the defeat of Germany.

The agreement did not hold up for long, and in many Eastern European nations important positions were going to the Soviets without the elections promised at Yalta. When the Big Three met at Potsdam in July of 1945, U.S. president Truman had recently learned that the atomic bomb had been tested and that it was functional, and this may have encouraged him to take a tough stance. Truman insisted that Stalin allow the promised free elections. Stalin refused, as he believed that such elections would result in anti-Soviet governments in the Eastern European countries. One reason why Stalin wanted pro-Soviet countries along his western border was that they would serve as a buffer against future German aggression, something Stalin greatly feared after the German invasion of Russia in World War II.

Truman and British prime minister Churchill were in no position to force Stalin to comply. At the same time, they could not simply ignore the situation. Truman cut off U.S. aid to Russia and declared that the United States would not recognize any government that was not freely elected. The Cold War era had begun. The United States and the Soviet Union both took control of areas that they occupied in Asia; the Soviet Union controlled the northern part of Korea, and the United States controlled the southern half of Korea, as well as maintaining occupation of Japan. The European countries remained in control of their colonies in Southeast Asia, and most of China's territory was restored to it.

The Cold War was so named because, although armed conflicts would erupt around the world between Soviet- and U.S.-backed factions and the leaders of these two nations would engage in tough talk, the two superpowers managed to avoid engaging in direct military conflict with each other. Thus, the war was "cold." However, during the Cold War in both the Soviet Union and the United States, a considerable amount of resources went into the military and the world lived with the constant threat that the conflict might become "hot." In the Soviet Union, more resources were channeled into the military than into any other sector of the economy, and it developed both atomic and hydrogen bombs.

After World War II, the Soviets had the most powerful forces in Eastern Europe, whose countries had largely been devastated by Nazi occupations and military actions. The Soviet alliance with the Communists in Vietnam provided it with bases for its naval fleets, while it also established an alliance with North Korea and briefly with China. Soviet influence also spread to other parts of the world, including Cuba.

Elections in Britain ousted Churchill from office, but he remained adamant in his opposition to Stalin. In one of his most famous speeches, he coined the phrase the **Iron Curtain** to describe the division of Europe into free democracies and states under Communist control.

The Truman Doctrine and the Marshall Plan

Truman developed the **Truman Doctrine**, which was a pledge of financial aid to countries threatened by the spread of Communism through force. Although the Truman Doctrine was initially directed toward Greece and Turkey, Truman's secretary of state, George C. Marshall, then offered economic aid under the **Marshall Plan** to European nations recovering from World War II. Truman believed that Soviet expansion was made possible partly through economic chaos in recovering nations, and he wanted to foster the economic recovery of Europe. The Marshall Plan mandated cooperation among recipients on tariff policies and other economic matters. The United States also created the Defense Department, the Central Intelligence Agency, and the Strategic Air Command, and also increased military spending.

Meanwhile, the Soviets thought that the Marshall Plan was simply imperialism in disguise. Stalin refused aid for the Eastern Bloc nations and solidified his control over them by removing all noncommunists from governmental positions. Such was the case in Soviet-occupied Czechoslovakia, which had attempted to restore a democratic-style government following the war.

Stalin then blocked access to Berlin. The Big Three had divided Germany into four zones, each zone controlled by a different nation. Berlin was situated in the zone controlled by the Soviet Union, but the city itself was also divided into zones. When the three powers that occupied West Germany worked toward economic unity and the formation of a West German government, Stalin blocked all movements through the Soviet zone of Germany to Berlin, and the United States and its allies launched the Berlin Airlift to bring supplies to West Berlin, despite the Soviet blockade. The airlift succeeded. The Soviet blockade of Berlin combined with the successful Communist revolution in China prompted the United States to change its foreign policy into one of containment of Communism.

NATO and the Warsaw Pact

In 1949, the United States and its Allies formed the **North Atlantic Treaty Organization (NATO)**. Its main purpose was to thwart the advance of Communism in Europe, partly by rearming West Germany. Stalin responded by strengthening his control over Eastern Europe in what would ultimately become known as the **Warsaw Pact** of Eastern European nations and the Soviet Union.

The Korean War (1950–1953)

The Marshall Plan ultimately failed to stop the spread of Communism; in response, during the period from 1946 to 1950, the United States formulated a new policy of

containment. For example, a revolution in China resulted in the establishment of a Communist Chinese government, and the United States eventually decided to prevent a Chinese Communist takeover of Taiwan. Events in Korea created further alarm. Following the 1905 war between Russia and Japan, Korea had been occupied by the Japanese until the end of World War II. The country was divided into two occupation zones after the war, with the Soviets occupying North Korea and the United States occupying South Korea at a boundary called the **38th parallel.** Independent elections were planned to establish a unified government, but as the Cold War escalated, two governments resulted: a Communist government in the north and a civilian anti-Communist republic in the south.

With the support of the Soviet Union, North Korea invaded South Korea in 1950. The United States responded with military aid, including troops from fifteen countries that were members of the United Nations, which had replaced the League of Nations after World War II. When these forces drove the North Koreans back and threatened the Chinese border, Communist China entered on the side of North Korea. The Soviet Union provided aid, but it did not directly enter the conflict, and the United States chose not to confront the Soviet Union openly, also to avoid a direct conflict. In October of 1950, the Chinese assault began and pushed the United Nations' troops back to the 38th parallel. The Chinese Communist and North Korean forces captured the South Korean capital of Seoul in January of 1951 and defeated the United Nations' troops.

Later that year, peace negotiations began and the parties agreed to a ceasefire. A **demilitarized zone** was created around the 38th parallel, which is still in existence today and is defended by North Korean troops on one side and South Korean and American troops on the other. No peace treaty was ever signed; the conflict was officially named a police action rather than a war. The impact of the Korean War on China was profound. China's intervention in the war resulted in greater determination by the United States to stop the Chinese from taking over Taiwan. Truman sent a naval fleet to Taiwan to block Chinese expansion, but the actions of the Chinese government had also cut it off from other Western powers and to economic and other assistance that they might have provided. China, then, was left to turn to Russia for assistance.

The Rise of Khrushchev and De-Stalinization

Stalin died in 1953 and, after a brief transitional period, Nikita Khrushchev took control of the Soviet Union and embarked on a policy of de-Stalinization and of "peaceful coexistence" with capitalist countries, a policy that created tensions with China. Krushchev's policies also stimulated rebellions against the Soviets, and Communism began to crumble in the Eastern Bloc.

Castro in Cuba

Krushchev's leadership was further challenged by events that unfolded in Cuba. In 1958, **Fidel Castro** led his supporters to a successful revolution in Cuba, establishing a Communist country within striking distance of the U.S. coastline. Tensions remained high, leading to the **Bay of Pigs** invasion in 1961. **President John F. Kennedy** authorized the invasion by armed Cuban exiles to overthrow the Castro government. The fighting lasted only two days, as the exiles did not receive the support of their fellow Cubans, nor of the Americans in the air or on the ground. Castro imprisoned several of the exiles involved, but twenty months later he released them in exchange for $53 million worth of food and medical supplies.

The Cuban Missile Crisis

The tensions of the Cold War continued to mount, culminating in the **Cuban Missile Crisis**, one of the major events of the Cold War. Khrushchev sent sixty ships to Cuba in 1962, with many carrying nuclear missiles and other weaponry. The Soviets wanted to shift the advantage in the buildup of nuclear arms from the United States and place missiles in Cuba that were capable of striking much of the continental United States. U.S. surveillance photos revealed that missile sites were in fact under construction in Cuba. The Soviets had not informed Washington of their intention to place missiles in Cuba, which greatly alarmed the U.S. administration.

After considering an attack on Cuba, the Kennedy administration publicly announced a naval blockade within 500 miles around the Cuban coast and demanded that the Soviet Union remove the nuclear missiles and dismantle the missile sites. Privately, the United States had little hope that Khrushchev would agree to its demands and expected that the situation might turn into a military confrontation. Khrushchev publicly declared that the United States had committed an act of aggression that could spark a nuclear war, but privately, he made two offers of settlement, promising to withdraw Soviet missiles from Cuba in exchange for a promise from the United States not to invade Cuba and to withdraw its missiles from Turkey, which were within striking distance of Moscow, the Soviet capital. After several tense days, Kennedy accepted both offers, and the crisis was over.

Détente

Khrushchev never recovered politically, since he had not only backed down in the face of U.S. threats, but he also initiated the crisis in the first place. In 1964 he was removed from power, and he died under house arrest in Moscow seven years later. As for Kennedy, some of his advisors believed that his response to the crisis was too weak to guarantee national safety. This was clearly the closest that the United States and the Soviets ever came to nuclear war in the Cold War era; however, Kennedy's choice of diplomacy over a military response had prevented both an invasion and a military conflict. The Cuban Missile Crisis also prompted the two superpowers to seek a better means of communication. They established a "hot line" between Washington and Moscow and developed a policy of **détente,** a loosening of tensions.

Leonid Brezhnev replaced Khrushchev and retreated from Krushchev's policy of peaceful coexistence. Brezhnev articulated a new policy known as the Brezhnev Doctrine, which pledged opposition to antisocialist forces. More funds were channeled into the military than any other sector of the Soviet economy under Brezhnev. Nevertheless, de-Stalinization had resulted in movement away from the Soviets in the Eastern Bloc. In Czechoslovakia, Alexander Dubček led reforms in 1968 known as the Prague Spring. These ended when the Soviet Union invaded Prague and took Dubček to Moscow to force him to accept Soviet demands. Gustav Husak, a dedicated Stalinist, eventually replaced Dubček. The events in Czechoslovakia prompted Soviet leaders to "re-Stalinize" at home by clamping down on protest movements. However, during this period a massive shift of the population in Russia was occurring as more and more people moved to cities. There, they were educated, and the class of professionals grew. As educational levels increased, protests also increased.

Rebellion brewed in East Germany as well. The Soviets crushed a workers' protest movement in 1953, and many sought refuge in West Germany. Most of the workers who fled to West Germany were highly skilled laborers, which created economic problems in East Germany. In 1961 the government attempted to block the steady stream of refugees by erecting the **Berlin Wall**, as most were entering West Germany through Berlin. East Germany was firmly in the Soviet camp throughout the Cold War era.

TEST TIP

Use the 10-minute reading period allotted for the document-based essay to carefully analyze each document provided. Also identify the point of view of the creator of each document.

The Vietnam War (1964–1975)

Both the Soviet Union and the United States had interests in Asia. The **Vietnam War** was another outgrowth of the Cold War, and in the United States the belief took hold that once Communism was allowed to flourish in South Vietnam, all of the other governments in southeastern Asia, such as those of Thailand, Laos, Cambodia, Malaysia, and Indonesia, would also fall to Communism. This idea was known as the **domino theory.** The United States, South Vietnam, Australia, and South Korea fought against North Vietnam and the National Liberation Front, a South Vietnamese guerrilla movement led by Communists. While Krushchev's policy of peaceful coexistence had resulted in the Soviets discouraging North Vietnamese aggression against South Vietnam, Brezhnev did not share the same views and actively supplied arms to the North Vietnamese. As in the Korean conflict, however, the Soviet Union did not directly participate in hostilities. China did not want to become directly involved either. While the Chinese verbally supported their fellow Communists, they quietly promised the United States that they would not enter the conflict unless U.S. military actions threatened their southern border. Moreover, they refused to allow the Soviets to transport goods to the North Vietnamese through Chinese territory, further deepening the divisions between China and the Soviet Union.

The Vietnam War originated with the French struggle in the First Indochina War against Communist Party leader Ho Chi Minh, who led a movement for independence of the colony of Vietnam from France. The Vietnamese Communist forces defeated the French army in 1954. Following this event, the French granted the colony independence. At a settlement reached in Geneva, Vietnam was divided into a Communist North and a non-Communist South, with hopes that the South would be a democracy. Elections in 1956 were intended to unify the two Vietnams, but the southern president Diem and U.S. president Eisenhower worried about a possible victory for Ho Chi Minh, and the elections were never held.

The Communists in the north launched a guerilla movement against the south known as the National Liberation Front. This movement was also known in the United States and in South Vietnam as the *Viet Cong*, from *Viet Nam Cong San*, meaning "Vietnamese Communist." The United States began sending support to the south, while the Soviet Union and the North Vietnamese communists, who viewed the conflict as a continuation of the colonial war first waged against the French, provided arms, advisors, and military to the Viet Cong along the Ho Chi Minh Trail.

The United States never declared war in Vietnam. In 1964, the Senate approved the Gulf of Tonkin Resolution, which authorized the use of armed forces in support of freedom in Southeast Asia. In 1965, U.S. president Lyndon Johnson sent 3,500 marines to South Vietnam, which escalated to over 500,000 troops by 1968. By that time, widespread protests against the war in the United States were contributing to President Johnson's unpopularity, and he did not seek reelection. Richard Nixon was elected president and initiated the Nixon Doctrine, according to which South Vietnam would be enabled to fight on its own. Although he gradually withdrew troops from Vietnam, Nixon continued air raids, and more U.S. troops eventually died during his presidency than during Johnson's tenure in office.

In 1970, Nixon ordered a strike in Cambodia against the Viet Cong. Protests against U.S. involvement in Vietnam had been escalating since 1966; further, events at Kent State University in Ohio in 1970 horrified many Americans, who were having increasing difficulty understanding the goals of the conflict and Washington's justification of its decisions. During a protest against the U.S. invasion of Cambodia on the campus of Kent State, the National Guard was called in and fired at students, killing four and wounding nine others. The conflict further escalated in 1971, when South Vietnam invaded Laos with the help of the United States. The following year, Nixon ended heavy bombing in North Vietnam, while at the same time tensions between the Soviets and China were increasing. Nixon traveled to China on a goodwill tour. Some historians believe that this visit contributed to the willingness of the North Vietnamese to enter peace talks, as they questioned whether their fellow Communists in China might no longer support their military actions. In 1973, the **Paris Peace Accords** officially ended U.S. involvement in Vietnam and in 1975, the U.S. Congress refused further aid to South Vietnam.

The North Vietnamese invaded South Vietnam in 1975, captured its capital, Saigon, and formed the Socialist Republic of Vietnam. Saigon became Ho Chi Minh City, a reminder of the U. S. failure in Vietnam to stop the spread of Communism. Meanwhile, the Communist Khmer Rouge seized power in Cambodia, beginning the infamous reign of terror of Pol Pot, who tried to return Cambodia to its ancient agricultural ways and to wipe out all religions. By the end of his regime, he had exterminated a sizable proportion of Cambodia's population in the infamous killing fields.

The SALT Treaties

Beginning in 1973, Soviet and U.S. leaders began to agree to a number of treaties, the most important of which were the **SALT treaties** resulting from the Strategic Arms Limitation Talks. By the end of the 1970s, however, détente was weakening. The United States established full diplomatic relations with the People's Republic of China in 1979 and announced the sale of weapons to the Chinese military in 1980. The diplomatic relationship between China and the United States was directed largely against efforts of the Soviets to expand their power in Asia. These new developments between the United States and China created hostility among the Soviets, who were themselves ignoring pledges that they had made to respect human rights in the Helsinki Conference (1975).

American president Ronald Reagan, who held office from 1980 to 1988, contributed heavily to the deterioration of Soviet–U.S. relations through his description of the Soviet Union as the "evil empire." He supported a massive military budget and the creation of the **Strategic Defense Initiative**, or "Star Wars," a system that, it was claimed, would have provided protection from nuclear attack. Soviet military intervention in Afghanistan also contributed to the decline of détente, and the United States once again came to believe in the need for a policy of containment.

The Soviets in Afghanistan

In December 1979, the Soviets invaded Afghanistan, further creating renewed tension with the United States. The previous year, a pro-Soviet faction of Muslims had taken power as the People's Democratic Party of Afghanistan (PDPA). The PDPA implemented radical reforms, leading to massive protests from Islamic leaders. The rebellions had become so intense that the Soviets intervened and installed Marxist Babrak Karmal as president. The United States supplied ground-to-air missiles to the *mujahideen*, the Islamic resistance in the countryside. In 1986 the Soviets replaced Karmal, who had not succeeded in quelling the revolt, with Muhammad Najibullah, who had been head of the Afghan Secret Police and had a close working relationship with the Soviets. This move was also unsuccessful, so in 1988, the Soviets agreed to a ceasefire and withdrew their forces. The *mujahideen*, however, disintegrated into tribal and ethnic factions who warred against one another. In 1996 the **Taliban**, an army of religious students, took control of the Afghan capital of Kabul and executed Najibullah, thus establishing the Islamic State of Afghanistan.

In 2003, the United States toppled the regime, accusing it of harboring the terrorists of the radical **al-Qaeda** organization responsible for terrorist attacks in the United States on September 11, 2001. Al-Qaeda had evolved out of the *mujahideen*; ironically, the United States had helped to train and provide weapons for many of the terrorists.

Gorbachev and the Soviet Union

In 1986, Soviet leader Mikhail Gorbachev initiated a radical period of reform, instituting **glasnost**, or "openness," and **perestroika**, or "restructuring." *Perestroika* allowed for freer prices and even for the creation of enterprises for profit. According to the new spirit of *glasnost*, free elections were held in Russia for the first time since the Revolution of 1917. *Glasnost* also allowed for free criticism of Soviet policies. In 1988, Gorbachev abandoned the Brezhnev Doctrine and allowed the Eastern Bloc countries to move away from Communism and even to adopt democracy.

The End of the Cold War: The Fall of the Soviet Union

Although Mikhail Gorbachev received the Nobel Peace Prize in 1990 and was elected as the first executive president of the Soviet Union, his detractors worried that he was leaning toward ending Communism. Gorbachev was surprised when ethnic tensions erupted as a result of *glasnost*. Lithuania responded to *glasnost* by declaring independence from the Soviet Union, and elsewhere in the Soviet Union ethnic movements were spiraling out of Gorbachev's control. In 1991 a force of Communist hardliners kidnapped him and detained him in the Crimea. Boris Yeltsin, elected president of Russia in 1991, convinced some of the armed forces to switch sides. He sent rescue forces to Gorbachev, who returned and arrested those who had attempted to oust him. Nevertheless, Gorbachev never fully regained control. Yeltsin, who had urged Gorbachev to implement more reforms, outlawed Communism in Russia. In 1991, Ukraine voted for independence, and soon thereafter, the presidents of Russia, Ukraine, and Belarus created the Commonwealth of Independent States. As Russia had in fact been the very heart of the Soviet Union, its declaration of independence ended its existence. Yeltsin served as president of Russia until 1999.

Anti-Imperialism and the Restructuring of States

In the post–World War II period, colonial empires were broken apart and nationalistic movements emerged. Other movements advocated the unification of people across national boundaries.

Nationalism in India and Pakistan

Britain had ruled India since the 1850s. World War I weakened the British Empire, leading to, among other things, a movement for Indian independence. The Indian National Congress was founded in 1885, and after World War I, it increasingly turned against the British. The **Muslim League**, founded in 1906, feared that Hindu domination would replace the British, and considerable conflict arose between Hindus and Muslims that still continues today. Wilson's Fourteen Points encouraged self-determination, and the Indian population eagerly embraced this ideal. The British responded with more repressive measures, creating a wave of rebellions and violence across the subcontinent of India.

Mohandas Gandhi emerged as an important leader. He was a Hindu who had been educated in law in London and had spent twenty-five years in South Africa, another British colony. While in South Africa, he had organized resistance to racial segregation within the Indian community. There he also developed his philosophy of nonviolence and passive resistance. He renounced worldly pleasures and, although he was a member of the merchant caste, he lived a life of simplicity. Gandhi returned to India in 1915 and became active in the Indian National Congress. In general, Gandhi opposed Western-style industrialization in India. Although he advocated nonviolence, the movements inevitably did result in violence, and the British arrested the offenders. In 1919, colonial troops dispersed an unarmed crowd with rifles and killed 379 demonstrators.

Gandhi helped to launch the Non-Cooperation Movement of 1920–1922 and the Civil Disobedience Movement of 1930. These were mass movements that boycotted British goods and British institutions. Gandhi urged the people to wear Indian-spun cloth as opposed to British-manufactured clothing. In 1921, the British government gave in and passed the **Government of India Act**, which gave India the institutions for a self-governing state. However, it also passed legislation limiting the production of salt to the British. In response, Gandhi led followers on a 230-mile march to the sea in 1930. He picked up salt from the shores and urged his supporters to refuse to follow the British law. Gandhi, only recently released from prison after being imprisoned for previous protests, was arrested again. While Gandhi opposed industrialization and considered it immoral, **Jawaharlal Nehru** did not, and he supported the creation of an independent nation-state in India. Nehru was a Brahmin Hindu educated in Western traditions. The Muslim League, led by **Muhammad Ali Jinnah**, however, rejected this compromise, as it feared Hindu domination. Jinnah advocated the formation of separate states, one for Hindus in India and another for Muslims in **Pakistan**, which would be the "land of the pure."

Transnational Movements

The Russian Revolution of 1917

Vladimir Lenin rose to prominence in the chaos of revolutionary Russia. From Karl Marx's *Communist Manifesto*, Lenin drew his first principle of revolution: that violent revolution was necessary to destroy capitalism. Lenin believed that revolution was necessary and possible even when a society such as Russia did not have a fully developed capitalistic economy. Further, he believed that a Communist revolution was possible even without a well-developed bourgeoisie class. With adequate leadership, such as what the **Bolsheviks** provided, he believed that revolution would succeed in Russia.

Only dedicated revolutionaries, with the intellect to fully understand the importance of revolution, could successfully lead a revolution. The proletariat (working class) were necessary instruments of the revolution, as leaders would need an organized army of workers. It would be up to the leaders, however, to keep the revolution on course to take control of a nation.

Leon Trotsky supported Lenin and urged him to overthrow the provisional government, which had been established after the Russian Revolution of 1917. Lenin's Bolsheviks succeeded in their attempt to topple the government, as the all-Russian Congress of Soviets officially handed over power to the Soviet Council of People's Commissars. They elected Lenin chairman and put Trotsky in charge of foreign affairs. Lenin moved quickly to solidify his position. He declared that the peasants had a right to seize land and he signed a treaty with Germany ending World War I for Russia. Lenin also attempted to spread Communism abroad and supported this through the creation of **Comintern** (Communist International).

In 1918, the Bolshevik government executed Tsar Nicolas II, his wife Tsarina Alexandra, their children, and their servants. Elections were held for the Constituent Assembly, which was to be the new Russian government. The Bolsheviks, however, did not manage to take a controlling majority in the elections, so Lenin used his Bolshevik troops to dismiss the Assembly and take control, leading to the creation of Soviet Russia, a Communist state.

By the 1920s, the Bolshevik revolution in Russia was complete. Lenin died in 1924, leaving the government scrambling to determine his successor. Trotsky was an obvious choice, having been so instrumental in the success of the revolution. However, **Joseph Stalin** was able to garner the support needed to become general secretary of the Central Committee, the most important committee in the government, and he used that position to gain even more power, influence, and supporters.

Trotsky believed that for the Communist revolution in the Soviet Union to last, the revolution had to be spread throughout the rest of Europe. This position did not sit well with a nation of war-weary people, however. Stalin held the opposite position, believing that the Soviet Union could stand on its own as a socialist nation, a position far more appealing than Trotsky's to party members. By 1927, Stalin achieved total power. He succeeded in exiling Trotsky in 1929 and had him assassinated a decade later. Stalin would ultimately be known as the gravedigger of the October Revolution, and his reign of terror in Russia resulted in the death of millions of Russians.

Pan-Africanism

Many Africans fought alongside the Allies in World War I, often as a result of force. The war caused many disruptions in the economy on a global basis, and in Africa these shortages were acutely felt. Following the war, the memory of these hardships created greater discontent when the European colonizers failed to reward their colonists for their sacrifices. Further, Western-style education brought by European colonizers had exposed Africans to revolutionary ideas, which erupted in Afrocentric agitation in the years following World War I.

These early Pan-African movements attracted many followers, but most of the Pan-African organizations were led by people, many of whom were African Americans, whose interests were different from those of Africans. Marcus Garvey and W.E.B. Dubois, who were African Americans, were influential in inspiring **Pan-Africanism**. Early efforts for Pan-Africanism failed to develop as its leaders envisioned, and African independence movements did not succeed until the period following World War II.

In 1946, long-time African nationalists Kwame Nkrumah of Ghana and Jomo Kenyatta of Kenya led a movement for African nationalism and founded the Pan-African Federation, which campaigned for land reform and political rights for Africans. It initially focused on negotiating with its imperialist rulers to gain independence for individual African colonies. In 1946, Kenyatta became president of the Kenya African Union, and the following year, Nkrumah became the prime minister of the independent state of Ghana.

Other African nationalist leaders succeeded in establishing independent African states, and by 1960 most of Africa was composed primarily of independent nations. However, Pan-Africanism was never successful in creating a united Africa. Ethnic conflicts continued to disrupt and ravage parts of Africa throughout the remainder of the twentieth century, and such conflicts are still ongoing.

Movements to Redistribute Land and Resources in Latin America

In the wake of World War II, many Latin American countries fought vigorously against U.S. and other foreign influences, and especially against U.S. intervention in their politics and economies. Most Latin American countries had enormous foreign debts. Thus, despite the movements to separate Latin America from U.S. interference, economic issues continued to force many Latin American areas to accept aid and therefore U.S. terms.

Brazil

Brazil, however, attempted to create a nationalized economy. Under the leadership of Getúlio Vargas (1930–1945), industrialization occurred rapidly, supported with high tariffs on imports. President Juscelino Kubitschek continued the policy of economic nationalism, and through heavy borrowing from international powers, Kubitschek attempted to achieve "Fifty Years' Progress in Five." In the 1960s, President João Goulart attempted to promote greater social equality by breaking up large estates and allowing those of lower classes, even those who were illiterate, to vote. The result was a conservative backlash in Brazil. The military took over in 1964.

Argentina

In Argentina, **Juan Perón** won the presidency in 1946 on the basis of his opposition to foreign, and especially U.S., intervention. Perón was the culmination of the increasing power of the military in Argentina's politics. His wife, Eva, was herself from the lower classes, and she personally and very publicly implemented aspects of his program of assistance to the poor. Perón also advocated industrialization and protection of workers' rights. Under Perón, the government controlled the banking, railroad, shipping, and other industries, and he was in many ways an authoritarian leader. While the couple was very popular with the lower classes of Argentina, others saw them as opportunistic and believed that they sympathized with Fascism. The military overthrew Perón in 1955 and he went into exile in Spain.

Demographic Shifts Resulting from Political Changes

Colonialism had had a profound impact on many regions of the world, especially in Africa, parts of Asia, and the Middle East. Western imperialists had often created arbitrary boundaries in places where they colonized; these arbitrary divisions often attempted to unite groups of people who had long been torn by ethnic and other rivalries. When the European colonizers departed, these ethnic rivalries erupted into many violent clashes in Africa, the Middle East, and India.

The Partition of India and Pakistan

World Wars I and II unleashed a tidal wave of colonial revolts, which resulted in the end of British rule in India after World War II. The Indian National Congress had failed to coalesce into a unified front, as Muslims disagreed with Hindus over the fate of India. The British made few attempts to reconcile the two groups, and in the end made decisions that ensured a permanent split.

The leader of the Muslim League, Muhammad Ali Jinnah, advocated a Day of Direct Action in 1946, and as rioting erupted, approximately 6,000 people died in the Great Calcutta Killing. Jinnah took a hard-line stance on the issue of Indian independence, rejecting any possibility that Hindus and Muslims might live and work together to build a new and united India. According to him, the only solution was to create a separate state for Muslims: Pakistan.

Mohandas Gandhi and Jawaharlal Nehru did not want to see India partitioned. In 1947, however, Britain partitioned India into two separate regions, creating an independent Pakistan for Muslims. By 1948, 10 million Muslims or Hindus had migrated to either India or Pakistan, amid tremendous violence. Gandhi went on hunger strikes to persuade Indians to protest Western imperialism and, as we said earlier, to use only Indian-made goods. He rejected all forms of Western culture as material, and believed that the Western notion of progress was bankrupt. He advocated a return to the simple agricultural life in India that existed before the arrival of the British. In the end he fell victim to an assassin's bullet.

Europe

The reconstruction of Europe after the devastation of World War II created a boom in the economy and a great demand for workers, particularly in Britain, Germany, and France. At first, people from other European countries who had been displaced during the war were able to meet this demand. With increasing demand for workers, Britain recruited immigrants from its colonies in the Caribbean and from India and Pakistan. Immigration was encouraged by the British Nationality Act of 1948, which allowed all Commonwealth citizens free entry into Britain. France recruited workers from its colony of Algeria. Because Germany no longer had any colonies, it recruited contract workers in countries adjacent to Western Europe, particularly from Yugoslavia and Turkey. Throughout the 1950s, about 10 million people immigrated to Europe.

Zionism

Since the 1890s, **Zionism** had been an important movement in Europe. Zionists fought against anti-Semitism and sought to create a homeland for Jews, an idea first suggested by Theodore Hertzl, a Hungarian Jew. Hertzl organized the first Zionist World

Congress in 1897, which created the World Zionist Organization. At first their interests were not centered on Palestine, as they planned the creation of a Jewish state in Africa; but gradually the focus of Zionism did become Palestine. The **Balfour Declaration** of 1917, which promised to establish a secure homeland for Jews in Palestine, was supported at the Paris Peace talks following World War I. In 1922, the League of Nations established a British mandate in Palestine. A mandate was a territory surrendered by Turkey or Germany to the victorious Allies in World War I and governed by a European power. Arabs resented the influx of both the British and the Jewish settlers, and rioting erupted in the 1920s and 1930s.

Anti-Semitism

In Germany, **anti-Semitism** was a founding principle of the Nazi Party. Once Hitler took control of Germany, life for the Jews became increasingly difficult. In 1935, the Nürnburg Laws were passed, declaring that anyone with at least one Jewish grandparent was Jewish and as such could not be a German citizen. By 1938 a quarter of all the Jews in Germany had fled to other European countries, with many of them making their way to the United States. The Jews who did not make it out of Germany or the areas conquered by Germany found themselves herded into ghettos, treated as subhumans, and forced to wear the Star of David to identify themselves as Jews. In 1941, Hitler enacted his "Final Solution" to the Jewish problem. German forces executed some Jews in the villages where they lived. Nazis shipped other Jews, as well as Gypsies and Communists off to the concentration camps, where the weak were sent straight to gas chambers. The Nazis worked the stronger ones literally to death. Some became test subjects in medical experiments. The **Holocaust** (from the Greek *holos*, or whole, and *kaustos*, or burnt), as this mass genocide came to be known, was unprecedented in modern history, resulting in the deaths of more than 6 million Jewish men, women, and children and millions of others.

As World War II progressed and Hitler's Final Solution threatened the very existence of European Jews, they flocked in increasing numbers to Palestine. Simultaneously, rising Arab nationalism in the wake of the formation of Arab states after World War II contributed to the hostility. The British tried to allay Arab fears by limiting Jewish immigration. In 1945, Jewish resistance to British rule began in earnest, led by the Haganah, an underground military organization founded to protect Jewish settlers and refugees. By 1947, the British had announced their intention to withdraw and allow the United Nations to decide the matter. The United Nations proposed to divide the area into a Jewish and a Palestine state and, before the Arab outcry could even be heard and the matter further debated, Jews took matters into their own hands and announced, in May 1948, the creation of the State of Israel.

The Partitioning of Palestine

Arab states mobilized in support of the Palestinians, and Egypt, Syria, Jordan, and Iraq declared war on Israel, beginning the Arab-Israeli wars. However, in 1949, the United Nations forged a truce and partitioned Palestine. Significantly, Jerusalem was partitioned between Israel and Jordan, with Jordan in control of East Jerusalem. The West Bank went to Jordan, while the Gaza Strip went to Egypt. Israel controlled the coastal areas of Palestine and the Negev Desert to the Red Sea. Many Palestinians fled their homelands and sought refuge in other Arab lands.

Pan-Arabism

Led by Gamul Abdel Nasser, the Egyptians deposed King Farouk in 1952. Nasser wanted to unite and lead the Arab world against the Israelis. Nasser also refused to become allied with any of the superpowers of the Cold War, and he terminated British rights to the Suez Canal in 1954. He then nationalized the Suez Canal, resulting in the combined attack of British, French, and Israeli forces. The United States condemned the military invasion of Egypt, as did the Soviets. The forces withdrew, and Nasser became the acknowledged moral leader of the Arab world. Nevertheless, Israel had not been toppled, and both the United States and the Soviet Union supported its right to exist. Nasser continued to promote **Pan-Arabism** and united with Syria in 1958 as the United Arab Republic. The union dissolved when Syrian leaders were toppled in a coup in 1961.

TEST TIP

Worried about whether your essay responses are scored fairly? Don't be. AP exam essay graders are experienced college professors and high school teachers who are specially trained in the subject they're scoring. Scores are checked to ensure that different graders score essays in a consistent, fair manner.

Opposition to War and Social Conflicts

The Arts

The carnage of the First World War was the worst that the world had ever experienced, and it left an indelible imprint on literature and other art forms. U.S. writer Ernest Hemingway's novel *A Farewell to Arms* and German writer, Erich Maria Remarque's *All Quiet on the Western Front* expressed the malaise and disillusionment of the postwar era and captured the seemingly meaningless suffering of the war. The belief that there were objective measures of good and evil was rejected by many in the arts. Some artists used non-European influences for their work, such as from Africa. Surrealist painter Salvador Dali, as well as other artists and writers, incorporated Freudian psychology into their works, often creating disturbing images of the world that matched the horrors of World War I.

Spanish painter Pablo Picasso's 1937 painting **Guernica** became an omen of the atrocities yet to come in World War II. Picasso had agreed to paint the centerpiece for the Spanish Pavilion of the 1937 World's Fair in Paris, whose official theme was the celebration of modern technology. The organizers of the fair hoped that the vision of the bright future that technology could bring to the world would help shake the economic depression and social unrest in the years that followed World War I. Picasso was living in Paris and trying to find inspiration for the painting as the Spanish Civil War was raging in his home country, with Generalissimo Francisco Franco and his Fascist forces fighting against the newly elected Republican government. While Picasso avoided politics, especially in his work, the events that occurred on April 27, 1937, so shocked the world—and Picasso himself—that he immediately found inspiration for his painting.

At the request of Franco, the German air force launched a massive bombing raid on the civilians living in the quiet Basque village of Guernica, in northern Spain. For more than two hours, the unsuspecting villagers were hit with highly explosive and incendiary bombs, which killed or wounded 1,600 hundred people—mostly women and children—and caused what was left of the village itself to burn for three days. Guernica was a religious and cultural center of the autonomous Basques in Spain, as well as a refuge for the Republican resistance, although it had no value as a military target to Franco or to Hitler. It essentially had been chosen as a target and tactical practice for Hitler's new military weapons and to create such utter devastation as to terrorize the Republican resistance to Franco into submission.

The unprecedented atrocities perpetrated on the Basque civilians by the bombing raid were met with outrage throughout the world. In Paris, more than a million people crowded the streets in protest. Picasso was so stunned when he read the eyewitness accounts and saw the stark photos of the events that filled the newspapers that he began almost immediately to make sketches in preparation for his painting, which he would name, simply, *Guernica*.

Guernica is a chaotic jumble of tortured images: suffering, grief-stricken, dead, and dismembered people, dying animals, daggers, destruction, and hidden symbols. Although there were and still are many interpretations of the painting and what its many symbols represent, it remains as one of the most enduring representations of the tragedies and suffering caused by war. Far from celebrating technology, as the organizers of the 1939 World's Fair intended, it is a reminder of the destructive forces that humans have unleashed on others through the use of technology.

Political Change through Nonviolence in the United States

In the United States, Baptist minister **Martin Luther King, Jr.,** emulated Gandhi's practice of passive nonresistance and boycotting to attain equality for black people. King led the Civil Rights Movement of the 1950s and 1960s, organizing acts of civil disobedience and peaceful protests to fight against segregation and discrimination against blacks. The demonstrations and activism of the **Civil Rights Movement** led to major changes in the legal system of the United States. The U.S. Supreme ruled in 1954 that segregation in public schools was unconstitutional, and later, the U.S. Congress passed the Civil Rights Act of 1964, a sweeping piece of legislation that banned major forms of discrimination based on race, color, religion, or national origin and gave the federal government the power to enforce desegregation. The Voting Rights Act of 1965 outlawed discriminatory voting methods that had been used to restrict voting by black citizens. King was assassinated in 1968 by a racist escaped convict; however, that same year the Civil Rights Act of 1968 was enacted, which prohibited discrimination in the sale, renting, and financing of housing.

Alternatives to the Existing Political and Social Order in China

After World War I, China hoped that Wilson's Fourteen Points and the Treaty of Versailles might end foreign domination of China's trade and obliterate the unequal treaties that had been imposed on it in the late nineteenth century. However, the Chinese were bitterly disappointed when the United States actually helped Japan to increase its activities in China. Resentment boiled over in China in the May Fourth

Movement of 1919, which was led by intellectuals and students. They protested foreign imperialism and wanted the restoration of national unity. The protestors believed that the United States had abandoned its own principles, especially in the context of China, and many of them turned to Communism. **Mao Zedong** was one of the most important members of the **Chinese Communist Party**, founded in 1921. He supported the equality of women, and fought against such practices as foot binding and arranged marriages, which had kept women from advancing. Sun Yat-sen organized the **Nationalist People's Party** in 1912 and by 1926, Communists accounted for one-third of its membership. Soviet advisors lent aid to the process.

Sun Yat-sen was elected president of what the Nationalist People's Party called the Republic of China in Guangzhou in southern China. He died in 1925, and Chiang Kai-shek replaced him as leader of the Nationalist People's Party. Chiang Kai-shek began a campaign, to unite China and establish Nationalist People's Party rule throughout the land. The Nationalist army's campaign was called the Northern Expedition. In 1926–1927, Chiang defeated thirty-nine warlords. He then moved on to Shanghai, where the Communists opposed his entry. He ordered a massacre of the Communists and took control of the city. Convinced that Sun Yat-sen's attempt to work with the Communists was dangerous, Chiang abandoned them. The Communists retreated to southern China, while Chiang marched on Beijing in 1928 and then established his headquarters in Nanjing. He declared the Nationalist People's Party the official government of a united China. Despite rhetoric to the contrary, however, China was not united. Chiang began a vicious battle to rid China of the Communist threat, and the Communists were forced to flee their retreat in southeastern Asia.

Mao Zedong emerged as the leader of the Communists in China and modified the teachings of Marx and Lenin about the revolutionary power of the urban, industrial proletariat to suit conditions in China. Among other things, he argued that the peasants were the foundation of revolution in China. The struggle between the Nationalists and Communists continued through World War II.

In 1949, Mao Zedong established the **People's Republic of China**, which was led by the Chinese Communist Party. As chairman of the party, Mao reformed Chinese society, using Soviet Russia as his model. Mao referred to this phase of China's history as the New Democracy, and he sought to encourage support of his program among the population. Communist China had a close relationship with the Soviets. Approximately one-half of Chinese exports went to the Soviet Union, and the Soviets further supported the development of Communism in China with loans. Although the relationship between China and the Soviet Union broke down in the 1960s, the Soviet model profoundly influenced Mao's programs in China.

Intensified Conflicts in Latin America

Latin America had been dominated by European powers since the Age of Exploration, and it then had to deal with constant U.S. intervention as the United States became more and more imperialistic. Argentine economist **Raul Prebisch** argued that Latin American economies, in fact, were damaged by their dependence on industrial nations, especially those of North America and Europe. Prebisch divided these nations into two groups, the "center" and the "periphery." In his opinion, Latin American nations on the periphery of international trade needed to diversify their domestic trade and promote their own industrial growth.

In the wake of World War II, many Latin American countries fought vigorously against U.S. and other foreign influences, and especially against U.S. intervention in their politics and economies. Despite the warnings of Prebisch and others, Latin American countries built up enormous foreign debts. During the recession of the 1970s and 1980s, the debt problem became worse. Despite the movements to separate Latin America from U.S. interference, economic issues continued to force many Latin American areas to accept aid and thus also to accept U.S. terms. U.S. investments in industries resulted in American control over the copper mining industry in Chile and Peru through the Anaconda and Kennecott companies; the oil industry in Mexico, Peru, and Bolivia; and the fruit industry through the United Fruit Company in Guatemala. Further U.S. involvement came as a result of the growing influence of Marxism in Latin America, with the United States supporting rebellions against many governments.

Chile

Chile was a clear example of U.S. interference. Chile suffered from serious economic difficulties, including the decline of the copper industry, which provided the bulk of the exports in Chile. In 1970, **Salvador Allende** was elected president. He nationalized the copper industry, largely owned by Americans, and socialized other industries. In response, U.S. president Richard Nixon cut off U.S. aid to Chile. Acting on Marxist ideology, Allende also broke up large estates. As in many other Latin American countries, a conservative backlash followed. Strikes were organized with U.S. support from the Central Intelligence Agency. Allende managed to control the strikes and even to increase his bloc in the elections of 1973. However, the military junta of Augusto José Ramón Pinochet took power in a U.S.-supported coup d'état. Allende, along with thousands of supporters, was killed.

Pinochet would lead Chile through massive economic reforms, called the **Miracle of Chile,** before open elections removed him as president in 1990. He remained commander-in-chief of the army until 1998. Pinochet's regime was one of severe brutality. Thousands fled to avoid torture and other abuses, while thousands more simply disappeared. Although Pinochet was arrested for human rights abuses in London in 1998, the British refused to extradite him to Spain, where his trial was to be held. The Chileans eventually dropped the charges against him. Some people viewed Pinochet as saving Chile from Communism and believed that his repressive measures were necessary in the face of increasingly violent resistance. However, Pinochet was one of the most brutal rulers in Chile's history. U.S. support of such figures is indicative of policy in this period, which sought to obtain political and other benefits for the United States, while often overlooking the miseries of the various populations governed by U.S.-supported governments abroad.

Guatemala

Similarly, Guatemala fought U.S. intrusion in its internal affairs. Foreign investors virtually controlled Guatemala's economy after World War II. The economy was heavily dependent on exports of coffee and bananas. In 1953, President Jacobo Arbenz Guzmán began a program of economic nationalism and took control of transportation and the electrical network. Arbenz then attempted to take unused lands from large estates, including a sizable amount of property from the United Fruit Company, which, as we said, was controlled by U.S. investors. Land was to be redistributed to peasants. Although he offered compensation for the land, U.S. president Dwight Eisenhower reacted by ordering the Central Intelligence Agency to overthrow the government. Eisenhower believed that Communist influences were at work behind the nationalization of the United Fruit Company land, and the U.S.-trained, non-Communist forces under Colonel Carlos Castillo Armas to combat the government. Armas toppled the government in 1954 and returned the land taken from the United Fruit Company. He also ruled as a military dictator, killing and torturing opponents. Under Armas, the deaths and disappearance of over 200,000 people were reported. These events were investigated by various agencies as acts of genocide against the Mayas. Armas' brutality resulted in intense rebel activity and his assassination in 1957.

Terrorism

Terrorism emerged in parts of the world both as an outgrowth of movements related to nationalism or to ethnic and religious identity, and as a response to increasing globalization. Members of the al-Qaeda ("the base") organization, for example, have intense feelings of resentment regarding the increasing American military presence in the Middle East. Many terrorist organizations in the Middle East fight for Palestinian autonomy against the Israeli occupation of Palestinian territories. Hamas, formed in 1987 during the Palestinian uprising against Israel, is just one of literally hundreds of terrorist groups in existence today.

The rise of terrorist organizations has created a sense of insecurity in various parts of the world. This is especially true of Americans, who once felt relatively immune from terrorism. Americans watched from afar as the **Palestine Liberation Organization** (PLO) launched innumerable terrorist attacks against Israel. Americans also watched the **Irish Republican Army** (IRA) carry out terrorist attacks against Britain and Protestant terrorists carrying out attacks against Irish Catholics in Ireland; however, it was not until the September 11, 2001 **(9/11),** attacks on New York City and Washington, D.C.—and aboard an airliner over Shanksville, Pennsylvania—that Americans recognized that their own security was at risk. American embassies had been bombed in the 1990s in Africa, for example, but nothing on such a large scale as the 9/11 attacks had ever occurred within U.S. borders. **Osama bin Laden's** al-Qaeda organization reflected the new global form of terrorism of the twenty-first century, as it has spawned operations by the Sunni extremists across the globe from Indonesia, to the United States, to the Middle East and Africa. Bin Laden rose to prominence as an American-funded *mujahideen* in Afghanistan, and he fled there after the attacks of 9/11. The United States pursued him there and toppled the Taliban regime. President George H. W. Bush's subsequent "war on terrorism" did not achieve the goal of finding bin Laden or of stopping continued al-Qaeda attacks elsewhere in the world. However, in 2011, a Navy Seal operation authorized by U.S. president Barack Obama killed bin Laden in the compound in which he had been hiding in Pakistan. Many experts believe that without bin Laden, the ability of the al-Qaeda core leadership to direct its extremist global movement will be diminished.

Effects of Global Conflicts on Popular Culture

Culture, as well as conflicts and politics, became increasingly globalized after the two World Wars and the Cold War. In some cases, the wars and conflicts themselves had profound effects on popular culture. For example, although the Cold War was a period of tension between two superpowers, the United States and the Soviet Union, it influenced events and ways of thinking in many parts of the world—not only in politics and military conflicts, but also in mainstream culture. People were fascinated by the Cold War throughout the decades of its duration, and various aspects of it began to be portrayed in 1953 in many movies, books, and other media that became widely available to people throughout the world. Both the espionage of the two superpowers and the threat of a nuclear war were themes or backgrounds of many popular movies and books, with some portraying fictional conflicts and events.

Perhaps the best-known example of the cultural preoccupation with the Cold War is the series of **James Bond** movies, which continue to be made and remain immensely popular throughout the world even today, with the character James Bond being one of the most recognizable icons of popular culture. British novelist Ian Fleming created James Bond in the 1953 novel *Casino Royale* and wrote eleven other Bond novels before he died in 1964. Other writers continued the Bond series after Fleming's death. The novels, set in the then-current political world atmosphere of the Cold War and the very real threats of a nuclear war, created widespread public intrigue about the world of espionage, first in Britain and then internationally.

Filmmakers in the United States acquired the rights to the Bond films, releasing the first one, *Dr. No,* in 1962. James Bond, British Secret Service Agent 007, was a dashing, steely, and cool-headed man of action who fearlessly saved the Free World from the machinations of villains who represented the Communist menace in the first stories. In *Casino Royale,* Bond's cover is a wealthy playboy who is assigned to gamble against a Frenchman involved in the Communist corruption of French trade unions. When Bond loses his money, a Central Intelligence Agent assigned as an observer slips him an envelope containing 32 million francs, "With the compliments of the USA," enabling Bond to go on to win 80 million francs that came from the Soviet-controlled trade union. This plot reflects the close alliance between Britain and the United States, and the necessity of U.S. money to defend the West from the Soviet threat.

Equipped with cutting-edge gadgets, the sharpest cars, and the most beautiful women in the world, the suave and self-disciplined Bond glamorized espionage as being a thrilling series of covert operations in exotic settings. Although the more mundane methods of signals interception and surveillance techniques were the actual means of espionage between the United States and the Soviet Union, the public embraced Bond as a superhero, and the Bond films remain the most successful and long-standing series in the history of filmmaking.

Chapter 21

New Conceptualizations of the Global Economy, Society, and Culture

Key Terms

apartheid

Archbishop Oscar Romero

Association of Southeast Asian Nations (ASEAN)

Bob Marley

Bosnia and Herzegovina

Deng Xiaoping

euro

European Union (EU)

F. W. de Klerk

Five-Year Plans

four modernizations

Great Depression

Great Leap Forward

Great Proletarian Cultural Revolution

green movements

Greenpeace International

Haile Selassie

international corporations

International Monetary Fund (IMF)

Kosovo

League of Nations

Liberation Theology

Mao Zedong

Nelson Mandela

New Deal

New Economic Policy (NEP)

North American Free Trade Agreement (NAFTA)

one-child policy

(continued)

Organization of Petroleum Exporting Countries (OPEC)

outsource

President Franklin Delano Roosevelt

Rastafarian

reggae

religious fundamentalism

Rwanda

Slobodan Milosevic

Social Security

Stock Market Crash

Tiananmen Square

United Nations (UN)

Universal Declaration of Human Rights

World Cup Soccer

World Health Organization (WHO)

World Trade Organization (WTO)

xenophobia

zaibatsu

Government Responses to Economic Challenges

The twentieth century was fraught with conflicts and wars. In the 1930s, the United States and the rest of the world were mired in a global depression. The United States responded by intervening in its free-market economy. In the Communist states of the Soviet Union and China, their governments responded by taking complete control of their national economies.

The United States

After World War I, the United States reacted against the lofty idealism of Woodrow Wilson, and in the 1920s the nation entered a period in which it sought to "return to normalcy." One of the main planks of the return to normalcy was rejection of former president Wilson's belief in the United States' international role and a renewal of the former stance of isolationism. In fact, by the mid-1930s, a Senate committee concluded that U.S. involvement in World War I had been a mistake, which contributed to U.S. reluctance to enter World War II.

In the 1930s, however, the nation, like the rest of the world, was in the midst of a global depression, called the **Great Depression**. The complex system of reparation demanded by the Treaty of Versailles was the basis for much of the economy in the 1920s, and Austria and Germany, for example, relied on U.S. loans to pay these debts. The French and British relied on reparation payments to pay their own loans from the

United States during the war. By 1928, U.S. lenders had started to withdraw capital from Europe, straining the financial system. Other factors contributed, as the use of oil began to undermine the coal industry, and techniques for using reclaimed rubber, perfected during the war, hurt the rubber export industry of the Dutch East Indies, Ceylon, and Malaysia. In fact, overproduction contributed to the global depression. During the war, European agricultural production had fallen, for obvious reasons. The United States and other parts of the world had expanded their production, and after the war, European production resumed. The result was a worldwide surplus. Demand declined and prices dropped. By 1929 the price of a bushel of wheat was at its lowest level in 400 years. This contributed to the inability of farmers to purchase manufactured goods, leading businesses to cut jobs.

The Stock Market Crash of 1929

On Black Thursday, October 24, 1929, investors across the world pulled out of the market, and stocks plummeted in what was known as the **Stock Market Crash.** Many people lost their life's savings, and banks began to call in loans. In the United States, by 1932, industrial production was at one-half the level of 1929, and the national income was also only one-half of what it had been. Almost half of the banks in the United States went out of business and took with them the deposits of millions of people. Because so much of the world was dependent on the U.S. economy, the world economy collapsed as well. Germany and Japan, as well as Latin American, African, and Asian countries were hard hit. These were nations that relied on exports. In Germany the unemployment rate reached 35 percent by 1932 and its production fell by 50 percent.

World production declined by 38 percent in the three years following the Stock Market Crash of 1929. Trade dropped by over 60 percent as nations imposed tariffs on imports in an attempt to become self-sufficient. In the 1930s, **President Franklin Delano Roosevelt** responded to the plight of many Americans with his **New Deal**, a massive program of social reform legislation based on federal intervention in the economy. The government created new jobs through the Works Progress (Projects) Administration, the Civilian Conservation Corps, and other agencies. It also created **Social Security** and other measures for the relief of its beleaguered population.

The Soviet Union

By the 1920s the Bolshevik revolution in Russia was complete and Lenin devoted his attention to controlling what remained of the country. Russia lay in ruins. Over half the people were starving as a result of famine brought on by drought combined with the devastation of war. The economy had been destroyed. The population, stretched to its limits, rioted once more. The Bolsheviks were still rebuilding Russian society when the global depression hit.

In 1921, Lenin issued the **New Economic Policy (NEP)**, which allowed for some economic freedom by encouraging cottage industries and small farms to produce food and goods and to trade among themselves. Major industries, however, remained under the control of the government. Lenin returned industries with less than twenty employees to the private sector. The NEP also allowed peasants to sell surpluses for free-market prices. By 1926 the economy had rebounded to its pre-1913 levels.

Lenin died in 1924, and Joseph Stalin had achieved complete power in the Soviet Union by 1927. Stalin quickly enacted several **Five-Year Plans**, intended to promote rapid economic development. The first plan focused on heavy industry, which was to become centralized through the efforts of the central state-planning agency. Stalin created collective farms and subsumed all private land into these units. Members shared the profits. Peasants revolted, and many starved to death on their own lands when they were unable to meet production quotas set by the government. By 1931, when the plan ended, half the land in Russia was contained within collective farms.

As the Soviet government focused on industry, consumer goods were virtually nonexistent. Rebellions emerged not only among those whose land was taken, but within the Communist Party as well. Stalin then embarked on a series of purges. Over two-thirds of the members of the 1934 Communist Central Committee and one-half of the army's highest-ranking officers were removed, while 3 million citizens died and 8 million were imprisoned.

China

The worldwide depression after World War I also affected China, as demand for its traditional exports of silk and tea declined. In the 1930s, most of China's industrial products were still made from the craft industries.

Mao Zedong

China's Communist leader, **Mao Zedong**, introduced his own version of the Five-Year Plan in 1955. Like Stalin, Mao wanted to transform China into an industrial nation that was self-sufficient. The policies of the first plan were modeled on those of Stalin, with a focus on heavy industry to the detriment of the production of consumer goods. Also like Stalin, Mao attempted to equalize land holdings in the countryside.

He took the land of the largest 10 percent of the landholders, who together owned 70 to 80 percent of the land in China. He redistributed the land to more than 300 million peasants. Each peasant received an equal amount of land, and these allotments are still visible in today's rural villages.

Mao's **Great Leap Forward** (1958–1961) moved China further along on the road to industrialization. He abolished private farms and created collective farms. Through small-scale industrial production on the farms, Mao hoped to bring China firmly into the industrial age. On the collective farms, families ate with other families in communal dining halls, and Communist propaganda worked against the traditional Chinese emphasis on family bonds. Individualism was discouraged. Mao emerged as even more radical than the Soviets in his effort to implement true Communism and to spread the Communist revolution abroad.

Just as Stalin's attempt to collectivize the farms of Russia resulted in disaster, however, Mao's Great Leap Forward resulted in a great leap backward. Production fell as the peasants could not meet quotas, and a series of bad harvests doomed the program. Mao refused to accept responsibility and blamed the failures on the eating habits of sparrows, which he called counterrevolutionaries. When he ordered the killing of sparrows, he left the way open for insects to devour the remaining crops. By 1962, the Great Leap Forward had resulted in the deaths by starvation of 20 million Chinese people.

Mao's **Great Proletarian Cultural Revolution** (1966–1976) was another attempt to weed out opposition to his reforms. By this time he had accused the Soviets of being "revisionists," a term that was very offensive within the Communist world. Mao then found revisionists throughout China and targeted the intellectuals, professionals, and others associated with foreign influences or bourgeois values. The so-called Cultural Revolution set China back many years, as it stripped China of its educated population and sent thousands to jails, to rural labor camps, or to their deaths.

Deng Xiaoping

Chairman Mao died in 1976, having brought China to its knees. **Deng Xiaoping** took power in 1981. One of the most controversial aspects of Deng Xiaoping's rule was the institution of the **one-child policy**, which remains in effect. China's population had exploded by the 1970s despite a series of famines and other problems. From 1949 to 1970, China's population increased by 270 million people. The effect of continuing at this birth rate would have been disastrous. The one-child policy applies to people living in cities and only to the Han Chinese. Ethnic minorities are exempt. Many people skirt the policy by abandoning their female children to orphanages, having abortions, or simply not reporting births. The policy remains controversial and is attributed to the disproportionate number of males to females in China. The Chinese government claims that the policy has prevented about 400 million births since its implementation.

More successful were a series of reforms known as Deng's revolution. Deng emphasized "**four modernizations**": in agriculture, industry, national defense, and technology. In agriculture, Deng allowed collectives to lease land to peasants. Whatever they were able to produce above the rent payment could be sold on the market. Industries similar to cottage industries were also tolerated in the countryside to provide an outlet for excess labor. By the 1980s, the average farm income doubled. Many peasants then valued the production of cash crops that might further their economic position, and thus inadvertently, the new agricultural policies detracted from the production of staple crops such as rice. Further, rural families were more willing to violate the one-child policy and pay the required fine so as to boost their farms' productivity. Nevertheless, the overall effect of the policies was to significantly elevate the standard of living in China. Per capita income dramatically increased. By the 1990s, the private sector in China produced 10 percent of the gross domestic product, China had an affluent middle class, and the government began to shut down state-run industries.

The more the standard of living was raised, however, the more the younger generation was inclined to protest. When Deng Xiaoping reversed Mao's isolationism and allowed foreign capitalist investments in China, he allowed many Chinese students to study at foreign universities. The exposure to new views, such as democracy, brought unintended consequences. In 1989, students staged a sit-down protest at **Tiananmen Square** in Beijing in front of the Forbidden Palace, once home to the emperors of China. Deng Xiaoping had himself been persecuted and condemned to labor during the Mao era, and he feared revolutionary movements of any kind. He responded with vicious force to the students in Tiananmen, with his troops mowing them down with tanks and guns. Many students died, while reporters filmed the events and showed them to a worldwide audience.

TEST TIP

There is no need to use all of the documents provided for your document-based essay; instead, choose the ones that you can use best to support your thesis. Using four or five documents effectively is better than using more documents less effectively.

Japan

The economy of Japan continued to grow at a rapid rate in the early twentieth century as a result of the Meiji reforms of the late nineteenth century. In the thirty years from 1900 to 1930, production of raw materials nearly tripled, leading to increased exports. Industries, which had received generous subsidies from the Meiji government, began to form conglomerates known as **zaibatsu**. By 1937, four of these *zaibatsu* controlled one-fifth of all banking enterprises, one-third of the shipbuilding industry, and 38 percent of commercial shipping.

Asia experienced an "economic miracle" after World War II, especially in Japan. The transformation of Japan made it one of the technological giants of the world. By 2009, Japan was the world's third-largest exporter of goods and services (behind Germany and the United States), falling to the fourth-largest in 2010, when China became the world's biggest exporter.

Agricultural reforms fostered by the U.S. occupation after World War II also broke up large landed estates with absentee landlords and spurred the growth of a class of yeoman farmers. Japan's transformation was remarkable, especially in light of the fact that the industrial base developed during the Meiji era was almost completely destroyed in World War II. The Allies, in fact, also tried to break up the *zaibatsu* conglomerates in the years following World War II, in the belief that the Meiji's centralization of industry contributed to the militaristic nature of Japan. Nevertheless, part of the *zaibatsu* structure was preserved under a new system of "interlocking arrangements." As the Allies worried about the spread of Communism in Asia, they looked to Japan to help them and became more willing to tolerate economic conglomerates.

Among the other reasons often cited for Japan's transformation after World War II is the fact that it was occupied and under the protection of the United States and therefore did not need to channel much of its wealth into its own defense. In fact, the total destruction of Japan's industrial plants actually promoted faster development, in contrast to development in other countries, which was often hindered by older machinery and plant structures. Further, the Japanese government continued to be heavily involved in promoting industry. The Ministry of International Trade and Industry controlled imports, while flooding foreign markets with goods priced below cost. By the late twentieth century, other countries in the Pacific Rim also built up very strong economies, including Taiwan, Singapore, South Korea, and Taiwan.

International Organizations

Organizations for World Peace and International Cooperation

The twentieth century saw the development of international organizations, starting with the **League of Nations** in 1918, which resulted from U.S. President Wilson's call for the creation of "a general association of nations," in the Paris Peace Conference that concluded World War I. The League of Nations was the first permanent international security organization. Its purpose was to maintain world peace. However, it had two basic flaws in its structure. First, it had no means to enforce its decisions, and second, it relied on the notion of collective security to preserve global peace. "Collective security" essentially meant that a threat to any one country was a threat to all, but because participation by the various powers was essential, the League could never attain its aims.

Many important powers were, at one time or another, absent from the League. Wilson had been the driving force for the formation of the League of Nations and for the treaty that would promise peace for Europe, but he was unable to deliver U.S. ratification of the treaty. The Senate was unable to agree with the terms of the League of Nations, and the rejection of the treaty also meant that the United States was not bound by its promise to come to the defense of France. Britain then refused to ratify its defense agreement with France as well. France was left with no defensive buffer zone and no promise of aid in the case of German aggression. Germany left the League in 1933, as it believed it to be dominated by the Allies. The Soviet Union joined in 1934 and was expelled in 1940. The League utterly failed to stop World War II and therefore collapsed in 1940.

The formation of the **United Nations (UN)** in 1945 was a response to the World Wars and the role of nationalism in the origins and events of those wars. The UN was founded to preserve international peace and foster international cooperation in solving the world's economic, political, and other problems. Although the member nations of the Security Council of the United Nations have often acted more out of their own self-interest than for the common good, the UN has nonetheless been an important force in world politics since 1945.

International Economic Institutions

The foundation of the **International Monetary Fund (IMF)** in 1944 helped to initiate a new era of global cooperation by encouraging free trade and high-growth rates. Free trade across borders was one of the most important issues that affected the post–World War II era. The 1947 General Agreement on Tariffs and Trade, supported by the United States, helped to establish the **World Trade Organization (WTO)**, which took the agreement's place in 1995. The end of the Cold War also created greater opportunities for trade, as China and the members of the former Soviet Union then entered international trade.

International Corporations

In the late twentieth century, many large companies became truly international corporations, having multinational ownership and management. **International corporations** now dominate the business world, including U.S. business giants Microsoft, McDonald's, and Coca-Cola, and Japan's Sony and Honda. Whereas international businesses earlier in the twentieth century took the form of multinational corporations, operating under the restrictions of a particular country but doing business abroad, international corporations today are operated from offices across the world. One of the motivating factors of international corporations is the search for cheap labor and places that impose few restrictions, thus lowering operating costs. Many global corporations are able to evade local tax laws, leading to a depletion of resources from tax revenues in various parts of the world. In fact, U.S. corporations are among the leaders of this trend, as are Japanese corporations, with many industries conducting some manufacturing in the United States. International corporations often farm their labor out across many national borders or pull up locations in one place in favor of another with cheaper labor. Further, some corporations located in one region **outsource** jobs to another region or country, where labor is cheaper. This often results in the loss of jobs in the home countries of international corporations.

Old alliances, however, are not easily undone, and various nations have formed trading blocs to protect their interests in the global market. The European Economic Community was first formed in 1957, and in 1993, the **European Union (EU)** was established with fifteen member nations. In 2002, twelve of the members implemented a system of common currency, the **euro**, with Britain most notably retaining its national currency, the pound. The **Association of Southeast Asian Nations (ASEAN)** was established in 1967, and the **Organization of Petroleum Exporting Countries (OPEC)** was formed in 1990. The United States, Canada, and Mexico signed the **North American Free Trade Agreement (NAFTA)** in 1993. These associations have tremendous power, as demonstrated by OPEC's embargo on oil shipments to the United States in 1973 in retaliation for U.S. support of Israel. The cost of a barrel of oil increased fourfold, triggering a global recession.

Humanitarian Institutions

When the UN was formed in 1945, its members proposed the establishment of a global health organization. The **World Health Organization (WHO)** came into being in 1948, with its stated objective being "the attainment by all people of the highest possible level of health." The WHO organizes international efforts to prevent, treat, and control outbreaks of infectious diseases. It provides global leadership on various health issues, setting the agenda for health-based research and standards. Other international organizations provide immediate assistance for health and humanitarian crises, such as the Red Cross and the Red Crescent, Doctors Without Borders, and Amnesty International.

Green Movements

Beginning in the 1960s, environmental activists began movements to protest the destructive consequences of population growth and industrialization on the environment. These so-called **green movements** raised public awareness about a variety of global environmental problems, such as deforestation, the extinction of animal species, and pollution. Green movements have been generally most effective in developed countries, where they form interest groups and put pressure on governments to implement measures to protect the environment. In developing countries, however, these movements have been less effective, and the destruction of rain forests and air and water pollution continue to be serious problems.

One of the most prominent green movements is Greenpeace, which emerged in the early 1970s from the antiwar movement and antinuclear protests in Vancouver, British Columbia. The group of activists originally came together to protest U.S. plans to test nuclear weapons in Alaska. Greenpeace gradually began to spread to other countries and staged protests against other environmental concerns, such as commercial whale and seal hunting and toxic waste. In 1979, **Greenpeace International** was established in Amsterdam with the merging of the Greenpeace groups in various countries. Greenpeace is known for taking direct actions against what it perceives to be threats to the environment, and for its success in raising public awareness of these issues, which in turn has resulted in some successes in pressuring both private organizations and governments to refrain from environmentally destructive practices. The actions of Greenpeace are often very controversial, such as members acting as human shields to protect whales from hunters and hanging protest signs on national monuments. However, it is these sometimes outrageous actions that draw attention to the organization and therefore to its missions.

New Conceptions of Societies and Cultures

Following both World Wars and continuing throughout the twentieth century and into the twenty-first century, conceptions changed about the roles of different people in societies throughout the world. Human rights became a global issue, as did women's rights and the rights of nonwhite members of various societies. Despite the increasing globalization of the world and increasing interactions among people of diverse cultures, various ethnic clashes, exclusionary reactions, and religious conflicts continue to rip at the fabric of unity.

Gains in Human Rights

Universal Declaration of Human Rights

After the atrocities of World War II and the establishment of the United Nations (UN), there was widespread consensus that there was a need to specify the individual rights of every person in the world. In 1948, the UN adopted the **Universal Declaration of Human Rights**, which identifies the nature of the rights to which every human being is entitled in its Preamble and thirty Articles. Some of these rights include the rights to life, to not be enslaved, to participate in society and politics, to freely practice religious and cultural beliefs, and to assemble. As of July of 2011, there were 193 member states of the UN, all of which have agreed to the terms of the Universal Declaration of Human Rights.

Women's Rights

Both World Wars liberated women in Western countries from the subservient roles that they previously had. With tens of millions of men fighting in both wars, women had to perform the jobs at home that kept the economies functioning. Women gained the right to vote in the Netherlands in 1917, in Canada and Sweden in 1918, in the United States in 1920, and in Britain in 1928, with other Western countries following suit in subsequent years. In the Soviet Union, women achieved suffrage in 1917; women in Austria, Czechoslovakia, and Poland gained the same rights in 1918, followed by women in Germany and Luxembourg in 1919.

Women gained the right to vote for the first time in Latin America in Ecuador, in 1929. Other Latin American nations soon followed, with women's suffrage being granted in 1932 in Brazil, in 1939 in El Salvador, in 1942 in the Dominican Republic, in 1945 in Guatemala, and 1946 in Argentina. By the 1990s, women had achieved impressive gains in Latin America, coming close to the rights of women in North America and Europe, especially in political office holding.

In India, women received the same suffrage as men from the British in 1935, while in the Philippines, women received the right to vote in 1937, in Japan in 1945, in China in 1947, and in Indonesia in 1955. As African colonies gained independence as autonomous nations following World War II, men and women typically were granted rights at the same time, as in Liberia in1947, Uganda in 1958, and Nigeria in 1960.

DIDYOUKNOW?

Margaret Thatcher became Britain's first female prime minister in 1979 and served an unprecedented three consecutive terms in that office. Thatcher developed a close political relationship with U.S. President Ronald Reagan, based both on their common mistrust of the Soviet Union during the latter part of the Cold War era and on free-market economic policies. The Soviets referred to her as the "Iron Lady".

Ethnic, Cultural, and Religious Conflicts

Simmering ethnic, cultural, and religious clashes occurred in various parts of the world in the late twentieth century and the early twenty-first century. Some conflicts were a continuation of long-standing differences, while others resulted from new cultural identities that emerged from the creation of new nations. Still others were caused by a resistance to the rise of globalism.

South Africa

In the nation of South Africa, the policy of **apartheid** (meaning "apartness") originated with European settlements being established there in 1652. In 1948, apartheid became law, followed by the Population Registration Act of 1950, which categorized South Africans as being either white, black African, or of mixed race, with a fourth category, Asian (referring to Indians and Pakistanis) later being included. The enactment of a series of laws during the 1950s reinforced apartheid: different races were assigned to specific residential and business sections in cities and to specific job categories; greater restrictions curbed the already limited rights of black Africans to own land and to participate in the government; most forms of social contact were prohibited between the races; public facilities were segregated; and separate standards of education were established.

Apartheid policies included government suppression of opposition and severe reprisals for ongoing resistance—which often was violent—by black political groups, with some support from sympathetic whites. The international community condemned apartheid in South Africa: in 1961, other members forced South Africa to withdraw from the British Commonwealth; the United Nations passed a resolution condemning South African apartheid policies in 1962; and by the late 1980s, Britain, the United States, and more than twenty other countries had imposed economic sanctions on it. Both internal and external pressures caused South African President **F. W. de Klerk** to begin to abolish some apartheid policies in the early 1990s. In 1994, a new constitution was in place in South Africa, with free general elections held for the first time in its history. **Nelson Mandela**, who had been a leading protester of apartheid and had therefore been imprisoned by the government for twenty-seven years, was elected South Africa's first black president and served in that office until 1999. He and President de Klerk had been jointly awarded the Nobel Peace Prize in 1993 for their efforts to end apartheid. In the following years, the government struggled to find effective policies to manage South Africa's new challenges in the face of national political and social changes, as well as changes within Africa. Adding to the difficulties that the South African government faced was the long-standing problem of migration and **xenophobia**, a fear or hatred of foreigners, which was far from being eradicated, despite the great progress that had occurred.

The problems of xenophobia that originated in South Africa's immigration policies persisted. Up until 1991, the government had required that official immigrants have specific abilities and characteristics to enable them to assimilate into its white culture, which blatantly excluded all black Africans. However, South Africa had a history (dating back to the nineteenth century) of allowing huge numbers of people from neighboring African countries—particularly Mozambique, Lesotho, Zimbabwe, and Malawi—to enter the country as contract migrant workers. Since the 1890s, the gold- and diamond-mining industries, and later, the commercial farming industry, had relied heavily on these workers as a cheap source of labor.

In the 1980s, Mozambique experienced a civil war, with about 350,000 of its people taking refuge in South Africa, which willingly accepted them. This acceptance had turned into resentment by 1994, however, when many South Africans came to view the refugees from Mozambique, as well as other African migrant workers, as outsiders. Tensions were fueled by widespread unemployment and competition for jobs; unemployment rates in South Africa were among the highest in the world, with an estimated rate of unemployment for all South African workers at 22 percent, and the rate for black Africans at a staggering 41 percent. Between 1994 and 2010, the South African government arrested and deported nearly 2 million migrant workers to bordering nations, a policy that was in striking contrast to national, regional, and worldwide human-rights expectations of the new government. The exportation policies were widely viewed as being no better than the openly discriminatory practices of the apartheid era, and xenophobia actually increased. Since 2000, the overall unemployment rate in South Africa has been estimated by some accounts to be as high as 36 to 42 percent, and tensions between South African citizens and foreign workers have been ongoing. In 2008, residents of working-class neighborhoods attacked foreign black contract workers in riots throughout South Africa, leaving sixty-two people dead. Although the South African government was pressured by governments and organizations throughout the world to stop the deportations and address the issue of xenophobia, it had thus far failed to implement meaningful changes, and incidents of violence against foreign workers and shopkeepers have continued.

The Former States of Yugoslavia

Bosnia and Herzegovina declared sovereignty in 1991 and independence from Yugoslavia in 1992, leading to a series of ethnic wars between Catholic and Orthodox Christians and Muslims. Serbian nationalism led Serb minorities in Bosnia and Croatia to attempt to secede, prompting furious fighting. In 1995, the UN sent forces to Bosnia to help implement the Dayton Agreement to a ceasefire. Today, Bosnia and Herzegovina are still divided along ethnic lines, but tensions have eased.

Similarly, the situation in **Kosovo** erupted into war in 1999 when Albanians protested Serbian rule. Kosovo had been declared an autonomous region of Serbia following World War II, and its boundaries were redrawn to form an Albanian majority. During the Kosovo War of 1999, many Serbs left, and **Slobodan Milosevic**, the leader of Serbia, became the first head of state to be prosecuted by the United Nations for war crimes in 2002, including genocide in Bosnia and war crimes in Kosovo and Croatia. Milosevic died before a verdict was reached in his trial, dashing the hopes of many that he would be held accountable for the deaths of more than 200,000 people.

Rwanda

Ethnic conflicts had been simmering between the majority Tutsis and the minority Hutus in **Rwanda** since 1962, when Belgium withdrew from the region and the independent states of Rwanda and Burundi were created. A civil war erupted in 1994, with more than 800,000 Hutus being killed in mass attacks of genocide by the Tutsis in the period of less than four months. The Tutsis won control of Rwanda, and a million Hutus, fearful of revenge, fled the country and took refuge in Zaire and Tanzania.

Religious Fundamentalism

The clash between Muslims and Christians in Bosnia and Croatia highlights the role played by religion in many modern conflicts. The rise of fundamentalist religious sects in many parts of the world is in part a result of their rejection of the tendency of globalization to produce a common identity, with religious groups wanting to retain their traditional identities. Further, globalization has promoted mass consumerism, which often conflicts with the values of religious fundamentalists. **Religious fundamentalism** exists among Hindus in India, Muslims in the Middle East and various other parts of the world, and Christians who are members of Protestant fundamentalist sects, especially in the United States and Latin America, but also in other parts of the world.

Liberation Theology

The increasing disparity between the wealthy and the poor in Latin America, combined with the existence of brutal regimes prior to the implementation of democracies, resulted in the development of **Liberation Theology** in the 1970s. Liberation Theology was developed by Roman Catholic priests in Latin America as a response to the needs of the poor. According to Liberation Theology, Jesus did not mean for the poor to suffer injustice and the Catholic Church had a duty to liberate them from oppression by becoming actively involved in politics to bring about social change. Clergy members such as **Archbishop Oscar Romero** of San Salvador advocated human rights and the need for reform. More radical proponents of Liberation Theology themselves became involved in politics and even supported violent revolutionary movements. Pope John Paul II vehemently objected to the highly politicized nature of the Liberation Theology and its blending of Marxist socialist ideals with Catholicism. He dealt severely with the movement, removing activist Catholic priests from their positions and closing Catholic institutions that taught Liberation Theology. Archbishop Romero became a martyr for the cause of Liberation Theology when he was assassinated as he was saying Mass in a cancer hospice in 1980. Throughout the 1980s and up to the present day, Cardinal Ratzinger, then the head of the Vatican's Congregation for the Doctrine of the Faith and currently Pope Benedict XVI, has prohibited the teaching of Liberation Theology in the name of the Catholic Church.

TEST TIP

You may only work on each section of the test during the stated time period. Looking ahead at the essays or trying to go back to check your multiple-choice answers when you're supposed to be working on something else can result in having your test scores canceled.

Globalization of Popular and Consumer Culture

During the twentieth century the globalization of popular culture became increasingly extensive and pervasive as a result of new communication technologies and the worldwide system of economic relationships. The World Wars and the Cold Wars contributed significantly to the spread of cultures, as these conflicts involved virtually all regions of the world to varying extents. Social movements, such as the human rights, antiwar, and environmental movements of the 1960s and 1970s, as well as struggles for equality based on ethnicity, class, and gender, became international movements. Even those who did not participate directly learned about them and followed them with interest through various media, including newspapers, radio, television, movies, books, and, later, the Internet and social networking sites.

While aspects of Western popular culture, particularly U.S. popular culture, have become immensely popular throughout the world since the 1950s, there has also been worldwide adoption of the music, dances, films, and fashions of other popular cultures. Today, for example, people throughout the world listen to reggae music, dance the salsa, and wear Rastafarian dreadlocks and hip-hop pants. They watch the international blockbuster Indian movie *Slumdog Millionaire* and other films produced throughout the world and promoted by such events as Robert Redford's Sundance Film Festival in Utah and the Cannes International Film Festival in France.

Reggae Music

Reggae music became a distinct genre in Jamaica in the 1960s, evolving from traditional Jamaican music including ska and mento, American rhythm and blues, and the heavy, back-beated rhythm of African music. At outdoor discos, Jamaicans who were too poor to afford radios or record players gathered to dance to reggae, meaning "coming from the people." Many Jamaicans of African descent practiced the **Rastafarian** religion, and reggae musicians often integrated Rastafarian beliefs into their songs.

Musicians such as Jimmy Cliff and Peter Tosh were influential in the spread of reggae, but it was a band of young men from the slums of the Jamaican capital of Kingston called the Wailers (since, as Marley said, "We started out crying"), led by the now-iconic **Bob Marley**, who made reggae a part of international popular culture. In the 1970s, the Wailers toured in the United States, Europe, Africa, and other places around the world, where many of their songs became hits. The unique and noncommercial music of the Wailers and Bob Marley's charismatic and soulful personality were internationally appealing—from black Africans struggling to overcome oppression to comfortable, white middle-class concertgoers in the United States. In troubled African states such as Mauritius and Zimbabwe, the Wailers' reggae message of standing up against racial discrimination and oppression inspired political resistance and a united sense of African identity. Marley often made his initial appearance onstage playing a West African drum and invoking a Rastafarian ritual, with a backdrop of banners showing Marcus Garvey, the Ethiopian flag, and a picture of **Haile Selassie**, the Ethiopian emperor who was remarkable in that he, as a monarch, advocated civil disobedience when it was necessary to remedy social injustices and free people who were oppressed.

Marley died in 1981 but remains a legendary figure throughout the world. He was posthumously inducted into the Rock and Roll Hall of Fame in 1994, and in 1999 the Wailers' 1977 album *Exodus* was named Album of the Century by the news magazine *Time*; their song "One Love" was named Song of the Millennium by the British Broadcasting Corporation (BBC). The appeal and power of reggae throughout the world, with Marley as its ambassador, is an example of how the globalization of popular culture is no longer dominated by the spread of Western culture to the rest of the world, but instead has become a two-way street.

World Cup Soccer

Sporting events, such as the Olympics and **World Cup Soccer**, also often represent the globalization of popular culture. At the same time, however, these sports events create passionate feelings of national and ethnic pride. In the present climate of the world, in which globalization is expanding and nationalism appears to be declining, the World Cup of Soccer remains a bastion of intense nationalism. Americans, who have been always been serious contenders in every major sport in the world except soccer, began in the 1990s to understand just how significant the World Cup is for nearly every other nation in the world, which call the game *football*—long before the American game of football usurped its name in the United States and called it soccer.

Held every four years in different countries who bid on hosting the event, the *Federation Internationale de Football Association* (FIFA) World Cup has long been the most widely viewed sporting event in the world. It is the ultimate sports tournament, with 32 national teams having to survive qualifying rounds involving more than 200 national teams that begin three years before the World Cup itself to compete for the much-coveted World Cup trophy. Throughout the month-long World Cup, in whatever region or country of the world the tournament takes place, citizens of all nations make plans—sometimes years in advance—to travel there to enthusiastically support their national teams. Fans in the stadiums and on the streets wave their national flags with pride and dress in their national colors, with many also painting their faces and bodies with team colors, singing their national anthems, dancing their national dances, and even playing national instruments—essentially making support of their teams a nationalistic performance art in the stands.

So strong is the patriotism exhibited in the World Cup that football (soccer) might very well be the only politically acceptable form of pure nationalism left in the world today. Those who normally feel that it is inappropriate to express emotional patriotism completely abandon such inhibitions when their national football teams are playing. The World Cup is a rare setting in which people throughout the world feel free to publicly express their love of their countries and to not only tolerate, but also to embrace such expressions by members of other countries, regardless of politics and even war.

Time for a quiz
- Review strategies in Chapter 2
- Take Quiz 6 at the REA Study Center
  (www.rea.com/studycenter)

Take Mini-Test 2
on Chapters 12–21
Go to the REA Study Center
(www.rea.com/studycenter)

Practice Exam

Also available at the REA Study Center *(www.rea.com/studycenter)*

This practice exam is available at the REA Study Center. Although AP exams are administered in paper-and-pencil format, we recommend that you take the online version of the practice exam for the benefits of:

- Instant scoring
- Enforced time conditions
- Detailed score report of your strengths and weaknesses

Practice Exam
Section I

(Answer sheets appear in the back of the book.)

TIME: 55 Minutes
70 Questions

Directions: Each of the questions or incomplete statements below is followed by four suggested answers or completions. Select the one that is best in each case and then fill in the corresponding oval on the answer sheet.

1. Which of the following examples of the patronage of the arts that flourished in the era of 1450–1750 was characterized by humanism as well as a display of political power and wealth?

   (A) Emperor Qinglong's printing of the Complete Library of the Four Treasures

   (B) Suleyman the Magnificent's commissioning of the Suleymaniye religious complex

   (C) Pope Julius II's commissioning of the painting of the Sistine Chapel's ceiling

   (D) Emperor Shah Jahan's commissioning of the Taj Mahal

2. All of the following were part of the pattern of the Columbian Exchange EXCEPT

   (A) Africa to the Americas: goats, chickens, bananas, coconut palms, coffee, and sugar cane

   (B) The Americas to Europe and Africa: corn, potatoes, tomatoes, squash, beans, pineapples, peppers, tobacco, and chocolate

   (C) Europe to the Americas: horses, cows, pigs, wheat, barley, sugar cane, melons, and grapes

   (D) Asia to Europe and Africa: spices, salt, rice, tea, sugar, oxen, and exotic animals

3. Which of the following was the main result of the Berlin West Africa Conference of 1884–1885?

   (A) European diplomats agreed to end the slave trade in Africa.

   (B) Belgium's King Leopold II established the Congo Free State and later seized it as the Belgian Congo.

   (C) Virtually all parts of Africa were colonized by Europeans by 1900.

   (D) Dr. David Livingstone, a Scottish missionary, spent three decades exploring the interior of Africa and setting up missionary outposts.

4. Which of the following characteristics do malaria, cholera, and tuberculosis share?

   (A) They are all associated with poverty.

   (B) They are all vector-borne infectious diseases.

   (C) They have all been eliminated in the most highly industrialized nations.

   (D) They all have strains that are multi-resistant to drugs.

5. Which of the following was a major reason for the Byzantine Empire's survival for almost a millennium after the Western Roman Empire collapsed?

   (A) The Byzantines taxed all goods that traders carried through their territory.

   (B) The Byzantines extracted gifts and money from neighboring realms and peoples.

   (C) Byzantine emperors were absolute rulers of both state and church.

   (D) The Byzantines established a merit-based bureaucracy that was well-educated, loyal, and efficient.

6. Which of the following was a distinct difference that set Judaism apart from Christianity?

   (A) Jews did not seek to convert others to their religion.

   (B) Judaism was a clearly monotheistic religion.

   (C) Judaism's appeal to ordinary people was comparable to that of Buddhism.

   (D) Jews viewed Jesus as the Messiah who would cleanse the Jewish religion of its rigid and haughty priests.

7. Which of the following helped lead to the complete subjugation of peoples in the Americas by the Spanish, but not by the English?

   (A) A hierarchical class system, with Europeans born in Spain at the top, followed by creoles, mestizos, mulattos, and then Native Americans and Africans

   (B) Individual colonies' being allowed to set up their own political structures similar to those in Spain

   (C) Well-coordinated communication between viceroys in the Americas and the Council of the Indies, whose members remained in Spain

   (D) A lack of elaborate bureaucracies in urban areas of the Americas

8. Which of the following best justifies the claim that military conflicts occurred on an unprecedented global scale at the beginning of the 20th century?

(A) Japan's victory in the Russo-Japanese War, its claiming of German territories after World War I began, and its invasion of Chinese Manchuria in violation of the Treaty of Versailles

(B) The formation of the major alliances of the Triple Entente (Russia, England, and France) and the Triple Alliance (Germany, Austria-Hungary, and Italy)

(C) Colonial disputes between Britain and Russia over Persia and Afghanistan, between Britain and Germany over eastern and southwest Africa, between Britain and France over the Nile River Valley and Siam, and between Germany and France over Morocco and western Africa

(D) Mussolini's appeal to Italian nationalism in his quest to recapture the glory of the ancient Roman Empire through military conquests

9. The photograph above of a statue created in second-century India represents which of the following?

(A) The Daoist core belief of balance between humans and nature

(B) The convergence of Greco-Roman culture and Buddhist beliefs

(C) Christianity's rejection of Roman and Hellenistic influences

(D) The unification of Confucianism, Hinduism, and Legalism

10. How did the James Bond films reflect the profound influence that global conflicts have had on popular culture?

   (A) They exposed the reality that espionage is all about covert operations and human intelligence, rather than the interception of signals and lengthy periods of surveillance.

   (B) They reinforced American concerns about Britain's intelligence operations after Kim Philby, the British Secret Intelligence Services liaison officer in Washington, was found to be a Soviet spy.

   (C) They allowed billions of people throughout the world to interpret the events of the Cold War without a Western bias, to realize that even close allies cannot be trusted, and to fear the intelligence capabilities of the United States.

   (D) They played on contemporary fears to show the reality of hidden enemies, explored the relationship between Britain in decline and the United States in ascendancy, and charted the history of the Cold War.

11. In which of the following ways did Social Darwinism facilitate and justify imperialism?

   (A) It questioned the assumptions of constitutional monarchies.

   (B) It brought about the rise of a large middle class in industrialized societies.

   (C) It enhanced the status of inherited titles of nobility based on land ownership.

   (D) It reinforced social class distinctions.

12. In which of the following ways did the spread of Islam cause changes in gender relations?

   (A) Women could inherit property, divorce their husbands, and engage in business ventures.

   (B) Women were confined to their homes to ensure the purity of the bloodlines of the elite class.

   (C) Women gave tribute to their leaders through textiles, pottery, and jewelry.

   (D) Women who died in childbirth were honored equally with men who died in battle.

13. All of the following innovations contributed to the economic revolutions of the Tang and Song dynasties EXCEPT

   (A) the development of paper money, checks, and letters of credit.

   (B) the invention of gunpowder, movable type printing, and the magnetic compass.

   (C) the adaptation of mathematics from the people they conquered.

   (D) the development of superior methods of producing iron and steel.

14. Of the following "gunpowder" empires in the Middle East and Asia, which had the least in common with the others?

   (A) The Mughal Empire

   (B) The Russian Empire

   (C) The Tokugawa Empire

   (D) The Ming Empire

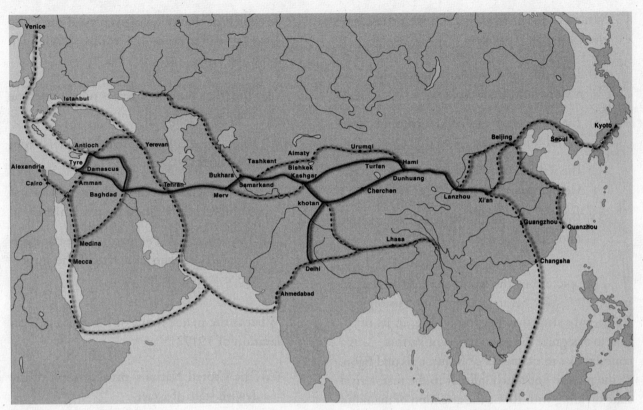

Source: The Stanford Program on International and Cross-Cultural Education.

15. The map above represents which of the following?

(A) The conquests of Alexander the Great

(B) The spread of cultures and trade along the Eurasian Silk Roads

(C) The influence of the Bantu migration in forming Trans-Saharan caravan routes

(D) The beginning of direct contact between the Western and Eastern Hemispheres

16. Many world historians have underrated the influence of which of the following on the transformation of global interactions in the 15th century?

(A) Queen Isabella and King Ferdinand's sponsorship of Christopher Columbus's voyages

(B) Vasco da Gama's founding of the maritime route to India

(C) Hernan Cortez's march to Tenochtitlán and his destruction of the Aztec Empire

(D) Prince Henry's establishment of a school for navigators

17. Which of the following was a major result of the Christian Crusades?

    (A) The entry of Europeans directly into the major world trade circuits

    (B) The isolation of the Turkish Muslims from inland trade routes

    (C) The fall of the Christian states in the Mediterranean

    (D) The recovery of the Middle Eastern holy lands for Christianity

"The picture of the world during the Roman period . . . put before students in 'Histories of Rome,' was defective, not to say false, in its omission to recognize the real position of Parthia . . . as a counterpoise to the power of Rome, a second figure in the picture not much inferior to the first, a rival state dividing with Rome the attention of mankind and the sovereignty of the known earth. Writers of Roman history have been too much in the habit of representing [Rome] as . . . a Universal Monarchy, a Power unchecked . . . having no other limits than those of the civilized world."

—George Rawlinson, English scholar and historian, 1873

18. The passage above suggests which of the following about Rawlinson's view of the historiography of Rome?

    (A) Historians have failed to recognize that Parthia was an empire as great or nearly as great as that of Rome.

    (B) Historians have exaggerated the glory of the Roman Empire.

    (C) Historians have largely rejected the idea that Parthia was a great empire.

    (D) Historians have placed too much emphasis on Rome to the exclusion of Parthia.

19. In which of the following ways did the Qing Dynasty differ from the earlier Mongolian Empire?

    (A) The Manchurian emperors ruled under the mandate of heaven.

    (B) The Manchu were foreign invaders from the north.

    (C) The Manchu kept their ethnic identity and prohibited the Chinese from assimilating it.

    (D) The Manchurian emperors were conquering warriors who understood the importance of military might.

20. What is the major result of the Balfour Declaration of 1917?

    (A) The United Nations' proclamation of the Jewish state of Israel

    (B) Large-scale immigration of Jews from Europe to Palestine

    (C) The beginning of the Holocaust

    (D) The downfall of the Turkish sultan who then ruled Palestine

21. What was the main reason for the abolition of slavery in Brazil in 1888?

    (A) Violent uprisings by the slaves

    (B) The overthrow of the monarchy by a democratic government

    (C) The refusal of army leaders to capture runaway slaves because slaves had served in the army

    (D) A bitter war that divided slave regions from non-slave regions

22. Many Latin American, sub-Saharan African, and Southeast Asian countries were unsuccessful in their attempts to create industrialized societies for all of the following reasons EXCEPT

    (A) the lack of government support and little investment capital.

    (B) the lack of an international division of labor.

    (C) their dependence on a single cash crop.

    (D) foreign investors owned and controlled their plantations.

"The great [Ghengis] Khan sent a baron . . . with a great force of horse and foot against this king of Champa . . . [who] was a very aged man, nor had he such a force as the baron had. And when he saw what havoc the baron was making with his kingdom he was grieved to the heart [and] bade messengers get ready and dispatched them to the great Khan. And they said to the Khan: 'Our lord the king of Champa salutes you as his liege lord . . . and will send you every year a tribute of as many elephants as you please. And he prays you in all gentleness and humility that you would send word to your baron to desist from harrying his kingdom and to quit his territories. These shall henceforth be at your absolute disposal.'

"When the great Khan had heard the King's ambassage he was moved with pity, and sent word to that baron of his to quit that kingdom with his army . . . . Thus it was then that this king became vassal of the great Khan, and paid him every year a tribute of twenty of the greatest and finest elephants that were to be found in the country."

—*Marco Polo, 13th century Venetian merchant, adventurer, and writer*

23. What main point would Europeans of the time likely have learned from the passage above?

    (A) Genghis Khan was one of the greatest military leaders in the world.

    (B) Once the Khan conquered people by brutal tactics, he was usually content to extract tribute from them.

    (C) The Khan, his empire, and his court were fascinating.

    (D) The Khan often allowed people he conquered to keep their own customs.

24. In which of the following ways did Mao Zedong's implementation of communism in China differ from Stalin's implementation of communism in Russia?

    (A) Mao's highly centralized control did not translate into totalitarian power.

    (B) Mao did not attain power by military force.

    (C) Mao emphasized internal economic development.

    (D) Mao believed in the importance of maintaining an agricultural-based economy.

25. The Olmec civilization was unlike other early river valley civilizations in that

    (A) its priests had the highest social status.

    (B) it did not have a well-developed irrigation system.

    (C) it was not politically united.

    (D) it practiced slavery.

26. Which of the following best represents the globalization and sharing of national and social aspirations?

    (A) Multinational corporations

    (B) The popularity throughout the world of Western fads and fashions

    (C) The Sundance Film Festival

    (D) World Cup Soccer

27. In which of the following ways were the Inca and Aztec societies alike?

    (A) They both developed from Mayan civilization.

    (B) They both had agricultural-based economies.

    (C) They both had elaborate political bureaucracies.

    (D) They both developed sophisticated forms of writing.

28. In which of the following ways did the Maya differ from the Teotihuacán?

    (A) They had a sophisticated form of writing that used both symbols and pictures.

    (B) They had prestigious warriors who often made slaves of their captives.

    (C) They were an urban civilization ruled by members of royalty and priests.

    (D) They had highly skilled professional architects and artisans.

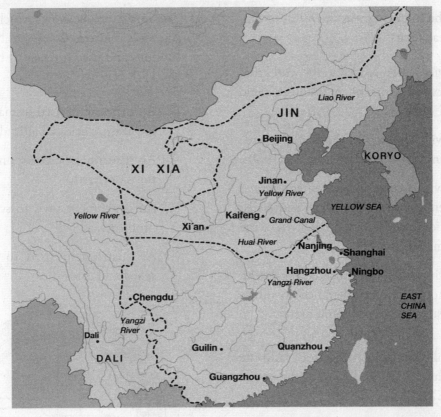

Source: The Metropolitan Museum of Art, New York.

29. The map above represents which of the following?

   (A) Before the Tang era, Buddhist monasteries held huge tracts of land and exerted great political influence in China.

   (B) The Tang conquest of southern China and Vietnam began a tremendous increase in agriculture with the cultivation of different strains of rice.

   (C) The Grand Canal connected the major rivers of China and vastly increased the amount and variety of internal trade.

   (D) The Tang built and maintained advanced road systems with inns, postal stations, and stables to accommodate travelers along the way.

30. Most historians would agree that increasing unrest about imperial authority and growing nationalism contributed greatly to all of the following movements EXCEPT

   (A) the Sepoy Rebellion of 1857.

   (B) the 1900 Boxer Rebellion.

   (C) the Taiping Rebellion of 1850.

   (D) the Greek Rebellion of 1821.

31. Which of the following was the result of Stalin's Five-Year Plans?

    (A) The Soviet Union proved to the world that the Marxist doctrine of communism could and did work.

    (B) The Soviet Union was the world's third-largest industrial power by the late 1930s.

    (C) The Soviet Union implemented *glasnost* to loosen censorship and allow nationalist minorities to address their concerns to the government.

    (D) The Soviet Union implemented *perestroika*, or economic reforms designed to infuse capitalism into the economic system.

32. The imperial societies in Afro-Eurasia and the Americas shared all of the following social structures EXCEPT

    (A) growing merchant classes.

    (B) agricultural-based economies.

    (C) patriarchal family structures.

    (D) increased equality among members of society.

33. Which of the following movements is most closely associated with the American and French Revolutions?

    (A) The Renaissance

    (B) The Enlightenment

    (C) The Scientific Revolution

    (D) The Protestant Reformation

34. The image below shows which of the following tools that was developed by classical civilizations and used extensively by Europeans in the 14th century?

    (A) An instrument used in marine navigation to measure celestial altitudes

    (B) An instrument used to find specific locations on Earth

    (C) An instrument used to solve astrological problems

    (D) An instrument used to measure wind speed and direction

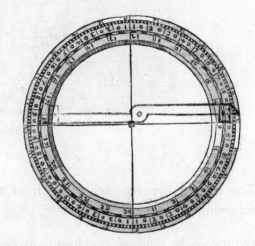

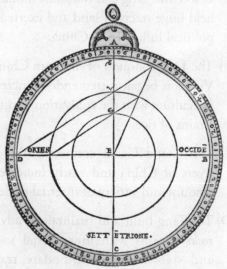

Source: Library of Congress,
Prints & Photographs Division.

35. Which of the following statements is true about the Opium Wars of 1839–1842?

    (A) The British East India Company grew opium in India and shipped it to China, causing a boom in trade once the Chinese developed addictions to the drug.

    (B) The British took over the Qing government by force after the Qing finally attempted to stop the opium trade.

    (C) The Treaty of Nanjing gave China control of Korea, Vietnam, and Burma in exchange for releasing control of Hong Kong to Britain.

    (D) The British agreed to stop the trade of opium in exchange for exclusive rights to trade in all Chinese ports.

36. The graph below represents which of the following?

    (A) The large growth of the population of Asia resulting from its isolationism

    (B) The recovery and rise of the population of Europe after the 14th century plague epidemic

    (C) The decimation of the population of western Africa caused by the slave trade balanced by the growth in the population on Africa's eastern coast

    (D) The decrease in the population of the Americas caused by their native populations' encounters with Europeans

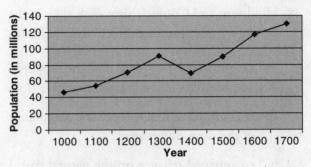

Source: Data from Bos, E.; Vu, M. T.; Levin, A.; and Bulatao, R. A. World Population Projections, 1992–93 Edition: Estimates and Projections with Related Demographic Statistics.

37. Which of the following factors was most responsible for the growth of trade along maritime routes from East Africa to East Asia?

    (A) Increased knowledge of the monsoon winds

    (B) The transformation of religious traditions

    (C) Innovations in farming and irrigation techniques

    (D) The development of Arabic numerals and the base-10 system

38. Hinduism and Confucianism were alike in the development of early societies in that they both

   (A) taught that changes in thought processes and lifestyles led to enlightenment.

   (B) encouraged self-knowledge and acceptance of the ways things were.

   (C) encouraged reliance on the natural world and veneration of ancestors.

   (D) accepted inequality as an important part of societal and political order.

39. Which of the following was one of the primary motivations for widespread European transoceanic voyages in the 15th century?

   (A) To regain hegemony in the Mediterranean

   (B) To reap large profits from commercial operations

   (C) To reinstitute tribute from people who no longer gave it

   (D) To restore internal trade and political administration

40. Which of the following was the major impact of the development of the theory of relativity and quantum physics in the early 20th century?

   (A) They led to the development of nuclear weapons.

   (B) They undermined Newton's model of a fixed and predictable universe.

   (C) They laid the foundation for chemically and genetically enhanced forms of agriculture.

   (D) They sparked the quest to explore the universe beyond the solar system.

41. In which of the following ways did the Ottoman Empire differ most from the Safavid and Mughal Empires?

   (A) It captured Christian boys and trained them to be skillful soldiers and bureaucrats.

   (B) It had its origins in the Turkic nomadic cultures of the central Asian steppes.

   (C) It had an absolute monarch with a court modeled on those of earlier Islamic dynasties.

   (D) It had a powerful army, but no navy.

42. Which of the following was a major reason for the fall of the Han, Western Roman, and Gupta Empires?

   (A) Attacks from the Huns

   (B) Internal political fragmentation

   (C) The decreasing importance of religious authority

   (D) The disruption of overseas trade resulting from conflicts

43. The major impact of the Safavid-Ottoman conflict was which of the following?

   (A) The spread of Buddhism to the Middle East

   (B) A temporary peace between Catholics and Protestants

   (C) The deepening of the rift between the Shi'a and the Sunni

   (D) The end of Legalism in China

44. In which of the following ways were the Mali and Ghana Empires similar?

    (A) They were major suppliers for the spice trade throughout Eurasia.

    (B) Their equal-field systems ensured that land distribution was fair and equitable.

    (C) Their wealth was largely based on gold.

    (D) They developed sophisticated methods of caravan organization.

45. Which of the following factors helped lay the foundation for the great cultural changes that began to occur in Europe in the 13th century?

    (A) The complicated network of lord-vassal relationships that laid the foundations for the early kingdoms of England and France

    (B) Ibn Battutu's detailed journal about his travels to Mesopotamia, Persia, Africa, and Asia

    (C) The wealth gained by Venice and Genoa from transporting knights of the Crusades across the Mediterranean and transporting goods on return voyages

    (D) The preservation of Constantinople as the center of the Eastern Roman Empire

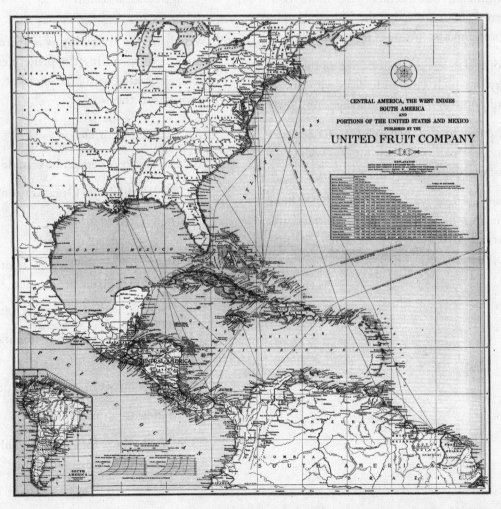

Source: Library of Congress, Geography and Map Division.

46. The image on the previous page represents which of the following developments in the emergence of global trade and production?

    (A) A large-scale transnational business

    (B) A limited liability corporation

    (C) A state's attempt to maintain preindustrial forms of economic production

    (D) An industrialized state developing new consumer markets for its finished goods

47. Which of the following factors best explains why Admiral Zheng He's voyages to India, the Middle East, and Africa came to an end?

    (A) Confucian bureaucrats were more concerned about protecting the Chinese Empire from nomadic invasions from the West.

    (B) Confucian leaders disapproved of the harsh way in which Zheng He dealt with pirates and political leaders who defied him.

    (C) Zheng He did not have the necessary navigational and maritime knowledge to sustain his voyages.

    (D) The Chinese emperor feared that Zheng He and his sailors would contract and spread diseases among the Chinese population.

48. All of the following were trends of immigration in the Americas in the latter decades of the 19th century EXCEPT:

    (A) Many Italians who immigrated to Argentina returned home partly because of the county's slow industrial development.

    (B) The Brazilian government paid for the passages of Italians who went to work on coffee plantations.

    (C) Thousands of Chinese immigrants worked as indentured laborers in sugarcane fields in Cuba.

    (D) Most Irish and German immigrants in the United States found permanent jobs in the agricultural sector.

49. Which of the following was formed for the purpose of spreading the principles and practices associated with free-market economics throughout the world?

    (A) The European Union

    (B) The North American Free Trade Agreement

    (C) The World Trade Organization

    (D) The United Nations

50. All of the following factors contributed to the rise of industrial production in England EXCEPT

    (A) the questioning of governmental authority by its citizens.

    (B) improvements in agricultural productivity.

    (C) an increase in urbanization.

    (D) many harbors for merchant ships and rivers for inland transportation.

51. All of the following resulted in part from the bubonic plague in many areas of the world during the 14th century EXCEPT

    (A) social unrest that led to rebellions.

    (B) a decline in agricultural productivity.

    (C) a near standstill in world trade.

    (D) the loss of rain forests and other natural habitats.

52. Which of the following enabled humans during the Paleolithic era to gradually migrate from their origins in East Africa to Eurasia, Australia, and the Americas?

    (A) The sharing of ideas among small bands of people about new survival skills

    (B) The disciplined social structure within small bands of people as they traveled

    (C) The creativity of individual bands of people to adapt to new climate regions

    (D) The discovery of fire and its many uses for survival

"Take up the White Man's burden—

Send forth the best ye breed—

Go bind your sons to exile

To serve your captives' need;

To wait in heavy harness,

On fluttered folk and wild—

Your new-caught, sullen peoples,

Half devil and half child.

"Take up the White Man's burden—

In patience to abide,

To veil the threat of terror

And check the show of pride;

By open speech and simple,

An hundred times made plain,

To seek another's profit

And work another's gain.

"Take up the White Man's burden—

The savage wars of peace—

Fill full the mouth of Famine

And bid the sickness cease;

And when your goal is nearest

(The end for others sought)

Watch sloth and heathen folly

Bring all your hopes to nought."

—*Rudyard Kipling, British poet*
who was born and lived much of his
life in India, 1899

53. Which of the following appears to be Kipling's message in the three stanzas of the poem above?

    (A) The British were exploiting the people of its colonies solely for profit.

    (B) British culture—and imperialist culture generally—improved the lives of people in the colonies it dominated.

    (C) The people of Britain's colonies should revolt against their British oppressors.

    (D) The people of Britain's colonies should retain their own cultures and live in peace with their British rulers.

54. The success of the Han Empire in the administration of its subjects was a result of a strong centralized government and which of the following factors?

(A) Scholar bureaucrats who obtained positions through civil service exams

(B) A grand palace and court to impress visitors and conceal political weaknesses

(C) The principle of the rule of law rather than rule by whims of the political leader

(D) A patron–client system whereby the wealthy supervised elaborate webs of people who owed favors to them

"Woman, wake up; the tocsin of reason is being heard throughout the whole universe; discover your rights. The powerful empire of nature is no longer surrounded by prejudice, fanaticism, superstition, and lies. The flame of truth has dispersed all the clouds of folly and usurpation. Enslaved man has multiplied his strength and needs recourse to yours to break his chains. Having become free, he has become unjust to his companion. Oh, women, women! When will you cease to be blind? What advantage have you received from the Revolution? A more pronounced scorn, a more marked disdain. In the centuries of corruption you ruled only over the weakness of men. The reclamation of your patrimony, based on the wise decrees of nature—what have you to dread from such a fine undertaking?"

—*Olympe de Gouges, playwright and political activist, 1791*

55. The passage above is a direct response to which of the following?

(A) The French Declaration of the Rights of Man and the Citizen

(B) The American Declaration of Independence

(C) John Locke's *An Essay Concerning Human Understanding*

(D) Montesquieu's *The Spirit of the Laws*

56. Which of the following factors caused the end of the Mongol Empire?

(A) Ghengis Khan could not conquer China for the Mongols during his lifetime.

(B) A severe drought in Central Asia forced the Mongols to migrate.

(C) The invasion of Europe lost its momentum when Genghis Khan's son died.

(D) The Mongols became assimilated into the cultures that they had conquered.

57. Which was an important consequence of the Viking invasions into many parts of Europe during the 8th and 9th centuries?

(A) Europeans began to form many different languages.

(B) Europeans shut themselves off from trade and became isolationist.

(C) Europeans established feudalism.

(D) Europeans learned to use longships to travel in coastal waters and rivers.

58. Which of the following was a factor that the United States and Russia shared as they began to develop industrialized societies?

   (A) Government control of industrialization

   (B) Cross-country railroads connecting parts of huge land masses

   (C) Economic autonomy

   (D) An abundance of laborers

59. The photo below, published in a newspaper in the 1880s, represents which of the following regarding global migration?

   (A) Chinese political intentions to dominate the global economy

   (B) American prejudice against Chinese and Irish laborer immigrants

   (C) The White Australia Policy restricting non-white immigration into Australia

   (D) Asian and European immigrants' fears that they would have to fight for jobs in North and South America

Source: Library of Congress, Prints & Photographs Division.

60. Feudalism in Europe differed from feudalism in Japan in that

    (A) feudalistic ties in Europe were sealed by negotiated contracts.

    (B) the feudalism system in Europe was based on political values that embraced all participants.

    (C) feudalism in Europe was highly militaristic and placed great value on physical courage and ritualized combat.

    (D) feudalism in Europe was based on collective decision-making teams that became part of the central government.

61. The map below represents which of the following?

    (A) The percentage of the population infected with influenza in the 1918 pandemic

    (B) The percentage of the population infected with polio before its vaccine was licensed in 1962

    (C) The percentage of the population infected with the Ebola virus in 1997

    (D) The percentage of the population living with AIDS/HIV in 2008

Source: 2010 Global Report, UNAIDS.

62. Pastoralist and agrarian societies that developed during the Neolithic Revolution were similar in that both

    (A) accumulated large amounts of material possessions.

    (B) intensively cultivated selected plants to the exclusion of others.

    (C) were important conduits for technological change through interactions with other societies.

    (D) were elite groups that created more hierarchical and patriarchal social structures.

63. The photo below is a result of which of the following wartime tactics that killed hundreds of thousands of people?

    (A) The incendiary bombing of Dresden by the U.S. and British air forces in World War II

    (B) The atomic bombing of Nagasaki by the U.S. air force in World War II

    (C) The stealth attacks of the United States during the 1991 Persian Gulf War

    (D) Trench warfare between the Allied forces and German forces in World War I

Source: Library of Congress, Prints & Photographs Division.

64. Most historians would likely agree that the fall of the Songhay kingdom mainly resulted from which of the following factors?

   (A) Disorganization of the political structure

   (B) A lack of prosperity

   (C) The support of Islam by the elite class

   (D) A lack of guns

65. Which of the following leaders of nationalist movements had the least in common with the others?

   (A) Sukarno in Indonesia

   (B) Gandhi in India

   (C) Pancho Villa in Mexico

   (D) Che Guevara in Cuba

66. Despite recent declines in the destruction of rain forests, the destruction continues at an alarming rate for which of the following reasons?

   (A) Environmental activist groups throughout the world are more concerned with global warming and pollution.

   (B) Political leaders of the most industrialized nations reward only environmental innovations that decrease the use of fossil fuels as sources of energy.

   (C) The countries in which the rain forests are located face an increasing demand for food.

   (D) The countries in which the rain forests are located have little influence in global politics.

67. Which of the following was a major factor in enabling the Greek city-states to expand their empires?

   (A) Dividing their armies into legions

   (B) Conquering but not enslaving other peoples

   (C) Superior seafaring skills

   (D) Superb engineering and architectural techniques

68. How was Islam able to hold together the Middle East, northern Africa, and southern Europe as a single region during the era 600 to 1450?

   (A) Muslims looted and destroyed their conquests' communities, churches, and monasteries.

   (B) Muslims bridged cultural differences and embraced literary, artistic, philosophical, and scientific traditions of others.

   (C) The structure of the caliphate that followed Muhammad's death survived political disunity.

   (D) Muslims forced the peoples they conquered to convert to Islam.

69. Which of the following elite classes had the greatest restrictions on their ability to focus on building armies at home as they confronted new challenges to affect the policies of their increasingly powerful monarch?

   (A) The zamindars in the Mughal Empire

   (B) The daimyo in Japan

   (C) The nobility in Europe

   (D) The boyars in Russia

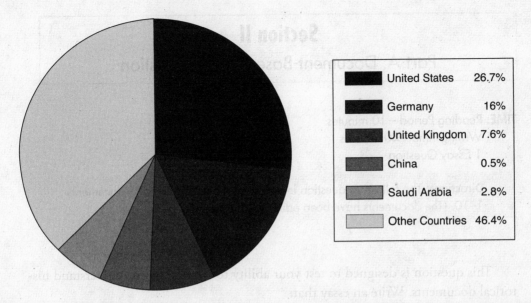

■	United States	26.7%
■	Germany	16%
■	United Kingdom	7.6%
■	China	0.5%
■	Saudi Arabia	2.8%
■	Other Countries	46.4%

Funds Pledged by Nongovernmental Organizations and the Public to Victims of the 2004 Tsunami (which killed more than 104,000 people in Indonesia and more than 5,000 in Thailand) by Country.

70. Which of the following conclusions can be made solely from the data in the graph above?

(A) U.S. nongovernmental organizations and its public pledged the greatest amount of money.

(B) The U.S. pledged the greatest amount of money per capita.

(C) China has few nongovernmental charitable organizations.

(D) Saudi Arabian nongovernmental organizations and the Saudi public choose not to spend much of their great wealth on aid to other countries.

STOP
This is the end of Section I.
If time still remains, you may check your work only in this section.
Do not begin Section II until instructed to do so.

Section II

Part A: Document-Based Essay Question

TIME: Reading Period—10 minutes
Writing Time—40 minutes
1 Essay Question

Directions: The following question is based on the accompanying documents 1–10. (The documents have been edited for the purpose of this exercise.)

This question is designed to test your ability to work with and understand historical documents. Write an essay that:

- Has a relevant thesis and supports that thesis with evidence from the documents.

- Uses all of the documents.

- Analyzes the documents by grouping them in as many appropriate ways as possible; does not simply summarize the documents individually.

- Takes into account the sources of the documents and analyzes the authors' points of view.

- Identifies and explains the need for at least one additional type of document. You may refer to relevant historical information not mentioned in the documents.

Using the following documents, analyze the various social and economic aspects that shaped the experiences of Chinese immigrants in California and their impact on the existing population, as well as on California politics and U.S. Chinese immigration policies. Identify an additional type of document and explain how it would help your analysis.

Document 1

Source: *Transcript of the Chinese Exclusion Act of 1882*

An Act to execute certain treaty stipulations relating to Chinese.

Whereas in the opinion of the Government of the United States the coming of Chinese laborers to this country endangers the good order of certain localities within the territory thereof: Therefore,

Be it enacted by the Senate and House of Representatives of the United States of America in Congress assembled, That from and after the expiration of ninety days next after the passage of this act, and until the expiration of ten years next after the passage of this act, the coming of Chinese laborers to the United States be, and the same is hereby, suspended; and during such suspension it shall not be lawful for any Chinese laborer to come, or having so come after the expiration of said ninety days to remain within the United States. . . .

SEC. 14. That hereafter no State court or court of the United States shall admit Chinese to citizenship; and all laws in conflict with this act are hereby repealed.

SEC.15. That the words "Chinese laborers," wherever used in this act shall be construed to mean both skilled and unskilled laborers and Chinese employed in mining.

Document 2

Source: *Chinatown, San Francisco: General Street Scene. California Historical Society, San Francisco. [SF Chinatown (iii): st.sc.: 330-B]*

Document 3

Source: The Chinese in California, 1850–1943 Timeline, The Library of Congress

1848	James Marshall discovered gold at John Sutter's sawmill on the American River at Coloma. This discovery triggered the California Gold Rush.
1850	Some 500 immigrants out of 57,787 arriving in California were Chinese. California state legislature passed the first Foreign Miners' Tax Law, levying a $20-per-month tax on each foreigner engaged in mining.
1852	Of the 11,794 Chinese living in California, only 7 were women. Chinese immigration increased to 20,000 with most going to mining regions. This number decreased to under 8,000 annually during the next two decades.
1854	*People v. Hall.* California Supreme Court ruled that a white man charged with murder could not be convicted on the testimony of a Chinese witness.
1862	Pacific Railroad Bill provided government aid to build a transcontinental railroad.
1865	Charles Crocker of the Pacific Railroad hired first 50 Chinese men in response to white workers' threat of a strike; within 2 years, 90% of the workforce on the railroad was Chinese.
1867	Railroad strike: Chinese laborers, without support of other workers, won concession over wages. 400 men (associated with Workingmen's Party) attacked Chinese in San Francisco. 12,000 Chinese were working in construction of the railroad.
1870	3,536 Chinese women had immigrated to California; 61% (2,157) listed as prostitutes. Foreign Miners' Tax represented 25 to 50% of all state revenue. Chinese constituted the largest racial group in the mines, 9,087 out of 36,339.
1871	Fifteen Chinese were hanged in anti-Chinese riots in Los Angeles.
1882	The Chinese Exclusion Act prohibited Chinese laborers from entering the United States.
1892	The Chinese Exclusion Act of 1882 was renewed in 1892 through the Geary Act. It was renewed again in 1902 and extended indefinitely.
1930s	Restrictions against Chinese immigrants began to ease. In 1930, Congress passed an act providing for admission of Chinese wives who were married to American citizens before May 26, 1924.
1935	Public Law 162 granted several hundred Asian veterans who served in the United States Armed Forces during World War I the right to apply for United States citizenship through naturalization.
1943	The Magnuson Act resulted in the repeal of the Chinese Exclusion Act.

Document 4

Source: The Appeal of a Chinese Merchant, Pun Chi, to the U.S. Congress, c. 1860; William Speer, The Oldest and the Newest Empire: China and the United States (Cincinnati: National Publishing Co., 1870), 588–601

The sincere and gracious attention of your honorable body is earnestly requested to the consideration of certain matters important to our peace as foreigners, the following statements of which may be relied upon as certainly true and correct:

We are natives of the empire of China, each following some employment or profession—literary men, farmers, mechanics or merchants. When your honorable government threw open the territory of California, the people of other lands were welcomed here to search for gold and to engage in trade. The ship-masters of your respected nation came over to our country, lauded the equality of your laws, extolled the beauty of your manners and customs, and made it known that your officers and people were extremely cordial toward the Chinese. Knowing well the harmony which had existed between our respective governments, we trusted in your sincerity. Not deterred by the long voyage, we came here presuming that our arrival would be hailed with cordiality and favor. But, alas! what times are these! —when former kind relations are forgotten, when we Chinese are viewed like thieves and enemies, when in the administration of justice our testimony is not received, when in the legal collection of the licenses we are injured and plundered, and villains of other nations are encouraged to rob and do violence to us! Our numberless wrongs it is most painful even to recite. At the present time, if we desire to quit the country, we are not possessed of the pecuniary means; if allowed to remain, we dread future troubles. But yet, on the other hand, it is our presumption that the conduct of the officers of justice here has been influenced by temporary prejudices and that your honorable government will surely not uphold their acts. We are sustained by the confidence that the benevolence of your eminent body, contemplating the people of the whole world as one family, will most assuredly not permit the Chinese population without guilt to endure injuries to so cruel a degree. We would therefore present the following twelve subjects for consideration at your bar. We earnestly pray that you would investigate and weigh them; that you would issue instructions to your authorities in each State that they shall cast away their partial and unjust practices, restore tranquillity to us strangers, and that you would determine whether we are to leave the country or to remain. Then we will endure ensuing calamities without repining, and will cherish for you sincere gratitude and most profound respect.

The twelve subjects, we would state with great respect, are as follows:

1. The unrighteousness of humiliating and hating the Chinese as a people.

We have heard that your honorable nation reverences Heaven. But if they comprehend the reverence that is due to the heavenly powers, of necessity they cannot humiliate and hate the Chinese. Why do we aver this? At the very beginning of time,

(continued)

Document 4 (*continued*)

Heaven produced a most holy man, whose name was Pwan-ku. He was the progenitor of the people of China. All succeeding races have branched off from them. The central part of the earth is styled by its inhabitants the Middle Flowery Kingdom. That is the country of the Chinese. The regions occupied by later races are distributed round and subordinate to it. Heaven causes it to produce in the greatest variety and abundance, so that of all under the sky this country is the greatest, and has bestowed upon it perfect harmony with the powers of nature, so that all things there attain the highest perfection. Hence we see that Heaven most loves our Chinese people, and multiplies its gifts to them beyond any other race. . . .

Document 5

Source: Workingman's Party, The Battle for Bread, c. 1879

At last a workingman, a drayman, Dennis Kearney, of San Francisco, immortalized by these words: "We will have a new party, the Workingman's Party. No great capitalist, no political trickster, no swindler or thief shall enter it. We will fill the offices with honest men who will make laws to protect themselves. We will send the Chinese home, distribute the land of the grabber, tax the millionaire, make a law to hang thieves of high as well as low degree, elevate the poor, and once more return to the simple virtue of honest republicanism. . . .

"When the thieves hear these things they will shake in their boots. They will do all they can to divide and defeat us. They will pervert the law to persecute us. They will try to cheat us, to count us out at the ballot-box, to bribe and corrupt the men we elect. They will provoke us to riot if they can, and set the military upon us. We must arm. We must resolve to fight, if need be. We must stand by each other to the death if necessary. We must swear that we will not be defeated. It is life or death. Either we must drive out the Chinese slave, and humble the bloated aristocrat, or we shall soon be slaves ourselves. There is no other solution to the problem. It is death or victory. We conquer or we perish. Arm! arm! and let our adversaries see that we are in earnest!"

Document 6

Source: Published at the Request of the San Francisco Methodist Preachers' Meeting, c. 1873 (San Francisco: Alta Printing House) and delivered in Platt's Hall, San Francisco, March 14, 1873. From The Bancroft Library, University of California, Berkeley [xF870.C5 G43].

Explanatory Note

On the 18th of February, the Hon. Frank M. Pixley, delivered a lecture in this city for the benefit of the "Church Union," subject, *"Our Street Araba. Who are responsible for them"*?

Mr. Pixley improved the occasion, to declaim against the immigration of the Chinese to this country, making use of some very violent and incendiary language, well adapted to excite the hatred and prejudice of the people against the Chinese.

On the 25th of February, the Rev. Father Buchard, a Jesuit Priest, addressed a large audience in this city, on "Chinaman or White man, which?"

He also declaimed against Chinese immigration, maintaining that the Chinese are an injury to the best interests of our country and people, because they cheapen labor, and because they are an inferior race. He charges that the most of the Chinese who come here are slaves—that they do not pay taxes—that they do not consume our products, but send their money home, thus draining our country of its wealth—that they are the careless authors of destructive fires—that they displace white laborers, driving them to pursue lives of beggary, prostitution and crime.

These two lectures, quite fully reported in our daily papers, with more or less of endorsement and commendation, were agitating the minds of the people. The hatred and prejudice of certain classes of our population against the Chinese were fully aroused, and many good citizens feared mob-violence in our city, as the result.

The "San Francisco Methodist Preachers' Meeting" having the matter under consideration, passed the following *Resolution:*

"The Rev. O. Gibson be requested to prepare an answer to the lecture delivered by Father Buchard on *"Chinaman or White man, which?"* at his earliest convenience, and that Rev. J. W. Ross, and Rev. A. J. Nelson be a committee to engage a hall and make arrangements for Mr. Gibson's lecture."

Document 7

Source: Miscellaneous Selections: Anti-Chinese Movement & Chinese Exclusion, 1867, Library of Congress, Prints & Photographs Division, reproduction number LC-USZC4-5758.

Political cartoon of gubernatorial candidate George C. Gorham, Union Party candidate for governor of California in 1867, who was "the only one that had the honesty and at the same time the imprudence to express himself opposed to the anti-Chinese movement, and had in consequence lost many votes and impaired his future political prospects." —Theodore H. Hittell, *History of California*, 1897, vol. 4, p. 405.

Document 8

Source: William Tell Coleman, organizer of the Committee of Public Safety (1877), which worked against the activities of the Workingman's Party to quash anti-Chinese riots, Statements, 1870–1893. Transcripts from The Bancroft Library, University of California, Berkeley [BANC MSS C-D 755].

Upon the sandlots bordering Market street was built two platforms round which between the hours of half-past seven and nine o'clock, eight or ten thousand persons packed themselves. The speeches were not incendiary. The struggle between capital and labor was bewailed, but it was agreed that violence was not the way to settle it. Selfish and unprincipled politicians, were the cause of the evil, the hirelings and tools of the magnates, ever ready as they were to sell themselves for money or political influence. The police were in attendance and did their duty admirable. There was nothing noteworthy in the meeting; their grievances were not so old as those at the east, and after free expressions of sympathy and sentiment, according to its rights, it adjourned.

Mingling with the crowd and hovering about its outskirts were certain lawless young men and boys, of ages ranging from fifteen to twenty, who lived as best they might, vagrant by day, abroad at night, pilfering, extorting, intimidating, picking up a little here and there, but ever carrying themselves with swagger and bravado, not unfrequently being caught in their petty raids and incarcerated.

Hoodlums they were called, from one Hood, who years ago upon the city front kept a low drinking-salon which was the rendezvous of the bad boys of that vicinity. These boys became the pest of the neighborhood and were known as Hood's boys, whence Hood'ums and finally hoodlums. They were the class, rapidly increasing of late, that fed the prisons and doubled taxation. They were born of the low European element which were deemed so advantageous to the nation's development, but which in truth caused more trouble and did a hundred times more harm than all the Asiatics that ever landed on these shores. They were no more laborers than the gad-fly that worried the draught-horse; they had no special sympathy with employer or employed, because they never worked. In the absence of a common enemy they would fight each other, and they would rob their own mothers as quickly as a Chinaman or a stock manipulator. They were the spawn of the low European, and other newly made American voters, reeking with whisky and garlic.

When first the people began to assemble, upon the occasion before mentioned, a pistol shot was heard from a point northeast of the city hall. Supposing it to be accidental little attention was paid to it. Half an hour later, while the speakers were addressing the meeting, three more shots were fired, wounding three spectators. From a bay window of a two-story frame house on McAllister street, some one said the shots came, and there the police found and arrested a half-drunken hoodlum, in whose possession was a five-shooter with four of the chambers empty.

(continued)

Document 8 (*continued*)

Shortly after nine o'clock, on the corner of Leavenworth and McAllister streets, an officer saw a man strike down a Chinaman. The fellow was promptly arrested, but almost immediately was rescued by some hundred associates. "To Chinatown! To Chinatown!" was now the cry, and off they ran up Leavenworth street, several hundred of them yelling like soldiers of Satan. On the south side of Tyler street, above Leavenworth stood some Chinese laundries; these the rabble bombarded, smashing doors and windows with bricks and stones. Thence they were driven by the police, but only to attack the unfortunate Asiatics in other quarters. The fiend-prince Mahu appeared to be in them urging to theft and demolition.

Breaking into a corner grocery the mobites supplied themselves with bottles of liquor and canned eatables, after which they demolished a Chinese tenement on Geary street, leaving it in flames. Fifteen other like places in that vicinity soon fell before them. The residence of Otis Gibson, of the Chinese mission, was stormed. Meanwhile the police several times met and dispersed them with their clubs, until finally the rioters retired, leaving the city quiet for the night.

Document 9

Source: Burlingame-Seward Treaty, 1868

Whereas since the conclusion of the treaty between the United States of America and the Ta Tsing Empire (China) of the 18th of June, 1858, circumstances have arisen showing the necessity of additional articles thereto, the President of the United States and the august sovereign of the Ta-Tsing Empire have . . . agreed upon the following articles . . .

ARTICLE IV

The twenty-ninth article of the treaty of the 18th of June, 1858, having stipulated for the exemption of Christian citizens of the United States and Chinese converts from persecution in China on account of their faith, it is further agreed that citizens of the United States in China of every religious persuasion and Chinese subjects in the United States shall enjoy entire liberty of conscience and shall be exempt from all disability or persecution on account of their religious faith or worship in either country. Cemeteries for sepulture of the dead of whatever nativity or nationality shall be held in respect and free from disturbance or profanation.

ARTICLE V

The United States of America and the Emperor of China cordially recognize the inherent and inalienable right of man to change his home and allegiance, and also the mutual advantage of the free migration and emigration of their citizens and subjects respectively from the one country to the other, for purposes of curiosity, of trade, or as permanent residents. The high contracting parties, therefore, join in

(*continued*)

Document 9 (*continued*)

reprobating any other than an entirely voluntary emigration for these purposes. They consequently agree to pass laws making it a penal offence for a citizen of the United States or Chinese subjects to take Chinese subjects either to the United States or to any other foreign country, or for a Chinese subject or citizen of the United States to take citizens of the United States to China or to any other foreign country, without their free and voluntary consent respectively.

ARTICLE VI

Citizens of the Untied States visiting or residing in China shall enjoy the same privileges, immunities or exemptions in respect to travel or residence as may there be enjoyed by the citizens or subjects of the most favored nation, and, reciprocally, Chinese subjects visiting or residing in the United States shall enjoy the same privileges, immunities and exemptions in respect to travel or residence as may there be enjoyed by the citizens or subjects of the most favored nation. But nothing herein contained shall be held to confer naturalization upon citizens of the United States in China, nor upon the subjects of China in the United States.

Document 10

Source: Harper's Weekly, Vol. 30, 1886. The Bancroft Library, University of California, Berkeley [MTP/HW: Vol. 30: 319].

STOP
This is the end of Section II, Part A.
If time still remains, you may check your work only in this section.
Do not begin Section II, Part B until instructed to do so.

Section II
Part B: Continuity and Change-Over-Time Essay

TIME: 40 minutes

1 Essay Question

Directions: You are to answer the following question. You should spend 5 minutes organizing or outlining your essay. Write an essay that:

- Has a relevant thesis and supports that thesis with appropriate historical evidence.
- Addresses all parts of the question.
- Uses world historical context to show continuities and changes over time.
- Analyzes the process of continuity and change over time.

1. Analyze continuities and changes in the development of political and military organization and the impact on other cultures of ONE of the following empires.

- The Mongols
- The Aztecs

STOP
This is the end of Section II, Part B.
If time still remains, you may check your work only in this section.
Do not begin Section II, Part C until instructed to do so.

Section II
Part C: Comparative Essay

TIME: 40 minutes

1 Essay Question

Directions: You are to answer the following question. You should spend 5 minutes organizing or outlining your essay. Write an essay that:

- Has a relevant thesis and supports that thesis with appropriate historical evidence.
- Addresses all parts of the question.
- Makes direct, relevant comparisons.
- Analyzes relevant reasons for similarities and differences.

2. Analyze similarities and differences in trade and communication during the period 1400–1750 in TWO of the following regions.

- Europe

- China

- The Middle East

END OF EXAM

Answer Key

Section I

1. (C)	19. (C)	37. (A)	55. (A)
2. (D)	20. (B)	38. (D)	56. (D)
3. (C)	21. (C)	39. (B)	57. (C)
4. (A)	22. (B)	40. (B)	58. (B)
5. (C)	23. (C)	41. (A)	59. (B)
6. (A)	24. (D)	42. (A)	60. (A)
7. (A)	25. (C)	43. (C)	61. (D)
8. (A)	26. (D)	44. (C)	62. (D)
9. (B)	27. (B)	45. (C)	63. (B)
10. (D)	28. (A)	46. (A)	64. (D)
11. (D)	29. (B)	47. (A)	65. (B)
12. (A)	30. (C)	48. (D)	66. (C)
13. (C)	31. (B)	49. (C)	67. (C)
14. (C)	32. (A)	50. (A)	68. (B)
15. (B)	33. (B)	51. (D)	69. (B)
16. (D)	34. (C)	52. (C)	70. (A)
17. (A)	35. (A)	53. (B)	
18. (D)	36. (B)	54. (A)	

Detailed Explanations of Answers

Section I

1. **(C)**

    Only the European Renaissance was characterized by humanism; Michelangelo, who painted the ceiling of the Sistine Chapel, was one of the Renaissance's artistic masters of the humanistic idealism of the human form.

2. **(D)**

    The Columbian Exchange developed among the continents of North America, South America, Europe, and Africa; it included all of the choices listed except trade from Asia to Europe and Africa.

3. **(C)**

    The Berlin West Africa Conference allowed European diplomats to carve Africa into European colonies. The slave trade of Africans by Europeans did end during this period, but not as a result of any formal agreement (A). King Leopold II's seizure of the Belgian Congo sparked the scramble to create African colonies in Africa that led to the Berlin treaty (B). Livingstone's exploration of Africa was unrelated to the Berlin treaty (D).

4. **(A)**

    Malaria is the only vector-borne disease among those listed (B). Tuberculosis has not been eliminated in the most highly industrialized nations, and the rate of its infection has a very high correlation with HIV/AIDS (C). Drug-resistant strains have developed only for tuberculosis (D).

5. **(C)**

    The Byzantine emperors' power as absolute rulers of both state and church was largely responsible for holding the empire together until the late 11th century. Ghana and Mali, not the Byzantines, taxed goods that passed through their territories (A). The Tang dynasty in China extracted gifts and money from other peoples (B), and the Song dynasty's highly centralized government depended heavily on its merit-based bureaucracy (D).

6. **(A)**

Jews viewed themselves as separate from others and did not seek to convert others to their religion, as many other religious groups did. There were other clearly monotheistic religions (B), including Christianity, whose appeal to ordinary people was comparable to that of Buddhism (C) and whose followers viewed Jesus as the Messiah who would cleanse the Jewish religion of its rigid and haughty priests (D).

7. **(A)**

The English colonies were allowed to set up their own political structures similar to those in Britain, whereas the Spanish colonies were not allowed such political freedom (B). There was much difficulty rather than coordination in communication between the viceroys and the Council of the Indies, thereby enabling the viceroys to rule their colonies with great independence from Spain (C). The Spanish did establish large bureaucracies in urban areas of their colonies in the Americas (D).

8. **(A)**

Although the Triple Entente contributed to tensions among European nations and specified conditions under which nations would go to war with one another for the purposes of self-preservation, it did not in itself cause the military conflicts that occurred at the beginning of the 20th century (B). Colonial disputes also were a source of tension among European nations, but compared with Japanese aggression, these conflicts were relatively minor (C). Although Mussolini advocated an extreme nationalism in the form of Fascism, which Hitler formed into Nazism in Germany, Mussolini did not himself cause major military conflicts.

9. **(B)**

Unlike typical Buddhist representations of the Buddha always sitting, usually portrayed without his feet and sometimes without his hands visible, this statue shows the Greco-Roman concentration of realistically portraying human anatomy. The convergence of Greco-Roman culture and Buddhist beliefs does not include any aspects of the Daoist belief in balance between humans and the natural world (A). Christianity retained many Roman and Hellenistic influences, including influences on art (C). Confucianism, Hinduism, and Legalism were not influenced by Roman and Hellenistic cultures at this time (D).

10. (D)

Bond perpetuated the popular glamorization of espionage as mainly consisting of covert operations and human intelligence, whereas in actuality it was the much more mundane interception of signals and surveillance techniques that dominated espionage (A). American concerns about Britain's intelligence operations were downplayed in the Bond films, with Bond portraying a defender of Britain and its seemingly well-functioning intelligence operations (B). The Bond films had a clearly Western bias toward the Cold War and portrayed a relationship of great trust between the British and American allies (C).

11. (D)

The Enlightenment, not Social Darwinism, questioned the assumptions of constitutional monarchies (A). The Industrial Revolution itself caused the rise of a large middle class in industrialized societies (B). The Industrial Revolution resulted in wealth being increasingly based on money and business success, but it did not change the status of inherited titles of nobility based on land ownership (C).

12. (A)

The spread of Islam enabled women to gain these freedoms, which were unusual in most other civilizations of the time. Chinese elites ensured the purity of their lines by confining women to the home (B). Incan peasant women gave tribute to their leaders in the form of their craft and artwork (C). Aztec women who died in childbirth were honored just as were men who died in battle (D).

13. (C)

All of the choices listed contributed to the economic growth and were characteristics of both the Tang and Song dynasties except that it was the Islamic states in northern India that adapted mathematics from the people they conquered, using their own Arabic numerals.

14. (C)

All of these empires had many things in common, such as large armies equipped with guns and independence from Western influence; however, the Tokugawa Empire of Japan was unique in that it was not land based, as were the others.

15. **(B)**

The Silk Roads were overland trade routes that extended from western China, across central Asia, to the Mediterranean area. Alexander the Great's conquests extended to Egypt, the Middle East, and the Persian Empire, which spread eastward only to the Indus River Valley (A). The Bantu migration (C) connected people of sub-Saharan Africa with people of eastern and southern parts of Africa. Although the Silk Roads spread goods and cultural influences from the Eastern to Western Hemispheres, the two hemispheres did not yet have direct contact (D).

16. **(D)**

Prince Henry of Portugal, known as Henry the Navigator, had a great but sometimes overlooked influence on innovations in navigation during this period, as the accomplishments of actual explorers were more celebrated. He did not go on voyages himself, but he established a school for navigators, whose students, including Diaz and da Gama, became some of the most skilled navigators in the world.

17. **(A)**

The societies of the Middle East were much wealthier and more sophisticated than European kingdoms were, and the knights of the Crusades returned home with goods from various parts of the world and created a demand in Europe for foreign goods. The Turkish Muslims continued to dominate inland trade routes (B). The Crusades resulted in no real gains or losses for Christians (C) (D).

18. **(D)**

While the passage expresses Rawlinson's view that historians have placed too much emphasis on Rome to the exclusion of Parthia, he does not suggest any of the other three choices.

19. **(C)**

Unlike the Mongolians, who assimilated the cultures and even the religions of the peoples they conquered, the Manchu kept their ethnic identity and prohibited the Chinese from assimilating it. The Manchu and the Mongolians were similar in all of the other choices listed.

20. **(B)**

   The United Nations' Declaration of the Establishment of the State of Israel was signed on May 14, 1948 (A). The Holocaust that Hitler began in 1933 was not sanctioned by any written document (C). The Turkish sultan who ruled Palestine did not suffer a downfall; it was his refusal to make any concessions toward the establishment of a Jewish state in Palestine that partly led to the Treaty of Balfour (D).

21. **(C)**

   Slavery ended in Haiti, not Brazil, because of violent slave revolts (A). The French Revolution was an overthrow of the monarchy by a democratic government (B). The United States experienced the bitter Civil War partly because of the division of opinion about slave states and nonslave states (D).

22. **(B)**

   Industrialization created an international division of labor as less-industrialized countries produced the raw materials needed by industrialized countries to produce manufactured products. All of the other choices listed did contribute to the lack of success in many Latin American, sub-Saharan African, and Southeast Asian countries' attempts to create industrialized societies.

23. **(C)**

   Up until the late 13th century, Europeans had neither direct knowledge of Chinese culture nor the magnificent and civilized court of the Khans in China, so they likely were more fascinated by Marco Polo's detailed accounts of his experiences with Genghis Khan and his court than with specific aspects of how he ruled his kingdom.

24. **(D)**

   Mao's implementation of Communism was similar to Stalin's in all of the choices listed except that Mao believed in the importance of maintaining an agricultural-based economy while Stalin focus on building an industrialized society.

25. **(C)**

   Unlike the other early river valley civilizations, the Olmecs were not united politically. They were similar to the other early river valley civilizations in all the other ways listed.

26. **(D)**

   Multinational corporations are not the best example of the sharing of social aspirations (A). Although Western fads and fashions are popular throughout the world, they do not represent the globalization and inclusive sharing of national and social aspirations (B). The Sundance Film Festival promotes films from around the world, but these films often are not part of mainstream culture (C), as soccer is in almost every country in the world.

27. **(B)**

   The Incas and Aztecs both had highly sophisticated, agricultural-based economies. Neither civilization developed from the Maya, whose empire flourished at about the same time (A). While the Incas had elaborate political bureaucracies to maintain contact with their subjects, the Maya were organized into city-states, with no central government (C). The Maya developed a system of writing, whereas the Incas did not (D).

28. **(A)**

   All of the choices listed were characteristics of both the Maya and Teotihuacán, except that the Maya had a sophisticated form of writing that made use of symbols and pictures, whereas the Teotihuacán did not develop a form of writing, but used a counting device to keep detailed records.

29. **(B)**

   The map shows the intricate river system of southern China and Vietnam, which became the source of the Tang's prosperous agricultural system. Because the map's emphasis is on this river system, none of the other choices are correct.

30. **(C)**

   Unlike the other three movements, the Taiping Rebellion was not really a movement characterized by dissatisfaction with imperial authority and a sense of nationalism, but rather a unique movement advocating the abolition of private property and equality for women.

31. **(B)**

   Stalin's centralized government with its brutal and nearly absolute control of its people bore little resemblance to the Marxist doctrine of Communism (A). Mikhail Gorbachev implemented *glasnost* in the 1980s to save the faltering Soviet Union from economic collapse (C). Gorbachev also implemented *perestroika* in the 1980s as another means to carry out economic reforms (D).

32. **(A)**

All of the choices listed were shared by the imperial societies in Afro-Eurasia and the Americas except that, in India, occupations were strictly dictated by caste and therefore its society did not include a growing class of merchants.

33. **(B)**

The American and French Revolutions were most strongly associated with the Enlightenment principle that philosophical and political ideas should seriously question the assumptions of absolute governments. The Enlightenment itself was part of the changes stimulated by the Renaissance, the Scientific Revolution, and the Protestant Reformation.

34. **(C)**

The instrument shown in the image is an astrolabe, which the Europeans used extensively in the 14th century to tell time, study the stars, and solve other astrological problems. A sextant was used to measure celestial altitudes (A), a compass was used to locate positions on Earth (B), and a weather vane was used to measure wind speed and direction (D).

35. **(A)**

Although the Qing surrendered after British attacks, the British did not take over the government, but instead forced the Qing to sign a treaty allowing the opium trade to continue (B). The Treaty of Nanjing gave the British control of Hong Kong and released Korea, Vietnam, and Burma from Chinese control (C). The British did not agree to stop the lucrative opium trade; the Qing government's attempt to finally stop the opium trade is what led to the Opium Wars.

36. **(B)**

Among all the choices listed, the sharp decline in the graph from the mid-1300s to 1400 and the slow increase until 1500, followed by a very sharp rise, can be indicative only of the recovery and rise of Europe's population after the plague epidemic of the 1300s.

37. **(A)**

The sailors of the Swahili city-states along the eastern coast of Africa used their knowledge of the monsoon winds to maneuver small trading boats through the Red Sea to the Indian Ocean to India and other parts of the Middle East. Although the other choices listed were important developments in the Middle East and African regions during this time, they were not major reasons for the growth of trade along maritime routes from East Africa to East Asia.

38. (D)

Hinduism emphasized the eternal existence of a universal spirit that guides all life on Earth, but only those in the highest caste could be reunited with the universal spirit, whereas Buddhism taught that changes in thought processes and lifestyles led to enlightenment (A). Confucianism and Daoism, but not Hinduism, encouraged self-knowledge and acceptance of the ways things were (B). A major belief of Hinduism was the reincarnation of the spirit, whereas Confucianism encouraged reliance on the natural world and the veneration of ancestors (C).

39. (B)

Inland travel was not practical for Europeans, and with Venice and Genoa having made great fortunes from sea travel, the Europeans made many transoceanic voyages to make large profits. Admiral Zheng He's voyages were intended to restore China's hegemony in Asia (A) and to reinstitute tribute from people who no longer gave it to China (C). The Tokugawa shoguns in Japan concentrated on internal trade and political administration rather than transoceanic voyages (D).

40. (B)

At the start of the 20th century, there was no threat of world wars and no impetus to develop nuclear weapons (A). The theory of relativity and quantum physics are unrelated to chemically and genetically enhanced forms of agriculture, which are based on chemistry and botany, not on physics (C). The theory of relativity and quantum physics were just the beginning of the questioning of Newton's model of a fixed and predictable universe; the quest to explore the universe occurred much later in the century (D).

41. (A)

All three empires had their origins in the central Asian Turkic nomadic cultures (B) and absolute monarch courts like those of earlier Islamic dynasties (C). The Safadid had a strong army, but no navy (D).

42. (A)

Attacks from the Huns were a major factor in the fall of all three empires. The fall of the Gupta was also a result of the breakdown of alliances with regional princes and political fragmentation, a feature not shared by the other two empires (B). Religion increased in importance rather than decreased as political authority decreased (C), and trade was somewhat disrupted but still survived and even increased in the Indian Ocean (D).

43. **(C)**

Buddhism did not spread to the Middle East but rather to China in this period (A). Europe remained deeply divided between Protestants and Catholics (B). Legalism had long since been abandoned by the Han emperors in the 7th century (D).

44. **(C)**

The wealth of both the Mali and Ghana Empires was largely based on their large gold deposits, not on spices, as the Melaka region was (A). It was the Tang dynasty in China that allocated agricultural land to individuals and families in the equal field system (B). Ghana and Mali taxed the goods that traders carried through their territories rather than actually transporting the goods via caravans; the nomadic Bedouins used caravans to transport goods through the deserts of Africa (D).

45. **(C)**

Europe experienced a dramatic growth in culture as its growing population satisfied its huge demand for foreign products sparked by the wealth that Genoa and Venice accumulated during their importation of foreign goods on return voyages from transporting the knights of the Crusades across the Mediterranean. The feudalistic systems of England and France laid the foundation for increased military power, not cultural changes (A). Ibn Battutu's detailed stories about his travels sparked European interest in Mesopotamia, Persia, Africa, and Asia, but they still did not bring Europeans into direct contact with these foreign cultures (B). Although Constantinople remained the center of the Eastern Roman Empire until the Muslims conquered it in 1453 and renamed it Istanbul, it did not spark changes in European culture (D).

46. **(A)**

The image, created in 1909, shows the area of influence of the transnational United Fruit Company, the largest banana company in the world, with plantations in Colombia, Costa Rica, Nicaragua, Panama, Santo Domingo, Cuba, and Jamaica. Limited liability corporations were financial instruments in which large sums of personal financial capital were invested in companies during this period, but the image does not represent this (B), nor does it represent any aspect of a single state (C) and (D).

47. **(A)**

After the death of Zheng He's sponsor, Emperor Yongle, Confucian bureaucrats gained control of the government. They wanted to continue to fund Zheng He's lavish voyages but were more concerned about using the money to protect the Chinese Empire from nomadic invasions from the West. The Confucian leaders were not concerned about the harsh way in which Zheng He dealt with pirates and political leaders who defied him (B) or about the spread of diseases among the Chinese population (D). Zheng He had excellent navigational and maritime knowledge, which was, at the very least, equal to those of the great European maritime explorers (C).

48. **(D)**

All of the choices listed were trends of immigration in the Americas in the latter decades of the 19th century except that most Irish and German immigrants in the United States found permanent jobs in industrialized big cities, not in the agricultural sector.

49. **(C)**

The European Union promotes freedom of enterprise and movement only of people whose European counties are members (A). The North American Free Trade Agreement removed most barriers to trade and investment only among the United States, Canada, and Mexico (B). The purpose of the United Nations is to facilitate cooperation in international law, security, economic development, social progress, human rights, and achievement of world peace, not with free-market economics throughout the world (D).

50. **(A)**

England was politically stable during this time and its citizens did not question Parliament's authority. The other three choices listed did contribute to the rise of industrial production in England.

51. **(D)**

The bubonic plague devastated many parts of the world in all of the ways listed except that it did not cause the loss of rain forests and other natural habitats; this occurred primarily because agricultural societies cleared the land to make way for fields to be used to grow crops.

52. **(C)**

Humans' success in settling in new areas was based almost entirely on their ability to figure out how to adapt to new environments, especially in the cultivation of crops. Migration of small bands of people occurred independently in different places, without communication with other peoples (A). Authority in these bands was based on family relationships, not a rigid social structure (B), and humans had been using fire for hundreds of thousands of years before this period (D).

53. **(B)**

Kipling's poem (e.g., "To serve your captives' need," "The end for others sought") is a justification of British (and, more broadly, imperial nations) domination of their colonies, including imposing their culture on the native peoples of the colonies for the latter's own good. The poem was actually a response to the United States' gaining the Philippines after the Spanish-American War. Kipling hoped that the U.S. would pattern itself on the British model of colonial rule over non-white populations in India and Africa.

54. **(A)**

During the Han era in China, scholar bureaucrats were an important part of the highly centralized government. The Gupta of India concealed their political weakness by a show of opulence in their courts and palaces (B). The principle of the objective rule of law was characteristic of Legalists, not the Chinese (C), and the patron–client system was Roman.

55. **(A)**

The passage is from "Declaration of the Rights of Woman, 1791" by Olympe de Gouges, who was a French political activist and feminist. She wrote the document shortly after the creation of the French Constitution of 1791 out of concern that the constitution addressed equal suffrage for men but did not address women's suffrage or rights. De Gouges viewed her "Declaration of the Rights of Woman, 1791" as the missing part of the French Constitution.

56. **(D)**

The Mongols adopted many customs and religions of the people they conquered, and their rulers were spread so far apart that they eventually lost contact with one another and became part of the cultures that they had conquered. Although Ghengis Khan did not conquer China in his lifetime, he did lay the foundation for his sons and grandsons to eventually do so (A). A drought in Central Asia caused the Mongols to initially migrate into China, before they created a great empire (B). Although the Mongol invasion of

Europe did lose its momentum after the death of Genghis Khan's son, this did not lead to the fall of the Mongolian Empire (C).

57. **(C)**

Numerous attacks from the Vikings convinced Europeans that protection of their territories was vital, so they each organized a network of lords and vassals that enabled them to build strong kingdoms with powerful armies. The Europeans retained their own languages; the Bantu migration caused the formation of many languages that developed in Africa (A). After the Ming revolt against the Mongols, China largely shut itself off from the rest of the world and turned to its internal development (B). The Vikings used longships to invade and savagely destroy parts of Europe, but Europeans did not adapt longships or any other part of Viking culture (D).

58. **(B)**

Capitalists were responsible for industrialization in the United States, where the economy was autonomous, whereas the government controlled industrialization and the economy in Russia (A) (C). Russia had an abundance of workers, while industrialization in the United States was somewhat delayed by the lack of laborers until the wave of European and Asian immigration began later in the 19th century (D).

59. **(B)**

The cartoon shows racist depictions of a Chinese immigrant and an Irish immigrant swallowing Uncle Sam, so the focus is on immigrants' impact on the U.S. economy, not on the global economy or China's ambitions (A), or on Australia's immigration policies (C). The racist caricatures of the Chinese and Irish immigrants and the depiction of them devouring Uncle Sam do not suggest any fear on their part of finding jobs in North America, much less South America (D).

60. **(A)**

The Europeans sealed their feudalistic ties with negotiated contracts, whereas the Japanese did not. The other listed choices were characteristic of the Japanese feudal system.

61. **(D)**

The 1918 influenza pandemic, associated with World War I, initially began in the Middle East, then spread to Spain, which experienced very high mortality rates, and then swept across Europe (A). Before the availability of the polio vaccine, polio was common worldwide and not concentrated in certain regions of the world (B). The outbreak of the Ebola virus in 1997, as with other previous outbreaks, was largely confined to Africa (C).

62. **(D)**

Both agrarian and pastoral societies had elite groups with hierarchical and patriarchal social structures. Members of agrarian societies were interested in acquiring material possessions (A) and in intensively cultivating selected plants (B); however, pastoral peoples were not, as their lifestyle was dictated by the need to constantly move in search of new pastures for their animals. Unlike the agrarian peoples, who were sedentary and settled into villages, the nomads did not have much interaction with other societies (C).

63. **(B)**

The incendiary bombing of Dresden by the U.S. and British air forces in World War II involved many individual planes dropping numerous bombs, which did not cause such concentrated destruction (A). The stealth attacks of the United States during the 1991 Persian Gulf War were conducted with single-seat, twin-engine stealth ground-attack aircraft that scored direct hits on 1,600 high-value targets and also did not cause such concentrated destruction (C). Trench warfare between the Allied forces and German forces in World War I consisted of troops sheltered in trenches to avoid the enemy's small arms fire and artillery (D).

64. **(D)**

The Songhay did not have guns and their empire fell when Moroccan soldiers used muskets to attack them in 1591. The Songhay had a highly organized political structure (A), were prosperous (B), and the empire's elite strongly supported Islam (C).

65. **(B)**

Gandhi is the only one of the choices listed who advocated passive nonresistance and boycotts to achieve equality. All of the others used violence to achieve these social goals.

66. **(C)**

Environmental activist groups throughout the world are very concerned with the destruction of rain forests, as this greatly contributes to global warming (A). Many political leaders of industrialized nations support global policies that will reduce the destruction of the rain forests (B). Some countries in which rain forest destruction is occurring, most notably Brazil, have a growing influence on global politics (D).

67. **(C)**

The Greeks had excellent seafaring skills that allowed them to easily navigate within the entire Mediterranean area. The Romans, not the Greeks, divided their army into legions (A) and built many monuments, roads, and sanitation systems with their superior engineering and architectural techniques (D). The slave trade had little to do with the expansion of the Greek Empire, as it did for the Roman Empire (B).

68. **(B)**

Muslims mixed their own Islamic culture with native cultures in a peaceful way that was conducive to trade, unlike the Vikings, who destroyed many cultural symbols of their conquests (A). Although the political structure of the Arab caliphate did not survive, Islam held the Middle East, northern Africa, and southern Europe together culturally (C). The Qur'an forbids forced conversions to Islam, so the Muslims allowed those they conquered to retain their own religions (D).

69. **(B)**

The Tokugawa of Japan required the daimyos, or regional lords, to spend every other year at the shoguns' courts, thereby restricting the daimyos' time and ability to focus on building their armies back home. The zamindars had few, if any, restrictions on their authority to collect taxes throughout the Mughal Empire (A). The monarchs of Spain, England, and France did restrict the power of the nobility while building up large armies too powerful for individual nobles to match, but these nobles still continued to build armies and loyalties of their own (C). The Russian tsars had much difficulty restricting the boyars, or Russian nobility, who often plotted against them (D).

70. **(A)**

While the graph itself indicates that U.S. nongovernmental organizations and the American public pledged the greatest amount of money to victims of the 2004 tsunami, none of the other conclusions listed can be supported by the graph without further information.

Sample Essays

Section II

Sample Answer to Document-Based Essay Question

As the Gold Rush began in California after the discovery of gold at Sutter's Sawmill in 1848, many Chinese men immigrated to California in search of gold and jobs. In 1850 alone, about 11.5 percent of all immigrants in California were Chinese, and by 1950, there were 20,000 Chinese immigrants living in California. While these immigrants certainly hoped to achieve success in this new country and expected to be treated with respect, instead they encountered many difficulties, including unjustifiable discrimination and persecution. This discrimination and persecution came not only from American citizens and other immigrants, but also from local governments, the courts in California, and even the U.S. government.

In the very first year of the first wave of Chinese immigration, the state legislature of California enacted a law that discriminated against immigrants by taxing every foreign miner $20 per month, an exorbitant amount for that time and, most likely, a great financial hardship on Chinese miners. Even the California Supreme Court discriminated against the Chinese, essentially stating that they were inferior to whites in its ruling that the testimony of Chinese against white men could not be used in some instances in courts of law.

With the U.S. government sponsorship of the construction of a transcontinental railroad in 1862 and the discriminatory mining tax forcing them out of working as miners, many Chinese immigrants took jobs as laborers for the railroad companies. They worked for less money than white laborers did, which led to resentment and hostility by white workers who felt that the Chinese were competing unfairly for jobs. Some young men and boys who did not have jobs or any interest in working—essentially vagrants and troublemakers with a mob mentality—cruelly persecuted the Chinese and committed violent acts against them.

The harsh treatment and lack of acceptance of the Chinese seems to have been mainly based on prejudice because their appearance and culture were distinctly different from those of Americans with European ancestry and from European immigrants. The Chinese immigrants were clearly hard workers and desperate for work, even for very low wages. Despite the challenges, some even became successful professionals, shop owners, and merchants.

Nevertheless, intense competition for jobs during the 1860s and 1870s heightened anti-Chinese sentiments. Men of various white segments of society in San Francisco, notably the Workingmen's Party, not only publicly blamed Chinese immigrants for taking jobs away from them but also made insulting and false accusations against them. These sentiments manifested themselves in part as an angry and irrational lashing out by white laborers against everything that they believed was conspiring against them. Newspapers printed political cartoons that expressed blatant racism toward the Chinese, and any brave politician who dared to oppose the anti-Chinese movement was doomed to failure. Tensions caused by anti-Chinese sentiment in California continued to mount, resulting in white mobs committing widespread acts of violence against the Chinese.

At the same time, the federal government wanted to establish U.S. power in Asia and to make inroads into the tremendously profitable trading opportunities there. To further these interests, the U.S. entered into the Burlingame-Seward Treaty with China in 1868. In addition to assurances of equality and mutual respect that would exist between the two countries and their citizens, the treaty also ensured the continuous flow of Chinese immigrant laborers into the United States. However, it also clearly stated that those laborers would have no right to U.S. citizenship. Given the reality of the treatment of Chinese immigrants, especially in California, the Burlingame-Seward Treaty was destined to fail.

In response to the growing racial problems in California and political pressure, the U.S. Congress passed the Chinese Exclusion Act of 1882, which banned Chinese immigration to the United States. As a result, the Chinese who already lived in California became increasingly isolated. With few suitable Chinese women having immigrated to California, most Chinese men did not have any reasonable hope of finding a wife and building a family. The Chinese Exclusion Act also made Chinese immigrants permanent aliens by excluding them from U.S. citizenship. Those Chinese men who were already married had little chance of ever reuniting with their wives or of starting families in their hostile new home. They remained marginalized as an almost all-male society in Chinatown and struggled outside of this safe haven to maintain their dignity and financial stability as they faced rampant racism and constant threats of mob violence. Although the Chinese were puzzled and resentful of such unwarranted treatment, they remained quiet and caused little trouble themselves. The entirety of their situation made it difficult—if not impossible—for the Chinese to assimilate into mainstream society for many decades, although some attempted to do so by adopting Western-style clothing and customs.

It was not until the 1930s that the Chinese living in the United States could begin to enter mainstream society in the United States, despite the fact that Chinese Americans had served in the U.S. Armed Forces in World War I, which began in 1914 and ended in 1919. In 1935, long after World War I, the U.S. Congress enacted a law giving Chinese and other Asian veterans of World War I the right to apply for U.S. citizenship. (To further explain how the Chinese began to assimilate into mainstream society in California, another document, such as an entry of a journal written by a Chinese American describing an ordinary day or a newspaper article describing an accomplishment of a Chinese American or someone from its community, would be necessary.) The Chinese Exclusion Act was not repealed until 1943.

Sample Answer to the Continuity and Change-Over-Time Essay Question

The Mongol invasions and conquests of the 13th century forever changed the map of the world, sparked intercontinental trade, created new nations, and affected the history of the world directly and indirectly in numerous other ways. At its height, the Mongol Empire was the largest empire in history, stretching from the Sea of Japan to the Carpathian Mountains just west of Central and Eastern Europe. This nomadic people from the steppes of Central Asia swept southward and eastward, conquering China, India, the Middle East, and Russia, and nearly conquering Europe as well. Although their brutal attacks initially disrupted many important trading routes, they ultimately brought peace and prosperity to the people whom they ruled.

The Mongols originally were pastoralists who relied on their animals for survival and moved several times a year in search of new sources of grasslands and water for their animals. They were loosely organized into family groups called clans, whose leaders later came to be known as khans. Their nomadic life style made them vulnerable to the heavy snow, ice, and droughts that regularly occurred in their original habitat. The Mongols' migration likely began as they searched for new pastures for their animals, and their skill as horsemen helped their migration succeed.

At the beginning of the 13th century, the Mongol khan Temujin unified all of the Mongol clans. He took the title Genghis Khan, whose meaning has been widely debated by historians, some believing that it means "supreme warrior" and others interpreting its meaning as "universal leader." In any case, this title is clearly an indication of Genghis Khan's ambitions for himself and his people. For 21 years, he led the Mongols in their conquest of vast parts of Asia. Under his leadership, the Mongols began to breach the Great Wall of China. However, Genghis Khan never conquered China, but he did the groundwork for its eventual defeat by the Mongols.

Genghis Khan is usually seen as one of the most talented military leaders in world history. Following the Chinese model, he organized his warriors into armies of 10,000, which were grouped into 1,000-man brigades, 100-man companies, and 10-man platoons. He ensured that all generals were either kinsmen or trusted friends, and they remained amazingly loyal to him. He used surprise tactics, like fake retreats and false leads, and developed sophisticated catapults and gunpowder charges.

After his death in 1227, Genghis Khan's sons and grandsons continued to expand the empire with many other conquests. The initial Mongol invasions had disrupted all the major trade routes, but Genghis Khan's descendents organized the vast empire so successfully that these routes rapidly recovered. The Mongols' governing structure included four political organizations called Khanates, with each one ruled by a different relative of Genghis Khan. The ruler of the original empire in Central Asia was the "Great Khan," who followed in the footsteps of Genghis Khan.

The death of Ogodai, the son of Genghis Khan and the Great Khan who was centered in Mongolia, halted the Mongol exploits in Eurasia. All the leaders of the empire traveled to the Mongol capital to choose Ogodai's successor, which drew attention away from the Mongols' plan to invade Europe. After seizing Baghdad and Damascus before Khan Hulegu departed for Mongolia, the Mongols were also held in check in the Islamic world by Egypt's Mamluk armies, whose horsemanship and military skills were equal to those of the Mongols. The Mamluks defeated the Mongols in battle in 1260 and drove them eastward before Mongol reinforcements could arrive. Hulegu decided not the press for further expansion at that time. The Mongols continued to clash with the Mamluks many times over the next 50 years until they signed a peace treaty in 1323.

Genghis Khan's grandson Kublai Khan led the Mongol forces in seizing the capital of the Song dynasty in China and establishing the new capital in Beijing, which he called Khanbaluk, meaning "City of the Khan." This was the great and sophisticated city that Marco Polo described so eloquently in his writings as the finest and richest in the entire world. Kublai Khan unified China and significantly expanded its territories. Mongols replaced the Song's top bureaucrats, but because of Kublai Khan's respect for many of the Chinese customs and political innovations, he allowed many lower-level Confucian officials to retain their positions. The Khan also admired the Song's cultural and organizational values but still placed the greatest value on the Mongols' skill in military affairs and conquests.

As Kublai Khan and his successors expended great effort in continuing to conquer more and more territories in Asia, they elevated the status of merchants. This caused deep resentment among the Confucian bureaucrats. They also disapproved of the Mongols' increase of tributes and their establishment of tax farming, which authorized middlemen to collect these taxes and, thus, led to corruption. Among other external difficulties that the Chinese faced, these problems initiated a conspiracy among the Confucian scholars, who led a revolt that defeated the Mongols.

Overall, the Mongols experienced relatively few military defeats, so what caused the decline of their empire? Once the Mongols conquered various peoples, most often using brutal tactics and trickery, they were usually content with extracting tribute from them. The Mongols were very open to and interested in other cultures and religions, so they often allowed these to remain in place in areas that they conquered. In addition, the Khans were located great distances apart within their huge empire, and it was difficult for them to stay in contact with one another. Most of them adopted the customs and, sometimes, even the religions of the people they ruled. Thus, the Mongol Empire eventually drifted apart rather than experiencing a devastating downfall. The Mongols themselves became assimilated into the cultures that they had once conquered.

Sample Answer to the Comparative Essay Question

During the period between 1450 and 1750, there was a trend toward a loss of power and influence in the older land-based empires, in contrast to the dramatic rise of power and prosperity of the new ocean-based European countries. However, the more established land-based Chinese Empire remained a powerful global force.

The Western Hemisphere and the Eastern Hemisphere began to maintain continuous direct contact with one another as a result of emerging new global trade patterns. Both Europe and China were at the forefront of establishing and rebuilding global trade. Innovations in maritime travel and techniques, economic prosperity, and strong, stable political organizations all enabled both regions to completely alter world trade patterns. As ocean-based trade grew in importance, Portugal, Spain, France, and England became major maritime world powers, as did China under the Ming and Qing dynasties.

In the middle of the 15th century, Europe was positioning itself to venture into the open oceans to seek great profits from trade. Although it had long been excluded from established trade routes because of the impracticality of inland travel, European leaders certainly had noted the success of Venice and Genoa as the first European city-states to make vast fortunes from maritime voyages in the Mediterranean Sea.

Inspired by the influence of Henry the Navigator's advanced knowledge of maritime techniques, advancements in mapmaking, innovations in the design of ships, new maritime technology and tools, and superior weapons, the Portuguese took over the trade routes of the Indian Ocean, which had been the domain of Arabs, Persians, Indians, and Asians. As Portugal dominated the trade of the Indian Ocean for most of the 16th century, Spain searched for an alternate route to the riches of India. Although the voyages of Italian sailor Christopher Columbus, sponsored by Queen Isabella and King Ferdinand of Spain, did not lead to the discovery of such a route, Columbus ended up in the Americas. This led to further exploration of the Americas by the Spanish and began a new era of incredibly lucrative world trade across the Atlantic Ocean for the Europeans.

However, the Europeans still had little participation in trade with Asia. At that time, there were no goods produced in Europe that the people of Asia wanted to buy. The solution to this barrier for European merchants was silver extracted from mines in the Americas. Europeans entered the trade markets in Asia by buying Asian goods with silver, which was a major factor in the commercialization and the creation of a global economy. European merchants also became specialists in transporting goods from one Asian market to another market in Asia or in the Indian Ocean region.

Overall, overseas trade between Europe and Asia expanded tremendously between the 16th and 18th centuries, generating great prosperity in European economies as well as in the economies of Asia, including China.

China's reasons for reestablishing overseas trade were very different from those of the Europeans. After the Ming overthrew the Mongols in 1356, they set about restoring the glory of Han China, first by reestablishing China's internal trade and political administration. The Ming emperors were wary of outsiders. They first allowed foreign merchants only to trade in the ports of Quanzhou and Guangzhou under close supervision by the government. Still, overseas trade had long brought prosperity to China, and the Ming realized that they could not afford to completely shut themselves off from the benefits of its wealth and influence. Markets in India and Europe were still eager to obtain silk, porcelain, and manufactured goods from China. Therefore, the Ming emperors allowed China to resume its place as the most powerful and influential trade empire in Asia.

Partly to restore Chinese prestige, Ming Emperor Yongle sponsored a series of naval expeditions between 1405 and 1433 under the command of Admiral Zheng He. The Chinese had a magnificent fleet of vessels, called junks, which were far bigger than the ships that the Portuguese and Spanish explorers were to sail only a few decades later. Zheng He's voyages greatly expanded China's maritime presence as he traveled to Southeast Asia, across the Indian Ocean to India, the Middle East, and Africa.

As the European nations continued to strengthen their wealth and power through overseas trade, the Ming empire began to decline in the 1600s. Piracy became common in the Chinese seas, just as it did in the Americas, especially in the Caribbean, but it had a greater negative impact on China. In addition, the land-based Silk Road trade dwindled during this era. Europe dominated the oceans, and trade was increasingly conducted by water.

Answer Sheet

Section I

1. Ⓐ Ⓑ Ⓒ Ⓓ
2. Ⓐ Ⓑ Ⓒ Ⓓ
3. Ⓐ Ⓑ Ⓒ Ⓓ
4. Ⓐ Ⓑ Ⓒ Ⓓ
5. Ⓐ Ⓑ Ⓒ Ⓓ
6. Ⓐ Ⓑ Ⓒ Ⓓ
7. Ⓐ Ⓑ Ⓒ Ⓓ
8. Ⓐ Ⓑ Ⓒ Ⓓ
9. Ⓐ Ⓑ Ⓒ Ⓓ
10. Ⓐ Ⓑ Ⓒ Ⓓ
11. Ⓐ Ⓑ Ⓒ Ⓓ
12. Ⓐ Ⓑ Ⓒ Ⓓ
13. Ⓐ Ⓑ Ⓒ Ⓓ
14. Ⓐ Ⓑ Ⓒ Ⓓ
15. Ⓐ Ⓑ Ⓒ Ⓓ
16. Ⓐ Ⓑ Ⓒ Ⓓ
17. Ⓐ Ⓑ Ⓒ Ⓓ
18. Ⓐ Ⓑ Ⓒ Ⓓ
19. Ⓐ Ⓑ Ⓒ Ⓓ
20. Ⓐ Ⓑ Ⓒ Ⓓ
21. Ⓐ Ⓑ Ⓒ Ⓓ
22. Ⓐ Ⓑ Ⓒ Ⓓ
23. Ⓐ Ⓑ Ⓒ Ⓓ
24. Ⓐ Ⓑ Ⓒ Ⓓ

25. Ⓐ Ⓑ Ⓒ Ⓓ
26. Ⓐ Ⓑ Ⓒ Ⓓ
27. Ⓐ Ⓑ Ⓒ Ⓓ
28. Ⓐ Ⓑ Ⓒ Ⓓ
29. Ⓐ Ⓑ Ⓒ Ⓓ
30. Ⓐ Ⓑ Ⓒ Ⓓ
31. Ⓐ Ⓑ Ⓒ Ⓓ
32. Ⓐ Ⓑ Ⓒ Ⓓ
33. Ⓐ Ⓑ Ⓒ Ⓓ
34. Ⓐ Ⓑ Ⓒ Ⓓ
35. Ⓐ Ⓑ Ⓒ Ⓓ
36. Ⓐ Ⓑ Ⓒ Ⓓ
37. Ⓐ Ⓑ Ⓒ Ⓓ
38. Ⓐ Ⓑ Ⓒ Ⓓ
39. Ⓐ Ⓑ Ⓒ Ⓓ
40. Ⓐ Ⓑ Ⓒ Ⓓ
41. Ⓐ Ⓑ Ⓒ Ⓓ
42. Ⓐ Ⓑ Ⓒ Ⓓ
43. Ⓐ Ⓑ Ⓒ Ⓓ
44. Ⓐ Ⓑ Ⓒ Ⓓ
45. Ⓐ Ⓑ Ⓒ Ⓓ
46. Ⓐ Ⓑ Ⓒ Ⓓ
47. Ⓐ Ⓑ Ⓒ Ⓓ
48. Ⓐ Ⓑ Ⓒ Ⓓ

49. Ⓐ Ⓑ Ⓒ Ⓓ
50. Ⓐ Ⓑ Ⓒ Ⓓ
51. Ⓐ Ⓑ Ⓒ Ⓓ
52. Ⓐ Ⓑ Ⓒ Ⓓ
53. Ⓐ Ⓑ Ⓒ Ⓓ
54. Ⓐ Ⓑ Ⓒ Ⓓ
55. Ⓐ Ⓑ Ⓒ Ⓓ
56. Ⓐ Ⓑ Ⓒ Ⓓ
57. Ⓐ Ⓑ Ⓒ Ⓓ
58. Ⓐ Ⓑ Ⓒ Ⓓ
59. Ⓐ Ⓑ Ⓒ Ⓓ
60. Ⓐ Ⓑ Ⓒ Ⓓ
61. Ⓐ Ⓑ Ⓒ Ⓓ
62. Ⓐ Ⓑ Ⓒ Ⓓ
63. Ⓐ Ⓑ Ⓒ Ⓓ
64. Ⓐ Ⓑ Ⓒ Ⓓ
65. Ⓐ Ⓑ Ⓒ Ⓓ
66. Ⓐ Ⓑ Ⓒ Ⓓ
67. Ⓐ Ⓑ Ⓒ Ⓓ
68. Ⓐ Ⓑ Ⓒ Ⓓ
69. Ⓐ Ⓑ Ⓒ Ⓓ
70. Ⓐ Ⓑ Ⓒ Ⓓ

Glossary

38th parallel the divisional boundary of Korea into two occupation zones near the end of World War II, with the Soviets occupying North Korea and the United States occupying South Korea.

9/11 attacks coordinated series of terrorist attacks spearheaded by al-Qaeda on the United States within its own borders on September 11, 2001.

Abbas I emperor of the Safavid Empire from 1587 to 1629, a time in which the empire was at its peak; reorganized, trained, and established a centralized administration for the army; drove out the Ottomans from Safavid territories and conquered most of Persia; continued efforts to eradicate the Sunni sect of Islam and forced his conquests to convert to Shi'ism.

Abbasid Caliphate established by Abu Abbas in 750 CE with Baghdad as its capital and important cultural center; Baghdad was captured as a result of Mongol expansion in 1258 CE, thus ending the Abbasid Caliphate.

absolutism rule by monarchy, with the king or queen having supreme power; reinforced by the belief in the divine right, or the god-given authority, of the monarchs to rule.

Achaemenid Empire established by the conquests of Cyrus the Great (from 550 to 539 BCE), during whose reign Persia expanded into the largest empire of the Near East.

Afrikaners Europeans who settled in South Africa; from the Dutch word for "African."

AIDS acquired immunodeficiency syndrome, caused by HIV (human immunodeficiency virus), that particularly threatens underdeveloped regions such as Africa.

Alexander III, Tsar Russian leader during whose reign Russia truly entered the Industrial Revolution in the 1890s.

Alexander II, Tsar Russian leader who implemented a program of social reforms, such as freeing the serfs, and modernization schemes during the latter half of the nineteenth century.

Allende, Salvador Chilean president who nationalized and socialized U.S.-owned and other industries; killed when the military junta of Augusto José Ramón Pinochet took power in a U.S.-supported coup d'état.

Allies in World War I, the nations who bound together to fight against the Central Powers; in World War II, the nations who fought against the Axis Powers.

al-Qaeda radical, militant, Islamic terrorist organization founded by Osama bin Laden; responsible for 9/11 attacks on the United States on September 11, 2001; evolved out of the *mujahideen*.

Amun-Re one of the most important deities worshipped throughout Egyptian history; was a fusing of the mythology of Amun with that of an earlier god, Re.

Analects a collection of the teachings of Confucianism.

Anthony, Susan B. social activist who organized movements based on women's suffrage.

antibiotics a medication that kills disease-causing bacteria without damaging healthy cells.

anti-Semitism hatred toward or discrimination against Jewish people as a religious, ethnic, or racial group; a founding principle of the Nazi Party.

apartheid "apartness"; policy of South Africa in which different races were assigned to specific residential and business sections in cities and to specific job categories; the rights of black Africans to own land and to participate in the government were limited; most forms of social contact were prohibited between the races; public facilities were segregated; and separate standards of education were established.

apostles a group of twelve men who were Jesus' original disciples.

appeasement policy of Britain in which Prime Minister Neville Chamberlain made concessions to Hitler and Nazi Germany in hopes of avoiding another world war.

apprenticeship a period of training to learn a craft or trade under the supervision of a skilled worker.

Aristotle a philosopher and student of Plato; believed in a realm that was not observable to humans through the five senses and, instead, advocated empiricism.

Articles of Confederation agreement between the thirteen founding states that established the United States of America and served as its first constitution; created a national system so weak that it barely had more power than the Congress itself.

artifacts objects made by human hands.

asantehene position created by the Akan people, to establish unity among the diverse clans; became their supreme political ruler and religious leader.

Ashante members of the Akan people who lived between the Atlantic coast and the northern trade center; rose to prominence in the seventeenth century as a result of the slave trade.

Ashoka emperor of the Mauryan Empire and the first Buddhist ruler of India; helped establish Buddhism as a widespread missionary belief system.

Association of Southeast Asian Nations (ASEAN) formed in 1967 by Indonesia, Malaysia, the Philippines, Singapore, and Thailand to promote political and economic cooperation and regional stability.

astrolabe a tool developed by the Arabs; allowed sailors to determine the altitude of the sun and thereby to plot latitude.

Athens city-state of classical Greece, dominated by wealthy aristocratic landowners; developed the world's first democracy in which all free adult male citizens could participate in politics.

atman the idea of the eternal self, which has always existed and always will exist, and cannot be destroyed.

atomic bomb a massive, destructive nuclear weapon used by the United States against Japan and the cities of Hiroshima and Nagasaki.

Aztecs wanderers for 150 years before settling on Lake Texcoco (modern-day Mexico City); built and expanded their empire through warfare.

Baghdad capital city and important cultural center of the Abbasid Caliphate.

Balfour Declaration 1917 public declaration made by Britain that promised to establish a secure homeland for Jews in Palestine.

Banana Republics countries that were exploited by—and whose economies were controlled by—industrialized countries.

Bantu African peoples who were the first to introduce the smelting of iron and the use of iron tools; the sub-Saharan trade route likely emerged from the Bantus.

basin irrigation the Egyptian system of irrigation that involved a series of dikes that held back floodwaters during periods of adequate rainfall and canals that allowed the water to flow to fields beyond the fertile strips of land along the river during periods of insufficient rainfall.

Battle of Tours turning point in European history, during which the Franks in 732 CE halted Muslim advances in present-day France.

Bay of Pigs the invasion by armed Cuban exiles—supported by the U.S. government—to overthrow the Castro government in Cuba.

Belgian Congo claimed for Belgium in 1876, the Congo River Valley was declared a free trade area by King Leopold II of Belgium, but his legacy of repressive rule there eventually forced the government of Belgium to take control of the colony in 1908.

Benin kingdom on the Slave Coast, east of the Gold Coast; in the beginning of the sixteenth century, the king limited the slave trade, preferring instead to trade in goods; by the eighteenth century, the desire of the nobility in Benin to acquire more wealth, along with pressure from European traders, led to Benin becoming prominent in the slave trade.

Benso di Cavour, Camillo leading figure in Sardinian politics from 1850 to 1861 and chief minister of King Victor Emmanuel; worked to unite northern and some of central Italy into a state dominated by Sardinia.

Berbers nomads of the Sahara; facilitators of the Saharan trade route through the domestication of camels, the invention of the camel saddle, and the use of camels as pack animals in desert caravans.

Berlin Conference meeting held in 1884–1885, where fourteen European nations and the United States determined that any European nation could found a colony in unclaimed territory if it notified the other nations of its intentions.

beys provincial governors of the Ottoman Empire who collected taxes from the tribal chiefs and who had both administrative and military control.

Bible Christian holy book containing the Old Testament of the Jews and the scriptures of the Christian New Testament.

Bill of Rights the first ten amendments to the U.S. Constitution that guaranteed individual rights.

bin Laden, Osama founder of the al-Qaeda organization, which reflected a new global form of terrorism of the twenty-first century as it spawned operations by the Sunni extremists across the globe from Indonesia, to the United States, to the Middle East and Africa; while hiding in a Pakistani compound, was killed in 2011 by a Navy SEAL operation authorized by U.S. president Barack Obama.

Bismarck, Otto von ministry head who united the people of Germany and transformed Prussia into the major power of Central Europe.

Black Hand secret, terrorist-like group that worked to unite all Yugoslavs within Serbia; was instrumental in planning and executing the assassination of Archduke Franz Ferdinand of Austria-Hungary and his wife Sophie in Sarajevo.

Bolívar, Simón Venezuelan military officer who worked to create an independent and unified Latin America; wrote the Letter from Jamaica, in which he advocated his ideas for a republican government and the unification of Latin America; advocated the idea that human freedom and rights are inalienable and natural and justified the violence in Latin America as being necessary for the revolutionaries to reclaim their natural rights.

Bolsheviks members of the Russian Social Democratic party, which seized power in Russia by the Revolution of November 1917.

Bond, James fictional character—British Secret Service Agent 007—created by Ian Fleming.

Book of the Dead collection of ancient poems illustrating the Egyptians' positive view of the afterlife.

Bosnia and Herzegovina former nations of Yugoslavia that declared sovereignty in 1991 and independence from Yugoslavia in 1992, leading to a series of ethnic wars between Catholic and Orthodox Christians and Muslims; the nations are still divided along ethnic lines today, but tensions have eased.

bourgeoisie middle class; used by Karl Marx to reference workers who would join together in a revolution against the industrialists who controlled the means of production.

Boxer Rebellion movement of antiforeign sentiment and Chinese nationalism led by the Society of Harmonious Fists.

boyars the nobility of Russia, many of whom were killed by Ivan the Terrible.

BP oil spill 2010 explosion and oil spill on a British Petroleum oil rig in the Gulf of Mexico; killed 11 men and injured 17 others working on the oil rig; the largest marine oil spill in history, releasing an estimated 5 million barrels of crude oil into the water.

Brahmanism the collective changes to the religious and social systems that resulted from the changes in Hinduism and Indian thought during the late Vedic period; characterized by the elevation of the Brahmin priests to a position of supreme power and privilege in society, even above the status of rulers and nobles.

bubonic plague the "Black Death"; symptoms include black swellings on victims' bodies caused by buboes, or internal hemorrhages; first recorded breakout was in the Byzantine Empire in the sixth century; an epidemic of the plague struck Europe in 1347, and a third of the population died.

Buddhism religion based on the ancient teachings of the prophet Siddhartha, who later became known as the Buddha, meaning the "Enlightened One."

Cabot, John a native of Italy who sailed under the English crown in 1497 and became the first English representative to reach North America; his voyages gave England claim to the North American mainland, which would lead to future English colonization.

Cabral, Pedro explorer who was sent in 1500 by King Manuel I of Portugal to set up trading posts in India; landed in Brazil, claimed it for the Portuguese crown, and then continued on to India, arriving in 1501.

caliphate form of government that was ruled by a caliph (successor of Muhammad), who was chosen by the leaders of the umma.

calpulli an organization based on households and kinship through which Aztec emperors summoned warriors to duty.

caravel sailing vessel that relied on wind power and was designed to carry large cargoes.

Carolingian dynasty dynasty established (750–887 CE) by a family of Frankish aristocrats to rule Western Europe; its most notable ruler was Charlemagne.

Carthage a wealthy, merchant-based city along the Mediterranean Sea that became the leader of the Phoenician colonies in the west and a full-fledged empire.

Central Powers in World War I, the powers—Germany, Austria-Hungary, Bulgaria, and the Ottoman Empire—that banded together to fight against the Allies.

Chamberlain, Neville prime minister of Great Britain who negotiated feverishly with Hitler to avert the almost-certain war, agreeing to Germany's immediate annexation of the Sudetenland.

Champa rice a strain of fast-ripening rice from Champa (present-day Vietnam), which produced both a summer and a winter crop each year.

Chang'an an ancient capital city of China that was a cosmopolitan urban center with a population that may have exceeded a million people by about 640 CE.

Charlemagne ruler of the Carolingian dynasty and Roman emperor; during his reign, the empire expanded greatly, united most of Western Europe; associated with the Carolingian Renaissance, a period in which art and culture were revived through the Catholic Church.

chattel property, such as how slaves were bought and sold.

Chavín early agricultural society (900–300 BCE) in the highlands of the Andes, in what is now Peru.

chinampas raised agricultural fields constructed by the Aztecs in swampy areas and in shallow water that resembled floating gardens.

Chinese Communist Party founded in 1921, the ruling political party in China.

Chinese Exclusion Act law that made the Chinese the only ethnic group in U.S. history to be specifically denied entry into the country; Chinese people were also prohibited by law from becoming U.S. citizens, testifying in court, owning property, voting, and having their families from China join them in the United States.

Christianity religion following the teachings of Jesus, who was a prophet, teacher, and, according to his followers, the promised Messiah and son of God.

Churchill, Winston British prime minister during World War II and an unyielding enemy of Hitler's Germany.

city-states in classical Greece, consisted of a central city protected by fortifications and surrounded by farmland and villages.

Civil Rights Movement political movement that fought for the rights of all before the law.

civilization a large society that has major cities and is a powerful state.

Cold War the ideological conflict between the Communist nations of Eastern Europe, led by the Soviet Union, and the Western democracies, led by the United States.

colonization the political, economic, and social structures created by Europeans in foreign lands that supported their efforts to dominate native cultures.

Columbian Exchange a global economy through the sea trade resulting from the European voyages of exploration; linked the continents of North America, South America, Europe, and Africa.

Columbus, Christopher an Italian explorer who believed he could more easily reach the East by sailing west across the seemingly limited expanse of ocean that separated Asia from the western coast of Europe than the Portuguese could reach it by sailing around the enormous continent of Africa; his explorations were financed by Spain, and in October 1492, he reached the Caribbean; led a total of four journeys to the islands of the Caribbean.

Comintern Communist International, created by Lenin in an attempt to spread Communism abroad.

communism Marxist theory of a society of equality and cooperation.

compass navigational device used during the Age of Exploration (but perfected by the Chinese many centuries earlier) that pointed north, which was an important means of location for ships traveling east to west.

Confucian scholar gentry those who acquired wealth in the Ming and Qing dynasties used it to educate themselves so as to acquire the status of a Confucian scholar; the focus on the Confucian literary classics, as opposed to the sciences, was a contributing factor in China's failure to develop a large manufacturing sector.

Confucianism religion based on the teachings of Confucius.

Confucius his teachings are the basis of Confucianism and the basis of Chinese culture; believed the most excellent models of virtue were to be found in the past and that respect for the past would restore balance, harmony, and order to society and to people's own lives.

Constantinople the capital of the Byzantine Empire and a major center of long-distance trading routes.

Constitution of the United States new government, established to replace the weak Articles of Confederation, in which the government's powers were divided among three branches: the legislative, judicial, and executive; established checks and balances to prevent any one branch from controlling the government.

constitutionalism a government according to constitutional principles; system adopted by England and the Netherlands, in which they each placed limitations on the power of the monarch.

containment policy of the United States that utilized numerous strategies to prevent the spread of Communism.

convict laborers in nineteenth-century Britain, persons who were sentenced to serve hard labor and leased to private companies in England under government contracts.

Córdoba a region in southern Spain, in which culture flourished under Muslim control.

Cortés, Hernando notary, farmer, and explorer who destroyed the Aztec monarchy, took possession of Tenochtitlán, and defeated most of the Aztecs in less than two years.

corvus pivotal bridge on Roman-built ships that could be swung out and extended for soldiers to march across and do battle.

Cossacks nomadic descendants of Russian peasants who had fled the taxes and other obligations of feudalism and who had acquired great military prowess and horsemanship.

cottage industry system in India in which brokers provided materials and money to artisans who worked at home in return for finished cloth products.

cotton gin invention of Eli Whitney that mechanically removed the seeds from raw cotton.

creoles individuals of European heritage who were born in the Americas.

Crimean War conflict between Russia and the allied forces of France and Britain for the territories of the crumbling Ottoman Empire.

Crusades four military expeditions led by Christian powers in the eleventh, twelfth, and thirteenth centuries to win the Holy Land from the Muslims.

Cuban Missile Crisis confrontation between the United States and the Soviet Union in 1962 after the U.S. discovered the building of nuclear missile sites in Cuba; President Kennedy decided to "quarantine" Cuba by placing a ring of ships around the island to prevent the delivery of the weaponry; crisis ended when the Soviets agreed to dismantle the weapon sites in exchange for a pledge from the United States not to invade Cuba; in a separate deal, which remained secret for more than twenty-five years, the United States also agreed to remove its nuclear missiles from Turkey.

cuneiform Mesopotamian, wedge-shaped writing, written with styluses on clay tablets.

da Gama, Vasco a Portuguese explorer and student of Prince Henry the Navigator; rounded the southern tip of Africa in 1487 and sailed east to reach India.

Dahomey kingdom seventy miles west of the Gold Coast that emerged in the seventeenth century by dealing in the slave trade; used profits from the slave trade to obtain guns, which it used to conquer smaller states and expand its kingdom; was the most highly centralized state in Africa at the time, with its kings being absolute monarchs.

daimyo vassals, in the Japanese system of feudalism.

Daoism religion based on the Dao, or the Way.

Dark Ages the period in Europe from about 500 to 1000 CE, during which much of the Roman civilization was lost, such as written language, innovative architectural and building techniques, organized government, and long-distance trade.

D-Day the invasion of Normandy, France, by the Allies in June 1944; the beginning of the liberation of France and Western Europe.

DDT insecticide with toxic effects that is banned in the United States and many other countries.

Declaration of Independence document drafted by Thomas Jefferson in which the thirteen colonies declared independence from the British monarchy.

Declaration of the Rights of Man document in which everyone in France was declared born free and equal in rights, especially those of life, liberty, property, security, and resistance to oppression.

deforestation the process of clearing forests, oftentimes to make room for more people and for the buildings, factories, and other structures that they desire.

de Gouges, Olympe French playwright who wrote the *Declaration of the Rights of Woman and of the Citizen*, which was modeled on the 1879 *Declaration of the Rights of Man;* echoed and extended the ideas of the *Declaration of the Rights of Man* to apply to women as well.

de Klerk, F. W. South African president who began the abolishment of some apartheid policies in the early 1990s.

Delhi Sultanate Muslim dynasties that ruled India from 1210 to 1526 CE.

demilitarized zone buffer zone running along the 38th parallel separating North Korea from South Korea; in general, buffer zone between two military powers in which military action is not allowed.

Deng Xiaoping Communist leader of China who implemented the one-child policy; enacted a series of reforms emphasizing "four modernizations": in agriculture, industry, national defense, and technology; responded with brute force to the student protest in Tiananmen Square.

détente a loosening of tensions, such as those between the United States and the Soviet Union.

devshirme a system in the Ottoman Empire of conscripting Christian boys from the provinces, raising them as Muslims, and using them as soldiers.

diaspora the scattering of the Hebrews of Israel throughout the Middle East and Afro-Eurasia.

Diaz, Bartholomew a Portuguese explorer and student of Prince Henry the Navigator; reached the tip of South Africa in 1487.

domino theory the belief that once Communism was allowed to flourish in South Vietnam, all of the other governments in southeastern Asia, such as those of Thailand, Laos, Cambodia, Malaysia, and Indonesia, would also fall to Communism.

Duma the representative body of the Russian government.

East India Tea Company company that was established to trade goods with the East Indies; however, the majority of trading was actually done with the India subcontinent and China.

Eastern Front in World War I, a theater of war in Central and Eastern Europe; in World War II, a theater of war with Germany and Austria-Hungary opposing Russia.

Emancipation Proclamation declaration made by President Abraham Lincoln that freed all slaves in the United States.

Emperor Constantine Roman emperor who ruled from 312 to 337 CE; established a second Roman capital in Byzantium, which he renamed Constantinople; was a convert to Christianity and allowed Christians to openly practice their faith.

empiricism reliance on the senses.

Enclosure system where wealthy landowners enclosed common fields, and a variety of crops were cultivated there on a continuous basis.

encomienda labor system in which Spanish conquistadors and Portuguese colonists with large land grants believed that they owned the native people who lived there and forced them to work on the plantations, while extracting tribute from them; the system lasted only during the sixteenth century.

Enlightenment reliance on reason above all else; era during which many thinkers began to question the authority of absolute governments and other accepted traditions and to focus on the rights of individuals; brought about by the Renaissance, the Scientific Revolution, and the Protestant Reformation.

Epic of Gilgamesh early Mesopotamian creation story in which the first immortal man, Utnapishtim, tells the hero Gilgamesh that the god Enlil sent a flood because humans were too noisy and irritated the gods.

euro basic unit of currency stabled by twelve members of the European Union.

European Union (EU) political and economic union of twenty-seven European countries.

extinction the process of becoming extinct, such as the eradication of an entire species of animal or plant.

factory system method of manufacturing adopted by the British during the Industrial Revolution; an assembly system in which each worker was responsible for a separate part of an item.

Fascists/Fascism a group of war veterans organized in Italy by Benito Mussolini with an ideology that was a blend of nationalism and socialism.

Ferdinand and Isabella king and queen of Spain, whom Christopher Columbus approached in 1485 with his plan of sailing west to reach the East; initially uninterested in Columbus's ideas, the pair grew eager to counter the rising power of the Portuguese that resulted from their initial voyages around Africa; the queen promised to finance Columbus's exploration in 1492.

Fertile Crescent the first settlements in Mesopotamia, dating back to about 5000 BCE.

feudalism a system of landholding and obligations that developed in Europe during the reign of Charlemagne; includes the complex social, economic, and political relationships that characterized much of Europe from the ninth century through the French Revolution.

Fidel Castro Cuban revolutionary who served as Cuba's prime minister (1959–1976) and president (1976–2008).

fiefdom the gift of a plot of land from a lord in a feudal society.

fiefs vast manorial estates that were divided into an area of land reserved for the lord and tracts reserved for peasants.

firebombing the process of dropping incendiary bombs.

First Industrial Revolution began in the late eighteenth century in Britain and later spread to other parts of Europe and to the United States.

Five Pillars of Faith the five duties at the heart of Islam, which represent a Muslim's submission to the will of God: there is no god but Allah, and Muhammad is his messenger; pray five times a day, facing Mecca; gives alms through a special tax to other Muslims who are less fortunate; fast during the month of Ramadan; and make a pilgrimage to Mecca at least once in a lifetime.

Five Year Plans plans enacted by Joseph Stalin shortly after taking over power of the Soviet Union, intended to promote rapid economic development.

fly shuttle invented by John Kay in 1733, a machine that was able to weave thread together better than a one-person loom.

foot binding process of breaking the bones of the feet and then binding the feet to ensure that they did not grow to normal adult proportions; common practice for upper-class women during the Song dynasty as it was a sign of wealth and status; restricted the ability of women to walk or to work and therefore led them to greater subservience to their husbands and confinement to the household.

foundational civilizations large, dense, hierarchical societies centered around cities, with complex institutions, sophisticated economic organizations, and specialization of labor.

four modernizations a series of reforms in China introduced by Deng Xiaoping focusing on agriculture, industry, national defense, and technology.

Franks Germanic peoples in Europe who migrated into what had once been the Roman Empire.

French Equatorial Africa created from the region on the north bank of the Congo, conquered by France.

French Indochina formed in 1887, the French-conquered Asian nations of Vietnam, Laos, and Cambodia.

French West Africa created by France out of various territories in West Africa.

Fukushima Daiichi nuclear power plant in Japan, at which an 8.9-magnitude earthquake in 2011 disabled its nuclear reactor's cooling systems and led to radiation leaks.

Funan important trading partner of India, whose capital was in what is today known as Vietnam; first state to arise in the area, and it controlled parts of the Malay Peninsula and Indochina.

Gandhi, Mohandas leader of the Indian nationalist movement against British rule; developed a philosophy of nonviolence and passive resistance as he worked for political and social reforms.

Garibaldi, Giuseppe fought for Italians and to liberate parts of Italy from foreign control; worked with Camillo Benso di Cavour for Italian unification.

Genghis Khan "universal ruler" of the Mongol tribes; established a fierce and brutal army to aid in his conquests.

Gestapo secret police of Nazi Germany.

Ghana a military kingdom of the Soninke people located directly on the trans-Saharan trade routes; flourished from 900 to 1100 CE.

glasnost a policy of openness initiated by Soviet leader Mikhail Gorbachev.

global warming the result of the amount of carbon dioxide, fluorocarbons, and other greenhouse gases that have risen into the ozone layer of the atmosphere; according to scientists, these gases have caused the average surface temperatures on Earth to rise, and will continue to do so for some time to come.

Government of India Act act passed by the British government in 1921 that gave India the institutions for a self-governing state.

Gran Colombia nineteenth-century republic that included Venezuela, present-day Colombia, Ecuador, Panama, and northern Peru, with Simón Bolívar as its president.

Grand Canal a 1,400-mile-long canal built by Yang Jian and his son that linked the Yellow and Yangtze Rivers.

Great Depression global economic depression of the 1930s.

Great Leap Forward campaign implemented by China's Communist leader, Mao Zedong, to move China toward modernized industrialization; was directly responsible for a famine from 1960 to 1961 in which anywhere from 18 to 45 million people died.

Great Proletarian Cultural Revolution socio-political movement initiated by Mao Zedong to enforce socialism in the country by removing capitalist, traditional, and cultural elements from Chinese society; Mao wanted revisionists throughout China removed, targeting the intellectuals, professionals, and others associated with foreign influences or bourgeois values; set China back many years, as it stripped the country of its educated population and sent thousands to jails, to rural labor camps, or to their deaths.

Great Pyramid at Giza constructed by the children and grandchildren of Pharaoh Sneferu with several internal passageways that appear to be aligned with constellations and important stars; one of the Seven Wonders of the Ancient World.

green movements movements protesting the destructive consequences of population growth and industrialization on the environment; raised public awareness about a variety of global environmental problems, such as deforestation, the extinction of animal species, and pollution.

Green Revolution research and development initiatives that resulted in increased agricultural production throughout the world.

greenhouse gases a gas in the atmosphere that absorbs and emits radiation.

Greenpeace International organization devoted to raising public awareness of threats to the environment, resulting in some successes in pressuring both private organizations and governments to refrain from environmentally destructive practices.

Guernica painting by Pablo Picasso based on the events of April 27, 1937, when the German air force launched a massive bombing raid on the civilians living in the quiet Basque village of Guernica, in northern Spain; for more than two hours, the unsuspecting villagers were hit with highly explosive and incendiary bombs, which killed or wounded 1,600 hundred people—mostly women and children—and caused what was left of the village itself to burn for three days.

guilds first formed in the twelfth century, organizations of artisans that regulated its members' activities.

gun and slave cycle the link between firearms and increased trading in slaves, leading to further acquisition of firearms and the renewal of the cycle.

gunpowder empires land-based empires that increased dramatically in size between 1450 and 1750, largely because of their immense armies and their use of guns; included the Ming and Qing in China, the Ottoman Turks and the Safavids in Southwest Asia, the Mughals in India, Japan, and the new Russian Empire.

Gupta Empire initially based around the Ganges River in eastern India but eventually extended to most of Northern India, the empire was in existence during the fourth and fifth centuries—India's classical age; imposed unity on society and fostered a flourishing of the arts; had a small bureaucracy with its emperors relying on local authorities to maintain order and collect tributes.

Haile Selassie Ethiopian emperor who advocated civil disobedience when it was necessary to remedy social injustices and free people who were oppressed.

Haiti after declaring independence from France in 1803, the nation became the second independent republic in the Western Hemisphere in 1804.

Hammurabi, Code of a set of 282 laws carved in forty-nine columns on a basalt stele, established by King Hammurabi.

Han dynasty established when the Han defeated the imperial army of the Qin as part of the mass rebellion that arose after the death of Emperor Qin; was in existence from 206 BCE to 220 CE; under the Hans, China officially became a Confucian state, established a rigid social class structure, and was a formidable military power.

Hangzhou southern capital of China and a large trading city with an ever-growing population during the Song dynasty.

Hanseatic League mercantile league of medieval German cities.

Harappan culture consisting of the twin capitals of Harappa and Mohenjo-Daro, nearly identical cities located 400 miles apart in the northernmost reaches of the Indian subcontinent.

Hellenization the intentional spreading of Greek culture.

Henry the Navigator Portuguese king and explorer who established a school for navigators that produced some of the most skillful navigators of all time, including Bartholomew Diaz and Vasco da Gama.

Henry VIII king of England who separated the English Church from the Catholic Church and Rome when the pope refused to grant him an annulment from his first wife, Catherine of Aragon.

hieroglyphs possibly the oldest form of writing, first developed around 3300 BCE and used by the Egyptians for the next 3,500 years.

Hinduism dominant religion of India; the integral parts of Hinduism's essential beliefs include the universal spirit and atman; reincarnation; the dharma; and karma.

Hiroshima city in Japan that suffered the first atomic bomb attack by the United States during World War II that resulted in approximately 150,000 deaths.

history the period of time during which there are written records of human activities.

Hitler, Adolf German chancellor and leader of the National Socialist German Workers' Party (Nazi Party); initiated World War II with his invasion of Poland in 1939.

Hittites pastoral Indo-Europeans who invaded and conquered the Old Babylonian Empire in Mesopotamia in the sixteenth century BCE; flourished from about 1600 to 1200 BCE.

HIV human immunodeficiency virus, the virus that causes AIDS.

Holocaust mass genocide of more than 6 million Jews and millions of others by Nazi Germany and its collaborators during World War II.

hominid human-like creatures.

Homo sapiens the modern human species.

Hong Kong and Shanghai Banking Company bank created in 1865 with one center in Hong Kong and one in Shanghai to meet the needs of European merchants who needed a local bank to finance the heavy transnational trade between China and Europe.

horse collar padded collar used on horses that contributed to more efficient agriculture as horses could pull more weight than oxen.

Huns a nomadic people from the steppes of Central Asia who, in the fifth century, migrated south and west, pushing the Germanic tribes who lived around the borders of the Roman Empire well into its borders.

hunter-gatherers individuals whose food is obtained through hunting, fishing, and foraging.

Hyksos "rulers of foreign lands"; a pastoralist group of people who came to Upper and Lower Egypt from Palestine during the Second Intermediate period (1567 to 1085 BCE).

Ibn Battuta fourteenth-century Moroccan historian and Muslim traveler who wrote a comprehensive history of the Eastern Hemisphere.

Ibn Rushd philosopher who believed in the principle of twofold truth—philosophy and religion are different kinds of knowledge, each with its own sphere of truth.

id according to German psychiatrist Sigmund Freud, the hidden, disorganized aspect of personality made up of desires that are not conscious but that often dictate human behavior.

imperialism the web of transoceanic colonial empires that the Europeans had built beginning in 1870.

Inca Peruvian civilization that settled primarily in the valleys of Huaylas, Cuzco, and Titicaca; controlled their population through a strong government, and unified the language and the religion of their subjects.

indentured labor the transportation of poor Indian peasants who were under contract to colonies in the Caribbean, East and South Africa, and the South Pacific island of Fiji to work for five years.

indentured servitude a legal agreement whereby shopkeepers, craftsmen, and merchants paid for the ship passages of young men and women (primarily from England and Germany, but also from Ireland and Scotland) who agreed to work for an indentured period of several years to pay their employers for the costs of their passages.

Indian Ocean trade routes developed around the same time as the Silk Road, these localized routes were less vulnerable to political conflicts, they were more secure, and they allowed for the transportation of larger quantities of goods.

indulgences payments to the Church that Catholics believed would ensure their eternal salvation in heaven.

insurance companies establishments formed to cover the losses resulting from both long-distance and internal trade, thereby reducing the risks involved in establishing and operating business ventures.

internal combustion engine any engine that operates by burning its fuel inside; its development led to the rise of the automobile industry in the early twentieth century.

international corporations large companies with multinational ownership and management and offices across the globe.

International Monetary Fund (IMF) economic organization of 187 countries, created to help initiate a new era of global cooperation by encouraging free trade and high-growth rates.

Internet an electronic communications network and global means of instant and frequent communication, which has furthered the interconnections between individuals and among groups and societies.

Irish Republican Army (IRA) revolutionary military organization that carried out terrorist attacks against Britain.

Iron Curtain term coined by Winston Churchill to describe the division of Europe into free democracies and states under Communist control.

Islam the last of the great religions to emerge (in the early seventh century); founded in Mecca by Muhammad, who traveled to a cave on Mt. Hira, where he was visited by the archangel Gabriel, who conveyed to him revelations from Allah, the one true god; the revelations became the Qur'an, which contains the fundamental beliefs of Islam.

Janissaries Christian slave soldiers who came to be the elite force of Ottoman infantry soldiers; their chief loyalty was to the empire, and they were taught to consider the sultan their father.

Jefferson, Thomas author of the Declaration of Independence and third president of the United States of America.

Juárez, Benito president of Mexico who attempted to curtail the influence of the Catholic Church and of the military in Mexico; under his leadership, Mexicans gained such civil liberties as freedom of speech and universal manhood suffrage.

Judaism religion developed among the ancient Hebrews, based on the concept of God as being limitless yet also loving and compassionate toward his people, and on the condition that its followers obey the Ten Commandments; its followers are a specially chosen people; was a major influence on the development of Christianity and Islam.

junk a ship with up to four sails designed during the Song dynasty around 960 CE.

Kaifeng northern capital of China, a major urban trade center, and a manufacturing center for cannons, movable-type printing presses, looms, and water-powered mills during the Song dynasty.

kamikaze during World War II, Japanese pilots who flew their planes loaded with just enough fuel to reach allied ships and then made suicide dives straight into them.

Kemal, Mustafa the commander of the Ottoman forces at the Battle of Gallipoli whose success made him a hero in Turkey, his homeland; led a nationalist movement against the division of Turkey by the Allies, formed the Turkish Republic, and became known as Ataturk, "father of the Turks"; became Turkey's first president in 1924.

Kennedy, John F. president of the United States who authorized the invasion by armed Cuban exiles to overthrow the Castro government in the Bay of Pigs affair; also led the United States through the Cuban Missile Crisis.

khanates political regions of the divided empire of Genghis Khan.

King Jr., Martin Luther leader of the Civil Rights Movement of the 1950s and 1960s, organizing acts of civil disobedience and peaceful protests to fight against segregation and discrimination against blacks.

Koryo dynasty arising in the tenth century, the Koryo followed the Chinese system of civil service examination and bureaucratic structures; slavery was an important aspect of Koryo society (differing from their Chinese models).

Kosovo country in southeast Europe that lost its autonomy in 1989 when Slobodan Milosevic imposed direct rule from Belgrade; Milosevic unleashed a brutal police and military campaign against the Kosovo Liberation Army (KLA), whose main goal was to secure the independence of Kosovo; over 800,000 ethnic Albanians were forced from their homes; a NATO military campaign was launched to halt the violence in Kosovo; U.N. Resolution 1244 suspended Belgrade's governance over Kosovo, established the United Nations Interim Administration Mission in Kosovo (UNMIK), and authorized a NATO peacekeeping force.

Kremlin large complex in Russia that houses the palaces of the tsar, the governmental administrative center, and other monuments.

Kublai Khan the grandson of Genghis Khan; continued the wave of conquests by attacking the Song dynasty and capturing surrounding regions; established the Yuan dynasty; failed to conquer Japan despite two attempts.

Lao Zi a wandering scholar of the fourth century BCE; thought to be the founder of Daoism.

Lascaux, cave of located in France, a possibly once-sacred site where archaeologists have discovered and studied remarkably realistic and colorful cave paintings of mainly large animals.

lateen sails triangular sails that were more effective than the traditional square sails in waters that were constantly exposed to the contrary monsoon winds.

League of Nations international security organization established to maintain world peace; flawed in that it had no means to enforce its decisions and in that it relied on the notion of collective security to preserve global peace.

Lenin, Vladimir led the October Revolution in which the Bolsheviks overthrew the Russian government; first head of the USSR.

Letter from Jamaica written by Símon Bolívar, in which he advocated his ideas for a republican government and the unification of Latin America; expressed his ideas using the language of Enlightenment thinkers such as Locke, Rousseau, and Montesquieu.

Liberalism based on the ideals of liberty and equality; belief system consisting of a representative government, equality before the law, freedom of speech, freedom of assembly, freedom of the press, and freedom from arbitrary arrest; promoted free enterprise and lack of governmental control of the economy.

Liberation Theology developed by Roman Catholic priests in Latin America as a response to the needs of the poor, a theological theory that combines a Marxist political philosophy with a theory of liberation from injustice; its advocates believed that the Catholic Church had a duty to liberate the poor from oppression by becoming actively involved in politics to bring about social change; its teaching is prohibited today in the name of the Catholic Church.

liege homage the pledge of homage by a vassal to a particular lord above all others.

lifestyle diseases preventable diseases associated with individuals' lifestyles.

limited liability system system that spreads the risks of a company, enabling businesspeople to invest in the company and earn profits while not having to face the possible loss of the entirety of their investments; investors are responsible for a company's debts and losses only to the extent to which they invested in the company.

Locke, John English philosopher who developed a natural rights theory of government, according to which the laws of government and of society were embedded in nature itself; believed that when the government did not respect the natural rights of man, people had a right—and even a duty—to rebel, which became part of the basis for the American Revolution.

Lombards Germanic peoples who invaded Italy in 568 CE; established a kingdom in the Po Valley.

long-range artillery weapons that are capable of long-range fire.

Louisiana Purchase the acquisition, by the United States, of French territories from the Mississippi River to the Rocky Mountains in 1803.

Luther, Martin a German monk who believed that the Catholic Church was corrupt and needed to be reformed; believed that no amount of outer penance could affect inner repentance and that humans could never do enough good to earn salvation; his writings, including his Ninety-Five Theses, initiated a massive social rebellion that

would ultimately fragment the Holy Roman Empire; his beliefs became known as Protestantism.

maceualtin a class of workers in the Aztec society to which failed warriors were relegated; landowners for life, they paid taxes and were required to work on imperial projects.

machine guns weapons with an ability to fire rapidly and continuously; came to symbolize World War I; over the course of the war, lighter, one-man machine guns were developed.

Magellan a Portuguese explorer who sailed under the Spanish crown and became the first European to circumnavigate the globe.

Magna Carta 1215 agreement limiting the power of the English monarch and placing him under the rule of law.

Magyars a nomadic civilization that traveled up the Danube River and plundered Bulgaris in the late nineteenth century and then ravaged Saxony, Germany, and other regions, traveling as far inland as Rheims in France; permanently settled in present-day Hungary.

Mahabharata a classic of Indian literature; the world's longest poem and a story about the power struggle of two clans; the Bhagavad Gita is one of its subsections.

maize corn; cultivated by the first agricultural settlement in Mesoamerica.

malaria an infectious disease caused by parasites that are transmitted to humans from female mosquito bites; also associated with poverty.

Mali one of the successor states to break away from Ghana, founded by the Mandike people.

Manchu members of the Jurchen dynasty of Manchuria.

Mandela, Nelson leading protester of apartheid in South Africa who was imprisoned by the government for twenty-seven years; in the nation's first free general election in 1994, Mandela was elected as the nation's first black president.

manifest destiny assumed that the democratic experiment in America was a superior form of civilization, and that the white people who brought it westward were superior to those people and cultures that they replaced.

manorial system agricultural system in which land was cultivated on vast manorial estates that were divided into areas of land reserved for the lords and tracts reserved for peasants.

Mao Zedong one of the most important members of the Chinese Communist Party and founder of the People's Republic of China; supported the equality of women and fought against such practices as foot binding and arranged marriages.

Marco Polo Italian traveler who served as Kublai Khan's ambassador to parts of China for seventeen years; upon his return to Italy, he was captured by the Genoans and imprisoned.

Marley, Bob leader of the Jamaican band the Wailers, who made reggae music a part of international popular culture; the reggae message of standing up against racial discrimination and oppression inspired political resistance and a united sense of African identity.

maroons former or escaped Haitian slaves.

Marshall Plan drawn up by Truman's secretary of state, George C. Marshall, program providing economic aid to European nations recovering from World War II; mandated cooperation among recipients on tariff policies and other economic matters.

Marxist socialism theory of Karl Marx in which he advocated the interests of the working people; Marx believed that capitalism exploited workers and widened the gap between the rich and the poor; he envisioned that the conditions of the working class in capitalist countries would eventually become so intolerable that workers would join together in a revolution against the industrialists.

Maurya, Chandragupta great military tactician who founded the Maurya Empire.

Maurya Empire well-organized and efficient empire encompassing all of India except for the southernmost area; founded by Chandragupta Maurya; lasted until about 185 BCE.

Maya heirs of the Olmec culture in Mesoamerica; ruled over much of what is today southern Mexico and Central America; had a sophisticated civilization that developed an elaborate system of hieroglyphic writing, several calendars, and other methods of timekeeping.

Mecca an ancient religious center and birthplace of Islam.

Medici a wealthy and powerful family in Florence, Italy, who helped fuel the Renaissance through their support of Michelangelo, Donatello, Botticelli, and many other artists.

Meiji reforms changes made by the Meiji regime in which trade rules favored exportation rather than importation; foreign loans were repaid and no more were taken out; revenue was raised through a new agricultural tax of 3 percent, and formerly private domains were ceded to those who worked the land.

Meiji Restoration revolutionary changes brought about in Japanese society, accomplished in a top-down, dictatorial manner.

Mein Kampf written by Adolf Hitler, articulated the fundamental ideas of the Nazis.

mercantilism a theory in which colonies supplied raw materials for the mother country and also could be subjected to taxes and other economic policies; articulated in detail by Scottish economist Adam Smith in his 1776 book *Wealth of Nations*.

meritocracy the idea that government should be run by those whose virtue and learning merit their positions of authority and respect.

Mesoamerica most of present-day Mexico, Guatemala, Nicaragua, Honduras, Costa Rica, and Honduras.

Mesopotamia "the land between two rivers"; located in Southwest Asia between the Tigris and the Euphrates Rivers.

mestizo individuals of mixed European and Native American ancestry.

metallurgy the science of metals.

Milosevic, Slobodan unleashed a brutal police and military campaign against the Kosovo Liberation Army (KLA) and implemented a campaign of ethnic cleansing where over 800,000 ethnic Albanians were forced from their homes; lost power in 2000, after which the U.N. charged him with crimes against humanity; he died in 2006 before the trial concluded.

Ming dynasty the last native dynasty to rule China, under which China experienced a great social and economic revolution; the first dynasty to interact with Europeans on a large scale.

Miracle of Chile massive economic reforms in Chile, led by Augusto José Ramón Pinochet.

mita system of forced labor adopted by the early Spanish conquerors to obtain Native American workers for the gold and silver mines.

Mitsubishi Company transnational corporation founded by Iwasaki Yataro.

Moche a wealthy, organized civilization of Andean South America that was in existence from 100 to 700 CE; ahighly developed society of skilled artisans and craftsmen that left behind a pictorial history of their culture rather than a written history.

moldboard an improved iron plow introduced in the ninth century.

Monasticism relating to the life of monks and nuns, often resembling a life of seclusion or simple asceticism; flourished in the age following Constantine's legalization of Christianity.

Mongols a nomadic people from the steppes of Central Asia; formed the largest empire in history.

Monroe Doctrine put the Western Hemisphere under U.S. domination in 1823, as President Monroe warned European nations against imperialist activity in the Western Hemisphere.

monsoon winds a periodic wind in the Indian Ocean that blows off the east coast of Africa from the southeast between April and October and from the northeast between November and March.

Montesquieu applied the scientific methodology of the seventeenth century to the idea of natural law; believed that England's government allowed the greatest amount of freedom for its people; his theories influenced the drafting of the U.S. Constitution.

Mughals descendants of the Mongols from Turkestan who brought further Persian influences to India, especially that of Sufi mysticism; ruled the Mughal Empire.

Muhammad Ali Jinnah leader of the Muslim League who advocated the formation of separate states, one for Hindus in India and another for Muslims in Pakistan.

Muhammad Ali pasha of Egypt under the Ottomans; considered the founder of modern Egypt.

mulatto individuals of mixed European and African ancestry.

Muslim League political organization whose original purpose was to safeguard the political rights of Muslims in India; under the leadership of Muhammad Ali Jinnah, feared that Hindu domination would replace the British and advocated the formation of separate states, one for Hindus in India and another for Muslims in Pakistan.

Mussolini, Benito founder of Fascism and leader of Italy from 1922 to 1943; led Italy into World War II as an ally to Nazi Germany and Japan.

myth of Osiris created the cult of the pharaoh; historians do not know whether Osiris was an actual historical figure.

Nagasaki city in Japan that suffered the second atomic bomb attack by the United States during World War II, resulting in approximately 80,000 deaths.

National Assembly group formed of the French Third Estate, the clergy, and the nobility.

national socialism policy of building Germany into one large community of Germanic, and only Germanic, people, advocated by the German Worker's Party.

nationalism the belief in cultural unity based on a common language, history, region, and ethnicity.

Nationalist People's Party political party in China organized by Sun Yat-sen in 1912; by 1926, Communists accounted for one-third of its membership; dominant in China from 1928 until 1949 under the leadership of Chiang Kai-shek; the official ruling party of Taiwan.

Nazi Party the National Socialist German Workers' Party; the political party founded in Germany in 1919 and brought to power by Hitler in 1933.

Nehru, Jawaharlal first prime minister of India; followed "neutralist" policies regarding foreign affairs.

Neolithic era "New Stone Age"; period of time beginning around 10,000 BCE, continuing until about 3500 BCE.

New Deal created by President Franklin Delano Roosevelt in the 1930s, a massive program of social reform legislation based on federal intervention in the economy; new jobs were created through the Works Progress (Projects) Administration, the Civilian Conservation Corps, and other agencies; also created Social Security and other measures for the relief of beleaguered citizens.

New Economic Policy (NEP) economic policy implemented by Vladimir Lenin that allowed for some economic freedom by encouraging cottage industries and small farms to produce food and goods and to trade among themselves; major industries, however, remained under the control of the government.

nonrenewable energy sources energy sources that cannot be replaced at all or they cannot be renewed quickly enough to keep pace with their consumption.

North American Free Trade Agreement (NAFTA) agreement removing most barriers to trade and investment among the United States, Canada, and Mexico.

North Atlantic Treaty Organization (NATO) organization formed by the United States and its Allies in 1949; its main purpose was to thwart the advance of Communism in Europe, partly by rearming West Germany.

nuclear power plants a thermal power station in which the heat source is one or more nuclear reactors; in 1956, Calder Hall in England became the first operational nuclear power station capable of generating enough electricity for commercial use; by 1960, seventeen power plants were generating electricity for commercial use in Britain, the United States, the Soviet Union, and France, and several other countries were in the process of developing nuclear power plants.

Olmecs ancient society originating around 1500 BCE at San Lorenzo, south of present-day Veracruz, Mexico.

one-child policy rule implemented in China by Deng Xiaoping stating that families can have just one child; applies to people living in cities and only to the Han Chinese (ethnic minorities are exempt).

open-field system dividing land in a manorial system into two or three units; modified to include three fields rather than two by the ninth century.

Opium Wars two wars between China and Western countries; started with the Chinese, who were desperate to stop the trade of opium, burning several tons of opium in Canton.

Organization of Petroleum Exporting Countries (OPEC) a permanent intergovernmental agency made up of twelve oil-producing countries (Algeria, Angola, Ecuador, the Islamic Republic of Iran, Iraq, Kuwait, Libya, Nigeria, Qatar, Saudi Arabia, United Arab Emirates & Venezuela), set up to unify the petroleum policies of the member countries and to determine the best means for safeguarding their individual and collective interests.

Ostrogoths a Germanic tribe and a branch of the Goths; established the kingdom of Italy; defeated by Emperor Justinian.

Ottomans a Turkish dynasty of the Sunni branch of Islam that rose to prominence when Mehmed conquered Constantinople in 1453.

Ottoman-Safavid conflicts ongoing wars between the Safavids and the Ottomans.

outsource the moving of jobs from one country to another, where labor is cheaper.

Pacific Island Laborers Act law that ended the practice of bringing laborers to the islands to work under slave-like working and living conditions on the plantations; specified that Pacific Islanders who were brought to the area as indentured laborers be returned to their homelands but that they could choose to stay in the colonies if they had lived there for twenty years or longer.

Paine, Thomas author of the *Common Sense,* which made the case for American independence from Britain; rejected institutionalized religion and argued against Christian doctrines; advocated the importance of the use of reason and freethinking.

Pakistan Islamic republic in South Asia; in 1947, Britain partitioned India into two separate regions, creating an independent Pakistan for Muslims; by 1948, 10 million Muslims or Hindus had migrated to either India or Pakistan amid tremendous violence.

Paleolithic era "Old Stone Age"; period of time that ended around 10,000 BCE.

Palestine Liberation Organization (PLO) political organization recognized as the sole legitimate representative of the Palestinian people by the United Nations; orchestrated innumerable terrorist attacks against Israel and was considered a terrorist organization until the Madrid Conference in 1991.

Pan-Africanism belief that African peoples share a common history and a common destiny.

Panama Canal canal built between 1904 and 1914 across Panama between the Atlantic and Pacific Oceans that linked oceans and seas and made trade between industrialized countries and their less-industrialized markets and sources of raw materials more profitable.

Pan-Arabism the movement toward the cultural and political unification of all Arab nations in the Middle East.

Pan-Slavic movement movement led by the Serbs, whose homeland was at the center of nationalist aspirations; wanted to unite the Slavic peoples who were under the control of the Austro-Hungarian Empire.

Paris Peace Accords "An Agreement Ending the War and Restoring Peace in Vietnam" signed by the United States, South Vietnam, Viet Cong, and North Vietnam; officially ended U.S. involvement in Vietnam.

pastoralism nomadic society whose members followed and domesticated animal herds; developed in Afro-Eurasia.

patriarchal social systems social system where men are the leaders and have the power within families, economies, and societies.

Pearl Harbor U.S. naval base in Hawaii on which Japan unleashed a surprise air attack in December

1941, resulting in a formal U.S. declaration of war on Japan the following day.

penicillin discovered in 1928 by Scottish biologist Alexander Fleming, a substance derived from mold that kills disease-causing bacteria without damaging healthy cells; known as the "wonder drug," it not only treated minor bacterial diseases but also a variety of virulent bacterial diseases, including bacterial pneumonia, scarlet fever, gonorrhea, and syphilis.

peninsulares the elite class of people who, during Spanish colonial times, lived in the New World but were born in Spain.

People's Republic of China established by Mao Zedong in 1949; a single-party state led by the Communist Party of China.

perestroika a reconstruction policy initiated by Soviet leader Mikhail Gorbachev.

Perón, Juan president of Argentina; advocated industrialization and protection of workers' rights; his government controlled the banking, railroad, shipping, and other industries, and he was in many ways an authoritarian leader; ousted by the military because some saw Perón and his wife Eva as opportunistic and sympathizers of Fascism.

Peter the Great Russian leader whose goal was to revolutionize the country's mainly agricultural economy and its culture by adapting Western systems.

Petrograd Soviet a collective group of workers and soldiers who were determined to give political power to the people of Russia.

Pizarro, Francisco explorer who first traveled to the New World in 1510 on an expedition to what is modern-day Columbia; in 1523, he left on an expedition that would lead him to discover Peru and the Incas; when the Inca king refused to convert to Christianity, Pizarro attacked and quickly defeated the Incas, overtaking the capital city of Cuzco.

Plato a student of Socrates and a teacher of Aristotle; developed his own philosophy in which he rejected the changeable, deceptive world that we are aware of through our senses and proposed, instead, a world of ideas, which were constant and true.

Poland Eastern European country whose independence was one of the fourteen points enunciated by President Woodrow Wilson during World War I; however, the Poles were largely responsible for achieving their own independence in 1918; in 1939, Germany and the Soviet Union signed the Ribbentrop-Molotov nonaggression pact, which secretly provided for the dismemberment of Poland into Nazi and Soviet-controlled zones, and Hitler's troops invaded on September 1, thus beginning World War II.

polydaemonism the belief in many spirits.

polytheism the belief in many gods.

power loom a steam-powered, mechanically operated version of a regular loom, an invention that combined threads to make cloth.

powered trip hammer tool used to pound, separate, and polish grain.

Prebisch, Raul Argentine economist who argued that Latin American economies were damaged by their dependence on industrial nations, especially those of North America and Europe.

prehistory the period of time before approximately 3000 BCE.

proletariat the working class, whose interests Karl Marx advocated for in *The Communist Manifesto*.

Punic Wars conflict that spanned more than a century (264–146 BCE) between the Roman Republic and the Carthaginians as the Romans sought to expand their empire.

Qin dynasty lasting only fourteen years, the Qins ended feudalism in China, adopted the philosophy of Legalism, built roads and bridges throughout China, and standardized the units of weights and measurement, the currency, and the form of writing.

Qing dynasty replaced the Ming in 1644 after devastating famine and plague created mass unrest in the countryside; during this time, the population of China exploded.

quantum mechanics a physics theory developed by Werner Heisenberg that mathematically describes the interactions of matter and energy.

Qur'an holy book containing the recitations of Gabriel, as told to Muhammad; contains the fundamental beliefs of Islam, expressed in the Five Pillars of Faith.

radicalism proposed drastic changes to existing governments and mainly advocated the narrowing of the gap between the rich and the poor.

Ramayana a classic epic of Indian literature, which tells about the wanderings of the banished prince Rama and the difficulties of his faithful wife Sita, before they are reunited and Rama is returned to his rightful throne.

Rastafarian an individual who follows Rastafarianism, which is a religious movement among black Jamaicans that teaches of the eventual redemption of blacks and their return to Africa.

Reformation a sixteenth-century split within Western Christianity initiated by Martin Luther and other early Protestants; was precipitated by centuries of general problems in the Catholic Church, dating back to the Babylonian Captivity of the fourteenth century and the Great Schism that followed.

reggae "coming from the people"; a distinct musical genre in Jamaica, evolving from traditional Jamaican music including ska and mento, American rhythm and blues, and the heavy, back-beated rhythm of African music.

religious fundamentalism strict adherence to a particular theological doctrine; exists among Hindus in India, Muslims in the Middle East and various other parts of the world, and Christians who are members of Protestant fundamentalist sects, especially in the United States and Latin America, but also in other parts of the world.

Renaissance a cultural movement and "rebirth" that began in Italy and lasted throughout the fourteenth to seventeenth centuries; perhaps best known for its developments in art, thanks to such patrons as the Medici family, there was also a flourish of literature, science, religion, politics, and learning.

reparations payment by a defeated nation for damages sustained by another nation as a result of hostilities with the defeated nation.

Rig Veda a collection of 1,028 hymns, revealing much about the early Aryans, Hinduism, and the Aryan culture, including the formation of the castes from the self-sacrifice of the deity Purusha.

river valleys areas of land where agriculture emerged, including Mesopotamia, Egypt, South Central Asia, and northern China.

Roman Empire created when Julius Caesar transformed the Roman Republic into a monarchy in 44 CE, lasting until 180 CE; time of great achievements in engineering, architecture, the arts, the military, and trade.

Roman Republic founded in 509 BCE and centered around Rome; based on the rule of the law, the governmental structure consisted of two consuls, the Senate, and the people; great expansion resulted in a large class of urban poor people and a wealthy merchant class who held the highest positions in government; fell when Julius Caesar transformed the Republic into a monarchy in 44 CE.

Romero, Archbishop Oscar bishop of the Catholic Church who advocated for human rights and the need for reform in El Salvador; closely aligned with Liberation Theology and became a martyr for the cause when he was assassinated as he was saying Mass.

Rome-Berlin Axis Agreement agreement between Italy and Germany, officially linking the two fascist countries.

Roosevelt, Franklin D. president of the United States who introduced the New Deal, a massive program of social reform legislation based on federal intervention in the economy.

Rousseau, Jean-Jacques French writer who believe that education should be left to nature, and that only when a person returns to nature can he or she truly learn.

Royal Road a 1,600-mile-long stretch of road, connecting the capital of Susa to Sardis, a Greek port.

Russian Revolution of 1917 a revolt against the Russian monarchy and the Russian government as it then existed; the revolutionaries were diverse groups with differing goals, values, and ideals with a common goal of removing the tsar.

Russo-Turkish Wars one of the longest conflicts in world history, continued sporadically throughout the nineteenth century as Russia fought with the Ottoman Empire in an ongoing attempt to dominate territories in the Balkans, the Crimea, and the Caucasus.

Rwanda African country that experienced ethnic conflicts between the majority Tutsis and the minority Hutus in Rwanda since 1962; a civil war erupted in 1994, with more than 800,000 Hutus being killed in mass attacks of genocide by the Tutsis in a period of less than four months; the Tutsis won control of Rwanda, and a million Hutus fled the country and took refuge in Zaire and Tanzania.

Safavids Iranian dynasty that ruled from 1501 to 1736; it began as a peaceful Sufi religious order that developed military and political traits later.

SALT treaties agreements on armament control reached after two rounds of talks—the Strategic Arms Limitation Talks—between the United States and the Soviet Union.

samurai professional soldiers of Japan.

Sanskrit early form of Aryan writing.

satrapy the area ruled by the governor of a province of ancient Persia.

savanna grassy plain.

Schlieffen Plan developed by Count Alfred von Schlieffen in 1905, which directed Germany's assaults on France and then focused on defending Germany from Russian attacks.

scientific racism based on the belief that basic differences existed among the races that made black people inherently inferior to whites, in an attempt to justify the inferior positions of black people in societies and economies; developed by Count Joseph Arthur de Gobineau.

Second Industrial Revolution begun in 1870 in Britain, brought about by the development of more efficient ways to produce iron with the steam engine.

Secretary of State for India replaced the East India Tea Company; was directly responsible to the British Cabinet.

sedentary a non-nomadic, nonmigratory lifestyle.

Self-Strengthening Movement advocated by scholar-administrators, established modern institutions in China, including capitalistic practices, and modernized the military, industries, communications, and transportation based on Western models.

Seljuk Turks a nomadic people who migrated to the northern border of the Persian Empire from the Asian steppes, converted to Islam, and unified the Turks of Central Asia.

Sepoy Mutiny rebellion of Indian troops against the British; chief cause was the refusal of the soldiers to use animal grease on the cartridges of their Enfield rifles (soldiers had to bite off the ends of the cartridges to load the rifles, which violated both Islamic and Hindu beliefs regarding animal products).

Seven Years' War the war between Great Britain and France in North America; also known as the French and Indian War.

sexual revolution movement that began in the late 1960s in the United States and then spread to Europe and other Western countries; challenged traditional attitudes toward sexuality and resulted in greater acceptance of sexual freedom, including sexual relationships outside of marriage; continuing into the 1980s, also led to an acknowledgment and some acceptance of homosexuality and the legalization of abortion in many countries.

shamanism a practice led by shamans, or high priests, who were revered as healers and as the links between the spiritual world and the natural world.

Shang dynasty the first solidly authenticated dynasty in Chinese history (1570–1045 BCE), centered in the Yellow River Valley.

Shari'a Muslim body of law that guided followers' ethical behavior and family life as well as their business and community practices.

Shi'a Muslims who believed that caliphs should be related to Muhammad; did not accept the Umayyads as their rulers and sought revenge for Ali's murder.

shogunate a feudal system of government in Japan established by clan leader Minamoto Yoritomo.

Siddhartha the Buddha, meaning "the Enlightened One"; a Hindu prince during the sixth century BCE who became disenchanted with Hinduism because it offered him no answers to the meaning of life; the revelations that came to him while sitting under a tree became the basic tenets of Buddhism.

Sikhism a new faith that emerged in India around 1500 CE, based on the belief that God is one with and present in all creation and that God can be directly apprehended by the human mind; Sikhs are disciples of the Guru.

Silk Road land-based trade connection between the east and the west of Central Asia, developed around 200 BCE.

Single Whip Reform the influx of silver from the Americas that allowed the Ming to take thirty or forty different types of taxes and reduce them to a single one payable in silver.

slash-and-burn agriculture a form of farming in which farmers would cut down all the vegetation from a piece of land and, once it dried, burn it to clear a field for the cultivation of food plants.

smart phones a cell phone with networking capabilities, such as e-mail and the Internet.

smog a dark, heavy fog combined with chemical fumes or smoke.

social Darwinism argued that stronger and more capable individuals competed better and so became more successful; white domination of less well-developed cultures was a natural and just situation.

Social Security federal relief program that includes numerous social welfare and social insurance programs.

Socialism belief system that advocated help for the poor, government control to ensure economic equality between the rich and poor, and the regulation or abolition of private property.

Socrates philosopher of the fifth century BCE and teacher of Plato; developed a philosophy of ethics and advocated a life of good and decent behavior; revolutionized many aspects of Western thought; taught his students to question conventional wisdom by using rational inquiry.

Song dynasty ruled China from 960 to 1279 CE; established a government monopoly on the tea trade and traded tea for horses from outlying regions where tea could not be easily cultivated.

Songhay state located in western Africa that, as a result of expansion, became a mixture of Islamic and native, polytheistic cultures;

conquered in the sixteenth century by Muslims from Morocco.

South African Republic republic formed as a result of conflicts between the Afrikaners and the native populations, in which the Afrikaners defeated the Zulu.

Spanish Armada the largest naval fleet ever assembled, launched by Philip II against his Protestant sister-in-law Queen Elizabeth I of England; England grounded the Spanish Armada before it could attack.

Sparta city-state of classical Greece that promoted equality by not allowing for the accumulation of wealth or land; a state where all people contributed to the military; the women had more equality with men and enjoyed relative freedom; Spartans were agricultural servants who were neither free citizens nor slaves.

spinning jenny a hand-powered multiple spinning machine that made it possible to spin more than one ball of yarn or thread.

square-pallet chain pump pump used by Chinese farmers to channel water to higher elevations, powered by a waterwheel or an ox pulling a mechanical system of wheels.

SS (Schutzstaffel) protection force for Adolf Hitler—his own personal bodyguards.

Stalin, Joseph supreme ruler of the Soviet Union for over 25 years; the gravedigger of the October Revolution. His reign of terror in Russia resulted in the death of millions of Russians.

Stanton, Elizabeth Cady social activist who organized movements based on women's suffrage; presented her Declaration of Sentiments at the first women's rights convention in Seneca Falls, New York.

steam engine invented by Thomas Newcomen in 1702 to help pump water out of coal mine shafts; transformed the iron industry in Britain, and the production of coal rose dramatically.

Stock Market Crash on October 24, 1929, U.S. stock prices fell and brokers sold stocks at a frenzied pace; at the end of the day, 13 million shares had been traded and the market dropped four billion dollars; ushered in the Great Depression.

storming of the Bastille French rioters stormed a fortress prison where the monarchy traditionally kept dissenters, releasing seven prisoners and forming a new municipal government, the commune.

Strategic Defense Initiative "Star Wars," a system supported by President Ronald Reagan that president said would have provided protection from nuclear attack.

strip-mining process of intensively mining deposits near the earth's surface, which destroys the natural habitat of the entire area and leaves huge gaping holes surrounded by waste rock.

sub-Saharan trade route significant route in the interregional trade of the late classical period, linking sub-Saharan peoples with societies in the eastern and southernmost parts of Africa; likely emerged from the Bantu people.

Suez Canal built between 1859 and 1869 in Egypt between the Mediterranean Sea and the Gulf of Suez, a northern part of the Red Sea.

Sufi a Muslim mystic.

Suleiman the Great sultan who extended the Ottoman Empire to Mesopotamia (in modern Iraq) and parts of present-day Central Eastern Europe; under his leadership, the empire reached its high point.

Sumerian the common customs and culture of the city-states of southern Mesopotamia (Sumer).

Sun Yat-sen organized and elected president of the Nationalist People's Party.

Sunni "the followers of tradition"; Muslims who believed that caliphs should continue to be chosen by Muslim leaders; wanted peace and therefore accepted the Umayyads as their rulers.

Sutra the text of Buddhism.

Taika reforms established a Grand Council of State and divided Japan into administrative districts based on Chinese Tang dynasty bureaucratic models and philosophical values.

Taiping Rebellion rebellion led by Hong Xiuquan, who, as a Christian, believed that the overthrow of the Manchu Qing dynasty would bring about the Kingdom of Heaven; after successfully defeating the attack led by the government, Hong Xiuquan declared that the Kingdom of Heavenly Peace had been founded; Taiping was to be a classless society with all wealth distributed equally and with women equal to men; the movement failed to maintain authority in the areas it conquered, and the twenty-year-long Taiping Rebellion was over with the suicide of Hong.

Taj Mahal monument built in northern India to commemorate the memory of the wife of Shah Jahan and to display the wealth and power of the Mughal Empire.

Taliban "Students of Islamic Knowledge Movement"; militant group who, in 1996, took control of the Afghan capital of Kabul and executed Muhammad Najibullah, thus establishing the Islamic State of Afghanistan; ousted from power in December 2001 by the U.S. military and Afghani opposition forces in response to the 9/11 attacks.

Tang dynasty from 618 to 907 CE, during which Chinese trade and culture flourished; overthrown by the Kirhgiz people.

Tanzimat a series of reforms that attempted to westernize the Ottoman world.

tecuhtli a high-ranking group of nobles in Aztec society who had won distinction as warriors; served as judges, governors of provinces, or generals.

Ten Commandments a set of rules that guide relationships both between people and between people and God; adhered to by the followers of Judaism and Christianity.

Tenochtitlán large capital city of Mesoamerica built on a raised island in Lake Texcoco.

Teotihuacán a major center of Mesoamerican civilization from around 300 BCE to 800 CE; the center of important religious functions with a population of about 150,000 people, supported by intensive agriculture and mining in the surrounding regions that it controlled.

tequiua a group of Aztec warriors/nobles who captured four prisoners or killed four enemies; were given a portion of the plunder.

terra nullius land belonging to no one.

terracing a series of horizontal levels formed in a hillside to conserve moisture and increase cultivable land.

terrorism the use of terror as a means of coercion.

textile manufacturing the chief industry of Britain and where the Industrial Revolution began.

theory of relativity Albert Einstein's theory that space and time are relative to the person measuring them; introduced the extraordinary idea that all the absolutes of past ages did not exist, and that reality or truth are merely mental constructs.

Tiananmen Square location of the Chinese Forbidden Palace and the student-initiated sit-down protest in 1989; Deng Xiaoping responded with vicious force and ordered his troops to attack the students with tanks and guns.

tlalmaitl a landless class of Aztec workers who were also required to perform military service.

Tokugawa Shogunate feudal regime of Japan, led by Ieyasu Tokugawa; the emperor lived in Kyoto, while the shoguns resided in Edo, a city that later became known as Tokyo; the emperor became a mere figurehead, and the daimyo became vassals of the shogun.

Torah the foundational text of Judaism, which includes the scriptures and the Old Testament of the Bible; believed to have been written by Hebrew leaders over several centuries, beginning in the tenth century BCE.

Toussaint, Francois Dominique led the Haitian revolt; by 1797, he controlled most of the island, and by 1801 he had created a constitution that granted equality and citizenship to all residents of the colony.

trans-Saharan caravan route established trade relationships between the people who lived in western Africa, south of the vast desert of the Sahara, to the civilizations of the Mediterranean and the Middle East.

Treaty of Hidalgo agreement in which the United States paid Mexico $15 million for Texas, California, and New Mexico.

Treaty of Nanjing agreement in which China handed over Hong Kong to the British, who held it until the late twentieth century, when it reverted back to China.

Treaty of Tordesillas agreement that redrew the line between Portuguese conquests and Spanish conquests at 370 leagues (1,770 km) west of the Cape Verde Islands; Portugal lost much in the Americas, as it received only Brazil; the Spanish became beneficiaries of the vast wealth of the Americas.

Treaty of Verdun 843 CE arrangement that divided Charlemagne's empire between his three grandsons.

Treaty of Versailles one of the peace treaties at the conclusion of World War I, ending the war between Germany and the Allied Powers.

trench warfare a system of warfare in which opposing forces fight from a relatively permanent system of trenches.

Triple Alliance alliance of Germany, Austria-Hungary, and Italy; became the Central Powers of World War I.

Triple Entente an agreement among Russia, France, and Great Britain; became the Allies of World War I.

Truman Doctrine pledge of financial aid to countries threatened by the spread of Communism through force; initially directed toward Greece and Turkey.

Type 2 diabetes chronic condition caused by a problem in the way the body makes or uses insulin; the body's cells do not respond correctly to insulin and, as a result, blood sugar does not get into these cells to be stored for energy; mostly affects people who are overweight when they are diagnosed as increased fat makes it harder for the body to use insulin the correct way.

umma coined by Muhammad, referring to the entire population of Muslim believers.

uncertainty principle developed by Werner Heisenberg, theory in which it is impossible to specify simultaneously the position and velocity of a subatomic particle; the more accurate the statement of a particle's position is, the less accurate the determination of the particle's velocity.

Union of Utrecht agreement signed in 1579 in which the seven northern provinces of the Netherlands became the United Provinces of the Netherlands and agreed to support each other against aggression by Spain.

United Fruit Company based in the United States, the largest banana company in the world when it was formed in 1899; also owned a fleet of steamships, called the Great White Fleet, as well as more than 100 miles of railroad track that connected the plantations to port cities.

United Nations (UN) international organization formed to preserve international peace and foster international cooperation in solving the world's economic, political, and other problems; founded in 1945 after the Second World War by fifty-one countries, the UN currently has 193 member states.

Universal Declaration of Human Rights UN declaration that identifies in its Preamble and thirty Articles the nature of the rights to which every human being is entitled; some of these rights include the rights to life, to not be enslaved, to participate in society and politics, to freely practice religious and cultural beliefs, and to assemble; as of July 2011, all 193 member states of the UN have agreed to its terms.

upper-middle class social class that developed in the nineteenth century in the form of the most successful industrial business families.

vaccine a biological preparation that improves immunity to a particular disease; Jonas Salk's polio vaccine was a polio virus that had been killed; it worked by immunizing people against polio without actually infecting them with the disease.

Vandals East Germanic peoples who established a kingdom in North African in the fifth century; defeated by Emperor Justinian.

vassals wealthy men who served as knights in a feudal society; pledged homage to their lords.

Vedas the sacred texts of Hinduism.

Venus figures feminine figurines with exaggerated female body parts associated with infertility; commonly found in Paleolithic caves.

Vespucci, Amerigo explorer who wrote about the "New World" reached by the Europeans, who, he realized, had not indeed reached the Indies but rather continents previously unknown, which led other European states to finance exploratory voyages.

viceroy the governor-general of India.

Vichy government French government formed after German forces took control of France, collaborating with the Axis powers from 1940 to 1944.

Vietnam War conflict between the United States, South Vietnam, Australia, and South Korea against North Vietnam and the National Liberation Front, a South Vietnamese guerrilla movement led by Communists; outgrowth of the Cold War and the belief that once Communism was allowed to flourish in South Vietnam, all of the other governments in southeastern Asia would also fall to Communism.

Vikings explorers and invaders from Norway, Denmark, and Sweden who raided, explored, and settled in many areas of Western Europe as well as Russia in the eighth and ninth centuries.

viziers political advisors who administered governments during the Abbasid Caliphate.

Voltaire prolific French writer and political activist who believed in the rights of individuals and the importance of ideas, knowledge, and rational thought; a strong advocate of the value of the careful observations of the natural world through science as a means of understanding the world.

Warsaw Pact a 1955 security pact between the Soviet Union and Eastern European nations.

water frame the first power-driven spinning mill, invented by Richard Arkwright, the father of the Industrial Revolution, in 1769.

Way the Dao; followers of Confucius were taught to follow the Way simply for the sake of the Way rather than for the sake of reward or punishment.

Western Front in World War I, trench systems that stretched from the coast of the North Sea southwards to the Swiss border; in World War II, generally the same area as in World War I.

White Australia policy restricted Chinese immigration to Australia and established poll taxes and other anti-Chinese policies.

Wollstonecraft, Mary an English writer who wrote *Vindication of the Rights of Women*, in which she argued that women deserved all of the rights that men had achieved in the French Revolution, including the right to equal education and participation in politics; argued that women were rational thinkers apart from their husbands and that equality should extend to women.

World Cup Soccer held every four years in different countries, the most widely viewed sporting event in the world with thirty-two national teams participating; representative of the globalization of popular culture as well as the passionate feelings of national and ethnic pride.

World Health Organization (WHO) proposed by members of the UN, a global health organization whose objective is "the attainment by all people of the highest possible level of health"; organizes international efforts to prevent, treat, and control outbreaks of infectious diseases and provides global leadership on various health issues, setting the agenda for health-based research and standards.

World Trade Organization (WTO) international organization that addresses the global rules of trade between nations; its main function is to ensure that trade flows as smoothly, predictably, and freely as possible.

World War I the first war to encompass more than half of the world; twenty-eight nations, the Allies and their Associated Powers, fought four other nations or empires known as the Central Powers: Germany, Austria-Hungary, Bulgaria, and the Ottoman Empire.

wu wei a tenet of Daoism; noninterference with the natural path of things and detachment from worldly affairs.

xenophobia fear or hatred of foreigners.

Yamato Kingdom present-day Japan, from where Prince Shotoku Taishi sent the first Japanese ambassadors to China in the early seventeenth century.

Yuan dynasty established by Kublai Khan; relegated the Chinese to a lower status than Mongols and other non-Chinese foreigners; its capital was Khanbaliq, to which Kublai Khan extended the Grand Canal of the Sui.

zaibatsu industrial and financial conglomerates in Japan that rose to prominence in the Meiji era.

Zheng He commanded seven expeditions to such places as Ceylon, Calcutta, South Vietnam, and Africa for the Yongle Emperor.

ziggurat a stepped, pyramid-like temple.

Zoroastrianism religion following the ancient teachings of the prophet Zoroaster; became the state religion of the Persian Empire following the conversion of the Persian kings.

Index

NOTES

NOTES

NOTES

NOTES